European Insolvency Law

European Insolvency Law

Reform and Harmonization

Gerard McCormack

Professor of International Business Law, Centre for Business Law and Practice, School of Law, University of Leeds, UK

Andrew Keay

Professor of Corporate and Commercial Law, Centre for Business Law and Practice, School of Law, University of Leeds, UK and Professorial Research Fellow, Deakin University, Melbourne, Australia

Sarah Brown

Associate Professor, Centre for Business Law and Practice, School of Law, University of Leeds, UK

Edward Elgar
PUBLISHING

Cheltenham, UK • Northampton, MA, USA

Published by
Edward Elgar Publishing Limited
The Lypiatts
15 Lansdown Road
Cheltenham
Glos GL50 2JA
UK

Edward Elgar Publishing, Inc.
William Pratt House
9 Dewey Court
Northampton
Massachusetts 01060
USA

A catalogue record for this book
is available from the British Library

Library of Congress Control Number: 2016949982

This book is available electronically in the **Elgar**online
Law subject collection
DOI 10.4337/9781786433312

Printed on elemental chlorine free (ECF)
recycled paper containing 30% Post-Consumer Waste

ISBN 978 1 78643 330 5 (cased)
ISBN 978 1 78643 331 2 (eBook)

Typeset by Servis Filmsetting Ltd, Stockport, Cheshire
Printed and bound in the USA

Contents

Contributors

AUTHORS OF THE STUDY

Gerard McCormack, Professor of International Business Law, University of Leeds, UK.
Andrew Keay, Professor of Corporate and Commercial Law, University of Leeds, UK and Professorial Research Fellow, Deakin University, Melbourne, Australia.
Sarah Brown, Associate Professor, University of Leeds, UK.

With assistance from **Judith Dahlgreen**, Lecturer in Law, University of Leeds, UK.

INTERNATIONAL ADVISORY GROUP

Cristina Amato, Associate Professor of Comparative Law and Chairman of the Centre of Comparative Studies, University of Brescia, Italy.

Jason Kilborn, Professor of Law, John Marshall Law School, United States; Consultant, Personal Insolvency and Over-indebtedness, World Bank.

Stephen Madaus, Professor of Civil Law, Civil Procedure and Insolvency Law, Martin-Luther-Universität-Halle-Wittenberg; Project Reporter, ELI Rescue of Business in Insolvency Law Project.

Rosalind Mason, Professor of Insolvency and Restructuring Law, Queensland University of Technology; Chair of the INSOL International Academic Forum.

Michael Murray, Legal Director of ARITA (Australian Restructuring Insolvency and Turnaround Association); Visiting Fellow, Queensland University of Technology; Consultant, Insolvency Management Practice, Ferrier Hodgson.

Johanna Niemi, Minna Canth Academy Professorship, Procedural Law and Gender, University of Turku, Finland.

Sophie Vermeille, Associate, Corporate Recovery and Restructuring, DLA Piper; Lecturer, University of Paris II Pantheon-Assas and Sciences Pro.

EU NATIONAL REPORTERS

Austria

Georg Kodek, Professor and Head of Department for Business Law, Vienna University of Economics and Business.

Belgium

Koen Byttebier, Professor, Vrije Universiteit Brussels; Partner, Everest Law.
Matthias Gesquière, Interim Professor, Vrije Universiteit Brussels; Partner, Portelio.

Bulgaria

Atanas Mihaylov, Senior Associate, Wolf Theiss, Sofia.

Croatia

Jasna Garašić, Professor, University of Zagreb.

Cyprus

Alexandra Kastrinou, Senior Lecturer, Nottingham Law School.

Czech Republic

Tomáš Richter, Commercial Law practitioner, Clifford Chance LLP, Prague.

Denmark

Camilla Hörby Jensen, Associate Professor, University of Southern Denmark.

Estonia

Signe Viimsalu, Chief Executive Officer, Estonian Business Angels Network.

Finland

Vesa Annola, Professor of Business Law, University of Vaasa.
Mikko Pihlajamäki, MBA Researcher of Business Law, University of Vaasa.

France

Jean-Luc Vallens, Bankruptcy Judge/Magistrate, Court of Appeal, Colmar.

Germany

Reinhard Bork, Professor, Universität Hamburg.

Greece

Alexandra Kastrinou, Senior Lecturer, Nottingham Law School.

Hungary

Tibor Tajti, Professor of Law, Central European University.

Ireland

Irene Lynch Fannon, Professor of Law, University College Cork.
Emilie Ghio, Ph.D Researcher, University College Cork.

Italy

Renato Mangano, Associate Professor, Università di Palermo.

Latvia

Agris Repšs, Partner, Sorainen Law Firm.
Raivo Raudzeps, Senior Associate, Sorainen Law Firm.

Lithuania

Lina Aleknaite-Van der Molen, Associate Professor, Kazimieras Simonavičiaus University.

Luxembourg

Corrado Malberti, Associate Professor, Université du Luxembourg.

Malta

Andrew Muscat, Professor, University of Malta.
Simon Pullicino, Associate, Mamo TCV Advocates.

Netherlands

Bas Kortmann, Professor and University President, Radboud University Nijmegen.
Michael Veder, Professor of Private Law, Radboud University Nijmegen.

Poland

Krzysztof Kazmierczyk, Banking and Finance Lawyer, Dentons.

Portugal

Catarina Serra, Professor, University of Minho.

Romania

Cătălin-Gabriel Stănescu, Attorney at Law, SCPA Bordianu and Associates.

Slovakia

Branislav Pospíšil, Principal, Pospíšil & Partners.

Slovenia

Pavle Flere, Senior Lawyer, UniCredit Slovenia.

Spain

Laura Carballo Piñeiro, Associate Professor, Universidad de Santiago de Compostela.

Sweden

Annina Persson, Professor of Private Law, Orebro University.

NON-EU NATIONAL REPORTERS

United States

Adrian Walters, Professor of Law, IIT Chicago-Kent College of Law.

Norway

Richard Sjøqvist, Partner, Advokatfirmaet BA-HR DA.
Peter Bugge Hjorth, Senior Lawyer, Advokatfirmaet BA-HR DA.

Preface

This book arises out of a research study that was generously funded by the European Commission through a competitive tender process (Tender No. JUST/2014/JCOO/PR/CIVI/0075). We thank the European Commission very much for their funding.

In 2015, the European Commission DG Justice commissioned a team from the School of Law at the University of Leeds to undertake a comparative study on substantive insolvency law throughout the EU, with a view to enhancing the knowledge base of the Commission and outlining the possibilities of harmonization and reform measures. The Leeds project team was made up of Gerard McCormack, Andrew Keay, Sarah Brown and Judith Dahlgreen, with Ruth Binns as project administrator. It worked alongside a team of 30 national reporters as well as an international advisory group. The national reporters represented each of the 28 EU Member States and two comparator countries, the United States and Norway. The national reporters and the members of the international advisory group are detailed in the list of contributors. The national reporters provided much of the raw material on which the study and the book is based, although we also carried out independent academic research and drew on other policy material. In the main, national reporters reported on the state of their national law up to October 2015 but in a number of cases we have been able to incorporate later developments.

The reform of insolvency law is very much at the top of the EU policy agenda. It forms an integral part of the Capital Markets Union project and the 'Five Presidents Report' of 22 June 2015 on *Completing Europe's Economic and Monetary Union* highlights the current state of insolvency law as being among the most important bottlenecks preventing the integration of capital markets. The European Commission's Single Market Strategy recognizes that impediments in the field of insolvency law can create a significant disincentive to entrepreneurial activity, and the potential impact of divergent personal insolvency procedures on cross-border credit relationships and investment has also been highlighted in the Commission's recent *Green Paper on Retail Financial Services*. Furthermore, on 12 July 2016, the Commission convened a major conference in Brussels, titled 'Convergence of Insolvency Frameworks within the European Union: The

Way Forward', and at this Conference there was substantial discussion and debate as to how insolvency law in the EU might be improved.

At the time of writing, specific legislative and other initiatives in the sphere of insolvency are being considered by the European Commission, including a strengthening of the EC Recommendation of March 2014 on a new approach to business failure and insolvency and its implementation in Member States (see https://webcast.ec.europa.eu/insolvency-conference and http://ec.europa.eu/justice/civil/files/insolvency/impact_assessment_en.pdf).

We hope that our study and this book will influence the future European reform agenda and also more indirectly the ongoing debates on reform of insolvency and restructuring law that are taking place in countries such as the United Kingdom, Australia and the United States.

Since the study was completed and in the course of transforming the study into a book, our academic gang of four became three, with Judith Dahlgreen leaving the University of Leeds for pastures new. We thank her for her work on initial drafts of Chapters 7 and 8. Since our study was completed, we have had the UK 'Brexit' Referendum of 23 June 2016. This event may cast a long shadow and the precise implications are as yet uncertain but we hope that it does not unduly dim the prospects for further European and international scientific research and co-operation.

In the course of the project we have incurred many debts: to Judith and to Ruth Binns, our very able project administrator, but also to the national reporters and to members of the international advisory group. We thank all these individual colleagues and friends who gave up their valuable time. We also thank colleagues at the University of Leeds, and in particular the Head of the School of Law, Alastair Mullis, for supporting us in our endeavours.

We take individual and collective responsibility for the contents of the book as a whole but for the sake of completeness we should perhaps point out that Gerard McCormack worked primarily on the Introduction and on Chapters 2, 3 and 6, and together with Andrew Keay on Chapter 5. Andrew Keay, as well as working with Gerard McCormack on Chapter 5, and contributing to the Introduction, worked primarily on Chapters 1 and 4. Sarah Brown worked primarily on Chapters 7 and 8.

On a personal level, Gerard McCormack would like to thank Presy, Amelia and Anthony, and Sarah Brown would like to thank Andy for his continuing support and patience, always there regardless of wherever he happens to be in the world.

Gerard McCormack
Andrew Keay
Sarah Brown
September 2016

Abbreviations

AFS	Accelerated Financial Sauvegarde
BIT	bilateral investment treaty
CJEU	Court of Justice of the European Union
COMI	centre of main interest
CVA	Company Voluntary Arrangement
DRO	debt relief order
EBRD	European Bank for Reconstruction and Development
EU	European Union
IOH	insolvency office holder
IP	insolvency practitioner
IVA	Individual Voluntary Arrangement
R&D	research and development
RPB	recognized public body
SME	small and medium-sized enterprise
UNCITRAL	UN Commission on International Trade

Introduction and background

THE PROJECT

In March 2015, the European Commission DG Justice commissioned a team from the School of Law at the University of Leeds to undertake a comparative study on substantive insolvency law throughout the European Union (EU). Insolvency law is regulated primarily in the EU through Regulation 1346/2000 (recast as Regulation 2015/848) and it is designed to facilitate cross-border insolvency proceedings and to ensure greater co-ordination of national insolvency proceedings. The Leeds project team has worked alongside a team of 30 national reporters as well as an international advisory group. The national reporters represent each of the 28 EU Member States and two comparator countries, the United States and Norway. The national reporters and the members of the international advisory group are detailed in the list of contributors.

The Leeds project team was required by the Commission to carry out four specific tasks. The first task was the collection of data about reforms in the EU Member States that implement Commission Recommendation 2014/135/EU, issued on 12 March 2014 on a new approach to business failure and insolvency. This builds on the study carried out for the European Commission by INSOL Europe involving a comparative analysis of the relevant provisions and practices on business failure and insolvency in Member States as of December 2013.

The second task was to collect data in order to enhance the comparative law information at the disposal of the Commission in respect of matters such as the regulation, status and powers of insolvency practitioners; the duties and liabilities of directors and the recognition of disqualifications, rules on the ranking of claims/order of priorities and the conditions under which certain detrimental acts can be avoided; conditions for opening insolvency proceedings and fast-track or standardized procedures for small and medium-sized enterprises (SMEs).

The third task was the collection of data about the procedures available to over-indebted consumers explaining how over-indebtedness is dealt with in the Member States including the conditions and timeframe for debt reduction and discharge. The data is intended to address the average length of the procedures; the involvement of creditors and the extent to which such procedures are publicized. It also considers issues such as the treatment of debtors who cannot afford to pay the costs of such procedures, and 'no income, no assets' debtors.

The fourth task was to carry out a horizontal cross-cutting analysis of the data, identifying areas where disparities in national laws produce problems that have impacts outside national boundaries.

The United States and Norway are used in this report as comparator countries. They are both advanced 'first world' economies with highly developed insolvency and regulatory frameworks. They also score well in international indices of 'best practices' such as the World Bank *Doing Business* project.[1] In the 'resolving insolvency' indicator of the 2016 *Doing Business Report*, the two comparator countries perform well on the indicator, at 5th and 6th, respectively. The project team recognize, however, that the particular solutions adopted in either the United States or Norway may not be suitable for adoption across Europe. Therefore, careful consideration has been given to the appropriateness of all elements of US and Norwegian law as far as an EU context is concerned.

The general evaluation and analysis is intended to be sensitive to the following goals:

- improving economic performance throughout the EU;
- promoting a more competitive business environment which encourages speed of resolution of distressed businesses;
- allocating assets to their most efficient use;
- building more stable and sustainable human capital;
- ensuring firm social and economic foundations for a Europe built upon equity and justice;
- ensuring that adequate accountability mechanisms are in place in respect of businesses, funders and insolvency practitioners;
- facilitating the exercise of the 'four freedoms' under the fundamental principles of the EU;
- preventing the abusive exercise of putative rights under EU laws.

The intention is to achieve a greater concordance between insolvency law, the regulatory instruments of insolvency practice, and the Europe 2020 growth strategy of fostering economic recovery and sustainable growth. The objective is to facilitate a situation where economic and social systems

---

[1]   See www.doingbusiness.org/.

are adaptable, resilient and fair; where economic activity is sustainable and where human values are respected.[2]

BACKGROUND: JUNCKER PLAN, CAPITAL MARKETS UNION AND SINGLE MARKET STRATEGY

The current European Commission President, Jean-Claude Juncker, said on taking office that his first priority was to put growth and jobs at the centre of the policy agenda of the European Commission. Addressing insolvency and business failures contributes to this policy in the following ways:

- Fewer insolvencies should mean that workers keep their jobs and businesses can contribute to growth across the EU.
- Reducing insolvencies will see creditors and other stakeholders incurring fewer losses thereby enabling them to assist in the growth process.
- Enabling individuals to recover from over-indebtedness should ensure that they can contribute to the overall economy.
- It should also mean less dislocation in local and national communities throughout the EU.
- Reducing the divergence of national insolvency frameworks could also assist growth by contributing to the emergence of pan European equity and debt markets thereby reducing uncertainty for investors who would otherwise have to assess investment risks on a country-by-country basis.

Furthermore, the Five Presidents' report of 22 June 2015 on *Completing Europe's Economic and Monetary Union* lists the area of insolvency law among the most important bottlenecks preventing the integration of capital markets.

On 30 September 2015, the European Commission released its Action Plan on Building a Capital Markets Union[3] in line with its top priority

---

    [2]   A. Keay, 'Balancing Interests in Bankruptcy Law' (2001) 30 *Common Law World Review* 206.
    [3]   COM(2015)468. For discussion of the Capital Markets Union see the symposium in (2015) 9 *Law and Financial Markets Review* 187 and see also Georg Ringe, 'Capital Markets Union for Europe: A Commitment to the Single Market of 28' (2015) 9 *Law and Financial Markets Review* 5.

of strengthening Europe's economy and stimulating investment to create jobs. The Action Plan stresses the fundamental importance of stronger capital markets in providing new sources of funding for business, helping to increase options for savers and making the economy more resilient. It also highlights the role of insolvency law in contributing to this process.

The free flow of capital is one of the core foundation stones on which the European Union is built. But, as the Action Plan points out, Europe's capital markets are still relatively underdeveloped and fragmented despite the progress over the past 50 years. While the EU economy is as big as that of the United States, the EU's equity markets are less than half the size of those in the United States and its debt markets less than a third the size. Moreover, there are even bigger gaps between individual EU Member States. The Action Plan suggests that more integrated capital markets will lead to efficiency gains. It will also support the EU's ability to fund growth, in particular by:

- unlocking more investment from the EU and the rest of the world;
- better connecting financing to investment projects across the EU;
- making the financial system more stable;
- deepening financial integration and increasing competition.

The Action Plan proposes taking forward a legislative initiative on business insolvency that will address the most important barriers to the free flow of capital and build on national regimes that work well. It is argued that differences in the implementation of the European Commission Recommendation on a new approach to business failure and insolvency means continuing legal uncertainty and additional costs for investors in assessing their risks. The Action Plan and the accompanying staff working document[4] refers to:

- persistent barriers to the efficient restructuring of viable companies in the EU, including cross-border enterprise groups;
- inefficient and divergent insolvency proceedings in the EU preventing speedier debt restructuring;
- non-performing loans being more difficult to resolve without effective restructuring and insolvency tools;

---

[4] See SWD(2015)183 final and SWD(2015)184 final. See in particular pp. 24–5 of the Action Plan and pp. 73–8 of the staff working document.

- difficulties for investors in assessing credit risk, particularly in respect of cross-border investments given the fact that there are 28 divergent insolvency regimes in the EU;
- incentives for companies in financial difficulty which do not have effective early restructuring possibilities in their home country to relocate to Member States with more effective systems;
- adverse effects on minority creditors by the application of a different insolvency regime than that originally expected by creditors even though business restructuring under a different regime could be beneficial to the general body of creditors and the company as a whole;
- high costs of relocation making it very difficult if not impossible for SMEs to benefit from better restructuring possibilities in other Member States.

On the other hand, convergence of insolvency and restructuring proceedings is seen as facilitating greater legal certainty for cross-border investors and encouraging the timely restructuring of viable companies in financial distress. An insolvency regime that encourages more debt restructuring may in turn enhance the creditworthiness of viable companies by facilitating their deleveraging. Shorter debt discharge periods for individuals enable families and households to recover more quickly from the financial crisis and to benefit from, and contribute to, economic development. Moreover, if debtors are not required to hand over income for an extended period, then this increases the incentive to work and contribute to the development of societal wealth.

The EU Commission's Single Market Strategy, published on 28 October 2015,[5] also recognizes that long discharge periods can create a significant disincentive to entrepreneurial activity. It reports that a regular complaint of SMEs is the fear of punitive bankruptcy laws. Uncertainty of a second chance, and potential legal and social consequences of bankruptcy, deter entrepreneurs from trying again.[6]

SMEs face a number of obstacles, including limited access to finance, complex regulation that is difficult to understand, and lack of support for innovation. The Single Market Strategy addresses this, building on the Commission Recommendation of 2014 on a new approach to business

---

[5] Communication from the Commission to the European Parliament, the Council, the European Economic and Social Committee and the Committee of the Regions, *Upgrading the Single Market: More Opportunities for People and Business* (COM(2015)550 final).

[6] *Ibid.* para. 2.2.

failure and insolvency.[7] The Commission Recommendation targets greater coherence between national insolvency frameworks as a goal. The aim is to foster early restructuring of viable companies in financial difficulties and promote a second chance for honest entrepreneurs, but with due support for the interests of creditors and investors, so encouraging cross-border investment. Efficient and consistent insolvency frameworks across the EU are also seen as allowing better assessment of credit risks and providing a reduction in cost in assisting over-indebted businesses.[8] This is further supported by the Action Plan on Building a Capital Markets Union[9] which, as has been noted, identifies divergent approaches to insolvency laws as a barrier to cross-border investment.[10]

The Single Market Strategy sets out the priorities of the EU Commission: increasing jobs, growth and investment. A number of initiatives, underpinned by 'better regulation', are being pursued, including restructuring and second chance. These will have the aim of encouraging innovation, whilst still accommodating failure, and so supporting entrepreneurial confidence to start again.[11]

The Banking Union Communication issued on 24 November 2015 also confirms that: (i) there is a need for greater convergence in insolvency law and restructuring proceedings across Member States; (ii) the inefficiency and divergence of insolvency laws make it harder to assess and manage credit risk; and (iii) enhancing legal certainty and encouraging the timely restructuring of borrowers in financial distress is particularly relevant for the success of strategies to address the problem of non-performing loans in some Member States.

METHODOLOGY

This report is based on the data which has been obtained from reporters in 30 countries. In the main, the 'cut-off' date for the supply of the data was 31 October 2015 but in a number of cases more updated information was provided. The report includes analysis of that data as well as a broader

---

[7]   C 2014 (1500).

[8]   *Ibid.* 3–4.

[9]   Communication from the Commission to the European Parliament, the Council, the European Economic and Social Committee and the Committee of the Regions, *Action Plan on Building a Capital Markets Union*, COM(2015)468 final.

[10]   *Ibid.* 24–5.

[11]   *Upgrading the Single Market: More Opportunities for People and Business*, COM(2015)550 final, para. 2.2.

consideration of the issues raised in the European Commission's Call for Tender (JUST/2014/JCOO/PR/CIVI/0075). The reporters reported on the position in all 28 Member States and two non-EU countries and identified areas where the disparity of national laws creates problems in relation to cross-border trade and investment. Collectively, the national reports investigated and analysed the various approaches on insolvency law matters in the EU Member States and the two non-EU countries used as comparators.

The national reporters were asked to prepare reports which were founded on questions and issues raised in two Questionnaires (see Appendices 1 and 2). The reports consisted of answers to those questions and issues and some other commentary that was considered relevant. The Questionnaires contained guidelines prepared by the Leeds project team to assist reporters in drawing up their reports and to achieve some common analysis of the relevant issues and a degree of uniformity of approach. Reports were received from all reporters and many reporters subsequently provided further information by way of clarification of, or additions to, their reports. The European Commission had a considerable input in approving the Questionnaires and in relation to information requests.

On receipt of the national reports, the Leeds project team commenced careful examination of the data, identifying key issues and exploring the different approaches taken in each of the Member States and the comparator states. The present report contains this analysis. Along with this introductory section, the report consists of eight substantive sections following the structure suggested by the Call to Tender. The chapter order is as follows:

1. Directors' liability and disqualification
2. Insolvency practitioners
3. Ranking of claims and order of priorities
4. Avoidance and adjustment actions
5. Procedural issues relating to formal insolvency proceedings
6. The Commission Recommendation on a new approach to business failure and insolvency
7. Second chance for entrepreneurs
8. Consumer over-indebtedness

The report attempts, *inter alia*, to identify and analyse where appropriate and possible:

- similar or different approaches in Member States on particular issues such as 'official' licensing procedures for insolvency practitioners;

- indicators of success of particular approaches to relevant issues, including indicators which have an internal market impact (e.g. restructuring procedures which encourage foreign investment or reduce debt overhang);
- 'best practices' in the way that Member States have addressed issues, supported by evidence relating to the indicators of success identified;
- 'difficulties' that exist or appear to exist in the way that Member States have addressed issues, in particular from the perspective of the need to ensure a smooth functioning of the internal market;
- gaps that may exist in the handling of specific matters in any or all of the Member States and the problems or potential risks they create;
- how insolvency law may facilitate responsible risk-taking by entrepreneurs even in circumstances where previous business ventures have failed, that is a second (or more) chance;
- inefficiencies in the way in which particular matters have been addressed, such as the absence of any effective mechanism for consumer debt discharge;
- advantages and disadvantages of different approaches in dealing with an issue such as simplified or specifically designed procedures for the relief of consumer over-indebtedness;
- possible impacts of different national approaches (including different levels of efficiency of insolvency procedures) on the functioning of the internal market.

The report builds on complementary policy initiatives by the European Commission and work done by other bodies such as INSOL, the European Bank for Reconstruction and Development (EBRD), the United Nations Commission on International Trade Law (UNCITRAL) and the World Bank.

For instance, the work done by INSOL and its constituent bodies provides a fertile source for comparative analysis.[12] INSOL Europe has carried out a comparative legal analysis on the approach to business failure and insolvency.[13] INSOL International has carried out a cross-country analysis on the avoidance of antecedent transactions and cross-border insolvency.[14] The countries examined include many of the leading European jurisdictions, as well as the United States. The INSOL

---

[12] See www.insol.org/.

[13] *Comparative Legal Analysis of the Member States' Relevant Provisions and Practices*, Tender No. JUST/2012/JCIV/CT/0194/A4, available at http://ec.europa.eu/justice/civil/files/insol_europe_report_2014_en.pdf.

[14] See www.insol.org/page/33/insol-publications.

International study forms a useful comparison point for our analysis. It suggests the ingredients of a possible common European approach for the avoidance of 'antecedent' transactions.

The insolvency law assessments carried out by the EBRD have also been considered as part of our comparative review. The EBRD regularly conducts assessments and surveys to measure both the extensiveness and effectiveness of insolvency laws in the countries in which it operates.[15] These countries include the EU Member States in central and Eastern Europe that form part of the old 'Soviet bloc'.

The EBRD measures the laws against international standards and best practices as represented by the UNCITRAL Legislative Guide on Insolvency Law and the World Bank's Principles and Guidelines for Effective Insolvency and Creditor Rights.[16] At the same time, the EBRD recognizes that the nature and content of insolvency laws will vary from country to country in order to accommodate the rich variety of legal and cultural traditions. The EBRD assessment is based on comprehensive guidelines, developed from the international benchmarks, measuring the extent to which a given country's laws and regulations are in compliance with these benchmarks and standards. The EBRD also aims to go beyond the 'law on the books'. It assesses how the laws in each country, together with the local institutional framework including rules of procedure for courts and insolvency administrators, work in tandem to create a functional insolvency regime.[17]

More recently, the EBRD has identified a set of principles that will guide law-makers in formulating and applying standards for the qualifications, appointment, conduct, supervision and regulation of insolvency practitioners. These principles single out the main issues that should be addressed in a legal regime that provides for the appointment of persons to take responsibility for the administration of an insolvent estate. They are not intended to be exhaustive, however, and simply serve as guidelines.[18] Nevertheless, they provide an indication of the sorts of measures that may be appropriate for adoption at the EU level in respect of the regulation of insolvency practitioners.

This report addresses these principles and also the Principles and Best Practices for Insolvency Office Holders (IOHs) in Europe developed by a team from Leiden University in conjunction with INSOL Europe. The

---

15 See www.ebrd.com/what-we-do/sectors/legal-reform/debt-restructuring-and-bankruptcy/sector-assessments.html.
16 See www.worldbank.org/ifa/ipg_eng.pdf.
17 See www.ebrd.com/what-we-do/sectors/legal-reform/overview.html.
18 See http://assessment.ebrd.com/insolvency-office-holders/2014/report.html.

Leiden Principles and Best Practices are intended to serve as a sound benchmark for the profession, as a way of strengthening public confidence and to focus the debate on possible future binding rules for IOHs at a European level.[19]

The analysis of the treatment of entrepreneurs and consumer over-indebtedness in this report also makes reference to the World Bank's *Report on the Treatment of the Insolvency of Natural Persons*.[20] The Report was published in 2013 by the World Bank's Working Group on the Treatment of the Insolvency of Natural Persons, convened by the World Bank's Insolvency and Creditor/Debtor Regimes Task Force. The study considers issues in relation to personal insolvency regimes, including, where appropriate, the treatment of entrepreneurs. Whilst this Report did not have, as its objective, recommendations for reform, it examines effective measures, potential issues and guidance on policy responses. This has been drawn upon at relevant stages of the analysis.

Our report identifies possible legislative and regulatory responses by the Commission but also has regard to the principles of subsidiarity and proportionality underpinning the EU Treaties, that is Community action is only appropriate where the objectives of the proposed action cannot be achieved satisfactorily at national level, and Community action should be proportionate to the aims to be achieved. The report will set out the advantages and disadvantages of particular types of legislative or regulatory action at European level to tackle deficiencies in the frameworks governing insolvency and consumer over-indebtedness in the Member States.

Our conclusions are sensitive to the jurisprudence emanating from the Court of Justice of the European Union (CJEU) that a mere disparity in national legislation appears insufficient to justify Community action, that is the 'Tobacco Advertising' case, C-380/03 *Germany* v. *European Parliament and Council*, judgment of 12 December 2006. The report is sensitive to local legal traditions and the history and traditions of Member States by avoiding simplistic solutions and a 'one size fits all' mentality. At the same time, we take note of the proposition that history is not destiny and that concrete measures to achieve real legal and regulatory improvements are possible.

---

[19]   See www.tri-leiden.eu/news/news-overview/semi-final-draft-of-the-insol-euro-pe-ioh-statement-published/. See also the INSOL Europe Turnaround Wing Guidelines for Restructuring and Turnaround Professionals.

[20]   World Bank, Insolvency and Creditor/Debtor Regimes Task Force, Working Group on the Treatment of the Insolvency of Natural Persons, *Treatment of the Insolvency of Natural Persons* (2013).

As far as our comparator nations are concerned, the report pays appropriate regard to the fact that solutions that work well in a US or Norwegian context may not be suitable for direct or indirect transplantation in the whole of the European Union. Moreover, insolvency law in the United States may undergo significant change in the next few years due to expansion in the use of secured credit, the growth of distressed-debt markets and other externalities that have affected the effectiveness of the current law. The American Bankruptcy Institute, one of the important actors in insolvency law reform in the United States, has established a review group which has reported on the reform of Chapter 11 of the US Bankruptcy Code (see www.commission.abi.org/full-report). Chapter 11 deals with the restructuring of ailing businesses. The review group has proposed reforms with a view to achieving a better balance between the effective restructuring of business debtors, the preservation and expansion of employment, and the maximization of asset values for the benefit of all creditors and stakeholders.

CASE STUDIES AND STATISTICAL COMPARATORS

In this report, we have made appropriate use of 'case studies' to facilitate analysis and to highlight particular points. These case studies draw on the case law of the CJEU and on national legal literature though we were not supplied by national reporters with numerous case studies. National insolvency/bankruptcy statistics and statistics drawn from the World Bank *Doing Business* project, rankings and database[21] have also, to some degree, informed our analysis. The great strength of the *Doing Business* database is that it facilitates cross-country analysis but we caution against unqualified acceptance of this database for reasons explained later.

In many cases, it has not been possible for us to draw firm conclusions in our analysis from the use of available national insolvency statistics. The reporters were generally not able to supply a significant amount of statistical information as there either seems to be a dearth of it or it is not readily available. Also, as far as the statistics that are available, they have often been compiled in a disparate way at the national level and this hampers the effectiveness of their use for comparative legal analysis.

In the United States, by contrast, national aggregate statistics are gathered by the Department of Justice and published quarterly.[22] These

---

[21]   See www.doingbusiness.org/.
[22]   See www.uscourts.gov/statistics-reports/caseload-statistics-data-tables/.

provide data on the number of bankruptcy filings (in aggregate and broken down into business and non-business filings) and the number of cases pending and terminated. It is the case, however, that these statistics are compiled more to gauge case volumes with an eye on court resources rather than to measure the overall health of the economy. In addition, the US Trustee programme collates and publishes in aggregate form the outcomes from Chapter 7 asset cases.[23] This data is derived from the final reports filed by trustees. Moreover, the dockets in all filed cases are publicly accessible via the Public Access to Court Electronic Records (PACER) system, thereby facilitating the production of a range of statistical information on Chapter 11 cases by academic and private providers. One of the best known of these is the UCLA-LoPucki Bankruptcy Research Database which provides information on the outcomes in large bankruptcy cases.[24]

The position in the EU should change in the direction of greater transparency and uniformity of approach with the 'full' coming into force of the recast Insolvency Regulation (Regulation (EU) 2015/848). Under the recast Regulation, Member States are required to publish certain information concerning insolvency proceedings in a 'free' and publicly accessible electronic register, though access to the register may be made dependent upon establishing a 'legitimate interest' to the competent authority.[25] What constitutes a 'legitimate interest' is obviously prone to different interpretations in different Member States and it is not clear whether an autonomous Europe-wide interpretation is envisaged. The information to be published includes information concerning the court opening the insolvency proceedings, the date of opening and closing of proceedings, the type of proceedings, the debtor and insolvency practitioner appointed, and the deadline for lodging claims.

There is, however, no requirement to publish details of claims that have been lodged or accepted. While individual States are not precluded from requiring additional information to be included on the registers, they may charge searchers a reasonable fee for accessing these optional extras.[26] Moreover, because of privacy concerns, States are not required to make available on the national register information concerning individuals not

---

[23]   See www.justice.gov/ust/bankruptcy-data-statistics/chapter-7-trustee-final-reports.

[24]   See http://lopucki.law.ucla.edu/.

[25]   Regulation 2015/848, arts 24–7. Under art. 86, Member States are required to provide a short description of their national legislation and procedures relating to insolvency and to keep this information regularly updated.

[26]   *Ibid.* arts 24(3) and 27(2).

exercising an independent business or professional activity, although they may do so.[27]

The European Commission is tasked with the responsibility of establishing a decentralized system for the interconnection of national insolvency registers and the European e-Justice Portal is intended to serve as the central public electronic access point to information from the system. The ambition of the project means that a longer period has been given to get the system up and running. In general, the changes made by the recast Regulation come into effect two years from the date that they are published in the *Official Journal*, that is from 26 June 2017. Member States, however, have 36 months to establish insolvency registers and 48 months to provide confirmation that the registers will form part of an interconnected EU Portal.[28]

WORLD BANK *DOING BUSINESS* PROJECT

The World Bank *Doing Business* database, reports and rankings have been used by the European Commission in its Action Plan on Building a Capital Markets Union.[29] They are also used as one of a number of points of reference in this report but, as explained already, we also caution restraint in the use of the report and rankings.[30]

The *Doing Business Reports* and rankings have been issued annually since 2004 and the rankings purport to measure a whole host of matters and not just 'getting credit' and 'resolving insolvency'. The *Doing Business* website explains the methodology behind the rankings. In terms of the 'getting credit' and 'resolving insolvency' indicators, the reports and rankings are based on a more sophisticated version of the 'legal origins' or 'law matters' thesis developed by four economists, La Porta, Lopez de Silanes, Shleifer and Vishny.[31] They also draw to a certain extent upon the

---

27   *Ibid.* art. 24(4) and see also art. 27(3).
28   *Ibid.* arts 24, 25, 87 and 92.
29   See the statement at p. 25 of the Action Plan, COM (2015)468: 'The 2015 World Bank Doing Business Report ranks countries on the strength of their insolvency frameworks on a scale of 0–16. The EU simple average is 11.6, which is 5% below the OECD average for high income countries (12.2). Some Member States score below 8.'
30   See generally G. McCormack, 'World Bank Doing Business Project: Should Insolvency Lawyers Take it Seriously' [2015] *Insolvency Intelligence* 119.
31   See R. La Porta, F. Lopez de Silanes, A. Shleifer and R. Vishny, 'Legal Determinants of External Finance' (1997) 52 *Journal of Finance* 1131, and by the same authors, 'Law and Finance' (1998) 106 *Journal of Political Economy* 113.

international standards in the field of insolvency and secured credit law that have been developed by UNCITRAL and the World Bank itself.

In general, EU countries perform well on the 'resolving insolvency' indicator and not so well on the 'getting credit' indicator.[32] On the 'resolving insolvency' report for 2016, Finland ranks 1st, with Germany 3rd and Portugal, Denmark, Belgium and the Netherlands ranked between 8th and 11th, respectively. The United Kingdom follows at 13th and Cyprus, Austria and Sweden come 17th to 19th, respectively. Slovenia is the first of the former 'Eastern bloc' countries and comes in 12th, followed by the Czech Republic at 22nd. Generally on the indicator Nordic and Western European countries score much better than Eastern European ones, though in fact Malta is the lowest ranking EU Member State at 83rd.

In relation to the 'getting credit' indicator, New Zealand is 1st with the United States, Colombia and Rwanda as joint 2nd, and Australia and Mexico as joint 5th. The highest ranked EU countries are Romania at joint 7th and then Poland, the United Kingdom, Latvia and Hungary at joint 19th. Germany, Ireland, Denmark, Estonia, the Czech Republic, Lithuania and Bulgaria are all bunched together and follow at equal 28th. But some other EU countries fare much poorer. For instance, France, the Netherlands and Greece are ranked equal 79th. Some of the results on the 'getting credit' indicator seem counter-intuitive. For example, despite the recent history of violence and political instability in these countries, Colombia and Rwanda score equal 2nd.

It should be noted that the *Doing Business* methodology and the underlying legal origins literature on which it is based has been criticized for a supposedly US-centric methodology.[33] Essentially, the *Doing Business Reports* use a creditor-centred approach with the highest grading given to countries that emphasize private contractual solutions rather than court-based ones. It may be that this approach is too one-dimensional. Certainly, it has been criticized for a preference for free market solutions and deregulation over other values.[34] As a World Bank Independent

---

The first three named authors refine the 'legal origins' thesis and defend it against criticisms in 'The Economic Consequences of Legal Origins' (2008) 46 *Journal of Economic Literature* 285.

[32] The reasons for the relatively poor performance on the 'getting credit' indicator are explored in Chapter 3.

[33] See generally R. Michaels, 'Comparative Law by Numbers? Legal Origins Thesis, Doing Business Reports and the Silence of Traditional Comparative Law' (2009) 57 *American Journal of Comparative Law* 765 and the literature referred to therein.

[34] See generally G. Sarfaty, 'Why Culture Matters in International Institutions:

Review Panel points out, the 'Doing Business project has, rightly or wrongly, been associated with a broad deregulation agenda'.[35]

The Independent Review Panel, commissioned by the World Bank, reported in 2013. Among other points, the Panel suggested that:

- The *Doing Business Report* had the potential to be misinterpreted.
- It relied on a narrow information source.
- It only measured regulations applicable to categories of business that could be captured through its methodology.
- Its data-collection methodology could be improved.
- It was not designed to help countries respond appropriately.
- The use of aggregate rankings was problematic.

The Review Panel was particularly concerned about rankings because they involve a process of aggregation across topics and this involved a value judgement about what was 'better' for doing business and how much better it was.

The criticisms on methodology apply with particular force to the 'getting credit' indicator. As the Review Panel has pointed out,[36] this indicator measures whether a country has a credit bureau system that has collected and distributed fundamental information about credit and a secured transactions legal regime that allows entrepreneurs access to credit using movable property. In reality, it does not measure directly what the indicator claimed to address.

The relevant data is gathered through questionnaire responses by local lawyers and insolvency practitioners and then verified through a study of laws and regulations as well as publicly available information on insolvency systems.[37] There is no attempt made to assess the

---

The Marginality of Human Rights at the World Bank' (2009) 103 *American Journal of International Law* 647.

[35] *Independent Panel Review of the World Bank Doing Business Report* (World Bank, 2013), p. 11. The Panel was chaired by Trevor Manuel, the former South African Minister of Finance. The *Doing Business Reports* appear to have made some adjustments in response to the Independent Panel report but the fundamentals of the project remain unaltered; see Foreword to the 2015 *Doing Business Report*, p. vii: 'Our attention has been drawn to many critiques by the Independent Panel on Doing Business, chaired by Trevor Manuel, which submitted its report in 2013. Following this report a decision was made to set a 2-year target to improve the methodology of Doing Business without damaging the overall integrity of this valuable publication.'

[36] *Independent Panel Review* (n. 35 above) 15.

[37] For some explanation of the methodology on 'getting credit' and 'resolving insolvency' see Word Bank 2016 *Doing Business Report*, pp. 137–9 and 155–9.

actual availability of credit in a particular economy. The assessment is based on the 'law on the books' rather than its actual application in practice.[38]

It may be that the 'resolving insolvency' rankings, and the methodology behind them, are no less problematic. The data is collected in the same way as for the 'getting credit' indicator, and in determining the rankings, two factors are equally weighted though the second factor was only introduced into the *Doing Business* methodology in 2015. It purports to measure the strength of the insolvency framework in a particular country. This factor depends both implicitly and explicitly on a set of normative assumptions that some aspects of insolvency law are better or more desirable than others. It could be argued that the assessment is relatively crude and depends largely on blunt 'all or nothing' measures. It assumes that particular legislative solutions are superior to others and misses out subtleties and nuances in the laws of a particular State. For example, it is considered desirable that undervalue pre-insolvency transactions should be subject to the possibility of avoidance in the insolvency proceedings. No attempt is made, however, to consider whether avoidance proceedings are easy to accomplish in practice or whether they are subject to conditions such as constraints on litigation funding that make the possibility of success in an avoidance action very difficult.

The first factor is the percentage recovery by secured creditors through restructuring, liquidation or debt enforcement proceedings and has been part of the 'resolving insolvency' rankings since their inception. The calculation takes into account whether the business emerges from the proceedings as a going concern or whether assets were sold piecemeal. Then the costs of the proceedings are deducted and, in line with international accounting practice, regard is also had to the value lost as a result of the money being tied up in insolvency proceedings for a particular period of time.

The recovery rate for creditors is seen as a function of the outcome, time and cost of insolvency proceedings in respect of a particular kind of local company. There is no attempt to measure whether this type of company is typical of the local economy or whether different outcomes and returns could be expected in relation to different types of company.

---

[38]   See the 2016 *Doing Business Report*, p. v: 'the report does not attempt to capture a number of dimensions of macroeconomic stability, the prevalence of corruption, antitrust policies or the skills of the workforce, important as all these factors are for establishing a foundation for sustainable economic development. Even within the relatively small set of indicators included in *Doing Business* the focus is deliberately narrow.'

The focus is also exclusively on returns to secured creditors. If the insolvency law in a particular country had a redistributionist element this would necessarily depress the returns to secured creditors and therefore lower a country's position in the rankings. For example, recital 22 of the Preamble to the recast Insolvency Regulation (Regulation (EU) 2015/848) refers to improving the preferential rights of employees at European level in the next review of the Regulation. Depending on the particular policy option adopted, this may worsen the position of EU countries in the rankings.

Moreover, an assessment of the 'recovery' rate depends in large part on the subjective views of survey respondents on the returns to creditors in their particular countries. In most countries, there will not be publicly available and accurate data on this matter.

SOME CONCLUSIONS FROM THE *DOING BUSINESS* PROJECT DATA

While this report has drawn attention to limitations in the methodology underlying the *Doing Business* project and accompanying database, the use of the database enables, nevertheless, comparisons to be drawn between countries and over time.

What is shown in Table I.1 is a simplified version of the *Doing Business* resolving data from 2006, 2011 and 2016. The 'strength of the insolvency framework' criteria were only introduced into the methodology and rankings from 2015 onwards and so we do not have data in respect of these matters for 2006 and 2011. The rank indicated in the table is the overall rank of the particular country on the 'resolving insolvency' indicator of the 2016 *Doing Business Report*.

The data covers the EU countries, though in respect of Cyprus, Luxembourg and Malta the data does not go back to 2006. The two comparator countries, the United States and Norway, are also included.

The 2016 *Doing Business Report* suggests that there is strong correlation between performing on the *Doing Business* indicators and also in other international data sets capturing different dimensions of competitiveness.[39] These include such measures as the Global Competitiveness Index and Transparency International's Corruption Perceptions Index. The report also points to a strong link between quality and efficiency and the

---

[39]   2016 *Doing Business Report*, p. 4.

Table 1.1 World Bank Doing Business resolving insolvency data (years 2006, 2011, 2016)

Economy	Year	Resolving insolvency									
		Rank	Recovery rate (cents on the dollar)	Time (years)	Cost (% of estate)	Outcome (0 as piecemeal sale and 1 as going concern)	Strength of insolvency framework index (0–16)	Commencement of proceedings index (0–3)	Management of debtor's assets index (0–6)	Reorganization proceedings index (0–3)	Creditor participation index (0–4)
Austria	DB2006	–	73.3	1.1	18	–	–	–	–	–	–
	DB2011	–	73.1	1.1	18	–	–	–	–	–	–
	DB2016	18	82.7	1.1	10	1	11	2.5	5.5	1	2
Belgium	DB2006	–	86.6	0.9	3.5	–	–	–	–	–	–
	DB2011	–	87.6	0.9	3.5	–	–	–	–	–	–
	DB2016	10	89.3	0.9	3.5	1	11.5	2.5	6	1	2
Bulgaria	DB2006	–	33.5	3.3	9	–	–	–	–	–	–
	DB2011	–	31	3.3	9	–	–	–	–	–	–
	DB2016	48	34	3.3	9	0	13	2.5	4	2.5	4
Croatia	DB2006	–	28.5	3.1	14.5	–	–	–	–	–	–
	DB2011	–	28.7	3.1	14.5	–	–	–	–	–	–
	DB2016	59	30.5	3.1	14.5	0	12	3	4	3	2
Cyprus	DB2006	–	–		–	–	–	–	–	–	–
	DB2011	–	70.4	1.5	14.5	–	–	–	–	–	–
	DB2016	17	71.4	1.5	14.5	1	13	3	4.5	2.5	3
Czech Republic	DB2006	–	17.8	9.2	17	–	–	–	–	–	–
	DB2011	–	55.9	3.2	17	–	–	–	–	–	–
	DB2016	22	66	2.1	17	1	13.5	3	5.5	3	2

Denmark	DB2006	—	67.2	3.3	4	—	—	—	—	—	—
	DB2011	—	89.4	1.1	4	—	—	—	—	—	—
	DB2016	9	87.8	1	4	1	12	3	6	1	2
Estonia	DB2006	—	39	3	9	—	—	—	—	—	—
	DB2011	—	35.5	3	9	—	—	—	—	—	—
	DB2016	40	40	3	9	0	14	2.5	5.5	2	4
Finland	DB2006	—	89	0.9	3.5	—	—	—	—	—	—
	DB2011	—	89.4	0.9	3.5	—	—	—	—	—	—
	DB2016	1	90.1	0.9	3.5	1	14.5	3	6	2.5	3
France	DB2006	—	47.5	1.9	9	—	—	—	—	—	—
	DB2011	—	45	1.9	9	—	—	—	—	—	—
	DB2016	24	77.5	1.9	9	1	11	3	6	1	1
Germany	DB2006	—	81.3	1.2	8	—	—	—	—	—	—
	DB2011	—	81.9	1.2	8	—	—	—	—	—	—
	DB2016	3	83.7	1.2	8	1	15	3	6	3	3
Greece	DB2006	—	45.9	2	9	—	—	—	—	—	—
	DB2011	—	43.2	2	9	—	—	—	—	—	—
	DB2016	54	34.9	3.5	9	0	12	2.5	5.5	3	1
Hungary	DB2006	—	35.7	2	14.5	—	—	—	—	—	—
	DB2011	—	37.9	2	14.5	—	—	—	—	—	—
	DB2016	65	41.7	2	14.5	0	9	2.5	5	0.5	1
Ireland	DB2006	—	88	0.4	9	—	—	—	—	—	—
	DB2011	—	87.4	0.4	9	—	—	—	—	—	—
	DB2016	20	87.7	0.4	9	1	10	3	4.5	1.5	1
Italy	DB2006	—	63.6	1.8	22	—	—	—	—	—	—
	DB2011	—	58	1.8	22	—	—	—	—	—	—
	DB2016	23	63.1	1.8	22	1	13.5	3	5.5	3	2

Table I.1 (continued)

Economy	Year	Rank	Recovery rate (cents on the dollar)	Time (years)	Cost (% of estate)	Resolving insolvency					
						Outcome (0 as piecemeal sale and 1 as going concern)	Strength of insolvency framework index (0–16)	Commencement of proceedings index (0–3)	Management of debtor's assets index (0–6)	Reorganization proceedings index (0–3)	Creditor participation index (0–4)
Latvia	DB2006	–	33.9	3	13	–	–	–	–	–	–
	DB2011	–	31.9	3	13	–	–	–	–	–	–
	DB2016	43	48.1	1.5	10	0	12	2.5	5	2.5	2
Lithuania	DB2006	–	49.8	1.7	7	–	–	–	–	–	–
	DB2011	–	48.3	1.7	7	–	–	–	–	–	–
	DB2016	70	42.8	2.3	10	0	8	2.5	4	0.5	1
Luxembourg	DB2006	–	–	–	–	–	–	–	–	–	–
	DB2011	–	43.7	2	14.5	–	–	–	–	–	–
	DB2016	80	43.8	2	14.5	0	7	2.5	3	0.5	1
Malta	DB2006	–	–	–	–	–	–	–	–	–	–
	DB2011	–	–	–	–	–	–	–	–	–	–
	DB2016	83	39.6	3	10	0	7.5	2.5	2	0	3
Netherlands	DB2006	–	88.4	1.1	3.5	–	–	–	–	–	–
	DB2011	–	82.5	1.1	3.5	–	–	–	–	–	–
	DB2016	11	88.9	1.1	3.5	1	11.5	2.5	6	1	2
Poland	DB2006	–	32.1	3	15	–	–	–	–	–	–
	DB2011	–	35.8	3	15	–	–	–	–	–	–
	DB2016	32	58.3	3	15	1	12.5	3	6	2.5	1

Country	Year										
Portugal	DB2006	–	74.7	2	9	–	–	–	–	–	–
	DB2011	8	72.6	2	9	1	14.5	3	5.5	–	–
	DB2016	–	73.4	2	9	–	–	–	–	3	3
Romania	DB2006	–	17.5	4.6	9	–	–	–	–	–	–
	DB2011	46	25.7	3.3	10.5	0	13.5	3	6	–	–
	DB2016	–	32.7	3.3	10.5	–	–	–	–	2.5	2
Slovak Republic	DB2006	–	38.6	4.8	18	–	–	–	–	–	–
	DB2011	33	55.3	4	18	1	13	3	4	–	–
	DB2016	–	54.7	4	18	–	–	–	–	3	3
Slovenia	DB2006	–	44	2	8	–	–	–	–	–	–
	DB2011	12	50.9	2	4	1	11.5	2.5	6	–	–
	DB2016	–	88.2	0.8	4	–	–	–	–	2	1
Spain	DB2006	–	74.1	1.5	14.5	–	–	–	–	–	–
	DB2011	25	70.5	1.5	11	1	12	3	6	–	–
	DB2016	–	71.2	1.5	11	–	–	–	–	2	1
Sweden	DB2006	–	74.9	2	9	–	–	–	–	–	–
	DB2011	19	77.3	2	9	1	12	3	6	–	–
	DB2016	–	76.6	2	9	–	–	–	–	1	2
United Kingdom	DB2006	–	85.3	1	6	–	–	–	–	–	–
	DB2011	13	88.6	1	6	1	11	3	5	–	–
	DB2016	–	88.6	1	6	–	–	–	–	1	2
United States	DB2006	–	80.2	1.5	7	–	–	–	–	–	–
	DB2011	–	81.5	1.5	7	1	15	3	6	–	–
	DB2016	–	81.5	1.5	7	–	–	–	–	3	3
Norway	DB2006	–	91.1	0.9	1	–	–	–	–	–	–
	DB2011	6	90.9	0.9	1	1	11.5	2.5	5	–	–
	DB2016	–	92.5	0.9	1	–	–	–	–	1	3

'resolving insolvency' indicator is singled out in this respect.[40] It is suggested that where there is a good legal framework for insolvency, then creditors will recover a larger share of the amount due to them at the end of the insolvency process. In this context, Finland is taken as an example. 'Resolving insolvency there takes 11 months on average and costs 4% of the debtor's estate, and the most likely outcome is that the company will be sold as a going concern. The average recovery rate for creditors is 90.1 cents on the dollar. This high recovery rate is paired with a high score on the strength of insolvency framework index.'[41] Finnish insolvency law is said to contain a range of good practices, including the fact that debtors are allowed to avoid preferential and undervalued transactions. All creditors are permitted to vote in judicial reorganization proceedings. New finance in connection with reorganization proceedings is also permitted with such finance only being granted priority over ordinary unsecured creditors.

The 2015 *Doing Business Report* in its review of the 'resolving insolvency' indicators also highlights the linkages between efficiency and quality.[42] It points out that the recovery rate measures the percentage recouped by secured creditors through insolvency proceedings and suggests that this is a measure of efficiency because time and cost are two important components. The strength of the insolvency framework index is said to be a proxy for quality because it measures how well insolvency laws accord with internationally recognized good practices. Very few economies are said to have an insolvency system that combines both high efficiency (a recovery rate of more than 50 per cent) and low quality (a score of less than 8 of the possible 16 points on the strength of insolvency framework index).

On the other hand, the correlation is not necessarily a strong one and it is possible to point to some anomalies and possible inconsistencies in the data. For instances, Austria, France and the United Kingdom score only the relatively low mark of 11 on the strength of the insolvency framework, yet have recovery rates in excess of 70 per cent. In the case of Austria and the United Kingdom, the recovery rates are in excess of 80 per cent. Bulgaria, on the other hand, scores 13 on the strength of the insolvency framework yet has a recovery rate that is below 50 per cent. The *Doing Business* team might explain Bulgaria as an example of an economy having 'an insolvency system with low efficiency and high quality. These are economies that have well-designed laws but face challenges in

---

[40]   *Ibid.* 9.
[41]   *Ibid.*
[42]   2015 *Doing Business Report*, p. 10.

implementing them effectively'.[43] Others may suggest that the example calls into question the reliability of some of the *Doing Business* data. For example, our research indicates that Bulgaria does not have an early stage restructuring law in line with the European Commission's new approach to business failure and insolvency, though there may be plans in the offing to introduce such a law.

Croatia, Greece, Estonia and Latvia are also countries which on the World Bank figures are said to have better designed laws than any of Austria, France or the United Kingdom, with respective scores of 12, 12, 14 and 12 on the strength of the insolvency framework measure. At the same time, these countries have recovery rates below 50 per cent. On a more positive note, however, encouraging signs can be drawn from the World Bank figures in relation to the improvements in recovery rates over time for certain countries. In the Czech Republic, Poland, the Slovak Republic and Slovenia, the recovery rates have improved significantly since 2006. This is partly counterbalanced, however, by the fact that in Greece and Lithuania recovery rates appear to have regressed somewhat.

---

[43] *Ibid.*

1. Directors' liability and disqualification

1.1 INTRODUCTION

This part of the study deals with the liability of directors and their possible disqualification from acting as directors, or in some other capacity. Directors, whether a one-tier board or a two-tier board approach is embraced by a jurisdiction, are critical to the lives of companies. One-tier boards involve a single board of directors consisting of both executive and non-executive directors, and with a two-tier board system there are two boards, a Board of Management and a Board of Supervision. Both types of approach are used across the European Union. Some Member States prescribe the use of two-tier boards,[1] some prescribe the use of one-tier boards,[2] and others permit either approach to be employed.[3] The directors will oversee the management of the company's affairs and make the most important decisions for the company, including designing strategy for the businesses the company owns; entering into transactions that involve the borrowing of funds; the sale of assets; the purchase of property necessary for the carrying on of business and the sale of what the company produces whether it be goods, services, technical advice or a combination of these. Importantly, directors formulate a particular strategy and then commit the company to it as well as determining how that is to be achieved. If the company has setbacks or experiences financial difficulties, the directors are the ones initially who have to decide what course of action needs to be adopted.

When a company is in financial difficulties then, as a matter of practical necessity, directors usually have to take some action to address the issues

---

[1] Such as Germany and Austria.
[2] Such as Ireland and the United Kingdom.
[3] Such as France and the Netherlands. For further discussion of the types of boards and their structure, see C. Gerner-Beuerle, P. Paech and E. Schuster, *Study on Directors' Duties and Liability* (prepared for the European Commission, London, LSE, April 2013), pp. 211–12 available at http://daccess-dds-ny.un.org/doc/UNDOC/LTD/V13/807/89/PDF/V1380789.pdf?OpenElement.

facing the company. Directors will have to engage in robust management and often have to make difficult decisions to ensure that the company survives.[4] Legal systems have prescribed, in different ways, what directors should do when a company is near to or actually insolvent and this report explores these various approaches. The World Bank, in its report titled *Principles for Effective Insolvency and Creditor Rights System*,[5] made it plain that laws governing director and officer liability for decisions detrimental to creditors made when an enterprise is in financial distress or insolvent should promote responsible corporate behaviour while fostering reasonable risk taking. At a minimum, standards should hold management accountable for harm to creditors resulting from wilful, reckless or grossly negligent conduct. We can see a response to these concerns in the laws of the EU Member States.

If they are involved in an insolvent company or precipitated the insolvency of the company, the directors might be disqualified from holding office as a director in existing and/or future companies or other offices in society. The disqualification might be seen as a protection of creditors and also, in some Member States, as a further penalty for a criminal offence. Regimes seem to exist in order to protect creditors by seeking to deter directors from acting wrongly and ensuring that miscreants are not, during the term of the disqualification, able to cause harm to other creditors.[6]

In its 2003 Action Plan, the European Commission stated its intention to propose a Directive to increase the responsibilities of directors which would include director disqualification.[7] But this did not occur, notwithstanding support at the public consultation stage. In 2006, the European Parliament proposed that the Commission should posit measures to enhance the cross-border availability of information on the disqualification of directors.[8] This was consistent with the suggestion made by the

---

[4] UNCITRAL, 'Directors' Obligations in the Period Approaching Insolvency' in *Legislative Guide on Insolvency Law* (Working Group V, 43rd session, New York, 15–19 April 2013), p.5, available at http://daccess-dds-ny.un.org/doc/UNDOC/LTD/V13/807/89/PDF/V1380789.pdf?OpenElement.

[5] World Bank, *Principles for Effective Insolvency and Creditor Rights System* (2001) B2 (p.13).

[6] K. Sorensen, 'Disqualifying Directors in the EU' in Hanne S. Birkmose, Mette Neville and Karsten Engsig Sørensen (eds), *Boards of Directors in European Companies. Reshaping and Harmonising their Organisation and Duties* (London, Wolters Kluwer, 2013), p.335.

[7] *Modernising Company Law and Enhancing Corporate Governance in the European Union: A Plan to Move Forward*, COM(2003)284 final, p.16.

[8] Resolutions on recent developments and prospects in relation to company law (2006/2051(INI)), para. 18.

Reflection Group on the future of EU company law.[9] It was noted by the
Group that the increase of cross-border mobility of companies did lead
to the risk that those who are subject to sanctions in one Member State
could simply continue their improper activity in another Member State.
Therefore, it called for greater access to information on the disqualification of directors. The Commission has endeavoured to broaden disqualification throughout the EU, and thus promote mutual recognition.[10]
This has been difficult to achieve because of the diverse disqualification
rules of the Member States and because of issues relating to the rights of
individuals.

One problem that often presents itself in addressing the issue of disqualification is that it falls into a grey area, somewhere between company
law and insolvency law. In this report the focus, as far as disqualification
is concerned, is on the breach of insolvency-related duties that might lead
to disqualification.[11]

1.2   WORK UNDERTAKEN BY UNCITRAL

In recent years Working Group V (Insolvency Law) of the United
Nations Commission on International Trade Law (UNCITRAL) has
been studying the obligations that might be imposed on directors in the
period approaching insolvency or where insolvency becomes unavoid-
able. As part of the study, the Working Group has sought to identify the
options that are available when a company is in the vicinity of insolvency
in order to inform policy-makers as they seek to devise appropriate legal
and regulatory frameworks.[12] The Group has referred to, and engaged
in some examination of, the developments in some jurisdictions which
have involved the shifting of directors' duties when insolvency is near or
actual, and which are discussed in this report.[13] The work of the Group

---

[9]   *Report of the Reflection Group on the Future of EU Company Law* (5 April
2011), pp. 34–5.
[10]   *Green Paper on the Approximation, Mutual Recognition and Enforcement
of Criminal Sanctions in the European Union*, COM(2004)334 final, p. 24; and
see similarly *Preventing and Combating Corporate and Financial Malpractice*,
COM(2004)661 final, p. 11.
[11]   Sorensen, 'Disqualifying Directors in the EU' (n. 6 above) 336.
[12]   The latest was UNCITRAL, 'Directors' Obligations in the Period
Approaching Insolvency' (n. 4 above).
[13]   It has not clearly endorsed the approach although there are comments in
recommendations that suggest that the Working Group seem to think that it needs
to be considered: *ibid*. 14–15.

has been brought together in Part 4 ('Directors' Obligations in the Period Approaching Insolvency') of UNCITRAL's *Legislative Guide on Insolvency Law* (2013).[14]

1.3 DUTIES OF DIRECTORS

This section addresses the duties of directors and the liability that might emanate from the breach of such duties. 'Duties' is interpreted in a broad way in the discussion and was the way that national reporters had considered it in their reports. Duties are invariably prescribed by statute, but some other duties may be provided for in judicial precedents, the company's constitution or pursuant to contracts between directors and their companies. Some of the consideration of duties in our study overlaps with, and builds on, the work done for DG Justice by a team from the London School of Economics in 2013.[15] This latter study focused solely on directors and board structure and did not consider insolvency save where it was related to a discussion of the duties of directors. The discussion in our report focuses on insolvency-related duties and does not really engage in consideration of duties that are only applicable to solvent companies. As we will see, in many Member States some of the duties of directors remain the same whether a company is solvent, near insolvent or actually insolvent.

Our study sought to ascertain the duties owed by directors across the EU and principally when directors' companies were insolvent or nearing insolvency. As directors are so crucial to the running of companies, corporate law lays down certain duties that regulate how the directors are to conduct themselves in carrying out their functions and powers. This is one way that the law endeavours to control directors and ensure that they are accountable to their company, the shareholders and stakeholders.

Directors are usually subject to general duties that are to guide them in their activities and more specific duties designed to address particular issues and circumstances, such as the need to keep proper accounting records. Duties are aimed at protecting the company, its shareholders and other stakeholders against mismanagement and misconduct. In some Member States, such as the United Kingdom and Ireland, there is

---

[14] Available at www.uncitral.org/pdf/english/texts/insolven/Leg-Guide-Insol-Part4-ebook-E.pdf.

[15] Gerner-Beuerle *et al.*, *Study on Directors' Duties and Liability* (n. 3 above) pp. 211–12.

an emphasis on acting for the benefit of the shareholders, whereas in the majority of states, where a stakeholder approach to corporate law tends to be adopted, the duties are aimed at benefiting all, or the most important, stakeholders, and this might mean, as it does in the Netherlands and Portugal, for instance, that the interests of creditors are taken into account even when a company is solvent. As one would expect, given that there is a significant degree of variation between the company laws of Member States, there is a diverse approach across the EU as far as the prescribing and formulation of duties is concerned.

Generally speaking, most Member States provide some duties of care and some duties of loyalty. The former encompasses requirements that directors act diligently and act with care in what they do. The latter includes the duty to act in good faith in respect of the interests of the company and ensuring that the directors do not have conflicts between their company's interests (which they must foster and protect) on the one hand, and their own personal interests on the other.

In most Member States there is no specific duty that requires directors to formulate plans to take preventative action to avoid insolvency or to identify possible insolvency problems, although it is arguably implicit that they do have some obligation in this regard as the directors should be managing the company responsibly and in such a way that is designed to ensure solvency; doing so will be in the interests of the company as well as those of the shareholders and other stakeholders. Also, in accordance with article 19 of the Second Directive,[16] Member States require the directors to convene a meeting of the shareholders if the company incurs a loss of half of its share capital. The German public companies' legislation is a good example and provides that:

> If upon preparation of the annual balance sheet or an interim balance sheet it becomes apparent, or if in the exercise of proper judgment it must be assumed that the company has incurred a loss equal to one half of the share capital, the management board shall promptly call a shareholders' meeting and advise the meeting thereof.[17]

The German approach is representative of the legislation found in the majority of Member States. It merely provides that the directors must call a meeting of shareholders when the relevant conditions exist. This is regarded as the minimum requirement under the Second Directive. Other

---

[16]   2012/30/EU, [2012] OJ L315/74.
[17]   Stock Corporation Act (Aktiengesetz), art. 92(1).

states' legislative response to article 19[18] demands more and requires the board of management or board of directors to call a meeting and have the company decide, upon losing half of its subscribed share capital, whether to recapitalize or liquidate/dissolve the company's business. The time that directors have in which to call a meeting varies across the EU. Most Member States provide a time period in which meetings should be convened, although some Member States, such as Portugal, merely provide that they should be held immediately. If directors fail to convene the meeting and/or other obligations connected with it, they can be personally responsible for the liabilities of the company that are incurred during the period in which the obligations of the directors are not met.[19] Also, the failure to call a meeting might lead to criminal liability.[20] The United States, in line with the position adopted in many common law countries, has no requirement that directors convene a meeting of the shareholders if the company's net asset value falls below a defined portion of share capital.

The company's insolvency might well coincide with the loss of half of the share capital and if so directors must not only take this action but other action that is required by legislation when the company is insolvent, such as filing for bankruptcy or seeking to minimize the loss of creditors. It is to be noted that in Italy, in order to foster corporate rescue, it is provided that, if directors had applied for some proceedings aimed at rescuing the company or for the judicial approval of a plan set down together by the company and its creditors, the directors are no longer obliged to activate the safeguards provided for the reduction or total loss of the capital mentioned above.[21]

In the majority of Member States there is no change in the nature of a director's general duties when the director's company is nearing insolvency or is in fact insolvent. In some states, however, such as the United Kingdom, Ireland, Malta and Cyprus, there is a clear change in the direction of duties.[22] Directors, whose focus tends to be doing what

---

[18] See Belgium, Cyprus, Czech Republic, Denmark, Estonia, France, Hungary, Italy, Latvia, Lithuania, Portugal, Spain and Sweden.

[19] An example is Sweden. See Companies Act 2005 (Aktiebolagstagen), s. 18.

[20] For instance, see Code of Commercial Companies, art. 523 (Portugal).

[21] Royal Decree of 16 March 1942 No. 267 (Legge Fallimentare), art. 182-*sexies*.

[22] See A. Keay, 'The Shifting of Directors' Duties in the Vicinity of Insolvency' (2015) 2 *International Insolvency Review* 140; D. Milman, *The Governance of Distressed Firms* (Cheltenham and Northampton, MA, Edward Elgar Publishing, 2013).

BOX 1.1 *LIQUIDATOR OF WEST MERCIA SAFETYWEAR LTD V. DODD* (1988) 4 BCC 30

D was the director of two companies, X and Y. X was the parent company of Y. At the relevant time both companies were in financial difficulty. X had a large overdraft that D had guaranteed and it also had a charge over its book debts. One debt owed to X was £30,000, and this was owed by Y. A few days before there was a meeting of the members of Y, which was going to consider a motion that Y wind up, D transferred the sum of £4,000 that had been paid to Y by one of its debtors to X's overdrawn bank account. On liquidation of Y, the liquidator sought from the bank repayment to Y of the £4,000. The bank refused and so the liquidator sought a declaration that D was guilty of breach of duty in relation to the transfer of the money to X, and repayment of the £4,000. At first instance, in the County Court, the liquidator failed. He then appealed to the Court of Appeal and succeeded on the basis that directors have a duty to consider creditor interests when a company is in financial difficulty, and in this case D breached his duty to Y in transferring the funds to X.

---

is best for shareholders when the company is clearly solvent and not experiencing financial stress, must consider the interests of the creditors when the company is nearing insolvency.[23] The only Member State that has legislation that incorporates this change in the nature of the duty of directors is the United Kingdom, and this is built on about 40 years of case law.[24] The imposition of this duty does not entail the directors having to take any specific preventative action. What action should be taken will depend solely on the company's circumstances[25] and of critical importance is the depth of the company's financial distress and its commercial context. The case study in Box 1.1, from the United Kingdom, explains how this approach works.

In some Member States, such as Slovenia, directors are required to demonstrate greater consideration of creditor interests when their company is nearing or in insolvency, and if a company is insolvent and directors do not act for creditors then the directors might be liable to those creditors.[26] Other Member States include various provisions, such as requiring directors to do that which is necessary to avoid insolvency when their company

---

[23] For example, see UK Companies Act 2006, s. 172(3) and Cypriot Companies Law, ss. 301, 303. For a discussion of the law in detail, see A. Keay, 'Directors' Duties and Creditors' Interests' (2014) 130 *Law Quarterly Review* 443.

[24] For a detailed discussion, see A. Keay, *Company Directors' Responsibilities to Creditors* (Abingdon, Routledge, 2007).

[25] Keay, 'Directors' Duties and Creditors' Interests' (n. 23 above).

[26] Supreme Court of Slovenia, no.111 Ips 145/2005 (14 June 2007).

is in financial distress;[27] a requirement that no payments are made except those that are compatible with what a prudent manager would make;[28] requiring creditors to be treated equally;[29] and to convene a meeting of the shareholders to consider what steps should be taken.[30] In one of our comparator jurisdictions, the United States, there is now generally no shift if a company is nearing insolvency, although there once was. Now there is only a shift in the nature of directors' duties once a company is insolvent.[31] The creditors of US companies can actually bring proceedings against the directors if the latter fail to fulfil their duty to take account of creditors' interests, although the former do so on behalf of the company by way of derivative action,[32] just as shareholders can in many jurisdictions in Europe and around the world when directors have breached their duties to their company.

When a company is insolvent or in a state that effectively means that it is insolvent, the majority of Member States require the directors to take some form of action, and this generally involves filing for insolvency in the courts. The time in which this must be done varies widely across the EU, from 14 days in Poland[33] (although this was to be extended to 30 days from 1 January 2016) to 60 days in Austria.[34] The average period tends to be 30 days. Some states do not actually state an exact period in which directors are to file proceedings. An instance is the Czech Republic which provides that the filing should occur without undue delay.[35] Likewise, Lithuania requires filing to be done immediately. Latvia also does not specify an exact time. There is some uncertainty in some states as to when the time period actually begins to run and this might be seen as unsatisfactory, especially given the fact that a failure to adhere to the requirement to file within the set period could lead to civil and/or criminal liability, as evidenced in Table 1.1. The problem is that defining insolvency is not easy, and is explained in different ways across the EU (as considered in section 5.2 below), and it has caused clear difficulties and uncertainty in many

---

[27] For example, the Czech Republic's Business Corporations Act 2012, s. 68.
[28] Germany's Stock Corporation Act (Aktiengesetz), art. 92(2).
[29] Insolvency Act (ZFPPIPP) (Slovenia), art. 34.
[30] Greece's Insolvency Code, arts 171 and 176.
[31] *North American Catholic Education Programming Foundation Inc.* v. *Gheewalla*, 930 A. 2d 92 (Del., 2007); *Quadrant Structured Products Co.* v. *Vertin*, 2015 WL 2062115 (Del. Ch., 4 May 2015).
[32] *Gheewalla* (n. 31 above); *Quadrant Structured Products Co.* v. *Vertin* (n. 31 above).
[33] Insolvency Law, art. 21(a).
[34] Insolvenzordnung (Insolvency Code), s. 69(2).
[35] There is no clear idea of what this expression means.

countries over the years. Even laying down the fact that insolvency entails cash flow (unable to pay debts as they fall due) or balance sheet insolvency (liabilities outweigh assets), as is most often done, does not resolve the problem, as it is problematic as to what liabilities can be taken into account in cash flow insolvency and particularly whether future liabilities are to be taken into account or not. With balance sheet insolvency there can be difficulties in valuing both assets and liabilities and determining what future liabilities and assets can be taken into account.

The difficulty with defining insolvency is manifest in the fact that it is expressed in different terms in Member States. For instance, in Germany, Austria and Bulgaria it involves the company being illiquid or over-indebted, and in Belgium[36] and Luxembourg[37] it entails the company ceasing to pay debts. Being illiquid in Germany involves not being able to meet one's debts as they fall due[38] and accords with the concept of cash flow insolvency. Over-indebtedness means that the company's assets do not cover the liabilities[39] and this is what is involved with the concept of balance sheet insolvency.[40]

Somewhat unusually, in Malta the directors do not need to file for bankruptcy if their company cannot pay its debts as they fall due, but they must convene a meeting of the shareholders who must consider the company's financial position. This has the benefit of ensuring shareholders do contribute to any decision that is taken concerning the company's financial problems, but it does mean that directors can effectively 'pass the buck', and also the convening of shareholder meetings can take a great deal of time and this might delay decisions about the future of the company, during which things could deteriorate substantially. In some Member States the duty to file for insolvency is coupled with a duty not to make payments.[41]

Table 1.1 shows the Member States that impose the requirement on directors to file for insolvency proceedings in the courts when their companies are in some form of insolvency, and the time period (if any) that is involved.

Our comparator jurisdictions of Norway and the United States tend to follow a different approach. In the former, while directors have to file insolvency proceedings when the company becomes insolvent, there is no

---

[36]   Belgian Bankruptcy Act 1997, art. 9.
[37]   Law on Commercial Companies 1915, art. 440.
[38]   Insolvenzordnung (Insolvency Code), s. 17(2).
[39]   *Ibid.* s. 19(2).
[40]   For further consideration, see Chapter 5.
[41]   Stock Corporation Act (Aktiengesetz), s. 84(3) para. 6 (Austria).

Table 1.1   Duty to file proceedings in court

Country	Provides requirement to file insolvency proceedings	Time in which directors must file	Nature of the circumstances that triggers requirement
Austria	√	Without negligent delay and at least within 60 days[a]	Illiquidity or over-indebtedness
Belgium	√	One month	Cessation of the payment of debts
Bulgaria	√	15 days	Suspension of payment of debts
Croatia	√	21 days	The occurrence of a bankruptcy reason (illiquidity or over-indebtedness)
Cyprus	None		
Czech Republic	√	Without undue delay	Directors learn that the company is insolvent
Denmark	None[b]		
Estonia	√[c]	20 calendar days	The company becomes permanently insolvent
Finland	No explicit obligation to file insolvency proceedings but directors' deliberate stalling may cause liability in damages for loss		
France	√	Within 45 days	Insolvency/cease paying debts
Germany	√	Without delay and at least within 3 weeks	Illiquidity or over-indebtedness
Greece	√	Without delay and no later than 30 days after trigger	Cease paying debts or there is a declaration that payments to creditors are suspended
Hungary	None		
Ireland	None		
Italy			

Table 1.1 (continued)

Country	Provides requirement to file insolvency proceedings	Time in which directors must file	Nature of the circumstances that triggers requirement
Latvia	√	There is no specific time period stated under law or in established court practice as to the time period in which an application should be filed	The company is unable to pay its debts when they come due
Lithuania	√	Immediately on becoming aware of the fact that the company is unable to pay its creditors	The company is or will be unable to pay its creditors or it has notified its creditors of its lack of ability or lack of intent to pay its debts
Luxembourg	√	One month	Company has ceased to pay its debts
Malta	None		
Netherlands	None		
Poland	√	30days[d]	The company is unable to perform its obligations (which is assumed where delay in performance of its payment obligations exceeds 30 days) or the total of its monetary liabilities (excluding future and contingent liabilities and financial indebtedness towards shareholders) exceeds the value of its assets and such state continues for over 24 months
Portugal	√	30 days	The company is unable to meet its debts as they fall due or assets are appreciably insufficient to cover liabilities

Table 1.1 (continued)

Country	Provides requirement to file insolvency proceedings	Time in which directors must file	Nature of the circumstances that triggers requirement
Romania	√	30 days	Unable to pay debts as they fall due (presumed where company has not paid one or more of its creditors within 90 days of the due date for payment of debts)
Slovakia	√	30 days	Indebtedness: company has more than one debt that cannot be paid and liabilities exceed the value of assets
Slovenia	√	3 business days	A shareholders' meeting does not increase equity when management has reported to it that financial restructuring is not likely to succeed due to the company's insolvency
Spain	√	2 months	The directors knew or should have known of insolvency (inability to regularly fulfil obligations)
Sweden	None		
United Kingdom	None		

Notes:
a   The 60 day period is only available if the directors endeavour to finalize a settlement with the creditors.
b   Proper management of the company might infer that the directors should file for bankruptcy on the insolvency of the company, but no specific duty applies.
c   Until 1 January 2015 directors' liability was criminal but now it is not.
d   The time was 14 days until 1 January 2016 when the law changed.

time period mentioned or any reference to a requirement to file without delay. The directors need to assess the company's financial position given the relevant circumstances. In the United States, there is no obligation on directors to file for bankruptcy when their company is insolvent.

As is manifest in Table 1.1, the majority of Member States oblige directors to file for insolvency proceedings within a certain time period following the advent of particular circumstances. The circumstances that trigger the need for directors to file is variously described, but effectively involves insolvency occurring. The time period that is prescribed varies between states, although the most common period invoked is 30 days/one month. Some states, while setting an upper time limit for filing, actually also mandate that the directors are to file without delay.

In some Member States, such as Finland, Germany and Sweden, the directors are actually empowered to file for bankruptcy when insolvency is near or imminent, even though it is not obligatory to do so. If they do not do so, then they might incur criminal penalties. In other Member States, such as the United Kingdom, the directors cannot file liquidation proceedings, as to liquidate the company is a decision for the members of the company in a general meeting. But the directors of UK companies could decide to place the company in administration, which is akin to several procedures in effect elsewhere, such as Chapter 11 bankruptcy in the United States and examinership in Ireland. The UK Insolvency Act 1986 permits entry into administration when a company is unable to pay its debts or is likely to become unable to pay its debts.[42] Entry into Chapter 11 bankruptcy in the United States is also permitted when a company is not insolvent. But if a company is not insolvent then entry into Chapter 11 proceedings is often tactical and to allow the directors to renegotiate pre-existing contracts, particularly with employees. Some Member States permit the directors to take a company into proceedings that involve possible restructuring if they believe that the company is near to being insolvent or insolvency is imminent.[43]

In those Member States where filing proceedings is required because of some event (usually insolvency), if the directors do not adhere to the law and fail to file within the prescribed period then they are going to be liable in some form or another. The nature of the liability varies from place to place and will usually involve, at least, civil liability to creditors for loss of company assets/funds that resulted from failing to file for insolvency on time. For instance, in Belgium the directors can incur liability in tort to the creditors. In other jurisdictions the liability could be criminal.

It might be thought that requiring directors to file for bankruptcy when the company is insolvent could be regarded in some cases as premature as it might prevent the company seeking to recover and so it might circumscribe any attempts to restructure and rescue the company. This is not a

---

[42]   Insolvency Act 1986, Sch. B1, para. 27(2)(a).
[43]   Such as Croatia, Greece, Hungary, the Netherlands, Portugal, Romania and Spain.

problem for Member States such as Germany, where filing for bankruptcy does not mean that the company is set on a particular course and will necessarily lead to the end of the life of the company. When insolvency proceedings are filed in Germany there are several options available and some involve a reorganization of the company and means that the company may continue to operate and rehabilitate itself. This kind of approach is thought to encourage debtor companies to file for insolvency before their circumstances become too dire.[44] This kind of thinking was, *inter alia*, behind the broadening of the process of administration in the United Kingdom in 2003.

Denmark has a hybrid approach whereby if a company gets to the point of no return as far as its finances are concerned, that is, the point where it is futile to keep the company operating, the directors have a duty to take into account creditors' interests, but it is implied that this will involve the cessation of the business of the company and the filing of process for bankruptcy. Italy also has dual coverage. In Italy, if a company is insolvent the directors must file for bankruptcy, but also if this state of affairs exists the directors have a kind of duty that is owed to the creditors.[45] Similarly, in Romania directors have a duty to file insolvency proceedings if their company is insolvent, but also they are liable for certain actions that are characterized, if committed, as wrongful trading and could lead to liability. Examples are continuing to trade their company for their own benefit and using the assets for the benefit of themselves.[46]

In Member States where there is not a formal requirement to file for insolvency within a specific time, most have some form of provision or case law which dictates that while companies may continue to do business when they are near to, or actually, insolvent (either on a cash flow or balance sheet basis), directors must modify their actions so as to halt a company's slide into insolvent liquidation and in order to protect creditors. This kind of provision, known as 'wrongful trading' in the United

---

[44] World Bank, 'Resolving Insolvency' in *Doing Business 2015* (29 October 2014), p.96, available at www.doingbusiness.org/~/media/GIAWB/Doing%20 Business/Documents/Annual-Reports/English/DB15-Full-Report.pdf.

[45] Civil Code, art. 2394.

[46] Gerner-Beuerle *et al.*, *Study on Directors' Duty and Liability* (n. 3 above), Annex, A.722, available at http://ec.europa.eu/internal_market/company/docs/ board/2013-study-reports_en.pdf. This kind of action would be regarded as a breach of duty in other Member States, and this liability is to be distinguished from wrongful trading as it is referred to in the United Kingdom.

Kingdom[47] and Malta,[48] and 'reckless trading' in Ireland,[49] can apply before the advent of insolvency, but where the directors can foresee the undoubted insolvent liquidation of their company occurring unless steps are taken to ameliorate the position of the company's finances. In the United Kingdom, directors are liable if they knew or ought to have concluded that there was no reasonable prospect that the company would not be able to avoid insolvent liquidation or insolvent administration, and in this context insolvent liquidation and insolvent administration means insolvency on a balance sheet basis, if they do not take appropriate action. This might mean filing insolvency proceedings for administration or liquidation.

A similar concept to wrongful trading is found in Hungary, where there is no duty to file for insolvency proceedings on the advent of insolvency, if there is what is referred to as 'threatening insolvency'.[50] With this action, a director can be held liable for not taking appropriate action when he or she knew or should have reasonably foreseen that the company would not able to pay its debts as they became due. Unlike wrongful trading in the United Kingdom, the focus is on liquidity. But, as with proceedings taken in the United Kingdom by a liquidator against miscreant directors, a director is able to defend a claim made against him or her successfully if the director takes action designed to mitigate the losses of creditors and which would be expected of a director in such circumstances. Under this kind of action, when a director knew or should have reasonably foreseen that the company would not be able to pay its debts on time, the directors should give priority to the interests of the creditors. Like wrongful trading in the United Kingdom, the actual point when directors need to consider creditor interests in Hungary and how they are to do so is not certain.

In Sweden, liability can ensue when directors carry on trading and in doing so lose company funds without any corresponding benefit when their company is insolvent or in palpable danger of becoming so. This liability is criminal and may result in imprisonment,[51] although it must be added that proceedings against directors are not common.

What seems to be expected of directors is that when there is concern over insolvency or possible insolvent liquidation they conduct the business activities of the company with the care of a prudent businessman and this will involve the careful monitoring of the financial position of their

---

[47]   Insolvency Act 1986, s. 214.
[48]   Companies Act 1995, art. 316.
[49]   Irish Companies Act 2014, s. 610.
[50]   Bankruptcy Act 1991, s. 333/A(1).
[51]   Penal Code (Brottsbalken), ch. 11, s. 3.

company. The view seems to be extant that wrongful trading and similar concepts are often not easy to establish and hence there are relatively few proceedings brought against directors for this and relatively few successes.[52]

A provision that is related to wrongful/reckless trading is found in a few jurisdictions, such as the United Kingdom, Ireland and Malta, and it provides for liability for fraudulent trading, that is, directors (and, in some Member States, others besides directors) are liable if it is found that they acted, prior to the advent of formal insolvency proceedings, with intent to defraud creditors. In this context the directors can be held liable both in civil and criminal law proceedings. Somewhat similarly, in some other Member States, such as in Italy,[53] directors may be held liable for intentionally making matters worse for the financial position of an insolvent or near insolvent company. This liability is criminal, whereas in Poland and Spain there will be civil liability for directors for intentionally causing their company to become insolvent. In Croatia, liability will be imposed where the directors caused the insolvency of their company.

As mentioned earlier, the United States includes no requirement on directors to file for bankruptcy when their company is insolvent. Nor does US law provide for any form of wrongful trading, but many of its States (although not (now) the most important State as far as companies are concerned, Delaware) impose a form of tort liability, known as deepening insolvency, if directors have acted improperly.[54] Directors can be held liable in the United States for wrongly prolonging the life of their distressed company and increasing its liabilities. This tort is most often considered when the directors have entered into contracts that the company, which is insolvent, cannot honour, usually by not being able to pay what is owed under the contract. This is akin in some ways to the tort liability imposed in some EU Member States, such as the Netherlands, where directors can be liable for damages when they entered into obligations for their company and they knew or should have known that the company

---

[52] See A. Keay, 'Wrongful Trading: Problems and Proposals' (2014) 65 *Northern Ireland Legal Quarterly* 63; R. Williams, 'What Can We Expect to Gain from Reforming the Insolvent Trading Remedy?' (2015) 78 *Modern Law Review* 55.

[53] Legge Fallimentare (Bankruptcy Law), arts 216–17.

[54] Delaware is widely regarded as the US State with the most sophisticated corporate law and the best specialist corporate law courts. Also, a majority of the leading US companies are listed in Delaware.

would neither be able to meet these obligations to the creditor nor would there be sufficient assets to discharge the obligation to the creditor.[55]

The general view amongst national reporters is that the divergent rules relating to duties of directors have not led to significant problems. However, some reports, notably those from Belgium, Sweden, Poland and Finland, recognized that the lack of uniform rules might well create problems, although none were specifically cited (and none have been supplied even on follow-up). It has been said that it is impossible to ascertain whether companies have located their business in particular jurisdictions because of the relevant law on duties. The Polish reporter has identified the fact that the liability of directors is a matter of substantive law and so it does not seem to fall under 'the law applicable to insolvency proceedings' within article 4(1) of the Insolvency Regulation (2015/848), thus not attracting the coverage of the Regulation and causing difficulty in the administration of an insolvent estate. Also, breach of duties is not clearly seen as either a company law or insolvency law issue where the directors' company is in financial difficulty and so it tends to 'fall between the cracks'.

Box 1.2 represents a good example of a situation where there was concern over whether actions of a director could be subject to the Regulation when the actions involved contravened company law and not insolvency law.

The provision in the German companies legislation discussed in Box 1.2 was such that it clearly contributed to 'the attainment of an objective which is intrinsically linked, mutatis mutandis, to all insolvency proceedings, namely the prevention of any reduction of the assets of the insolvent estate before the insolvency proceedings are opened'.[56] The provision was regarded as being similar to a rule laying down the unenforceability of legal acts that are detrimental to the creditors under article 4(2)(m) of the Regulation (see Chapter 4).[57] But there might well be other company

---

[55]   The relevant rule in the Netherlands is called the '*Beklamel* rule' (DSC, 6 January 1989, NJ 1990) and named after the case that decided that directors could be liable on the basis discussed in the article: M. Olaerts, 'Directors' Duties and Liabilities from a Dutch Perspective', available at http://www.google. co.uk/url?sa=t&rct=j&q=&esrc=s&source=web&cd=1&ved=0CCIQFjAAahU KEwijh9C9-trGAhUNLNsKHYK_D2Y&url=http%3A%2F%2F; http://www. maastrichtuniversity.nl%2Fweb%2Ffile%3Fuuid%3D02bfef4f-a6bb-4a77-b420-c928409c61b0%26owner%3Dd005c32e-a803-49d1-8486-63ebc78749b1&ei=YS 2lVePSGo3Y7AaC_76wBg&usg=AFQjCNHWrfulfqyHm2hZUIDajmyq8Th QUA.

[56]   C- 594/14 *Kornhaas* v. *Dithmar* (2015), para. [20].

[57]   *Ibid.*

BOX 1.2   C-594/14 *KORNHAAS* V. *DITHMAR* (2015)

A company, X, was incorporated in England and Wales but then it established a branch in Germany and began to operate primarily in Germany. The company was subject to liquidation and a liquidator brought proceedings against K who was a director of X. K resided in England. The action was based on the fact that K had made payments out of X's funds after the point when she was required by German companies legislation to apply for the opening of insolvency proceedings. This legislation provides that directors are in breach if they do not apply for such opening forthwith after the company becomes insolvent, or three weeks after this time, at the latest. The liquidator demanded that K reimburse X for the payments that she had made after the insolvency of X. Insolvency proceedings were opened in Germany as the place where its centre of main interests was located. Under article 4 of the Regulation, German law would apply to the insolvency and hence the provision in the companies legislation referred to above would apply. The German courts were uncertain as to whether German company law could apply to an insolvency matter where the action is to be brought against a director of a company that was incorporated under the laws of another Member State, and thus whether it was consistent with EU law. Hence the matter was referred to the CJEU.

The CJEU held that the action was permissible. The provision in the companies legislation can clearly be categorized as being covered by insolvency law, thus the provision must be regarded as being covered by the law that applies in the insolvency proceedings and their effects within the meaning of article 4(1) of the Regulation. More generally, the Court said that national provisions, such as the companies legislation provision that was the subject of this case, which have the effect of penalizing a failure to fulfil the obligation to file for the opening of insolvency proceedings, must be considered to fall within the scope of article 4.

---

law provisions, the object of which is not as clear as the one considered in *Kornhaas* v. *Dithmar*, and thus there might remain concerns as to whether it would apply in insolvency proceedings under the Regulation.

The Slovakian and Spanish views were that a uniform approach in relation to the liability of directors across the EU would be beneficial. The former saw the following possible benefits in such action. First, the directors of an insolvent company would not seek to change the centre of main interests (COMI) of its company so that insolvency proceedings could be opened in a state where the responsibilities of directors are low and, hence, either actions will not be taken against directors or if they were they might well be unsuccessful. Second, as with any uniform or harmonized approach, an insolvency practitioner (IP) does not need to investigate the rules of which Member State apply to the actions of miscreant directors. Third, if there were uniform rules, it would reduce the transaction costs for the financial sector when deciding whether to lend money to a company which does or is likely to carry on business in more than one jurisdiction and if the duties imposed on directors were uniform and rigorous it could encourage lenders to lend and creditors to extend credit even where companies were in financial difficulty although not insolvent. Fourth, conceivably, if the duties imposed on directors were uniform and rigorous, it would raise the standard of directorial actions across the whole of the EU and that would be advantageous for all stakeholders. While of the view that a uniform approach would be beneficial, the Spanish reporter was of the opinion that the case law of the CJEU and the recast Insolvency Regulation have established a situation where there is a reduction in the effects of divergence.

The Polish reporter said that having an express regulation either providing for a harmonized conflict of law rule or a substantive law rule across the EU addressing the liability of directors would bring transparency and clarity to the area.

1.4 DUTIES OF DIRECTORS IN INSOLVENCY PROCEEDINGS

Generally in the EU, it will depend on what insolvency procedure is commenced in relation to a company as to whether the directors are no longer subject to any duties once that begins. In most Member States and Norway, if the company enters liquidation/bankruptcy then the directors either lose office or their powers largely cease or are heavily restricted, and they then owe no duties as they have passed their functions to the IP.[58] Where the procedure is a restructuring/reorganizing type process, the directors will often keep their offices and will be subject to duties. Duties might be limited to ensuring that they do not act in such a way as to prejudice the interests of creditors during the restructuring process or inhibit the work of the IP.

In insolvency procedures that involve the appointment of an IP, the directors generally still have certain duties to ensure that the insolvency proceedings are handled efficiently and comprehensively. For instance,

---

[58]   This is the term that is used in art. 2(5) of the recast European Regulation on Insolvency Proceedings (Regulation (EU) 2015/848 of the European Parliament and of the Council of 20 May 2015 on insolvency proceedings (recast), [2015] OJ L141/19, 5 June 2015) to refer to persons occupying all types of office, involving the oversight of the affairs of insolvent companies or individuals, rather than the term 'liquidator' which was used in the previous version of the Regulation (art. 2(b)). This is discussed in more detail in Chapter 2 which focuses on insolvency practitioners.

directors in nearly all Member States have an express duty to co-operate with the IP and, where relevant and/or appropriate, the court, and this duty usually includes a prohibition against concealing assets, destroying documents and disposing of assets of the company. If they do not co-operate or engage in actions that indicate a lack of co-operation, then they can be subject to either or both civil and criminal liability as well as being disqualified as a director for a certain period of time (prohibiting appointment to other companies).

1.5   SANCTIONS FOR BREACHES

The term 'sanctions' is interpreted broadly in this report. There are a broad range of sanctions that can attach to directors for their pre- or post-insolvency action. Sanctions for breaches of duty are varied and range from orders made for monetary sums in civil courts to imprisonment in criminal proceedings.

Directors can be the subject of legal proceedings in which the claimant(s), usually the IP administering the affairs of the insolvent company, ask that directors be ordered to contribute to the discharge of their company's debts because they breached their duties, such as the duty of care. In many Member States, such as Belgium and the Netherlands, directors can be held liable in tort by a creditor with whom they entered into a contract on the company's behalf when the directors knew or should have known that the company would neither be able to meet its obligations to the creditor nor would there be sufficient assets to discharge the obligation to the creditor.[59]

In some jurisdictions the insolvency of a company debtor is classified as either non-culpable/fortuitous or culpable.[60] The latter occurs where the insolvency eventuated or happened because of gross negligence or intentional conduct (the latter is known as fraudulent bankruptcy in some states, such as Romania[61] and Spain[62]). Presumptions are laid down sometimes to make it easier to establish culpable insolvency. If there is culpable insolvency the directors might be held liable wholly or partly for the claims of creditors. An instance is Spain, where those who hold positions as directors up to two years before the opening of insolvency proceedings

---

[59] As to the '*Beklamel* rule' in the Netherlands, see n. 55 above. This is also broadly the position in other states, such as Belgium and Portugal.

[60] For example, Denmark, Spain and Portugal.

[61] New Criminal Code, art. 241.

[62] Insolvency Act (Ley Concursal), art. 172.

can also be held liable.[63] With culpable bankruptcy, directors might even be subject to criminal prosecution. In fact, in some jurisdictions directors can be subject to criminal prosecution or disqualification even where there are non-culpable bankruptcies and where the directors did file within the prescribed period.

If directors incur liabilities for their company without a reasonable basis for doing so and hence worsen their company's financial position before entering formal insolvency proceedings they will be liable in civil proceedings,[64] and might be subject to criminal penalties in some Member States, examples being Finland, Latvia, Poland, Sweden and Italy, even if there is no intent but there is negligence (although it might have to be gross negligence).

In some jurisdictions, such as Germany, an IP may bring proceedings against directors who have made payments out of company money after the point where they should have filed for insolvency proceedings.[65]

Civil proceedings during formal insolvency procedures that are claims that either the company is entitled to or are seen as collective claims for creditors, must be brought in most Member States by IPs who act on behalf of the insolvent estate, and proceedings initiated by creditors or others in relation to collectively suffered losses are not permitted. But in some jurisdictions creditors and shareholders can take action, and this might occur where the IP has failed to take action against the directors within a certain specified period of time after the occurrence of a particular event, such as the request made by creditors for the IP to institute proceedings against the directors.[66] It is possible in some Member States, such as Portugal and Slovenia, for creditors to bring actions on their own behalf in relation to their own losses. In the United States, where a company is subject to Chapter 11 bankruptcy, a creditors' committee might well bring proceedings against directors.

If an IP is not amenable to bringing proceedings for whatever reason(s) (perhaps he or she feels that there is insufficient funding to bring proceedings) he or she might assign the action to a creditor who might be willing to initiate proceedings. In Norway, shareholders might even take an assignment of an action if creditors do not wish to do so, but one would envisage this to be a very rare occurrence as the claim would have to bring in sufficient funds to pay off all creditors in full before shareholders would

---

[63] *Ibid.* art. 164.

[64] For example, Latvia. See Judgment of the Supreme Court of Latvia, Case no. PAC-0164, 16 December 2013.

[65] For example, see *Kornhaas* v. *Dithmar* (n. 56 above).

[66] For example, see Insolvency Act, art. 172 (Spain).

be entitled to share in the proceeds of the action. In some states, such as Portugal, the court itself may open proceedings against directors on its own volition.

In some Member States, a public authority has power to take action against directors for breach of duties. But in other states, such as the United Kingdom, there is no such authority and no such power.[67] This is also the case in the United States.

Table 1.2 sets out the sanctions that may be visited on directors who fail to file for bankruptcy (within time or not at all) where they are required to do so. The table also indicates any domestic law and sanctions that apply in Member States where there is a prohibition against some form of wrongful trading. Some states do not require filing for bankruptcy or prohibit wrongful trading. There might be other requirements on directors in these jurisdictions and sanctions will apply. For instance, in Cyprus emphasis is placed on directors not engaging in fraudulent trading, and if they do then there will be penalties, and either civil or criminal action may be brought against errant directors.

Norway also exacts sanctions for not filing proceedings when the company is insolvent. Directors may face both civil liability (in tort) and criminal liability.

Overall it would seem that the most common situation where directors are liable is where they fail to act at a time when they should have done so, whether it be filing for insolvency or taking action that will mitigate the losses of their companies, and hence creditors.

1.6 OBSTACLES TO ENFORCEMENT

While the law might provide for sanctions against directors who breached their insolvency-related duties, clearly not all directors are subject to proceedings. A number of reasons have been given for the fact that proceedings have not been taken against directors and Table 1.3 sets out the ones that are seen as primary. All Member States were said to have experienced some obstacle(s), except for Germany. Less frequently referred to obstacles are mentioned after Table 1.3.

The reason that directors against whom proceedings have been taken lack funds to pay any award that might be made against them and, therefore, they are impecunious, might often be due to the fact that

---

[67] For criticism of this, see A. Keay, 'The Public Enforcement of Directors' Duties: A Normative Inquiry' (2014) 43 *Common Law World Review* 89.

Table 1.2   *Sanctions for failing to file proceedings and for wrongful trading*

Country	Sanctions for not filing for bankruptcy in time when company is insolvent	Sanctions for wrongful/reckless trading
Austria	Civil liability and would also include liability for continuing to do business	
Belgium	Civil liability for damages (under tort law)	
Bulgaria	Civil liability for damages Criminal liability (up to 3 years' imprisonment or fine)	
Croatia	Civil liability to the creditors for any damage caused to creditors by omission to adhere to this duty Criminal liability	
Cyprus		
Czech Republic	Civil liability to creditors: damages consisting of the difference between the amount of creditors' claims and their dividend in the bankruptcy	
Denmark	No liability for failing to file for bankruptcy but civil liability for intentionally or negligently causing damage to company, for example by not having filed for bankruptcy at the point in time when it must be considered futile to keep the company going without further losses to creditors	
Estonia	Civil liability	Directors are personally liable
Finland	Civil liability for loss of creditors after the time when insolvency proceedings should have been filed (damages claim)	Criminal liability, with the possibility of imprisonment Prohibition to pursue a business Civil liability
France	Disqualification order Civil liability for company debts	
Germany	Civil liability in tort (damages claim) Criminal liability	
Greece	Civil liability for loss of creditors during the time between when insolvency proceedings should have been filed until the court's	

Table 1.2   (continued)

Country	Sanctions for not filing for bankruptcy in time when company is insolvent	Sanctions for wrongful/reckless trading
Greece	declaration of bankruptcy of company (damages claim) Criminal liability	
Hungary		Civil liability to the creditors for the loss sustained by creditors because of a diminution of company assets as a result of not taking action in light of threatening insolvency
Ireland		Civil liability for loss suffered by creditors in light of directors engaging in reckless trading and fraudulent trading. Also disqualification and restriction
Italy		
Latvia	Civil proceedings (liable for loss of the company) Administrative liability Criminal liability with the possible imposition of a fine Disqualification	
Lithuania	Civil proceedings brought by creditors who suffered loss due to late filing Disqualification	
Luxembourg	Criminal proceedings	
Malta		Civil proceedings to obtain a court declaration that directors make payments towards the company's assets
Netherlands		
Poland	Civil liability for the company's liabilities (including tax liabilities) and thus liability to the company creditors for damages Criminal action leading to a fine or imprisonment Disqualification	
Portugal	Civil liability in relation to loss suffered by creditors Disqualification	

Table 1.2   (continued)

Country	Sanctions for not filing for bankruptcy in time when company is insolvent	Sanctions for wrongful/reckless trading
Portugal	Criminal liability (imprisonment likely to be replaced by fines)	
Romania	Criminal liability: imprisonment of 3–12 months or fine	Civil liability
Slovakia		
Slovenia	Duty to compensate the creditors for damage caused by the management because they did not file for bankruptcy in timely manner	
Spain	Civil liability Criminal liability: imprisonment up to 8 years and/or fine	Civil liability for the outstanding debts not satisfied by the debtor's estate
Sweden	Civil liability	Criminal liability: imprisonment
United Kingdom		Civil liability in relation to loss suffered by creditors Disqualification

they have transferred assets to family members and/or friends. One would think that such actions could be attacked on the lines discussed in Chapter 4 dealing with avoidance provisions, but it is not always easy to bring, or be successful with, such proceedings, for a number of reasons discussed under the section addressing the avoidance provisions. The time element included in Table 1.3 primarily relates to the slowness of court procedures which discourages IPs from taking proceedings.[68]

Lack of evidence often points to the fact that there are no documents to support a claim and the age-old problem of information asymmetry, in that the directors will know more about the affairs and transactions of the company than anyone else, even the IP who has to try and reconstruct the affairs of the company, often with little assistance and poor records. Furthermore, the evidence available might not be sufficient to establish that the directors were responsible for any loss sustained by the company. The burden of proof can be a particular obstacle in relation to many actions, but especially for those that require proof of dishonesty

---

[68]   For example, Bulgaria, Slovakia and Poland.

Table 1.3 Obstacles to enforcement

Country	Impecunious directors	Cost	Time	Lack of evidence	Burden of proof	Lack of funding
Austria	√					
Belgium	√	√				√
Bulgaria	√		√			
Croatia			√	√		
Cyprus					√	
Czech Republic	√					
Denmark				√		
Estonia	√	√	√	√	√	√
Finland		√		√		
France	√			√		√
Germany						
Greece	√	√	√	√		
Hungary	√	√	√	√	√	√
Ireland	√	√		√		√
Italy						
Latvia						
Lithuania				√		
Luxembourg	√	√				
Malta		√		√	√	√
Netherlands						√
Poland				√		
Portugal	√	√	√	√		
Romania						
Slovakia	√	√	√			
Slovenia		√				
Spain						
Sweden				√		
United Kingdom	√	√		√	√	√

and in criminal proceedings in general where a higher level of proof is demanded.

Besides the obstacles that are set out in Table 1.3, other less commonly cited obstacles are:

- pressure from the courts to complete administrations (Belgium);
- lack of incentive on the part of the IP; for instance, the unlikely granting of penalties by courts (Latvia) or the time and cost to the estate of investigating and the creditors receiving little or no benefit (the Netherlands);

- courts having difficulty in determining whether directors have acted improperly (Denmark);
- determining the amount of loss suffered as a result of the directors' actions (Slovakia);
- establishing a causal link between the actions of the directors and the losses of the company (Poland, Spain);
- determining when liability exists being difficult to predict (Sweden).

As far as comparator jurisdictions are concerned, the Norway report identifies the poor prospect of the estate benefiting from any action and the issue of costs, and the United States report also refers to problems of cost and the lack of incentive for the IP in taking action.

A further potential obstacle to enforcement could be that in some situations the IP or the courts might be uncertain whether company law might be applicable in a cross-border insolvency situation and thus the Insolvency Regulation might not apply. This obstacle was manifested in the recent case of *Kornhaas* v. *Dithmar*[69] which was discussed earlier.

Where criminal proceedings are to be instituted by public prosecuting authorities, the fact that there tends to be insufficient funds and a lack of knowledge and understanding of the relevant facts mean that few proceedings are taken. Also, the prosecution of insolvency offences may well be low on the authority's list of priorities.

While lack of funding can be an obstacle to proceedings in France, an application can be made for the public funding of any action. The delegated judge for the bankruptcy makes the decision whether to order the provision of public funding.[70] This is rather a novel approach in EU jurisdictions. This strategy has been used elsewhere in the past in other nations, such as Australia.[71]

While many reports communicated several obstacles that exist against the taking of legal proceedings, the most common was the cost involved.

Overall there appears to be relatively few cases brought against directors, in civil or criminal law, in most Member States.

---

[69] See n. 56 above.
[70] Commercial Code, art. L663-1 (France).
[71] This is both under the Fair Entitlements Guarantee Recovery Programme, and under the Assetless Administration Fund.

1.7 DISQUALIFICATIONS

Over the years, many jurisdictions have considered and perhaps implemented a procedure for the disqualification of directors, particularly where directors have been involved in insolvent companies. Table 1.4 seeks to display whether disqualification exists in EU Member States, whether there is a public register that contains disqualifications, what are the insolvency-related reasons for disqualification, and the term of disqualification that is permitted to be ordered. It is emphasised that in some Member States there might be other reasons that could lead to disqualification besides those related to insolvency, but they have not been mentioned in this report as the focus is on insolvency and breaches of insolvency-related duties and obligations. Table 1.4. only addresses reasons for disqualification that are linked to insolvency.

Nearly all Member States have some form of disqualification regime operating. Only Greece and Italy appear not to have any kind of regime. The rigour and depth of the disqualification procedures that do exist vary, as one would expect. Many Member States provide for disqualification as an adjunct to their criminal law, that is, directors who are convicted of certain offences are disqualified to some extent from acting as directors in other companies and/or holding certain offices. The German system provides a good example of that. There appears to be some move in various places in the EU to the formulation of disqualification regimes that are not based on criminal convictions but conduct that is not illegal per se and falls short of criminal conduct. The Dutch presently have such a regime before their Parliament. These regimes might be additional to any regimes that are presently in place and related to the commission of criminal offences. The problem potentially with having a regime that is an adjunct to, and dependent on, criminal proceedings is that it might be hard to obtain disqualifications as the burden of proof will be high, because it is dependent on securing a criminal conviction. If a disqualification regime was civil in orientation and depended only on civil liability then the burden of proof would not be as demanding, and that might encourage the relevant government authority to take action against directors.

Besides providing for the disqualification of people from acting as directors, some Member States, such as Austria, Belgium, Germany, Latvia, Lithuania, the Netherlands and Romania, may also exclude directors from acting in some professional capacity or assuming some specific offices. A small number of Member States only provide for the disqualification of directors in this latter situation and have no general disqualification framework.

A good number of Member States have disqualifications recorded in

Table 1.4 Disqualification regimes

Country	Disqualification exists	Public register of disqualifications	Reasons for disqualification	Disqualification period
Austria	√ (but limited)[a]	None	Failure to file for bankruptcy in specified time	3 years (but can be lifted if directors demonstrate they are reliable)
Belgium	√	None	Gross fault contributing to the bankruptcy of the company	3–10 years
Bulgaria	√	√	Their company was dissolved in insolvency proceedings	Indefinite
Croatia	√	√	Causing bankruptcy, giving preferential treatment to creditors, receiving and giving bribes during the bankruptcy proceedings	5 years (and not including any time that the director spent in prison)
Cyprus	√	None	Fraudulent trading Breach of duties Fraudulent behaviour	Up to 5 years
Czech Republic	√	√[b]	Directors' actions caused the insolvency and prejudiced creditors	Up to 10 years
Denmark	√	None[c]	Unfit to act due to grossly irresponsible business conduct	Up to 3 years[d]
Estonia	√	√[e]	Insolvency Fraud, etc.	From the time of the declaration of bankruptcy until the end of the bankruptcy proceedings plus 3 years if decided by the court

52

Country				
Finland	✓	✓	Breach of duties. May be rendered disqualified based on gross negligence towards statutory responsibilities related to being a director or if the director is found guilty of a crime, which relates to business	3–7 years
France	✓[f]	✓[g]	Failure to file for bankruptcy within the time limit Failing to co-operate with the liquidator[h]	Up to 15 years
Germany	✓	None	Offences connected to insolvency Fraud	5 years
Greece	No			
Hungary	✓	✓	Where directors are liable pursuant to court order for paying company losses	5 years
Ireland	✓	✓	Unfit to be involved in the management of a company Fraudulent trading Reckless trading Several other grounds including breach of duty and breaches of the Companies Act	2–10 years
Italy	No			
Latvia	✓	✓[j]	Failure to file bankruptcy proceedings when the company was insolvent Causing the company's insolvency Breaching insolvency proceedings' regulations	1–3 years (up to 5 years for breaches of criminal law)
Lithuania	✓	✓	Breach of duties including failing to file for bankruptcy within the specified time	3–5 years

Table 1.4 (continued)

Country	Disqualification exists	Public register of disqualifications	Reasons for disqualification	Disqualification period
Luxembourg	√	√	Gross negligence contributing to the insolvency of the company Guilty of criminal offence related to insolvency	1–20 years
Malta	√	√	Director of a company which became insolvent and following his or her conduct, the court deems him or her unfit to be involved in the management of a company	1–15 years
Netherlands	√[k]	None[l]	Certain criminal offences related to bankruptcy	Up to 5 years
Poland	√	√	Failure to file for bankruptcy within the time limit Intentionally causing insolvency Failure to disclose assets and books after declaration of insolvency Concealing assets Obstruction of insolvency proceedings	1–10 years
Portugal	√	√	Causing or aggravating the company's insolvency	2–10 years
Romania	√	√	Incurring the liabilities that led to insolvency	10 years
Slovakia	√	None[m]	Failure to file for bankruptcy within the time limit	3 years 1–10 years

Country		Grounds for disqualification	Length of disqualification
Slovenia	√	Intentional or negligent actions relating to the insolvency of the company (criminal action)	2 years
		Liability to pay damages to the creditors for their losses	None
Spain	√	Company's insolvency classified as fraudulent	2–15 years
Sweden	√	Found to have acted with gross impropriety towards the creditors or otherwise breached obligations in connection with the insolvent company's business	3–10 years
United Kingdom	√	Unfitness to act (following acting as a director in a company that became insolvent)	2–15 years
		Breach of duties	
		Wrongful trading	
		Fraudulent trading	

Notes:

a Austria does not have a formal disqualification regime. Directors are only disqualified if they fail to file for insolvency proceedings within the time prescribed.

b A disqualification order will be archived in the file kept for company records and is placed on the insolvency register, and these are available to the public, but these cannot be searched easily by the public.

c While records are not open to public access, disqualification details are kept by the Danish Business Authority. The purpose of the register is to prevent persons who are subject to disqualification from being registered as members of the management in a company, and to ensure that any existing records in the system of the persons concerned are deregistered. The register is open for other public authorities (the police, the prosecution authority and the bankruptcy court), when necessary for the performance of their tasks. The Danish Business Authority informs the Danish tax authorities about registrations in the disqualification register.

Table 1.4 (continued)

Notes: (continued)

d   Directors can be disqualified more than once at the same time and the period of disqualification expires at the end of 10 years from the time of the last disqualification order.

e   E-Business Register.

f   Disqualification can be limited to a particular sector of commerce or activity.

g   Presently they are registered in the commercial law register. From 1 January 2016 a database will be held by the National Council of Clerks of Commercial Courts of all disqualification orders.

h   Together with other actions.

i   Ireland also has a restrictive order scheme which can prevent a person acting as a director of a company unless the company has a minimum capital of 100,000 euros for private companies and 500,000 euros for public companies. Under this scheme, directors can be stopped from being involved in companies unless they have the aforementioned capital for up to 5 years.

j   Information is available from the Commercial Register which enters disqualifications even though there is no separate database for disqualifications.

k   The system is based on criminal convictions. There is a proposal to introduce a disqualification regime that is based on civil law presently before the Dutch Parliament.

l   The proposal presently before the Dutch Parliament (referred to in the previous note) proposes registration of the disqualification in the Commercial Register of the Chamber of Commerce (Kamer van Koophandel) in The Hague. This register is publicly accessible. The disqualification will only be listed in the register for the length of the disqualification, thus preventing any unnecessary reputational damage after the disqualification has ended.

m   The disqualifications are kept on a register, but it is not public. Concerned persons might apply to get an extract from the register and this is confined to whether or not they are included on it.

some kind of public register. The ease of access tends to be variable. While many states do not have a public register that enables people to ascertain whether a person has been disqualified from acting as a director, some do require the order to be registered with the relevant office that oversees the registration of companies and the filing of required documents by companies, such as the appointment and registration of directors. States which do have a public register often require the order of disqualification to be registered with the authority which oversees or regulates companies.

As can be seen from Table 1.4, the time for which a person might be disqualified from acting as a director varies widely. Most Member States provide for a range and leave it to the discretion of the court as to how long the period should be. Member States like Spain and the United Kingdom have a broad range (2–15 years) while other states have a narrower range. The shortest period of disqualification that can apply is in Luxembourg and Malta and that is one year. The longest possible prescribed period is 20 years in Luxembourg, and 15 years in France, Malta, Spain and the United Kingdom. However, Bulgaria has the most rigorous regime when it comes to penalties as directors can be disqualified indefinitely.

As for our comparator jurisdictions, the United States does not have any form of disqualification regime, although the Securities Exchange Commission is empowered to disbar a person from acting as a director of a registered securities issuer. Norway does have such a regime. Under this regime directors may be disqualified if they commit offences that are related to bankruptcy or they are deemed unfit to manage companies.[72] The disqualification period is two years and relates to the disqualification of persons from taking up future appointments. However, the court can decide that directors should be removed from holding existing positions in companies that have not become insolvent. Disqualification can only apply to directors of Norwegian registered companies. Notification of disqualification is given on a public register, namely one held at the Norwegian Company Registry. As with many EU Member States, the officers at the Norwegian Company Registry will check that all those to be registered as directors of companies are not already disqualified. There is no provision for checking disqualifications in foreign jurisdictions and no provision for sharing Norwegian disqualifications with other nations.

While some Member States require their company registering authority to check whether a director is disqualified when he or she is appointed to a company, new or existing,[73] and other states require a person taking up

---

[72] Bankruptcy Act, s. 142.
[73] For example, France, Hungary, Malta, the Netherlands, Poland and Sweden.

a directorship to declare that he or she is not subject to disqualification, generally reliable procedures for ensuring that disqualified directors are not appointed as directors in other companies are not as robust as one would like. There is evidence that in several Member States persons who are disqualified are engaged in running or controlling companies even though they are not registered as a director. This might be done by relying on nominees or influencing registered directors. This is notwithstanding the fact that many Member States make it an offence for a director to breach a disqualification order and/or make them liable for the debts of the company for which they hold office. Consequently, there appears to be merit in disqualifying persons from managing or controlling companies as well as acting as directors. This might require the use of the concept of de facto and shadow directors and including in disqualification orders prohibition on acting as either a de facto or shadow director of a company.

Most Member States rely on court orders for the disqualification of directors. The order might be the decision of the bankruptcy court that orders the bankruptcy of the company or oversees other insolvency proceedings or the decision of a separate court. The United Kingdom has introduced a different or extra approach. While disqualification can be ordered by a court, a director may agree to provide an undertaking not to act as a director for a period of time if it is made clear to him or her that it is the intention of the authorities to bring disqualification proceedings against the director. This process is faster, as it obviates the need to institute proceedings in the courts, waiting for a hearing date and then having a trial, and it is less costly for both directors and the UK authorities. It also means that the director is not subject to the same publicity. This might be regarded as a positive thing for the director, but not for the community, which might demand that any errant directors' actions are made as public as possible. But having said that, any undertaking given is included on the register of disqualifications that is available to the general public so the effect is the same as obtaining an order. Also, as with orders, the giving of undertakings is usually published in government media releases.

As far as foreign disqualifications are concerned there is little done in most Member States to apply them within their own jurisdiction. This is the case in relation to the United States and Norway as well. Nevertheless it is much easier now for companies to operate in another Member State and they might do this while having disqualified directors as part of their boards. Generally only directors of companies registered, or having their real seat, in the home jurisdiction will be subject to disqualification orders. There tends to be no checking as to whether foreign directors have been disqualified or disqualification orders sought in other countries when they are registered as directors in the relevant Member State. Belgium may impose a criminal prohibition, restricting directors from acting in certain professional capacities, if a director has been convicted of bankruptcy offences in foreign courts. In Estonia, the Ministry of Justice is empowered to establish a list of disqualification orders in foreign states whose legislation is recognized in Estonia. Foreign orders will only apply in Germany if the order relates to intentional offences which are comparable to those which will lead to disqualification under the German Criminal Code. In some Member States foreign directors may be disqualified. In the United Kingdom, foreign directors of foreign companies (companies who are incorporated or having their real seat outside of the United Kingdom) that are being liquidated or capable of being liquidated in the United Kingdom may be disqualified.[74] In Hungary, foreign directors may be disqualified if their company has its real seat in Hungary, and in Ireland and Slovakia a person may be disqualified from acting as a director if he or she was disqualified in a foreign jurisdiction and the Irish and Slovakian courts are satisfied that the conduct of the person that led to his or her disqualification abroad would mean disqualification could be ordered in Ireland or Slovakia. So it seems eminently possible for a state to disqualify a director based on what he or she did in another Member State. The drawback might be obtaining sufficient evidence about what actually occurred in another jurisdiction.[75]

There is little in the way of provision for the recognition of disqualification orders in other Member States. An exception is Ireland: where a person is disqualified in a foreign state and he or she is a director in Ireland this must be noted on the Irish company's register or else it is an offence.[76] Also Luxembourg makes some provision for disqualifying directors disqualified in other states.[77] But the problem of recognition appears to lie more with the fact that states do not advise other states concerning disqualification orders that have been made. Perhaps the interconnectedness of national insolvency registers required by article 25 of the recast EU Insolvency Regulation[78] would overcome this. It would appear that the network of national registers under article 24 of the recast Insolvency Regulation, and provided through the European e-Justice Portal, would not automatically encompass disqualification orders. Article

---

[74] *Re Eurostem Maritime Ltd* [1987] BCC 190; *Re Seagull Manufacturing Co. Ltd (No. 2)* [1994] 1 WLR 453; *Official Receiver* v. *Stojevic* [2007] EWHC 1186 (Ch).

[75] Sorensen, 'Disqualifying Directors in the EU' (n. 6 above) 339.

[76] Companies Act 2014, ss. 149(8), 150.

[77] Law on Commercial Companies 1915, art. 444-1.

[78] See n. 58 above.

24(3) provides that the information detailed in article 24(2) and required to be included in national registers 'shall not preclude Member States from including documents or additional information in their national insolvency registers, such as directors' disqualifications related to insolvency'. This, therefore, permits the inclusion of disqualifications in the register, but it does not compel it. Thus, there seems to be provision to have an EU register of disqualifications but it will take movement from each Member State. In this respect each Member State would need to provide access online to information concerning disqualified directors.

In Estonia, it has been reported by insolvency practitioners that (automatic) recognition of disqualification of directors, business bans or other restrictions to act as manager, director, etc. does not work or is complicated as there is no (official) information exchange or this information is not available to IPs and relevant institutions dealing with directors' liability.

If an order of disqualification of a director is made in a Member State, then one would think that provided that it could be regarded as an order deriving directly from the insolvency proceedings against the director's company and is closely linked with the insolvency proceedings it should, according to Insolvency Regulation, article 25,[79] be recognized in other Member States. This would be the case even if the disqualification order was delivered by a court other than the one in which insolvency proceedings were opened (article 25(1)). The issue that might be in doubt is whether the disqualification application and order can be said to be closely linked with the insolvency proceedings. But if the disqualification order results from the insolvency of the company that is the subject of the insolvency proceedings then it is likely that it could be seen as being linked provided that it can be said that it is closely connected with the insolvency proceedings.[80] The *Report on the Convention on Insolvency Proceedings* ('Virgos-Schmit Report') gives as examples of judgments that would be recognized those judgments given in relation to claims to set aside transactions that cause detriment to the creditors; actions relating to the admission or the ranking of a claim; and disputes between the IP and the debtor on whether an asset belongs to the bankrupt's estate.[81] Perhaps there might be some doubt as to whether criminal proceedings that are taken and that lead to disqualification might be encompassed by the foregoing, although

---

[79]   Council Regulation on Insolvency Proceedings (EC) 1346/2000, 29 May 2000. In the recast Regulation it is art. 32.

[80]   *Report on the Convention on Insolvency Proceedings* ('Virgos-Schmit Report'), para. 196.

[81]   *Ibid.* para. 196.

if the disqualification does follow from the insolvency of the director's company, as is the situation in many cases, one might think that it should not matter. Nevertheless, while an order should be recognized, the order might not be enforced in practice, which is another issue. Recognition and enforcement of any order will always fall under the exclusive authority of the courts of the Member State where the measure is to be executed.[82]

The Reflection Group on the future of EU company law did have some misgivings about the making of information easily available across borders as it caused, potentially, a number of issues such as language problems, problems linked to the fact that the grounds for disqualification differ between Member States, and problems related to personal privacy, data protection and fundamental rights.[83] These are all matters that might need to be addressed if there is to be an EU-wide provision for disqualification.

There has been some concern as to whether disqualification falls within company law or insolvency law. Insolvency and/or the breach of insolvency-related duties is the principal or only basis for the disqualification of directors in most Member States, and so this suggests that disqualification is better considered under an insolvency law umbrella as far as the EU as a whole is concerned.

1.8   CONCLUSION AND DIVERGENCE ISSUES

While there are differences in the structuring of boards of directors across the EU, all jurisdictions impose some kind of duties on directors and all but a couple of Member States provide for disqualification procedures to be brought against errant directors. Importantly, all Member States provide that directors have certain obligations when their company is insolvent or even when it is near insolvent. In most Member States there is no specific duty that requires directors to formulate plans to take preventative action to avoid insolvency or to identify possible insolvency problems, although it is arguably implicit that they do have some obligation in this regard as the directors should be managing the company responsibly and in such a way that is designed to ensure solvency.

When a company is insolvent, then in all Member States there is a need for directors to do something that is different from what they have been doing. What that involves varies across the EU. In some Member States there is a shift in the nature of the duties of directors when a company is

---

[82]   *Ibid.* para. 201.
[83]   *Report of the Reflection Group* (n. 9 above) 34–5.

near insolvent or actually insolvent, but in the majority of states there is not. In these latter Member States, directors are usually obliged to file for bankruptcy if their company is insolvent. This involves filing proceedings within a set period of time from a particular point, usually when the company becomes insolvent, but the period of time differs between states, although 30 days/one month seems to be the most common period employed. Also, in some states directors are obliged to modify their management approach and to take certain action if they know that their company is heading for insolvency in order to minimize creditor losses. In this last instance, if directors do not take action then they might be held liable for what is often referred to as wrongful trading. In some Member States directors are obliged not to enter into obligations which they knew or ought to have known that their company could not fulfil; if they do then they might be held liable in tort. The difference in approach between Member States is quite marked. For instance, there is a lot of difference between saying that the duties of directors must change when insolvency occurs or is near, on the one hand, and requiring directors to file insolvency proceedings when they know or ought to know that their company is insolvent. Arguably, the big difference is that with the latter the opportunity for the directors to seek to restructure is limited. Any form of informal restructuring will effectively not be permitted, which might be seen as a drawback as informal restructuring is generally less costly and saves time. But even in states where there is no obligation to file for insolvency proceedings when directors know or ought to know that their company is insolvent, directors might be restricted in the formulation of restructuring plans, since if the plans are not approved and implemented then the directors could be liable for breach of their duties or wrongful trading.

Sanctions for breaches of duty vary across the EU. Some Member States only provide for civil liability, while others provide for both civil and criminal liability. In some places director disqualification can result from a breach. Disqualification might be ordered in the insolvency proceedings themselves, whereas in other Member States separate proceedings have to be instituted.

All reporters (save for one) recognized that there were several obstacles to the enforcement of breaches of duties. Most reporters identified a number of obstacles, with the fact that the directors are impecunious, proceedings can be costly and the time delay in getting a hearing of proceedings being the most frequently cited.

All but a couple of Member States have some form of disqualification process for directors and it is generally seen as an important element in the monitoring and control of directors. The approach taken to disqualification differs across the EU, and is reflected in the time periods prescribed for disqualification, the reasons for making a disqualification order and whether there are other consequences, besides disqualification from acting as a director, from the handing down of an order. While a number of Member States do not have public registers which note who is disqualified and which are easily accessible, many do. Clearly there is a problem with recognition of disqualification orders made in other Member States. It would seem that generally speaking the fact that a director is disqualified in Member State X will not bar him or her from acting as a director in Member State Y, and there are few, if any, checks on whether a person who presents himself or herself for appointment as a director in one Member State is disqualified in another. Thus, disqualified directors might move their residence to a Member State where they are not disqualified and continue to act as directors in their new home jurisdiction. It would seem that often disqualified directors in one state might run a company in another state through nominees. It might be possible that in the situation where a disqualification order can be said to derive directly from the insolvency proceedings against the director's company and is closely linked with the insolvency proceedings, it should, according to Insolvency Regulation, article 25,[84] be recognized in other Member States. This would be the case even if the disqualification order was delivered by a court other than the one in which insolvency proceedings were opened (article 25(1)).

The fact that breaches of directors' duties and disqualification are not clearly seen as falling within either the domain of company law or insolvency law means that there is some confusion where directors have acted on behalf of an insolvent company, as the regulation of such directors seems 'to fall between the cracks', that is, between company law and insolvency law. A good example of this is the decision in *Kornhaas* v. *Dithmar*,[85] which was discussed earlier. In this case, a director had made payments out of her company's funds after the point where, according to Germany's relevant companies' legislation, she should have filed for insolvency proceedings. The German courts were unsure whether a liquidator of the company who was appointed could bring proceedings against the director under the Insolvency Regulation as this covered insolvency law and yet the director had fallen foul of the companies' legislation. This manifests the concerns that can occur where a matter involves the intersection of company law and insolvency law. It can, clearly, cause uncertainty.

It might be thought possible to introduce a Directive that provided for minimum standards to be applied by the law of each Member State, but

---

[84] See n. 79 above.
[85] See n. 56 above.

if it were part of insolvency law this might be problematic as some jurisdictions permit disqualification of directors for reasons other than those
related to the insolvency of the directors' companies.

There are different approaches across the EU in relation to directorial liability and disqualification. The concerns over divergence was a
major point made in INSOL Europe's report in 2010, *Harmonisation of
Insolvency Law at EU Level*,[86] where it reported that differences between
national laws did create obstacles and problems for companies to engage
in cross-border activities within the EU as well as increasing forum shopping and reducing good corporate governance.[87] Some reporters seem to
support such a view, believing that harmonization would bring clarity
to the area, and also it could possibly raise the standard of conduct of
directors, although many other reporters do not see problems with different regimes applying, while at the same they did recognize deficiencies in
national approaches. Perhaps the major concern is that there is a need for
some uniform approach as far as either the framing of disqualification law
or the recognition by Member States of any disqualification determination
made concerning directors in another Member State.

---

[86]   INSOL Europe, *Harmonisation of Insolvency Law at EU Level* (April 2010),
p. 8, available at www.europarl.europa.eu/meetdocs/2009_2014/documents/empl/
dv / empl _ study _ insolvencyproceedings _ empl _ study _ insolvencyproceedings _
en.pdf.

[87]   *Ibid.* 9.

2. Insolvency practitioners (administrators, liquidators, supervisors, mediators, etc.)

The institutional framework is crucial in the operation of a properly functioning insolvency system. The role played by insolvency practitioners (IPs) is fundamental in this regard. As the UNCITRAL *Legislative Guide on Insolvency* points out,[1] the IP has 'a central role in the effective and efficient implementation of an insolvency law, with certain powers over debtors and their assets and a duty to protect those assets and their value, as well as the interests of creditors and employees, and to ensure that the law is applied effectively and impartially'.

As the European Bank for Reconstruction and Development (EBRD) has suggested, an insolvency process cannot be imagined without the involvement of an IP who in many respects is the lynch pin of the process – the link between the court, creditors and the debtor.[2]

2.1 TERMINOLOGY

The IP is known by different names in different countries. Expressions such as 'administrators', 'trustees', 'liquidators', 'supervisors', 'receivers', 'mediators', 'curators', 'officials', 'office holders' or 'judicial managers' or 'commissioners' are used across the European Union. The European Regulation on Insolvency Proceedings 1346/2000 used the expression 'liquidator' and defined this as meaning any person or body whose function is to administer or liquidate assets of which the debtor has been divested or to supervise the administration of his affairs.[3] The person who took control of a debtor's affairs after insolvency proceedings had been

---

[1] UNCITRAL, *Legislative Guide on Insolvency* (2013), p. 174.
[2] See C. Bridge, 'Insolvency Office Holders: A New Study by the EBRD Provides Insight into Creditors' Rights In Insolvency' [2014] *Law in Transition* 2.
[3] Council Regulation on Insolvency Proceedings (EC) 1346/2000, 29 May 2000, art. 2(b).

opened was referred to throughout the Regulation as a liquidator even though that person might be charged with the task of preparing a restructuring plan. This terminology was also reflected in the Report prepared by the European Parliament with recommendations to the European Commission on insolvency proceedings in the context of EU company law. The recast Insolvency Regulation (Regulation (EU) 2015/848) opts however, for more neutral terminology and uses the expression insolvency practitioner throughout rather than liquidator.[4] This terminology, as indicated earlier, will be followed in this Report.

2.2 WORK DONE IN THIS AREA BY THE EUROPEAN PARLIAMENT

In a Report to the Commission in 2011, the European Parliament suggested harmonization of general aspects of the requirements for the qualification and work of liquidators (IPs).[5] It suggested that the IP must be approved by a competent authority of a Member State or appointed by a court of competent jurisdiction of a Member State. The IP must be of good repute and have the educational background needed for the performance of his/her duties. The IP must be competent and qualified to assess the financial situation of the debtor entity and to take over management duties. Finally, the IP had to be independent of creditors and other stakeholders in the insolvency proceedings and, in the event of a conflict of interest, had to resign from office.

An earlier INSOL Europe study for the European Parliament was much more cautious in its conclusions.[6] It noted the fact that in many EU Member States there were different rules on the qualifications and eligibility for appointment, licensing, regulation, supervision, professional ethics and conduct of IPs. It also noted that certain functions were in practice reserved to local lawyers, which put a practical restriction on the

---

[4] Insolvency Regulation, art. 2(5). 'Insolvency Practitioner' is defined as meaning 'any person or body whose function, including on an interim basis, is to: (i) verify and admit claims submitted in insolvency proceedings; (ii) represent the collective interest of the creditors; (iii) administer, either in full or in part, assets of which the debtor has been divested; (iv) liquidate the assets referred to in point (iii); or (v) supervise the administration of the debtor's affairs.'

[5] European Parliament Resolution of 15 November 2011, with recommendations to the Commission on insolvency proceedings in the context of EU company law, 2011/2006(INI), para. 1.4.

[6] See *Note on Harmonisation of Insolvency Law at EU Level* (2010), prepared by members of INSOL Europe.

free movement of services in the EU. Nevertheless, in its view, and because of the substantial differences between EU Member States, there was no merit in seeking to harmonize these issues until a further harmonization of substantive insolvency law and company law had been achieved. This view may require re-evaluation.

2.3   INTERNATIONAL CONSENSUS

It is the case that the EBRD, UNCITRAL and INSOL Europe[7] are all working, or have recently worked, on principles for insolvency practitioners/office holders and to guide IPs in the performance of their functions. Moreover, there is a high degree of consensus about the contents of these principles and guidance.

These principles are expressed at a high level of generality. For instance, UNCITRAL has suggested that an IP should be appropriately qualified and possess appropriate knowledge and experience.[8] This will help to ensure the effective and efficient conduct of the proceedings as well as confidence in the insolvency regime. UNCITRAL recognizes that the qualifications required of an IP may vary depending on the role that the IP plays in the insolvency proceedings, whether the proceedings are liquidation or restructuring proceedings, and the level of court supervision. In the case of private sector IPs, it suggests that a balance needs to be struck between stringent requirements leading to the appointment of a highly qualified person; widening the pool of persons considered appropriately qualified for appointment; ensuring that costs are kept within reasonable bounds; and guaranteeing the quality of the service required. UNCITRAL also points out that because of the complexity of many insolvency proceedings it is highly desirable for IPs not only to have knowledge of the law but also adequate experience in accounting and commercial and financial matters generally. It notes that different approaches are taken in ensuring that IPs have appropriate qualifications, including a 'requirement for certain professional qualifications and examinations; licensing where the licensing system is administered by a government authority or professional body; specialized training courses and certification examinations; and

---

[7]   See INSOL Europe, *Statement of Principles and Guidelines for Insolvency Office Holders in Europe* (8 April 2015), available at www.insol-europe.org/down load/resource/167. The INSOL Europe statement is based on research conducted by Leiden University.

[8]   See the discussion at UNCITRAL, *Legislative Guide on Insolvency Law* (2013), pp. 174–6.

requirements for certain levels of experience'. Another point made by UNCITRAL is that IPs should be able to demonstrate independence from conflicts of interest, including those of an economic, familial or other nature.

The EBRD has used the following principles for benchmarking the IP profession, though it prefers use of the expression 'insolvency office holders' (IOHs) rather than insolvency practitioners (IPs):[9]

- Licensing and registration: IPs should hold some form of official authorization to act.
- Regulation, supervision and discipline: given the nature of their work and responsibilities, IPs should be subject to a regulatory framework with supervisory, monitoring and disciplinary features.
- Qualification and training: IP candidates should meet relevant qualification and practical training standards. Qualified IPs should keep their professional skills updated with regular continuing training.
- Appointment system: there should be a clear system for the appointment of IPs, which reflects debtor and creditor preferences and encourages the appointment of an appropriate IP candidate.
- Work standards and ethics: the work of IPs should be guided by a set of specific work standards and ethics for the profession.
- Legal powers and duties: IPs should have sufficient legal powers to carry out their duties, including powers aimed at recovery of assets belonging to the debtor's estate.
- Information: IPs should be subject to a duty to keep all stakeholders regularly informed of the progress of the insolvency case.
- Remuneration: a statutory framework for IP remuneration should exist to regulate the payment of IP fees and protect stakeholders. The framework should provide ample incentives for IPs to perform well and protection for IP fees in liquidation.

In general, Member States perform well against these benchmarks but there is considerable variation in terms of detail. For example, most EU Member States do not have a separate IP profession with its own separate code of ethics and discipline. In practice, however, IPs tend to be lawyers or accountants and subject to the codes and ethics of their

---

[9]   See EBRD, *Assessment of Insolvency Office Holders: Review of the Profession in the EBRD Region* (2014), available at www.inppi.ro/arhiva/anunturi/download/196_1f89a9d9c30bb669c1a3020f0960c8da.

so-called principal profession. Appointment systems also vary greatly. In the majority of cases the court makes the appointment of the IP but in other countries there is to some extent a greater role for creditors in the appointment process.

At a high level of generality, the responses of the national reporters to the questionnaire are summarized in Table 2A.1.

2.4 COURTS

Most countries do not have specialist insolvency or bankruptcy courts; the most that can be said is that cases are heard by commercial court judges with substantial experience of business law matters. Typical in this regard would be Ireland and Croatia where there are no specialist courts as such but courts hearing insolvency matters have a high degree of commercial experience. Germany also illustrates the general approach in that insolvency courts are a special division of the local courts and judges in insolvency matters should have documentable knowledge in the areas of insolvency law, commercial law, company and partnership law, as well as a basic knowledge of the aspects of labour law, social law, tax law and accounting that are required for insolvency proceedings. A judge whose knowledge of these areas is not documented may only be assigned the duties of an insolvency judge if he or she can legitimately be expected to acquire this knowledge in the near future.

Few, if any, EU countries go so far as the United States (which has specialist bankruptcy courts staffed by federally appointed bankruptcy judges). It may be, however, that the bankruptcy courts are best characterized as specialist units of the federal district courts with each of the 94 federal districts having a bankruptcy court operating under its auspices. Bankruptcy judges are appointed for a 14-year fixed term of office pursuant to Congressional powers in article I of the US Constitution. It is the case, nevertheless, that bankruptcy judges have a lesser constitutional status than federal district judges and federal appellate judges who are appointed under article III, section 1 of the US Constitution with life tenure and other protections, and in whom the judicial power of the United States is vested.

The other comparison country, Norway, is more typical of the EU norm in that the district court where the debtor is located decides on the commencement of bankruptcy proceedings, except for the capital city Oslo which has a specialist insolvency court.

While courts hearing bankruptcy cases in most EU countries may not be specialist there is no reason to believe that they do not approach their

---

BOX 2.1 *DAN CAKE (PORTUGAL) SA V. HUNGARY*, ICSID CASE NO. ARB/12/9, DECISION ON JURISDICTION AND LIABILITY, 24 AUGUST 2015

A Portuguese investor had acquired a majority shareholding in a Hungarian subsidiary company. The subsidiary experienced liquidity issues and creditors initiated liquidation proceedings against it in Hungary, leading the Hungarian Bankruptcy Court to declare the company insolvent and appoint an IP (liquidator). The Bankruptcy Court ordered a public auction of the company' assets within 120 days of the liquidation order notwithstanding the company's attempt to settle its debts with the creditors by agreement.

The investor claimed a breach of the Portugal-Hungary Bilateral Investment Treaty (BIT) and the ICSID arbitral tribunal found in its favour. The tribunal found that the Hungarian court had frustrated the company's attempts to reach an agreement with its creditors. It found that the Hungarian court's conduct of the liquidation proceedings amounted to a breach of Hungary's obligations under the BIT in respect of the fair and equitable treatment of the foreign investor. The court's conduct was described as 'shocking' and in 'flagrant violation' of Hungarian law, constituting a clear denial of justice and a breach of the treaty.

The Bankruptcy Court, acting as an organ of the Hungarian state, had made the sale of the company's assets inevitable. Under international law its conduct was attributable to Hungary which was considered to have violated its obligation to treat the foreign investor in a fair and equitable manner. The Bankruptcy Court's decision was 'tainted by unfairness' and therefore Hungary had also failed to ensure that the foreign investment was not impaired 'by unfair or discriminatory measures'.

The arbitral tribunal did not consider why the Hungarian Bankruptcy Court had acted in the way that it did but it was considered to have removed any possibility for the foreign investor to have a fair chance of saving its investment. It should also be noted that the foreign investor did not bid for the company's assets at the auction. There may have been factors which rendered such a course of action unrealistic or impracticable but the arbitral tribunal did not speculate on the reasons for this.

---

work with the utmost professionalism. There may be occasional exceptions, however, as illustrated in Box 2.1.

In most EU countries, IPs are specialist lawyers but not a separate regulated profession, though countries like Ireland, France, the United Kingdom and Cyprus are exceptions.

2.5 INSOLVENCY PRACTITIONERS AS A SPECIALIST AND REGULATED PROFESSION

IPs are normally natural persons, i.e. an individual or individuals rather than a legal entity though Hungary is an exception in this regard. In

Hungary, IPs can only be legal persons (either a private limited company or a private company limited by shares).

It is the case also that in the majority of countries, IPs do not constitute a separate and independent regulated profession. Germany typifies this approach in that the facility of special licensing and registration as an IP is not available but courts normally will only appoint as the IP or insolvency office holder a lawyer who is specialized in insolvency law. In order to acquire this qualification, a lawyer will have to attend special courses, sit a particular examination, and establish some practical experience in insolvency proceedings. Moreover, to maintain the qualification, the lawyer has to participate in some theoretical training every year. Italy and Luxembourg are also illustrative of the European mainstream in that there is no specific and regulated profession of 'insolvency practitioner' but IPs are usually part of another regulated profession such as lawyers and accountants.

There are countries, however, that have introduced a separate legal code dealing with the licensing and registration of IPs. Romania took this approach in 2006; Portugal in 2013; Ireland followed suit in 2014; and Cyprus in 2015. The Portugal statute contains provisions on training and accessing the profession, professional powers and duties, remuneration, monitoring and supervision of IPs, etc. Essentially, the Irish Act requires that IPs should be lawyers or accountants or members of another professional body recognized by the supervisory authority. There is, however, a 'grandfathering' clause allowing for existing IPs who may not have actual professional qualifications to continue their practice. The Act also recognizes the role of the relevant professional bodies in disciplining their members where the IP is a member of such a body.

In Cyprus, an Insolvency Practitioners Law was enacted in 2015 that sets out minimum standards of qualification and regulation for persons fulfilling the role of IP. To obtain authorization to act as an IP, an individual must be licensed and a member of a recognized professional body and have at least three years' experience as a lawyer, chartered accountant, officer or examiner in the national insolvency service or have equivalent experience in the financial sector.

The Irish and Cypriot approaches combine statutory foundations with a substantial element of self-regulation. In this respect they follow the same general trend as the United Kingdom where, since the Insolvency Act 1986, it is an offence for an unqualified person to act as an IP in relation to a company.[10] One may obtain the appropriate qualification through passing the examinations and satisfying the other requirements of one of

---

[10] See also Insolvency Act 1986, s. 388.

the recognized professional accountancy bodies[11] or the Law Society.[12] The UK government's Insolvency Service acts as an oversight regulator and may withdraw recognition from a professional body. Changes made with effect from October 2015 allow for the partial authorization of IPs. Currently, IPs are authorized to take on both corporate and personal insolvency work but under the new regime they may be authorized to act in relation to either companies or individuals or for both.[13]

In the United Kingdom, it is usually accountants who become IPs and they in turn work closely with solicitors and other professionals. This is in contrast to many other countries where it is often lawyers who take the appointments and consult accountants.

There is clearly much merit in endeavouring to ensure that IPs are appropriately qualified. If it is possible to act as an IP without holding any relevant professional qualifications or having any previous experience, this could be exploited by unscrupulous persons to their own advantage. For instance, the controllers of a company could elect to put the company into liquidation and arrange to have a sympathetic IP appointed who, through ignorance, inexperience or complicity, would agree to the sale of the company's business at a low price to another company controlled by the same persons. This stratagem would allow the controllers to continue the business free from the burden of existing debts and, meanwhile, the creditors of the old company are left with claims that, in all probability, will never be paid.

This is an issue that has ramifications across national frontiers. Clearly, at least at a theoretical level, the problems associated with poorly qualified or regulated IPs do not stop at national boundaries. While national reporters have not, however, identified any specific examples of poorly qualified or regulated foreign IPs acting in their respective countries, the potential for abuse clearly exists.

The EU Insolvency Regulation, both in its original and recast versions, implements a philosophy of EU universalism.[14] Main insolvency proceed-

---

[11] Guidance notes indicate that 'independence' is a further requirement. If, e.g., one of the partners of an individual who is otherwise qualified to act as an insolvency practitioner has in the previous three years been the auditor of a company, that individual is not qualified to act as an insolvency practitioner in relation to that particular company.

[12] Insolvency Act 1986, s. 390(2).

[13] Deregulation Act, s. 17 which inserts a new s. 390A into the Insolvency Act 1986.

[14] Regulation on Insolvency Proceedings, Preamble, recital 12 and recast Insolvency Regulation, Preamble, recital 23. For the universalism/territorialism debate, see G. McCormack, 'Universalism in Insolvency Proceedings and the

ings opened in one Member State where the debtor has its centre of main interests (COMI) are stated to have universal scope and aim at encompassing all the debtor's assets wherever they are situated throughout the EU. Subject to local law and procedural conditions, IPs in main proceedings have the same powers in other Member States as they have under the law of the main proceedings. They may 'repatriate' assets to the state where main proceedings have been opened.[15]

There is the possibility of opening secondary insolvency proceedings in a state where the debtor has an establishment and these proceedings may protect creditors with priority rights under the relevant national law. Nevertheless, any creditor, wherever located, may submit claims under the main proceedings or in any secondary proceedings. Ill-trained or incompetent IPs under one national law or regulatory regime may disadvantage creditors throughout the EU. It is the case that disparities between national insolvency laws and practices on IP qualifications can create obstacles, competitive advantages and/or disadvantages and difficulties for companies having cross-border activities or ownership within the EU, as well as for the creditors of these companies.

The relationship between main and secondary proceedings was considered by the Court of Justice of the European Union (CJEU) in C-116/11 *Bank Handlowy and Adamiak*,[16] where the court referred to the mandatory rules of co-ordination in the text of the Regulation, as well as to the principles articulated in recitals 12, 19 and 20 of the Preamble to Regulation 1346/2000. The court stressed the dominant role of the main proceedings and the fact that the IP in the main proceedings had certain prerogatives at his disposal, which allowed him to influence the secondary proceedings. The court also referred to a principle of sincere co-operation in the context of the main and secondary proceedings.

The recast Regulation extends the principles of co-operation that apply in the context of main and secondary proceedings to insolvency proceedings that involve different companies within the same group. IPs and courts are obliged to co-operate and the co-operation may take different forms depending on the circumstances of the case. IPs should exchange relevant information and co-operation by way of protocols is explicitly

---

Common Law' (2012) 32 *Oxford Journal of Legal Studies* 325 and S. Franken, 'Three Principles of Transnational Corporate Bankruptcy Law: A Review' (2005) 11 *European Law Journal* 232.

[15] Regulation on Insolvency Proceedings, art. 18 and recast Insolvency Regulation, art. 21.

[16] ECLI:EU:C:2012:739 [2013] OJ C26/4.

mentioned: article 41(1) (main and secondary proceedings) and article 56(1) (groups).

In certain cases, however, co-operation between IPs from different Member States appears to be an aspiration rather than a reality, as Box 2.2 illustrates.

It remains to be seen whether the strengthened duties of co-operation between IPs in the recast Insolvency Regulation will improve the sort of situation revealed in this case and/or whether mandatory requirements in respect of qualifications and training of IPs at EU level will have a beneficial effect.

Prima facie, there appears to be a case for the EU moving towards some form of licensing or recognition system that would build on existing strengths and good practice in most EU Member States where IPs are highly qualified and specialized lawyers and accountants. A new recognition and regulatory regime might require professional qualifications and/or membership of professional associations and it might also address issues of supervision and discipline.

A licensing system need not go so far as requiring the creation of a separate and independent IP profession. It is noteworthy that neither of the comparison countries has an independent IP profession as such, though the US corporate bankruptcy system in practice relies heavily on qualified professionals.

Oversight of the entire US bankruptcy system is carried out through the US Trustee Program, a component of the US Department of Justice.[17] US trustees are required to do the following:

- establish, maintain and supervise a panel of private IPs (trustees) who are eligible and available to serve as trustees in cases under Chapter 7 of the Bankruptcy Code (the liquidation chapter);
- perform the duties of a trustee in a case under the Bankruptcy Code when required under the Code to serve as a trustee in such case;
- supervise the administration of cases and trustees in cases under the Bankruptcy Code.[18]

In carrying out their supervisory duties, US trustees may intervene in various ways in the system and in the administration of corporate bankruptcy cases.[19] US trustees may also appoint one or more individuals to

---

[17] 28 USC 581–9.
[18] 28 USC 586(a).
[19] 11 USC 586(a)(3).

BOX 2.2   C-341/04 *RE EUROFOOD IFSC LTD* [2006] ECR I-3813

Eurofood was registered in Ireland in 1997 with its registered office in the International Financial Services Centre in Dublin. It was a wholly owned subsidiary of Parmalat SpA, an Italian incorporated company and its principal objective was the provision of financing for companies in the Parmalat group.

In December 2003, in accordance with a specially enacted law, Parmalat SpA was admitted to insolvency proceedings (extraordinary administration proceedings) in Italy and an Italian IP was appointed to the company. On 27 January 2004, a major creditor instituted liquidation proceedings in respect of Eurofood in Ireland and an Irish IP (provisional liquidator) was appointed to the company. The IP was given powers to take possession of all the company's assets, manage its affairs, open a bank account in its name, and instruct lawyers on its behalf. In February 2004, extraordinary administration proceedings were, however, opened in respect of Eurofood in Italy and the same Italian IP that acted for Parmalat was appointed to the company.

Basically, there was a clash between the Irish and Italian courts about where the centre of main interests (COMI) of Eurofood might lie. In February 2004, the Italian court took the view that Eurofood's COMI was in Italy and that it had international jurisdiction to determine whether Eurofood was in a state of insolvency. However, the Irish courts took the view that the COMI of Eurofood was in Ireland and that the appointment of the provisional liquidator constituted the opening of main insolvency proceedings in Ireland which therefore predated the opening of the proceedings in Italy. It was also held that the circumstances in which the proceedings were conducted before the Italian court were manifestly contrary to public policy under the terms of the Insolvency Regulation and therefore justified a refusal to recognize the decision of the Italian court.

The Irish Supreme Court referred certain questions to the CJEU for a preliminary ruling. On the basis of the responses from the CJEU it could be concluded that main insolvency proceedings had been opened in Ireland before such proceedings were purportedly opened in Italy. The Court noted that a Member State could refuse to recognize insolvency proceedings opened in another Member State where the decision to open the proceedings had been taken in flagrant breach of the fundamental right to be heard which a person concerned by such proceedings enjoyed.

The proceedings in the case were marred by a general lack of co-operation between the Italian and Irish IPs and the Irish Supreme Court castigated the conduct of the Italian IP stating (at para. 35 of its judgment) that his behaviour was 'extraordinary' and should be criticised 'in the strongest terms'. (Please note that we are not in any way impugning the competence, qualifications or integrity of the Italian IP, merely noting the comments of the Irish Supreme Court.)

---

serve as standing trustee in their region in individual bankruptcy cases under Chapter 13 of the Bankruptcy Code.[20]

---

[20]   11 USC 586(b).

Rules made by the Attorney-General govern eligibility for membership of panels that are established by US trustees[21] and lawyers in good
standing and certified public accountants are eligible for appointment to
a panel. While it is not strictly necessary for a person to be a member of
the legal or accountancy practice to qualify for panel membership, the
vast majority of private trustees are lawyers or accountants.[22] US trustees
have the power to 'hire and fire' panel members, but administrative decisions to terminate a private trustee's panel membership are subject to judicial review.[23] There are further requirements laid down in the Bankruptcy
Code that govern eligibility of a person to be appointed trustee in a
particular bankruptcy case.[24] Trustees, for example, are required to file
a bond with the court conditioned on the faithful performance of their
duties.[25]

In Norway, the system is less formally regulated though the law does
prescribe that when bankruptcy proceedings are opened, the court shall
appoint a qualified person to oversee and manage the bankruptcy estate.
While a lawyer will normally be appointed, there are no formal qualification rules for such appointment.

2.6 DISCIPLINARY ACTION AGAINST INSOLVENCY PRACTITIONERS

A robust and effective system for supervision and discipline, where appropriate, is important for building and maintaining trust and confidence
in the integrity and competence of the IP profession. Disciplinary action
against IPs may be the responsibility of a state agency or a professional
body depending on how what might be termed 'the IP profession' is constituted in a particular state.

In the Czech Republic, for example, while IPs are not a separate
profession (the majority of them are lawyers) they are regulated by the
Ministry of Justice. Nevertheless, the regulatory regime is perceived to be
ineffective because the Ministry does not have enough statutory powers
and because it is not adequately staffed and equipped to supervise and

---

[21] The rules are contained in 28 Code of Federal Regulations s. 58.3.
[22] For a list of current panel trustees, see www.justice.gov/ust/chapter-7-12-
13-private-trustee-locator. The Chapter 7 bankruptcy trustee community has its
own professional association, the National Association of Bankruptcy Trustees.
[23] 11 USC 586(d)(2).
[24] 11 USC 321–2.
[25] 11 USC 322.

discipline the actual number of IPs. Reforms, however, are in the process of being considered. Other countries have also considered the reform option, such as the United Kingdom where, in June 2013, a new system was established whereby all complaints in relation to the regulated work of a licensed IP are directed to the Insolvency Complaints Gateway hosted by the Insolvency Service.[26] The system was intended to provide a common, independent method under which complainants may access the complaints system. If the complaint falls within the scope of the system, the Insolvency Service will then pass it to the relevant professional body which authorized the IP.

Other countries typically apply the approach of holding that since IPs are normally members of other regulated professions such as lawyers and accountants, they are subject to the codes of professional ethics and disciplines of these professions and may be sanctioned for failure to observe these standards. The Netherlands is an example in this respect. Most IPs in the Netherlands are lawyers and are governed by the lawyers' own code of professional discipline and ethics. Moreover, Dutch IPs are invariably members of the Dutch Association of Insolvency Practitioners, INSOLAD, which has its own internal disciplinary code. Normally, where a disciplinary committee or tribunal decides that a complaint has been proved or where it is admitted, it will then decide on the appropriate sanction based on the particular facts of the case. These sanctions may range from an unpublished caution or warning; reprimand; severe reprimand; suspension or withdrawal of a licence to practice. The sanctions also include monetary fines.

These examples of different approaches in different states highlight two dilemmas in any system for complaints handling and monitoring of IPs. First, if the function is entrusted to a state agency there is the task of ensuring that this agency is properly resourced and staffed to fulfil its functions and that it is not prone to regulatory capture. Secondly, if complaints handling and adjudication is the function of professional bodies there is the task of ensuring that the body approaches its function with the required level of detachment, objectivity and independence. The complainant may have the perception that since the IP is being judged by fellow IPs, the complaint will not be taken sufficiently seriously or approached with rigour, in other words, that the complainant will not necessarily get the fairest and most impartial hearing. One way of dealing with this is to

---

[26] See http://webarchive.nationalarchives.gov.uk/20121212135622 and http://www.bis.gov.uk/insolvency/contact-us/IP-Complaints-Gateway/ and see also the R3 publication, available at www.creditorinsolvencyguide.co.uk/.

require the appointment of 'non-IPs' to adjudication panels or to build some other more independent element into the adjudicatory process.

2.7   INSURANCE

Insurance for IPs appears to be required more or less across the board in EU Member States though there are suggestions in some states that IPs find difficulty in locating suitable insurance at competitive rates. A number of different approaches can be seen. In some states insurance is required as a matter of law, whereas in other states it is more a matter of practice and professional regulation, i.e. IPs are invariably either lawyers or accountants and since the professional bodies regulating these professions require insurance as part of the relevant professional licence, insurance is therefore required for IPs. Some other states draw a distinction between fidelity insurance and professional negligence cover. One may be required as a matter of course but not the other, which is seen as more a matter of professional regulation. Fidelity insurance in the form of posting a bond would cover possible fraud or misappropriation of funds from the estate, whereas professional negligence insurance would cover actions taken in good faith by the IP that were nevertheless mistaken and caused loss to the bankruptcy estate. An example might be the failure to take appropriate advice from real estate professionals and the sale of corporate assets at a price substantially below the market value as a result of the failure to take appropriate advice and consequent faulty marketing. Clearly, however, ensuring that an IP maintains an appropriate level of insurance cover is very important in practice and it is also an area where there is already a high degree of de facto uniformity throughout the EU.

2.8   CONFLICTS OF INTEREST

Member States are also more or less at one in requiring that IPs should be independent and free from conflicts of interest that would inhibit them from carrying out their statutory and professional functions. The relevant regimes vary quite a lot in terms of details, however. Some laws content themselves with more or less a general statement prohibiting conflicts of interests. These prohibitions may be laid down in a Bankruptcy or Insolvency Act or as part of general fiduciary law or in codes of professional bodies. They may even be part of a specific statute regulating the IP profession, as in Portugal, which has also established a system for ensuring compliance with these rules through a Commission for the Monitoring of Court Officers and Auxiliaries.

Others, however, go into a lot of details concerning the kinds of relationships that are deemed conflicting, or potentially conflicting, and constitute grounds for precluding the appointment of a particular person as an IP in a certain case. Estonia, for example, is a country where the relevant laws are quite detailed and prescriptive. The danger with a very prescriptive approach is that potentially conflicting relationships are missed out inadvertently but the very comprehensiveness of the prohibitions leads to the inference that those situations not expressly prohibited are in fact permitted. This risk is, however, mitigated if the specific preclusions are said merely to be examples of a more general prohibition on conflicts of interest.

It is difficult to gauge the extent to which prohibitions on conflicts of interest are observed in practice or whether state agencies or professional bodies are proactive or active in policing the prohibitions. In the Czech Republic, while there is a general prohibition against conflicts, in practice the suspicion has been voiced that conflicts seem to be widespread and are not policed properly either by the courts or by the Ministry of Justice. Enforcement is a product of culture and resources.

In the United Kingdom, there have been concerns about sales of company assets to connected parties where there has been no open marketing of the assets. The term 'pre-pack' is used to refer to a sale negotiated in advance of the company entering insolvency proceedings but carried out afterwards. The concerns led to the formulation of Statement of Insolvency Practice (SIP) 16 by the IP representative bodies after these bodies were pressed into action by the Insolvency Service. To demonstrate that the IP has acted with due regard for their interests, SIP 16 requires that creditors be provided with a detailed explanation and justification of why a pre-pack sale was undertaken within seven days of the transaction. The IP must disclose information about the terms of the sale; marketing activities undertaken; alternative courses of action considered by the IP with an explanation of what their possible financial outcomes would have been; why it was not possible to trade the business and offer it for sale as a going concern; and any connection between the purchaser and the directors or others involved in the company. An IP should also keep a detailed record of the reasoning behind the decision to undertake a pre-pack. In the case of pre-packaged sale to a party connected with the debtor, the IP may ask for an opinion from a member of the 'pre-pack pool'. The pool is an independent body of experienced business people who will offer an opinion on the purchase of a business and/or its assets by connected parties. In these circumstances, the connected party may also be asked to prepare a statement about the future prospects for the viability of the business.[27]

2.9 APPOINTMENT OF INSOLVENCY PRACTITIONERS

As a broad generalization, the court appoints the IP in the majority of cases but many countries facilitate creditor involvement in the appointment process. There are at least two reasons for this. First, article 2(5) of the recast Insolvency Regulation recognizes that an IP represents, at least partially, the collective interests of creditors. Secondly, in the majority of cases the remuneration and expenses of an IP should come out of funds that would otherwise go to creditors.

The extent of creditor involvement in the IP appointment process varies greatly, however, from country to country in the EU. In Austria, for example, IPs are chosen by the court and while creditors can petition for appointment of another IP it appears that this is done only rarely. In Slovakia, the IP is appointed by the court but creditors can then replace the court appointee without reason.

Creditors can nominate or directly select the IP in about one-third of countries. This includes the United Kingdom, where in the most important insolvency cases in practice, the IP is ether appointed directly by creditors or the latter control the appointment process by having a veto on the identity of the person appointed. In some countries, the involvement of creditors is restricted to either the nomination or selection of a permanent IP after the court has appointed an initial or temporary IP at the commencement of the proceedings.

In Portugal and Estonia, for example, the court will make the appointment of an initial or temporary IP and creditors have the task of subsequently electing a permanent IP. It is not clear, in practice, how often creditors take the step of replacing the court-appointed IP. The insolvency proceedings may be far advanced, with important decisions already taken, by the time that the creditors meeting is held and creditors have the opportunity of replacing the IP.

In 2012, German insolvency legislation was amended to give creditors a certain role and to make provision for the establishment of a preliminary creditors' committee in respect of debtors of a certain size. While the IP

---

[27]   For further information on how the 'pre-pack pool' operates, see www.prepackpool.co.uk/.

is chosen by the court, the preliminary creditor committee must be heard and the court is obliged to appoint an IP proposed unanimously by the provisional creditors' committee unless the person proposed is not suitable for the office. The court decision on the appointment of an IP is not appealable but the first creditors' meeting subsequent to the court appointment may replace the court nominee with somebody else. The court may then only refuse the appointment of the creditors' appointee on the basis that that person is unsuitable but the court decision on unsuitability may be appealed.

In other countries, creditor influence over the appointment process may be less overt or manifested in less formalized and structured ways. In the Netherlands, the court selects an IP in a particular case from a list that is ranked in terms of the expertise and experience of IPs. In practice, the debtor or creditors may suggest appointment of a particular IP but the court is not obliged to accept the request.[28]

To militate against perceptions of favouritism in court selection and appointment, some countries have adopted randomized methods for the appointment of IPs, though Portugal appears to be the only example of this in respect of the 'older' EU Member States. In Portugal, the appointment is made by the court using computer tools which help to ensure the randomness of the choice. Hungary, Lithuania and Slovakia are also examples of countries that use randomized methods of appointment making use of electronic or computer technology.

Randomized methods of appointment have the superficial appearance of fairness but they are obviously something of a lottery and may not match up individual IPs with suitable cases. As an EBRD commentator has remarked, a randomized appointment system not only does not match an IP to a case, it may remove the incentive for an IP to perform to a high level as:

> future appointments are not dependent on performance. In systems where . . .
> [IPs] are appointed on the basis of reputation and merit, it is likely that they
> will work hard to maintain their reputation and perform to the best of their

---

[28]   In certain other countries, including the Czech Republic, France, Romania and the United Kingdom, debtors in certain cases may make an initial or temporary appointment of an IP, but generally the creditors have a more decisive role in the appointment process. This reflects the fact that in an insolvency procedure, creditors are 'out of the money' and a debtor-dominated appointment process may carry agency and 'moral hazard' risks for creditors. The French reporter refers to the fact that debtor nominated IP may have a greater familiarity with the debtor's business, but the Czech reporter highlights the proposition that a debtor nominated IP may be inclined to give precedence to non-creditor interests.

abilities. Exemptions introduced by Slovenia to the automatic system for medium and large-sized enterprises suggest that it may not be appropriate for companies of higher economic importance.[29]

As mentioned at the outset of this section, there is a case for facilitating greater involvement by creditors in the IP appointment process, as has been done recently in Germany. Creditors have a direct interest in the outcome of the insolvency proceedings. The EBRD have made the persuasive point that opening up the system of appointing IPs to those stakeholders that stand to lose most financially from the insolvency may:

> encourage greater competition and better performance from those within the profession . . . [IP] remuneration is generally paid from the funds available in the debtor's estate, in priority to unsecured creditors and also sometimes preferential and secured creditors. It is therefore particularly important for creditors that they receive 'value for money' for an [IP's] services since they may be paying for these services from proceeds which would otherwise be available for distribution to creditors.[30]

2.10 INSOLVENCY PRACTITIONERS FROM OTHER MEMBER STATES

It is very rarely the case that an IP from another Member State would be appointed. This is despite EU Directive 2005/36 on the recognition of professional qualifications. For instance, in the United Kingdom, the Directive has been implemented by the European Communities (Recognition of Professional Qualifications) Regulations 2007.[31] The IP needs to apply to a recognized professional body (RPB) in the United Kingdom but the RPB would be obliged to recognize equivalent professional qualifications obtained in the state where the applicant has been authorized to act.

The vast majority of national reporters comment that they have not come across the appointment of an IP from another Member State, though the theoretical possibility of such an appointment is not precluded. Lithuania provides an example, however, of a case where a foreign IP was appointed. The case involved a leading bank with international operations, Snoras, and a UK IP was appointed jointly to act alongside a local IP. It should be noted, however, that a large part of the insolvency

---

[29] See Bridge, 'Insolvency Office Holders' (n. 2 above) 6–7.
[30] *Ibid.*
[31] SI 2781/2007.

proceedings involved asset recovery work in 'offshore' Caribbean jurisdictions with a common law heritage and a leading UK practitioner may be seen as particularly versed in this type of work.

The main factor inhibiting the appointment of a foreign based IP is the lack of familiarity with national insolvency law. Since substantive insolvency law has not been harmonized across Europe, it is assumed that a foreign IP would not be acquainted with the detailed nuances and practices of local insolvency law. Essentially, the IP profession is organized on a national basis.

Another factor that operates in particular in the Baltic countries is local language requirements. An IP is required to be proficient in the national language and it is unlikely that a foreign qualified IP will be able to demonstrate the necessary command of Estonian or Latvian, as the case may be. In other countries, national linguistic competence may be expected as a matter of practice of prospective appointees rather than formally required by law.

2.11 INSOLVENCY PRACTITIONER REMUNERATION

IP remuneration is undoubtedly a sensitive topic in many countries. Such remuneration generally ranks as an expense of the insolvency proceedings and it is payable out of the insolvency estate with a high level of priority. At the very least, it is payable ahead of unsecured creditors and may in fact be payable ahead of priority creditors, for example, unpaid taxes and employee claims. There may be a concern, particularly among shareholders, unsecured creditors and other stakeholders, that they are receiving poor, if any, pickings from the insolvency estate whereas the IP is being handsomely rewarded for his/her services, perhaps on the basis of generous professional hourly rates. On the other hand, it seems unfair to equate the position of IPs and unsecured creditors. The IP knows that the entity to which he or she is appointed is, or may be, insolvent and few, if any, IPs would accept appointment if there was little prospect of them being remunerated for their services. It is a truism that IPs are not charities and cannot reasonably be expected to provide professional services if the chances of getting paid are slim. The EBRD have made the point that a competitive level of remuneration is essential for the development of the IP profession:[32]

---

[32]   Bridge, 'Insolvency Office Holders' (n. 2 above) 7.

It provides an incentive to satisfy often burdensome, as well as costly, admission requirements for the profession, including specialised study and training. Remuneration is also a potential tool by which the higher performers within a profession may be rewarded for their efforts, or the specialist sector skill or experience held by certain professionals is reflected.

Nevertheless, the level of IP remuneration and the method of calculating this remuneration has generated controversy in some Member States. The controversy sometimes centres on the absolute levels of remuneration and in other cases on obscure or hidden top-ups or side payments to IPs. This controversy is not necessarily confined to Europe. For instance, in the United States there is a perception that Chapter 11 cases are expensive and involve wealth transfers from creditors to professionals.[33] Certainly, in some northern European countries fee levels may seem high by Southern or Eastern European comparisons. In Sweden, for example, there are about 400 lawyers who accept assignments as IPs, with the remuneration rate being 300–500 euros per hour. The IP's fee is, however, set by the court and it is for the court to decide whether the amount claimed is reasonable in accordance with certain special statutory rules. In Denmark, the level of fees appear to be similarly high. There, the IP fees are determined by the court and based on an overall assessment that has regard to the scope of work; the nature of the estate; the responsibility associated with the work; and the result achieved in the particular case. But in Denmark there has been recent discussion and concern about an apparent lack of scrutiny exercised by the Bankruptcy Court over the bills that they receive from the IP. In one recent and notorious case, there was nothing left in the estate for unsecured creditors after the IP's bills had been paid. In Hungary, there has also been controversy over what counts as costs of administering the insolvency proceedings over and above the IP fees.

In many countries, remuneration is set by the court and creditors have limited rights of participation. There may be a strict tariff system which the court uses in fixing fees, either a fixed fee or a variable fee with different thresholds. In some countries, there is also a performance element built into the fee structure, with the possibility of the IP obtaining addi-

---

[33]   See generally, Nancy Rapoport, 'Rethinking Fees in Chapter 11 Bankruptcy Cases' (2010) 5 *Journal of Business and Technology Law* 263; Lynn LoPucki and Joseph W Doherty, 'Rise of the Financial Advisors: An Empirical Study of the Division of Professional Fees in Large Bankruptcies' (2008) 82 *American Bankruptcy Law Journal* 141; Stephen J. Lubben, 'Corporate Reorganization and Professional Fees' (2008) 82 *American Bankruptcy Law Journal* 77.

tional fees if certain performance targets are met. In the Netherlands, for example, the fee is determined by the court on a time spent basis. In 2015, the basic hourly rate has been set at 200 euros but this figure may be adjusted based on the experience of the IP, complexity of the case and total realized proceeds.

In Germany, the level of IPs' fees is regulated by statutory instrument. The fees are fixed not by the hour but by the percentage of the realized insolvency estate. In other words, the fee depends on success not time, but the fixed fee can be increased by top-ups or subject to discounts in exceptional cases. It has been said that the statutory fee base and the fixing of the remuneration by the court guarantees the reasonableness of the fee.

France, Italy and Spain adopt variants of this approach. In France, the amount of IP remuneration is determined by the court on the basis of detailed rules which set out a scale of fees (specific rules grant fees for specific tasks), checking of claims, etc. In Italy, remuneration is based on a scale established by statute and is calculated on the basis of the value of the estate and the amount realized. There are minimum and maximum parameters that take into account the work done; the results obtained; the importance of the proceedings; and the promptness with which they were carried through. In Spain similarly, IP remuneration is determined by the court on the basis of a tariff system that takes into account the value of assets; the extent of liabilities; the number of creditors, etc. Moreover, the fee may be reduced by the court if the IP is considered to be negligent in the performance of its functions.

The tariff system has the advantage of transparency and appears to be fair. Nevertheless, unless moderated by some performance element, it may either over-reward or under-reward IPs depending on how simple or complex a particular case may be. Other countries may distinguish between different types of proceedings in setting IP fees, i.e. whether these proceedings are liquidation or restructuring proceedings or may pay greater attention to the hourly rate. In Austria, for example, the level of IP fees is fixed by statute and is a flat fee based on a certain percentage of the value of the insolvency estate. The court may depart from the statutory tariff in unusual cases but, to avoid controversy, it normally sticks to the tariff. If the IP runs the debtor's business, however, he is entitled to be paid at an hourly rate. In the United Kingdom, IP fees are settled by creditors' committee or by the court or creditors where there is no such committee. The fee is normally based on standard professional fee rates and is calculated on an hourly basis. Under new rules, however, where an IP wishes his fees to be based on time costs he is required to provide an upfront estimate of his fees for creditor approval. IPs have to provide details of the work and an estimate of the time taken to undertake the work. The estimate serves as an effective cap on fees, since IPs are not able to draw more remuneration in excess of the estimate without creditor approval.

The risk associated with a system that determines IP fees primarily by reference to hourly rates is that IPs are incentivized to carry out work that has little likelihood of benefit to the insolvency estate. The IP fees are enhanced but creditors and other stakeholders do not necessarily see any returns. Requiring the IP to provide an up-front estimate of fees may mitigate against this risk but the estimates may be pitched at a high level.

2.12 CONCLUSIONS ON INSOLVENCY PRACTITIONERS

It is fundamentally important for the proper functioning of an insolvency regime that IPs are appropriately qualified and display appropriate standards of competence, expertise, integrity and professionalism in relation to the conduct of the proceedings. Whatever the country, the IP will have a range of legal duties imposed either by specific statutes or the general law. The IP is at the very heart of the insolvency proceedings. Because of the principle of mutual recognition of insolvency proceedings in the Insolvency Regulation, the issue of incompetent or poorly qualified IPs in one Member State has potential ramifications throughout the EU.

A number of international and European standard setting bodies are working or have worked on a set of principles laying down parameters for the qualifications and training of IPs and formulating guidelines for the performance of their functions. While sometimes formulated at a high level of generality, there is a considerable degree of commonality about the nature of these standards and guidelines. It may be that the European Union could leverage the work of these other organizations with a view to formulating a set of rules for adoption on a pan-European basis. For instance, the principles developed by the EBRD could provide a useful starting point for discussion on a common European framework. These principles have been set out earlier and for convenience are repeated below:[34]

---

[34]   See EBRD, *Assessment of Insolvency Office Holders* (n. 9 above).

- Licensing and registration: IPs should hold some form of official authorization to act.
- Regulation, supervision and discipline: given the nature of their work and responsibilities, IPs should be subject to a regulatory framework with supervisory, monitoring and disciplinary features.
- Qualification and training: IP candidates should meet relevant qualification and practical training standards. Qualified IPs should keep their professional skills updated with regular continuing training.
- Appointment system: there should be a clear system for the appointment of IPs, which reflects debtor and creditor preferences and encourages the appointment of an appropriate IP candidate.
- Work standards and ethics: the work of IPs should be guided by a set of specific work standards and ethics for the profession.
- Legal powers and duties: IPs should have sufficient legal powers to carry out their duties, including powers aimed at recovery of assets belonging to the debtor's estate.
- Information: IPs should be subject to a duty to keep all stakeholders regularly informed of the progress of the insolvency case.
- Remuneration: a statutory framework for IP remuneration should exist to regulate the payment of IP fees and protect stakeholders. The framework should provide ample incentives for IPs to perform well and protection for IP fees in liquidation.

Of course, a considerable amount of work is required to operationalize these principles. For example, in relation to complaints handling against IPs, there are two basic approaches with many variations. The first is to give the task of considering, investigating and adjudicating upon complaints to some official agency, but in this situation the agency must be properly motivated and resourced. If a self-regulatory approach is adopted, with complaints handling dealt with by the relevant professional bodies, some independent element must be built into the investigatory and adjudicatory function to ensure rigour and objectivity and to maintain public confidence in the efficacy of the system.

APPENDIX: DATA TABLE

Table 2A.1   Summary of questionnaire concerning insolvency practitioners

Country	2 (a) Specialist courts and IPs	2 (b) IPs, regulated profession?	2 (c) Disciplinary action against IPs	2 (d) Liability insurance	2 (e) How IPs are chosen from other states	2 (f) IPs and conflicts of interest	2 (g) Remuneration of IPs
Austria	Specialist courts but no IP profession	No, normally specialized lawyers	Depends on the profession IP is part of	No legal rules, depends on rules of professional organization, variable in practice	IPs chosen by the court Creditors can petition for appointment of another IP but done only rarely IPs from outside Austria only rarely appointed	IP has to be independent of debtor and creditors	Fixed by statute, flat fee based on certain percentage of proceeds. If IP runs business entitled to be paid at hourly rate Court can depart from scheme in unusual cases but to avoid controversy normally sticks to scheme
Belgium	Commercial courts some of whom have specialist bankruptcy divisions No specialist IP profession but most IPs are specialist lawyers who are appointed	Most courts will appoint IPs from a special list and to get on the list a lawyer must have attended a specific training course, and give guarantees of	Supervision by the court and by the public prosecutor's office	Lawyers are obliged to carry liability insurance	Generally appointed by the court In theory IPs from other Member States may be appointed in certain circumstances	Conflicts of interest governed by the Bankruptcy Act	Generally based upon (i) a percentage on assets realized by the receiver, with a minimum amount of 750 euros, and (ii) a fixed fee for administrative costs

	on a regular basis, and are therefore able to gain and enlarge their experience in the field of insolvency	competence There is no entrance examination and no officially recognized training courses for IPs					
Bulgaria	Specialist IPs but no specialist courts	Yes, special law	Governed by special law, supervised by Minister of Justice	Mandatory professional liability insurance	Done initially by court but creditors can then appoint	Rules in statute to prevent appointment of conflicted person	Determined by creditors
Croatia	Commercial court with some judges specialized in bankruptcy proceedings	Not a separate profession	No formal disciplinary system	Yes	On a random basis by the court but court may choose another IP if the particular case requires special expertise IPs from other Member States in practice not appointed	Bankruptcy Act contains rules on conflicts of interest	Determined by the court on the basis of a statutory scale subject to a cap but court may increase remuneration if IP was considered to perform particularly well
Cyprus	No specialist court	New Insolvency Practitioners Law 2015 sets out minimum standards of qualification and licensing for IPs, seems to be modelled on UK	Monitored by relevant professional body who issued licence	Yes	By court IPs from another state can act provided they are authorized to act as an IP in Cyprus	Subject to general law and to conflict of interest rules of relevant professional body	Set out in a statutory scale but in certain circumstances this scale can be departed from

Table 2A.1 (continued)

Country	2 (a) Specialist courts and IPs	2 (b) IPs, regulated profession?	2 (c) Disciplinary action against IPs	2 (d) Liability insurance	2 (e) How IPs are chosen from other states	2 (f) IPs and conflicts of interest	2 (g) Remuneration of IPs
Cyprus		system and so normally accountants or lawyers					
Czech Republic	Licensed IPs (but not separate profession) and specialized insolvency judges	Regulated by a special Act and subject to special requirements but are members of other professions, normally lawyers	Monitored by the insolvency courts and under an administrative regime run by the Ministry of Justice but regime is perceived as ineffective	Must carry liability insurance	Chosen by the court on an automated random basis but creditors can then replace the IP IPs from other Member States normally act on an occasional or temporary basis	General prohibition against conflicts of interest but in practice suspicions of conflicts seem to be widespread and not to be policed properly either by the courts or by the Ministry of Justice	Statutory scale based on (i) amount of claims verified; (ii) payout to creditors in liquidation; and (iii) debtor's turnover in restructuring. If the estate does not generate enough value, the state will pay a certain amount
Denmark	Specialized courts	Most IPs are lawyers, can get special certification on voluntary basis but no specialist profession as such	Would be subject to rules of relevant profession	Bankruptcy Act requires professional liability and fidelity insurance, also relevant profession requires insurance	Formally appointed by the court but creditors have a strong say IPs from other Member States rarely seen	General prohibition on conflicts of interest	Fee determined by the court based on overall assessment having regard to scope of work, nature of the estate, responsibility associated with the work and result achieved. Recent concern over level of scrutiny and level of fees

	Courts	Competency/Regulation	Supervision	Professional liability insurance	Appointment	Conflicts of interest	Remuneration
Estonia	No specialized courts	Specific statutory requirements but in practice members of other professions Oral and written proficiency in Estonian required	Subject to supervision by courts, Ministry of Justice, and Chamber of Bankruptcy Trustees/Bar Association	Professional liability insurance required but not against liability arising from intentional violation of obligations	Chosen and appointed by the court but must have the confidence of creditors Estonian language requirements may in practice deter foreign appointees	General prohibition on conflicts of interest	Calculated by the court on the basis of the value received by the bankruptcy estate, volume and complexity of the work and the IP's skills
Finland	No special bankruptcy courts, general competency requirements for IPs	General competency requirements for IPs in insolvency legislation but no special profession	Subject to insolvency legislation. If IP is a member of the Bar, the Bar Code of Conduct applies	Not required by legislation. Bar Code of Conduct requires general liability insurance for its members	Appointed by the court but main creditors have an opportunity to be heard	Prohibition on conflicts of interest in insolvency legislation	Set by the creditors, guidelines recently issued by the Bankruptcy Ombudsman suggest a fee based on a fixed element and an additional part based on value of estate
France	Specialized IPs	IPs regulated in a detailed legal framework contained in the Commercial Code	Specific disciplinary rules	Yes, required	IPs appointed by court from those registered on official lists, takes into account competence and ability to act in specific case In theory IPs from other Member States may be appointed	No specific provisions but general rules of civil and criminal liability	Remuneration determined by court on the basis of detailed rules containing a scale of fees, specific rules grant fees for specific tasks, checking of claims, etc.

Table 2A.1 (continued)

Country	2 (a) Specialist courts and IPs	2 (b) IPs, regulated profession?	2 (c) Disciplinary action against IPs	2 (d) Liability insurance	2 (e) How IPs are chosen from other states	2 (f) IPs and conflicts of interest	2 (g) Remuneration of IPs
Germany	Specialist courts and in practice specialist lawyers	Special licence and registration are not available Normally, however, courts only appoint as IP a lawyer specialized in insolvency law and to get this qualification a lawyer has to participate in special courses, sit a special exam and show some practical experience	General supervision by the court	In practice liability insurance is required	IP chosen by the court but the creditors committee may replace court nominee in practice IPs from other Member States not generally appointed	IP required to be particularly experienced in business affairs and to be independent of creditors and debtor	Regulated by statutory instrument, not by the hour, by percentage of realized insolvency estate, depends on success not time; fixed fee can be increased by top-ups or subject to discounts in exceptional cases; statutory fee base and fixing of remuneration by court guarantees reasonableness of fee
Greece	No specialized courts or IPs	IP must be a qualified lawyer with certain experience and generally	Greek Insolvency Code provides for civil and criminal liability of IPs	No professional liability insurance	Appointed by the court from a list provided by the local Bar Association. In theory IPs	Must comply with lawyers' code of conduct	Determined by court taking into account value of the estate, length of proceedings and beneficial effects of IP activities

Hungary	Specialist insolvency courts. Legal entities may be IPs. Appointed from special lists maintained by local court. Rules for legal entities to have at least 2 persons with specialist liquidator qualifications	Also possibility of disciplinary action by Bar Association. General supervision by the court and by government minister	Appropriate insurance required	From other Member States may be appointed. Since 2014 chosen randomly by the court from the list of registered liquidators using an electronic selection method. Only Hungarian branches of foreign legal entities may be registered as liquidators in Hungary	Regulated in detail by the Insolvency Act. Policed by the court and the relevant Ministry	Based on a percentage of realizations, but expenses are left to the court and some controversy over the amount claimed in respect of expenses
Ireland	Commercial division of the High Court deals with insolvency matters. IPs normally accountants who specialize in this type of work. Companies Act 2014 now requires that certain qualifications necessary for appointment as IP. Members of recognized professional bodies	Supervision by relevant professional body	Requirement of professional indemnity insurance for certain types of IP	Generally by the court but creditors have a strong say in the identity of the person appointed	Rules laid down in the Companies Act 2014 and general scrutiny by the creditors' committee or the court	Determined by creditors committee or the court. A number of ways in which remuneration may be calculated including by reference to time spent on the proceedings
Italy	Specialist courts and in practice specialist IPs. No specific and regulated profession but IPs are usually part	General law provisions and regulations of professional associations	IP is usually part of another regulated profession	Generally chosen and appointed by the court and/or administrative	Laws regulating the different insolvency proceedings also specifically	Based on a scale established by statute and calculated on the basis of value of estate, amount realized and

Table 2A.1 (continued)

Country	2 (a) Specialist courts and IPs	2 (b) IPs, regulated profession?	2 (c) Disciplinary action against IPs	2 (d) Liability insurance	2 (e) How IPs are chosen from other states	2 (f) IPs and conflicts of interest	2 (g) Remuneration of IPs
Italy		of another regulated profession such as lawyers and accountants	provide for procedures to enforce the disciplinary liability of their own members	and this profession will require insurance	authority that supervises the insolvency proceedings No evidence of cases where non-Italian citizen appointed as IP	govern the conflicts of interest of the IPs	extent of liabilities. Minimum and maximum parameters that take into account the work done, results obtained, importance of proceedings and promptness
Latvia	No specialist courts IPs licensed by Association of IPs	Yes, certain pre requisites for licensing including formal training and a professional exam, usually lawyers	Set out in the Insolvency Law	Compulsory professional indemnity insurance	Appointed by the court from a list of IPs IPs from other Member States can theoretically practice in Latvia but no precedents	Governed by Insolvency Law and supervised by Insolvency Administration, a state entity, and a court	Provision for remuneration to be calculated on a scale but IP can agree with creditors on a different remuneration model
Lithuania	No specialist courts	Formal requirements, including language, to become an IP. Legal person may become IP	Set out in Bankruptcy Law Provision for supervisory authority to bring proceedings in certain circumstances	Compulsory insurance	Selected by the court on a random, computerized basis	Rules to prevent conflicts of interest in Bankruptcy Law IPs from other Member States may be appointed	Determined by the creditors, may be a lump sum, monthly salary or dependent on amounts recovered by IP; court may evaluate whether amount chosen is just and reasonable

	Specialist courts / IPs	Regulated profession	Disciplinary / sanctions	Professional insurance	Appointment	Conflicts of interest	Fees
Luxembourg	No specialist courts IPs generally lawyers	No specific qualification rules but normally lawyers or members of other regulated professions	Some specific sanctions and in addition the sanctions applicable to the regulated profession of which the IP is a member	Professional insurance of the specific regulated profession to which the IP belongs will apply	Appointed by the court	Court should avoid any conflicts of interest in appointing IPs	Fees determined by the court as a variable percentage of assets sold by IP, determined according to different thresholds No recent controversies about remuneration
Malta	No specialized courts or IPs	No regulated profession but liquidators as distinct from corporate recovery practitioners required to be a certified accountant or lawyer or a person registered with the Registrar as fit and proper to exercise the function of a liquidator	Court and Registrar of Companies, a public entity, may exercise a general supervisory jurisdiction	No such rules	Depends on the type of procedure but creditors will have a strong say on the appointee Non-Maltese individual may be appointed as IP	General rules on conflicts of interest	No hard and fast rules, depends on the type of procedure whether court or creditors determine and could be a fixed fee, an hourly rate and would depend on the complexity of the case, etc.
Netherlands	No specialist courts Most IPs members of INSOLAD (Dutch	Not a regulated profession as such but generally only specialist lawyers	INSOLAD has its own internal disciplinary code and lawyers are subject to their	IPs are obliged to carry sufficient professional indemnity	Court selects IPs from a list ranked on their expertise and experience. In practice, debtor or	IP obliged to act independently and court will endeavour to ensure that	Determined by the court on a time spent basis For 2015 basic hourly rate is 200 euros but may be adjusted based

Table 2A.1 (continued)

Country	2 (a) Specialist courts and IPs	2 (b) IPs, regulated profession?	2 (c) Disciplinary action against IPs	2 (d) Liability insurance	2 (e) How IPs are chosen from other states	2 (f) IPs and conflicts of interest	2 (g) Remuneration of IPs
	Association of IPs) but not a statutory requirement to act in insolvency proceedings	appointed by the court, and INSOLAD is a self regulatory body	own code of professional discipline and ethics	insurance	creditors can suggest appointment of a particular IP but court not obliged to accept request IP from another Member State could be appointed in theory	no conflicts of interest exist	on experience of IP, complexity of case and total realized proceeds
Poland	In practice, special bankruptcy courts and IPs	Special statute governs licensing of IPs, may be legal persons as well as natural persons. Can be citizens of EU Member States but sufficient knowledge of Polish language is required	Rules set out in the Insolvency Act and in the IP licensing statute which contains provisions for suspension or withdrawal of license	Mandatory insurance	Appointed by the court from a list kept by the Minister of Justice	Prohibition on conflicts of interest	Determined by the court on the basis of a scale fixed by reference to the value of the bankruptcy estate; may be adjusted upwards or downwards depending on success and whether remuneration is disproportionate
Portugal	Usually special courts which deal with	A regulated profession, IP statute from	The rules that govern disciplinary	In theory yes but no official order	IP generally appointed by the court but may also	Rules that govern conflicts of interest are	When IP is appointed by creditors the remuneration is

commercial matters generally	2013 which contains provisions on training and accessing the profession, professional powers and duties, remuneration, monitoring and supervision of IP, etc.	determining the extent of cover required	be appointed by the creditors, in a creditors' meeting The appointment by the court is by computer tools to ensure the randomness of the choice, court may also take into account names forwarded by the debtor and the creditors' committee In some cases, after the IP has been appointed, the creditors may replace him by another IP of their choice, regardless of the fact that his name is not on the official list; may only occur due to company's size, activity or complexity of the proceedings IPs from other Member States in practice not appointed	laid down in the IP Statute Compliance with these rules is ensured by the Commission for the monitoring of court officers and auxiliaries	determined by creditors When the IP is appointed by the court, remuneration is calculated according to the values set down in a ministerial order. In addition, there is a variable remuneration depending on how successful the IP is in achieving the rescue outcome or liquidation outcome
	action against IP are laid down in the IP Statute, which covers rules on fines, loss of status as IP and warnings for poor conduct Given the character of the profession (acting as court officers), the disciplinary actions are of a public nature It is up to the control body which oversees the work of IPs (the Commission for the monitoring of court officers and auxiliaries) to commence disciplinary proceedings whenever necessary, on account of malpractice and breach of duties				

Table 24.1 (continued)

Country	2 (a) Specialist courts and IPs	2 (b) IPs, regulated profession?	2 (c) Disciplinary action against IPs	2 (d) Liability insurance	2 (e) How IPs are chosen from other states	2 (f) IPs and conflicts of interest	2 (g) Remuneration of IPs
Romania	Specialist division of courts and specialist IPs	Regulated profession under 2006 Act	Governed by the 2006 Act but complaints are to the professional body representing IPs and so there may be a lack of independence in the adjudicatory mechanism	Required	Varies depending on the nature of the procedure; in certain cases the debtor nominates someone and in other cases the court makes a random selection from lists but the creditors can then appoint someone else Foreign IPs can in theory be proposed	Conflicts of interest are governed by insolvency law, the law governing IPs and the Criminal Code	Negotiated between the IP and the creditors, court has some involvement May be in the form of a lump sum (including monthly fees), success fee or a combination of fixed and success fees
Slovakia	Specialized courts IPs can be natural or legal person	Licensed and regulated profession governed by statute	Supervision by a special section of the Ministry of Justice and to a certain extent by the court	Required	For bankruptcy proceedings appointed by the court on the basis of a random computer generated selection, but creditors can then replace the court appointee without reason	Regulated by the statute governing the licensing of IPs	In bankruptcy proceedings determined by the court, partly fixed fee and partly depending on the nature and value of the assets in the bankruptcy estate
Slovenia	No specialist courts but specialist IPs	Statute governing licensing by	A range of sanctions in the legislation	Insurance required	Appointed by courts from lists Foreign IPs	Rules on conflicts of interest set out in the	Determined by the court on the basis of a statutory tariff which

		the Ministry of Justice	for disciplinary offences but proceedings may only be commenced by the President of certain courts		may be licensed but knowledge of Slovenian language required	Insolvency Act	takes into account the value of the estate, the amount realized and for carrying out certain functions
Spain	Specialist courts and qualified IPs An IP may be a natural or legal person	New Spanish law provides for registration of IPs in a public insolvency registry; provision for professional exams and accreditation of prior experience; IPs normally members of regulated professions such as lawyers or accountants	Provision is made for disciplinary sanctions and these may be sought by debtor and creditors	Liability insurance required	Chosen by the courts from lists and provision is made for big or complex cases where list may be varied Foreign IPs may in theory be appointed	Insolvency Act contains provisions to prevent conflicts of interest	IP remuneration is determined by the court on the basis of a tariff system that takes into account value of assets, extent of liabilities, number of creditors, complexity of proceedings, etc. and the fee may be reduced by the court if the IP is considered to be negligent in the performance of his functions
Sweden	No specialized courts but specialist IPs who are lawyers	State supervisory authority and stringent requirements to be met	Disciplinary proceedings may be instituted by state supervisory	Mandatory insurance	Appointed by the court, some use of lists, must have special insight and experience which the assignment demands	Rules to prevent conflicts of interest	About 400 attorneys in Sweden who can accept assignments, remuneration rate is 300–500 per hour. Fee set by the court, for the

Table 2A.1 (continued)

Country	2 (a) Specialist courts and IPs	2 (b) IPs, regulated profession?	2 (c) Disciplinary action against IPs	2 (d) Liability insurance	2 (e) How IPs are chosen from other states	2 (f) IPs and conflicts of interest	2 (g) Remuneration of IPs
Sweden		before deemed suitable to accept appointments	authority, debtor, creditor or Swedish Bar Association		and in all other respects be suitable for the assignment Rare for foreign IPs to be appointed		court to decide whether the amount claimed is reasonable in accordance with certain special statutory rules; if there is a shortfall in the estate to make up remuneration, it is covered by the state
United Kingdom	No specialist courts as such but courts hearing insolvency matters have a high degree of commercial experience Specialist IPs	Regulated professions Elaborate system of self-regulation with a state oversight regulator	Complaints against IPs directed through a common complaints gateway operated by the self-regulatory bodies; range of disciplinary sanctions may be administered	Mandatory fidelity insurance and IPs would invariably have professional indemnity insurance	In bulk of cases it is effectively the creditors who make an appointment though the court has a certain role IPs from other Member States have to obtain authorization to act in the UK in accordance with Directive 2005/36. IP needs to apply to a recognized professional body (RPB) in the UK but the RPB would be obliged to recognize equivalent	Rules on conflicts of interest	Settled by the creditors' committee or by the court or creditors where there is no such committee. Normally based on standard professional fee rates and calculated on an hourly basis. Under new rules where an IP wishes his fees to be based on time costs he is required to provide an upfront estimate of his fees for creditor approval. IPs have to provide details of the work and an estimate of the time taken to undertake the work (an effective cap). IPs not able to draw more

					professional qualifications obtained in the state where the applicant has been authorized to act		remuneration without creditor approval
United States	Specialist insolvency courts and no concept of licensed IP as such System in practice relies on specialist professionals	Corporate bankruptcy trusteeship is a de facto profession Concept of debtor in possession	Monitoring of and disciplinary action against panel trustees is a matter for the US Trustee and is governed by administrative agency rules	Professional liability insurance and fidelity insurance in practice required	Depends on the type of proceedings but US trustee normally makes initial appointment in bankruptcy case though creditors may replace the nominee. In Chapter 11 it is debtor in possession	Conflicts of interest are regulated by fiduciary law and professional regulation	Chapter 7 or 11 trustees are entitled to reasonable compensation but within fixed limits based on a descending percentage of realizations. Chapter 11 debtor in possession must seek court approval to retain professional to assist, their fees subject to court approval but no statutory ceilings; perception that Chapter 11 cases are expensive and involve wealth transfers from creditors to professionals
Norway	Certain amount of specialization at court level but court will normally appoint a lawyer to act as IP	No separate and regulated profession	No such specific rules A lawyer appointed as IP is subject to normal ethical rules for lawyers whose breach may lead to disciplinary action	Bankruptcy estate has an obligation to take out liability insurance	IP normally chosen from a list of active IPs considered qualified, may act on a suggestion from creditors In theory foreign IPs could be appointed but rarely practical as knowledge of Norwegian insolvency law required	General rules of bankruptcy law and principles of ethics that apply to legal practitioners	Set by the court on IP application; debtor and creditors may be heard on the requested level of remuneration

3. Ranking of claims and order of priorities

3.1 INTRODUCTION

Question 3 concerns the ranking of claims and order of priorities. Recital 22 of the Preamble to the recast Insolvency Regulation[1] acknowledges the fact that:

> as a result of widely differing substantive laws it is not practical to introduce insolvency proceedings with universal scope throughout the Union. The application without exception of the law of the State of the opening of proceedings would, against this background, frequently lead to difficulties. This applies, for example, to the widely differing national laws on security interests to be found in the Member States. Furthermore, the preferential rights enjoyed by some creditors in insolvency proceedings are, in some cases, completely different.

This study has indeed revealed very different approaches in Member States on the priorities enjoyed by the holders of security interests (secured creditors) and preferential (priority) claimants in an insolvency.[2] This conclusion has important implications in the context of the Insolvency Regulation. Under the Regulation, main insolvency proceedings may only be opened in the EU Member State where the debtor has its centre of main interests and secondary proceedings may be opened in states where the debtor has an 'establishment'.

Main insolvency proceedings have universal effects and apply to all assets of the debtor, whereas the effect of secondary proceedings are limited to assets of the debtor within the territory of which state secondary

---

[1] Regulation (EU) 2015/848 (recast Insolvency Regulation). The equivalent in Regulation 1346/2000 on Insolvency Proceedings is recital 11.
[2] In this report, the expression 'priority claimants' is used rather than preferential claimants. Use of the expression 'preferential claimants' may cause confusion with those claimants who are asked, in the course of transactional avoidance proceedings, to repay payments that they have received from the debtor in the course of pre-insolvency transactions, 'preferential payments'.

proceedings are opened.[3] The Regulation contains rules on the coordination of main and secondary proceedings but, nevertheless, it is vitally important to determine whether assets fall within the scope of the main or secondary proceedings. The Regulation not only allocates jurisdiction to open main and secondary insolvency proceedings but also determines applicable law in respect of each of the proceedings.[4] The applicable law governs, amongst other matters, the rules governing the lodging, verification and admission of claims, as well as the rules governing the distribution of proceeds from the realization of assets and the ranking of claims. In the *Nortel* case, it was important to determine where assets were located so as to determine which law to apply in respect of the distribution of assets (see Box 3.1).

In some countries secured creditors are paid first after the costs of the insolvency proceedings have been taken care off. Indeed, secured creditors can effectively opt out of the insolvency proceedings and realize their secured property (collateral) separately. Germany and the United Kingdom basically take this approach. Recital 68 of the Preamble to the recast Insolvency Regulation (Regulation 1346/2000, recital 25) refers to the proprietor of a right *in rem* being able to assert its right to segregation or separate settlement of the collateral security.

In other countries, employee claims are treated as priority claims and may get paid first even ahead of secured creditors. France and, to a certain extent, Italy and Portugal, take this approach. However, countries differ on the extent to which employee claims are treated as priority claims and the monetary limits that may be applicable. Countries also differ on whether tax claims should have any preferential status in insolvency proceedings. Germany and the United Kingdom have removed the preferential status of tax claims – in Germany's case in 1982 and in the United Kingdom some 20 years later. Many other countries stick robustly to the line that since the revenue authorities are, to an extent, involuntary creditors their claims should have some element of priority in the insolvency of a taxpayer entity.

At the risk of over-generalization, there appears to be a broad split between Germanic/Anglo-Saxon and Nordic countries on the one hand, and 'Latin' countries on the other hand. The first camp assigns much greater priority to security interests in insolvency proceedings than the

---

[3] Insolvency Regulation, Preamble, recital 23 and art. 3(2) and Regulation 1346/2000, Preamble, recital 12, art. 3(2).

[4] Insolvency Regulation, art. 4(2) and Regulation 1346/2000, Preamble, recital 12, art. 7(2).

BOX 3.1   C-649/13 *NORTEL NETWORKS SA* V. *ROGEAU*,
ECLI:EU:C:2015:384[2015] OJ C270/4

The Nortel group was one of the leading providers of telecommunications network solutions in the world. The group as a whole was headquartered in Canada and a Canadian company Nortel Networks Limited (NNL) controlled a majority of the group's worldwide subsidiaries. This included Nortel Networks SA (NNSA), a company that was incorporated under French law.

The Nortel group pursued extensive research and development (R&D) activities through specialist subsidiaries ('the R&D centres') and NNSA was one of those subsidiaries. The intellectual property resulting from the R&D activities was registered (mainly in North America) in the name of NNL as the legal owner but NNL granted the R&D centres free exclusive licences to exploit the intellectual property. The R&D centres retained beneficial ownership of the intellectual property, in a proportion based on their respective contributions to the R&D activities. The legal relationships between NNL and the R&D centres were organized through an inter-company agreement, known as the Master R&D Agreement (MRDA).

The Nortel group began to experience serious financial difficulties and, with a view to maximizing realizations through a co-ordinated sale of group assets, insolvency proceedings were opened simultaneously in Canada, the United States and the EU. Main insolvency proceedings were opened in the United Kingdom in respect of all the group companies incorporated in the EU, including NNSA. This was on the basis that the centre of main interests (COMI) of the respective companies was in the United Kingdom but secondary proceedings in respect of NNSA were later opened in France.

Following strike action by NNSA employees in France a settlement agreement was reached under which severance payments, including deferred severance payments, became payable to the employees. The funds to make these payments, however, could only come from assets located in France and certain preliminary questions on the determination of the location of assets were referred to the Court of Justice of the European Union (CJEU) by a French court.

The CJEU ruled that the courts of the state in which secondary insolvency proceedings have been opened have concurrent jurisdiction, alongside the courts of the state in which the main proceedings have been opened, to rule on the determination of the debtor's assets falling within the scope of the effects of those secondary proceedings. It also ruled that the debtor's assets that fall within the scope of the effects of secondary insolvency proceedings must be determined in accordance with article 2(g) of the Regulation on Insolvency Proceedings (1346/2000).

There are problems highlighted by the case, however. First, there is the risk of incompatible judgments, but the CJEU noted that, in accordance with article 25 of the Regulation, a national court should recognize the earlier judgment of another national court with jurisdiction over the same subject matter. It also noted that both national courts will apply the same set of rules, thereby minimizing the risk of incompatible judgments. Secondly, the rules for determining the location of assets in article 2(g) seemed to contain gaps. The court suggested that article 2(g) established a hierarchy of rules that must be applied (at para. 54) but, unlike the Advocate General, avoided direct consideration of the question whether the rules set out in article 2(g) were an exhaustive set. In this connection, it may also be noted that article 2(9) of the recast Insolvency Regulation contains a more extensive set of 'localization' rules than article 2(g).

second camp. Eastern European countries have largely reformed their laws on secured interests and bankruptcy (in some cases under US influence) and tend to fall into the first camp.

3.2 INTERNATIONAL BACKGROUND ON PRIORITY RIGHTS AND RANKING OF CLAIMS

The importance of secured creditor rights, particularly in insolvency proceedings, has been stressed in the influential 'legal origins' or 'law matters' thesis developed by four economists, La Porta, Lopez de Silanes, Shleifer and Vishny.[5] The original creditor rights index constructed by La Porta *et al.* measured four powers of secured lenders in bankruptcy: (1) whether there are restrictions, such as creditor consent, when a debtor files for reorganization; (2) whether secured creditors are able to seize collateral after the petition for reorganization is approved, that is there is no stay imposed by the court; (3) secured creditors are paid first out of liquidation proceeds; and (4) whether an insolvency practitioner (IP), and not management, is responsible for running the business during the reorganization period. If a country's laws and regulations entrust each of these powers to secured creditors, then a value of 1 is added to the creditor rights index. The scores are then aggregated and vary between 0 (poor creditor rights) and 4 (strong creditor rights).

The *Doing Business Reports*, issued annually since 2004 through the World Bank Group,[6] build on the legal origins literature and employ a more sophisticated version of the same methodology employed by La Porta *et al.* The lack of priority accorded security interests in insolvency

---

[5] See R. La Porta, F. Lopez de Silanes, A. Shleifer and R. Vishny, 'Legal Determinants of External Finance' (1997) 52 *Journal of Finance* 1131 and by the same authors 'Law and Finance' (1998) 106 *Journal of Political Economy* 113. The first three named authors refine the 'legal origins' thesis and defend it against criticisms in 'The Economic Consequences of Legal Origins' (2008) 46 *Journal of Economic Literature* 285.

[6] See www.doingbusiness.org.

may be a reason why some EU Member States perform relatively poorly in the 'getting credit' component of the *Doing Business Reports*. The methodology section of the reports explains how the reports are compiled and how certain features of collateral/secured transactions laws are considered desirable by the World Bank. The incorporation of these features in a country's laws will result in a positive score and the corollary also holds good. In other words, if some or all of the features are absent, the country will get a poor grade.

The 'getting credit' indicator includes both 'legal rights' and 'sharing of credit information' features. The first feature purports to ascertain the extent to which certain elements are contained within the secured credit (collateral) and corporate insolvency (bankruptcy) laws of a particular country. The second feature addresses the coverage, scope and accessibility of credit information that is available through credit reporting service providers, such as credit bureaus or credit registries. Sixty per cent of the overall proportion of the ranking is made up of the 'legal rights' element and the remaining 40 per cent is attributed to the 'sharing of credit information' element.

The 'legal rights' index purports to measure ten features of collateral law and two aspects of bankruptcy law. The index assigns a score of 1 for each of the following aspects of the law in a country:

- The economy has an integrated or unified legal framework for secured transactions that extends to the creation, publicity and enforcement of four functional equivalents to security interests in movable assets: fiduciary transfer of title; financial leases; assignment or transfer of receivables; and sales with retention of title.
- The law allows a business to grant a non-possessory security right in a single category of movable assets (such as machinery or inventory), without requiring a specific description of the collateral.
- The law allows a business to grant a non-possessory security right in substantially all its movable assets, without requiring a specific description of the collateral.
- A security right can be given over future or after-acquired assets and extends automatically to the products, proceeds or replacements of the original assets.
- A general description of debts and obligations is permitted in the collateral agreement and in registration documents, all types of debts and obligations can be secured between the parties, and the collateral agreement can include a maximum amount for which the assets are encumbered.
- A collateral registry or registration institution for security interests granted over movable property by incorporated and non-

incorporated entities is in operation, unified geographically and with an electronic database indexed by debtors' names.

- The collateral registry is a notice-based registry, a registry that files only a notice of the existence of a security interest (not the underlying documents) and does not perform a legal review of the transaction. The registry also publicizes functional equivalents to security interests.
- The collateral registry has modern features such as those that allow secured creditors (or their representatives) to register, search, amend or cancel security interests online.
- Secured creditors are paid first (for example, before tax claims and employee claims) when a debtor defaults outside an insolvency procedure.
- Secured creditors are paid first (for example, before tax claims and employee claims) when a business is liquidated.
- Secured creditors are subject to an automatic stay on enforcement procedures when a debtor enters a court-supervised reorganization procedure, but the law protects secured creditors' rights by providing clear grounds for relief from the automatic stay (for example, if the movable property is in danger) or setting a time limit for it.
- The law allows parties to agree in the collateral agreement that the lender may enforce its security right out of court; the law allows public and private auctions and also permits the secured creditor to take the asset in satisfaction of the debt.

In changes made in 2014, two components were added on what type of collateral registry operates in the country and on how it operates. The scoring also now penalizes countries for not having an automatic stay on enforcement during reorganization procedures so as to ensure that a viable business can continue to operate. Further, the index takes into account new elements relating to out-of-court enforcement procedures, such as the types of auctions allowed. Scores are then aggregated, with the higher scores signifying that the collateral and bankruptcy laws in a particular jurisdiction 'are better designed to expand access to credit'. As explained in the Introduction to this report, in general EU Member States do not rank particularly well on the 'getting credit' indicator, with Romania being the highest ranked EU country at joint 7th. Poland, the United Kingdom, Latvia and Hungary follow at joint 19th and Germany, Ireland, Denmark, Estonia, the Czech Republic, Lithuania and Bulgaria are all bunched together at equal 28th. But France, Netherlands and Greece are only ranked at equal 79th. New Zealand is number 1 in the rankings, and despite the perceived violence and instability in Colombia and Rwanda, they rank equally with the United States as joint 2nd.

It is difficult to escape the conclusion that unless a country has laws on secured transactions that are modelled on the relevant US provisions (article 9 of the US Uniform Commercial Code), then it will not do very well in the World Bank survey. New Zealand, Australia and Canada all have laws modelled on article 9, and along with the United States rank in the top ten in the survey.[7] Article 9 has often been held out as 'state of the art' by secured credit reformers worldwide. Certainly, it has proved a lasting monument for the largest economy in the world and it has been tried and tested in mercantile practice and judicial interpretation. Its basic philosophy facilitates access to credit in terms of easy-to-comply-with rules for the creation of security interests and making those rules effective against third parties. Moreover, almost all kinds of assets may be collateralized. It has however, to be viewed against the backdrop of US bankruptcy law, which reins in the enforcement of security during bankruptcy and restructuring proceedings.

One of the main selling points of UCC, article 9 is its track record of keeping the credit markets unlocked, and partly for this reason it has been indirectly copied in Canada, New Zealand and Australia. Even more indirectly, its ideas and substance has been reflected in the contents of Model Laws and Guiding Principles from international organizations, including UNCITRAL and the World Bank in its *Doing Business* survey. For example, the *Doing Business* project hails recent reforms in Colombia, stating:[8]

> Colombia improved access to credit by adopting a new secured transactions law that establishes a functional secured transactions system and a centralized, notice-based collateral registry. The law broadens the range of assets that can be used as collateral, allows a general description of assets granted as collateral, establishes clear priority rules inside bankruptcy for secured creditors, sets out grounds for relief from stay of enforcement actions by secured creditors during reorganization procedures and allows out-of-court enforcement of collateral.

Nevertheless, as has been pointed out in the Introduction to this Report, the *Doing Business* methodology and the underlying legal origins literature on which it is based has been criticized for an ostensible US orientation.

---

[7]   It appears that Colombia and Rwandan law has also been remodelled along US lines, see www.doingbusiness.org/reforms/overview/economy/colombia and www.doingbusiness.org/reforms/overview/economy/rwanda.

[8]   See www.doingbusiness.org/reforms/overview/economy/colombia/.

The deregulatory and free market agenda was quite explicit in the first *Doing Business Report* in 2004, which purported to show that a 'heavy' regulatory regime produced the worst results in terms of economic outcomes because it was usually associated with inefficiency within public institutions, long delays in reaching decisions, high costs of administrative formalities, lengthy judicial proceedings, higher unemployment and more corruption, less productivity, and lower investment.[9] The report also said 'Common law countries regulate the least, countries in the French civil law tradition the most. However, heritage is not destiny'.

There was some surprise and disappointment about the poor ranking given to the French legal system. The Association of the Friends of French Legal Culture published two critical commentaries[10] and a research institute has also been established to demonstrate the attractiveness of French law.[11]

The Introduction to this Report has also pointed out that many of the criticisms of the World Bank project and its methodology are reflected by the Independent Review Panel commissioned by the World Bank report and which reported in 2013.[12] The Review Panel was particularly concerned about rankings because they involved aggregation across topics and a value judgement about what was 'better' for doing business and how much better it was.

The Panel was also concerned about the naming, in particular, of the 'getting credit' indicator since it did not measure directly what the indicator claimed to address.[13] The *Doing Business Reports* appear to have made some minor adjustments in response to the Independent Panel report but the fundamentals of the project remain unaltered.

---

[9]   See the 2004 *Doing Business Report* at 83: 'Heavier regulation of business activities generally brings bad outcomes, while clearly defined and well-protected property rights enhance prosperity.'

[10]   See Association Henri Capitant des amis de la culture juridique Française, '*Les droits de tradition civiliste en question. A propos des rapports Doing Business* (Paris, Societé de Législation Comparée, 2006), available at www.henricapi tant.org. See the comment in R. Michaels, 'Comparative Law by Numbers? Legal Origins Thesis, Doing Business Reports and the Silence of Traditional Comparative Law' (2009) 57 *American Journal of Comparative Law* 765, 774: 'Somewhat typically, almost all of these contributions were published in French, leaving them with almost no impact in the international sphere.'

[11]   Fondation pour le droit continental, see www.fondation-droitcontinental. org.

[12]   Independent Panel Review of the World Bank, *Doing Business Report* (World Bank, 2013). The Panel was chaired by Trevor Manuel, the former South African Minister of Finance.

[13]   *Ibid.* 15.

3.3   BASIC RULES: SECURED VERSUS UNSECURED CLAIMS

EU Member States (as well as the comparison countries Norway and the United States) invariably draw a distinction between secured claims (claims under security interests) and unsecured claims. There is no universally accepted definition of security rights or interests but it is generally taken as meaning something equivalent to a right over property to ensure the payment of money or the performance of some other obligation. The property over which security is taken is referred to as 'secured' or 'collateralized'.

Secured claims generally have priority over unsecured claims but the extent of this priority may vary. There may be a certain proportion of the realizations under secured claims set aside for the benefit of unsecured claimants. In some laws, including Sweden and the United Kingdom, a distinction is drawn between security interests over all the assets of a business (an enterprise or floating charge) and other types of security interest, with the carve-out in favour of unsecured creditors being confined to the universal security.

Under UK law, a certain percentage of floating charge realizations is set aside for the benefit of unsecured creditors. The percentage is calculated by secondary legislation on a sliding scale, but subject to a global ceiling of £600,000.[14] Moreover, the carve-out is inapplicable if the company's net property is less than a prescribed minimum and where the IP considers that the cost of making a distribution to unsecured creditors would be disproportionate to the benefits received.

It might be argued that provisions of this nature constitute a fair concession to unsecured creditors without destroying the notion of security in its entirety. They are admittedly blunt instruments since they benefit all unsecured creditors and not merely non-adjusting creditors, that is those who are unable to adjust the explicit or implicit lending terms to take into account the fact that the borrower has granted security.[15] Fixed ceilings, however, allows attendant risks to be calculated.

The idea of 'carve-outs' for the benefit of unsecured creditors failed to gain acceptance when the relevant provisions of US law (UCC, article 9) were mostly recently revised in full. The carve-out advocates, including the well-known bankruptcy law Professor, Elizabeth Warren (now an

---

[14]   See Insolvency Act 1986 (Prescribed Part) Order 2003, SI 2003/2097. See also, A. Keay, 'The Prescribed Part: Sharing Around the Company's Funds' (2011) 24(6) *Insolvency Intelligence* 81.

[15]   See V. Finch, 'Security, Insolvency and Risk: Who Pays the Price?' (1999) 62 *Modern Law Review* 633, 652.

influential US Senator), pointed out that while the US Bankruptcy Code recognized security rights to their fullest, nevertheless there were a number of rules, doctrines and practices that effectively operated to erode the priority of secured claims in bankruptcy.[16] For example, Chapter 11 of the US Bankruptcy Code imposes restrictions on the enforcement of security interests in the course of proceedings for the restructuring of ailing businesses and, during this time, the value of the collateral may fall.[17]

Critics suggested, however, that the carve out would be factored into the borrowing base and secured creditors would extend less credit as a result. This would have a particularly adverse impact on marginal businesses, resulting in further bankruptcies. In their assessment, the denial of full priority might detract from the capacity of entrepreneurs to attract investors. It was suggested that while secured creditors might lose profits under a carve-out regime, the biggest losers would be debtors, who would receive less funding.[18]

3.4 FINANCIAL CLAIMANTS VERSUS COMMERCIAL CLAIMANTS

To the extent that financial claims are secured, they have priority over unsecured commercial or trade claims. Financial claimants are more likely to take security than commercial claimants. To a large extent, therefore, the distinction between financial claimants and commercial claimants mirrors the distinction between secured and unsecured claims. Accordingly, the financial claimants, *prima facie*, have priority over commercial claimants.

In many countries, however, commercial claimants may benefit from 'quasi-security' devices such as a retention of title clause in a sale of goods

---

[16]   See L. Bebchuk and J. Fried, 'The Uneasy Case for the Priority of Secured Claims in Bankruptcy' (1996) 105 *Yale Law Journal* 857; L. Bebchuk and J. Fried, 'The Uneasy Case for the Priority of Secured Claims in Bankruptcy: Further Thoughts and a Reply to Critics' (1997) 82 *Cornell Law Review* 1279; E. Warren, 'Making Policy with Imperfect Information: The Article 9 Full Priority Debates' (1997) 82 *Cornell Law Review* 1373, 1377.

[17]   See D. Baird and T. Jackson, 'Corporate Reorganizations and the Treatment of Diverse Ownership Interests: A Comment on Adequate Protection of Secured Creditors in Bankruptcy' (1984) 51 *University of Chicago Law Review* 97, 112–14.

[18]   S.L. Harris and C.W. Mooney, 'Measuring the Social Costs and Benefits and Identifying the Victims of Subordinating Security Interests in Bankruptcy' (1997) 82 *Cornell Law Review* 1349, 1357.

contract or the supply of equipment under a finance or operating lease. 'Quasi-security' may be described as a form of legal mechanism that is not strictly speaking security but serves many of the same economic functions. If goods are sold, or equipment supplied, to a business under a retention of title clause or finance lease, then, in the event of the business becoming insolvent, the seller or supplied can repossess the goods or equipment.[19] In theory, the seller or supplier does not have to compete for the assets with the other creditors of the business. The business never became the owner of the assets and the seller or supplier is simply seeking the return of its own property. The claim of the seller or supplier is based on ownership. Article 9 of the Directive on late payment in commercial transactions (Directive 2011/7/EU) provides:

> Member States shall provide in conformity with the applicable national provisions designated by private international law that the seller retains title to goods until they are fully paid for if a retention of title clause has been expressly agreed between the buyer and the seller before the delivery of the goods.

While the meaning of the Directive may be ambiguous, especially the reference to private international law, many states go far in recognizing retention of titles claim, in particular Germany and the Netherlands.

3.5   WHY SECURED CLAIMS ARE GIVEN PRIORITY

Essentially, there are two sets of arguments for giving security creditors priority over the unsecured creditors. The first set is based on property rights and freedom of contract. The second set is based on the proposition that recognizing the priority of security rights will lead to more credit and at lower cost and this in turn will help to stimulate economic activity and lead to better economic conditions for all.

The first argument proceeds on the basis that the secured creditor has bargained for property rights and priority in respect of the debtor's assets. A social market economy should, in the normal run of things, respect property rights and freedom of contract and recognize this manifestation of the parties' contractual freedom. Security is seen as a fair exchange for the credit; the secured creditor has bargained for security and priority, whereas other creditors have not. Consequently, it does not seem unfair to

---

[19]   See generally P. Omar, 'Insolvency, Security Interests and Creditor Protection' in I. Davies (ed.), *Security Interests in Mobile Equipment* (Aldershot, Ashgate, 2002), ch. 8, pp. 293–334.

privilege the secured creditor over other creditors who equally could have contracted for security but chose not to do so.

On the other hand, there may be involuntary creditors, that is creditors not in a contractual relationship with the debtor, who are not in a position to bargain for security. Moreover, there may be other non-adjusting creditors, or poorly adjusting creditors, where it is unrealistic to suppose that they could bargain for security or where the transaction costs of doing so are too great. These creditors in a weak bargaining position are perhaps most likely to be the ones that will be hit hardest by the debtor's insolvency. The insolvency may impact disproportionately on them in that they are not very capable of sharing or passing on the costs of the loss. Large financial institutions which are most likely to take security are in a much better position to pass on losses.

In the second set of arguments, security interests are seen to function as a risk reduction device that increases the availability, and lowers the cost, of credit. The minimization of risk should encourage lenders to make loans and to reduce the risk premium they might otherwise factor into the calculations of interest rates. According to the World Bank:[20]

> Economic analysis suggests that small and medium sized businesses in countries that have stronger secured transactions laws and registries have greater access to credit, better ratings of financial system stability, lower rates of non-performing loans, and a lower cost of credit.

The overall effect, however, of recognizing security rights is to improve a creditor's hand in dealing with adverse selection, moral hazard and uninsurable risk issues.

In UNCITRAL's view:[21]

> The key to the effectiveness of secured credit is that it allows borrowers to use the value inherent in their assets as a means of reducing credit risk for the creditor. Risk is mitigated because loans secured by the property of a borrower give lenders recourse to the property in the event of non-payment. Studies have shown that as the risk of non-payment is reduced, the availability of credit increases and the cost of credit falls. Studies have also shown that in States where lenders perceive the risks associated with transactions to be high, the cost of credit increases as lenders require increased compensation to evaluate and assume the increased risk.

---

[20] See *Secured Transactions Systems and Collateral Registries* (Washington, DC, World Bank, 2010), p. 8.

[21] *Draft Legislative Guide on Secured Transactions, Report of the Secretary General*, A/CN9/WG VI/WP 2 (2002), addendum 1, para. 4.

The argument is that banks and other financial institutions will not engage in large-scale lending activities if their position as secured creditors in the liquidation of their borrowers is not sufficiently certain, or sufficient means for the enforcement of security are not available. Economists suggest that security plays a crucial role in lending decisions by addressing the problems of adverse selection, moral hazard and uninsurable risk.[22] The incentives of creditors and borrowers are aligned and a credible commitment is added to the relationship.[23]

Adverse selection refers to the fact that some borrowers may turn out to be over-optimistic or unreliable. A lender cannot simply raise interest rates to screen out these borrowers because honest borrowers with sound projects will drop out of the picture as well. The potential pay-off from the project may not be enough to meet the borrowing costs. Where security is taken, however, adverse selection problems are addressed more powerfully. The lender can back up its assessment of the borrower and the soundness of the business plan with information on the value of the collateral. As well as the revenues generated from the project, the lender can look to the collateral for repayment. Moral hazard refers to the possibility that a borrower may abscond with the loan. The larger the loan, the greater the moral hazard, but if the borrower provides security, the lower are the lender's costs in monitoring moral hazard. The borrower has given the lender a hostage against flight risk in the shape of security. Security reduces certain risks, that is the borrower not being able to repay due to loss of key customers, or losses on foreign exchange, that may not be easily insurable, or insurable at all. Uninsurable risk is reduced in unsecured lending through 'spreading', that is through making smallish loans to a large number of borrowers. Security allows more concentrated lending and reduces uninsurable risk since the security serves as an alternative repayment mechanism.[24]

On the other hand, within the European Union, it seems that no two national priority systems are exactly identical. This may be because of the influence exerted by powerful groups of creditors; the inertia of legal

---

[22]   See generally J. Stiglitz and A. Weiss, 'Credit Rationing in Markets with Imperfect Information' (1981) 71 *American Economic Review* 393. See also G. Akerlof, 'The Market for "Lemons": Qualitative Uncertainty and the Market Mechanism' (1970) 84 *Quarterly Journal of Economics* 488.

[23]   See generally O. Hart and J. Moore, 'Default and Renegotiation: A Dynamic Model of Debt' (1998) 113 *Quarterly Journal of Economics* 1.

[24]   See G. McCormack, *Secured Credit and the Harmonisation of Law* (Cheltenham and Northampton, MA, Edward Elgar Publishing, 2011), ch. 3.

tradition, or as a result of the conscious and deliberate choice to promote certain values.[25]

Table 3.1 provides a brief snapshot indication of the divergent rules on priorities and the ranking of claims in the EU Member States and in the two comparator countries.

3.6 EMPLOYEE CLAIMS

Employees and self-employed agents are typically non-adjusting, or poorly-adjusting, creditors. In other words, they cannot realistically be expected to bargain for security over the debtor's assets in response to the fact that financial institutions may have taken security. Their own bargaining power is too weak or the economic and other costs associated with taking security would be too great.

Different EU countries have different ways of protecting such creditors, whether through social safety nets, or insurance schemes, or the like. It is the case, however, that the treatment of self-employed agents is far different from the treatment of employees. Self-employed agents are invariably treated as normal trade creditors and have unsecured status in the liquidation of a business entity. Spanish law, however, constitutes an exception in that the self-employed are given preferential status in certain circumstances. It may be that other Member States need to respond to changing patterns of employment and equate the treatment of employees and self-employed agents subject to certain conditions.

Unpaid employees invariably have preferential status, subject to certain monetary limits, which gives them priority over unsecured claims. Preferential claims are generally paid in the third tier of priority, that is after expenses of the insolvency proceedings and then secured claims. In some countries, however, most notably France but also including Portugal, Italy and Greece, employee claims are payable ahead of secured claims. The reason for this, it seems, is largely redistributionist and to protect the weaker party. It has been argued in France that employees should not be treated merely as unsecured creditors and that it is:

> morally desirable to favour employees over financial creditors (which may in any case have protected themselves against the risk of their borrower's default). Moreover, when the company goes bankrupt, employees may suffer additional

---

[25] See J.M. Garrido, 'No Two Snowflakes are the Same: The Distributional Question in International Bankruptcies' (2011) 46 *Texas International Law Journal* 459, 460–61.

Table 3.1   Priorities and the ranking of claims

Country	Certain employee claims rank above secured creditors?	Certain tax claims have preferential status, i.e. rank above general unsecured creditors?	Shareholder loans are subordinated to loans due to other creditors?
Austria	No	No	Yes
Belgium	No	Yes	No
Bulgaria	No	Yes	No
Croatia	No	No	No
Cyprus	Yes but only in limited circumstances, e.g. over floating charges	Yes	No
Czech Republic	No	No	No
Denmark	No	No	No
Estonia	No	No	No
Finland	No	No	No
France	Yes	Yes	No
Germany	No	No	Yes generally
Greece	Yes	Yes	No
Hungary	Yes	Yes	Partial subordination
Ireland	Yes but only in very limited circumstances, e.g. over floating charges	Yes	No
Italy	Yes	Yes	Yes but under specific conditions
Latvia	No	Yes	No
Lithuania	No	Yes	No
Luxembourg	No	Yes	No

Table 3.1 (continued)

Country	Certain employee claims rank above secured creditors?	Certain tax claims have preferential status, i.e. rank above general unsecured creditors?	Shareholder loans are subordinated to loans due to other creditors?
Malta	Yes	Yes	No
Netherlands	No	Yes	No
Norway	No	Yes	No but subordination may be specifically agreed upon by the relevant parties
Poland	No	Yes	Yes in certain circumstances treated as disguised contributions of capital
Portugal	Yes in certain circumstances	Yes	Yes
Romania	No	Yes	Yes in certain limited circumstances
Slovakia	No	No	No
Slovenia	No	Yes	Yes
Spain	Yes in certain circumstances	Yes	Yes
Sweden	No	No	Yes
United Kingdom	Yes but only in respect of very limited circumstances, i.e. floating charges	No	No
United States	No	Yes	No

costs, e.g., costs incurred as a result of a change of location to find a new job. These costs are not taken into account when calculating the amount of their claims as part of the bankruptcy procedure. For this reason insolvency law should have a redistributive purpose.[26]

But law-makers are faced with the challenge of determining the extent to which insolvency law should have such a redistributive purpose and, in any event, the satisfaction of employee claims through preferential status is very uneven. It depends on there being sufficient assets within the debtor's coffers to meet the claims. Recital 22 of the Preamble to the recast Insolvency Regulation states that at the 'next review of this Regulation, it will be necessary to identify further measures in order to improve the preferential rights of employees at European level'.

The different levels of protection of the preferential rights of employees in the different EU Member States is often the motivation behind the opening of secondary proceedings under the Insolvency Regulation. The applicable law in respect of the secondary proceedings is the law of the state where the proceedings are opened, including local priority rules in respect of the distribution of assets.[27] Secondary proceedings therefore protect local preferential creditors whose claims would be treated as non-preferential under the law that applies to the main proceedings. Secondary proceedings, however, qualify the universality of the main insolvency proceedings. Moreover, they add to the overall cost of the insolvency process and may make the job of the IP in the main proceedings more difficult and certainly more complex. IPs in main proceedings have developed strategies to overcome some of the disadvantages associated with secondary proceedings, and courts in certain states, particularly the United Kingdom, have recognized and implemented these strategies (see Box 3.2).

The recast Insolvency Regulation has now formalized some of the practices developed in cases such as *Re Collins and Aikman* since, as the European Commission has pointed out,[28] such a practice was not previously possible under the law of many states. Under the recast Regulation, the court seised of a request to open secondary proceedings may turn down the request if the IP in the main proceedings gives an

---

[26]   See Sophie Vermeille, *The Legal System and the Development of Alternative Methods of Financing to Bank Credit; Or How French Law has Failed to Adapt to the Evolution of the Economy and Finance* (2012), para. 167, available at http://papers.ssrn.com/sol3/papers.cfm?abstract_id=2090036. It is fair to say, however, that the author is critical of certain aspects of French bankruptcy law.

[27]   Regulation 1346/2000, arts 4(2)(i) and 28 and Insolvency Regulation, arts 72(2)(i) and 35.

[28]   Proposal for a New Regulation, COM(2012)744, para. 3.1.

BOX 3.2   *RE COLLINS AND AIKMAN* [2006] EWHC 1343

In this case, the UK court developed the notion of 'synthetic' secondary proceedings, holding that the UK Insolvency Act 1986 was sufficiently flexible to enable UK
IPs to honour promises made to creditors in other EU Member States that local
priorities would be respected in return for not opening secondary proceedings in
these states. In this case, local creditors effectively got the benefits of secondary
proceedings without the trouble of having to open them. These secondary proceedings were 'synthetic' or 'virtual' rather than actual.

The case concerned a group of companies, headquartered in the United States,
which supplied components to the automotive industry. The US holding company
filed for Chapter 11 bankruptcy reorganization in the United States and insolvency
(administration) proceedings were opened in the United Kingdom in respect of
companies in the European arm of the group on the basis that the centre of main
interest of these companies was in the United Kingdom. The European arm was
made up of 24 companies spread over ten countries and 27 operational sites with
4,000 employees and an annual turnover of about US$1 billion. The IPs were
strongly of the view that the best returns to creditors would be achieved through a
co-ordinated approach to the continuation of the businesses, to the funding of the
administration and to the sale of the businesses and assets. They were also of the
view that the opening of secondary proceedings would make it more difficult to
continue to trade the businesses, fund the administrations and conduct sales processes on a group basis. Accordingly, the IPs gave oral assurances to the creditors
that if there were no secondary proceedings in the relevant jurisdiction then their
respective financial positions as creditors under the relevant local law would be
respected in the UK proceedings. The UK court held that there was sufficient flexibility in UK insolvency law to enable the IPs to implement these assurances and
to depart *pro tanto* from the application of ordinary provisions of UK law, which was
the law of the main proceedings.

undertaking that adequately protects the general interests of local creditors (articles 38(2) and 36).

The new provision, however, comes with a lot of complexity in its
detailed design. For instance, the undertaking has to be approved by the
known local creditors. Rules on qualified majority and voting that apply
in the state where the secondary proceedings could have been opened
apply for the approval of the undertaking. It is certainly not a complete
solution to differences in the priority or preferential rights of employees
under national insolvency law. It is more a patchwork solution to overcome particular difficulties in respect of the coordination of main and
secondary insolvency proceedings.

Protecting employee claims through a social insurance or guarantee
fund arguably offers a more uniform and potentially complete protection
than priority or preferential status under insolvency law. Employees are

also likely to be paid much more promptly their arrears of salary and other entitlements from such a fund. The alternative is for unpaid employees to wait a potentially long time before an IP establishes the value of an insolvent estate and the extent of the liabilities owed by the estate. Establishing a guarantee fund, however, requires a substantial administrative commitment and there are also 'moral hazard' and financing issues, that is whether the fund should be financed through *ex ante* or *ex post* contributions from employers.[29]

Directive 2008/94/EC on the protection of employees in the event of the insolvency of their employer requires the establishment of such a fund by Member States. Essentially, the Directive is designed to protect employees who have a claim for unpaid remuneration against an employer who is in a state of insolvency. Member States are obliged to establish institutions that guarantee payment of employee claims and, where appropriate, severance pay on termination of employment relationships. Ceilings may be set on the payments made by the institution but these ceilings must be sufficiently high to contribute to the social objective of the Directive.

Member States, however, have a substantial measure of discretion in the implementation of the Directive in terms of potential exclusions from coverage, determination of reference periods for calculation of unpaid remuneration, and whether employers contribute to funding costs for the institution.

In many, if not most, Member States, the first resort for employees of an insolvent entity is to make a claim against the guarantee fund. Once the claim is met, the Fund will then stand in the shoes of the employee and seek full or partial reimbursement from the insolvent estate. According to the European Commission:[30]

> 3.4 million workers who have benefited from the safety net provided by the intervention of the guarantee institutions in the last four years, mostly in times of economic crisis, prove its usefulness.

It may be that the best way forward in terms of enhancing employee protection in the event of employer insolvency would be to strengthen the provisions of the Directive and the guarantee fund whose establishment it

---

[29]   See generally J. Armour, 'The Law and Economics Debate about Secured Lending: Lessons for European Lawmaking?' (2008) 5 *European Company and Financial Law Review* 3, and J. Armour, 'Should We Redistribute in Insolvency?' in J. Getzler and J. Payne (eds), *Company Charges: Spectrum and Beyond* (Oxford, Oxford University Press, 2006).

[30]   COM(2011)84 final, para. 9.

mandates. Possible approaches would be to end some of the opt-outs, to remove some of the scope for variation in terms of reference periods for calculation of remuneration, and to require employer contributions to the fund.

3.7 UNPAID TAXES AND SOCIAL SECURITY CONTRIBUTIONS

There are two basic differences in approach on this issue in EU Member States. Some countries, led by Germany but also including Austria, the United Kingdom, Croatia, the Czech Republic, Denmark, Estonia, Finland and Sweden, have removed the preferential status of tax and social security claims. Essentially, this means that the state authority claiming the unpaid official contributions is in the position of an unsecured creditor with no priority over general creditors. The other approach which is followed in the majority of countries is to give these claims by the state authorities a preferential status, perhaps subject to certain monetary limits or in respect of certain types of taxes or claims. This approach is also exhibited in the two comparison countries, Norway and the United States. In the United States, tax claims have priority unsecured status subject to certain limits which means that they are payable ahead of general unsecured creditors. The same basic approach is followed in Norway.

The main justifications given for tax priority centre around the social costs of non-collection and the importance of minimizing losses for the public purse.[31] Moreover, it has been argued that insofar as the state is claiming unpaid taxes and social security contributions, it is an involuntary creditor who has not consciously assumed the risk of the debtor's insolvency. It is also argued that the state authorities are not in a position effectively to monitor the debtor's behaviour and to assess the risk of default or insolvency.

The reasons for not giving priority are that the state is generally in a much more powerful position than unsecured creditors and it is therefore unfair to prioritize its claims. Moreover, not giving priority to the state authorities means that they are much more likely to monitor the debtor's behaviour and enforce payment discipline. The state authorities are also

---

[31] See generally, A. Keay and P. Walton, 'The Preferential Debts Regime in Liquidation Law: In the Public Interest?' [1999] *Company, Financial and Insolvency Law Review* 84.

likely to have powerful and coercive collection tools available outside of insolvency proceedings.

The priority status of tax and other 'public law' claims have been considered by many countries of different political persuasions, including in Singapore by a government appointed Insolvency Law Review Committee.[32] The committee considered that the priority status of such claims visited hardship upon the general body of creditors while producing benefits that were insignificant in terms of total government receipts. It also suggested that there were greater gains to the government if the tax which would otherwise be paid in priority to the government was distributed to other creditors so that they, in turn, could continue their economic activities and pay their taxes, and that the state was not alone in being an involuntary creditor. The committee concluded, however, by saying that this was an 'issue which is intertwined with the policies and financial considerations of the Government and the Committee defers to the views of the Government'.[33]

3.8   SHAREHOLDER CLAIMS

The standard position throughout the EU is that insofar as shareholders are seeking compensation for the value of their shares in the insolvency proceedings, their claims are subordinated to those of the unsecured creditors. They cannot receive anything in return for their shares unless creditor claims are met in full. If, however, shareholders are seeking reimbursement for loans they have made to the insolvent debtor, it depends on whether the loans are secured or unsecured. If the loans are secured then the shareholder is treated as a secured creditor, subject to the possibility of the IP challenging the loan as a voidable transaction if it is made during a 'suspect' period. The fact that the loan has been made by a shareholder may mean that the transaction is deemed an 'insider' transaction and therefore easier to challenge, something considered in Chapter 4.

If the shareholder loan is unsecured, then the claim for recovery of the loan is generally treated in the same way as other unsecured claims and payable rateably with these claims. A few countries, however, such as Germany and Austria, but also including Spain, Sweden, Italy, Poland

---

[32]   Insolvency Law Review Committee, *Final Report* (2013), available at www.mlaw.gov.sg/content/dam/minlaw/corp/News/Revised%20Report%20of%20the%20Insolvency%20Law%20Review%20Committee.pdf.

[33]   *Ibid.* 21.

and Romania, apply a doctrine of 'equitable subordination'. This means that, in certain circumstances, a shareholder loan may be deemed to constitute a disguised capital contribution and is therefore subordinated to ordinary unsecured claims on this basis. Alternatively, a more general principle of subordination may apply.

If the debtor is not insolvent, then the expectation is that all creditor claims, whether secured or unsecured, would be met in full. If creditors and shareholders bargain over the debtor's assets when the solvency of the debtor is threatened but in a situation outside formal insolvency proceedings, then the parties bargain in the shadow of the law and the expectation is that normal liquidation priorities would be respected. The nature of restructuring proceedings in some countries means that shareholder claims have a 'hold-up' or obstruction value over and above their strict liquidation entitlements. Therefore, it is not uncommon for existing shareholders to receive or retain some 'equity' in a restructured business entity. This also helps to ensure their continued co-operation and may reduce valuation disputes which have the potential of slowing down the restructuring process.[34]

This 'hold up value' operates in practice in many countries, including even one of the comparison countries, the United States, where the so-called 'absolute priority' principle is enshrined in Chapter 11 of the Bankruptcy Code. The 'absolute priority' principle mandates that unless creditors are to be paid in full, or unless each class of creditors consents, the company's old shareholders are not entitled to receive or retain any property through the restructuring process on account of their old shares.[35] The case study in Box 3.3 highlights some of the issues.

The American Bankruptcy Institute, in its 2014 report on possible

---

[34] Nevertheless, in respect of many restructuring procedures, the shareholders in a company facing financial difficulties would, at best, expect to see their shareholding in a restructured entity diluted substantially. In many cases, their shareholding may be eliminated entirely; see J. Payne, *Schemes of Arrangement: Theory, Structure and Operation* (Cambridge, Cambridge University Press, 2014), p. 159, referring to the UK scheme of arrangement. In the impact assessment that accompanies the European Commission's Recommendation on a new approach to business failure and insolvency, it is suggested that a procedure modelled along the lines of the UK scheme would make restructuring 'procedures less cumbersome, less costly and speedier than they are currently in some Member States', see Recommendation Impact Assessment, SWD(2014)61, p. 38.

[35] Bankruptcy Code, s. 1129(a)(7). For a suggestion that the 'absolute priority' principle in the United States is less absolute than it might superficially appear, see Mark J. Roe and Frederick Tung, 'Breaking Bankruptcy Priority: How Rent-Seeking Upends the Creditors' Bargain' (2013) 99 *Virginia Law Review* 1235.

BOX 3.3   *IN RE GENCO SHIPPING AND TRADING LTD*

In Re Genco Shipping and Trading Ltd, available at www.nysb.uscourts.gov/sites/
default/files/opinions/249024_321_opinion.pdf Genco sought approval of a
Chapter 11 plan that would convert the outstanding senior secured debt into equity
in the reorganized entities, pay general unsecured trade creditors in full, and
provide a small recovery for existing equity.

Genco was a leading provider of maritime transportation services for 'dry bulk'
cargoes, such as iron ore, coal, grain and steel products. The Genco plan, which
received more or less unanimous creditor approval, contained the following main
features:

- Approximately US$1.2 billion of secured debt would be converted into equity
  in the restructured entity.
- New capital would be invested through a US$100 million rights offering.
- The maturity dates for two existing secured lending facilities would be
  extended.
- General unsecured claims would be reinstated and paid in the ordinary
  course of business.
- Existing equity holders would receive options to obtain up to 6% of the equity
  in the restructured entity.

The Genco plan was premised on the assumption that the value of the enterprise
was between US$1.36 billion and US$1.44 billion. But shareholders objected to
confirmation of the Genco plan on the basis that the debtors' enterprise value was
actually between US$1.54 billion and US$1.91 billion. They argued that, because
the debtors were solvent under its valuation, existing shareholders were entitled to
greater recoveries than those provided under the Genco plan.

The Bankruptcy Court, however, concluded that the debtors' value did not
exceed US$1.48 billion, the amount at which existing equity holders would be
entitled to any recovery. Therefore, it approved the Genco plan.

---

reforms to Chapter 11,[36] recommended retention of the basic 'absolute
priority' principle but subject to certain modifications. These included
provision for stakeholders who are 'out of the money' at the time of
confirmation of a restructuring plan to receive 'redemption option value'.
This is the value of a hypothetical option with a three-year lifespan to
purchase the entire company and with an exercise price equal to the face
value of the senior claims. The Recommendation is intended to address
the fact that bankruptcy proceedings may take place during an economic

---

[36]   See American Bankruptcy Institute, *Commission to Study the Reform of
Chapter 11 2012–2014, Final Report and Recommendations* (2014), pp. 207–11,
available at www.commission.abi.org/full-report.

downturn, resulting in a lower company valuation and lower recoveries for junior creditors. The report explains that:

> the valuation may occur during a trough in the debtor's business cycle or the economy as a whole, and relying on a valuation at such a time may result in a reallocation of the reorganised firm's future value in favour of senior stakeholders and away from junior stakeholders in a manner that is subjectively unfair and inconsistent with the Bankruptcy Code's principle of providing a breathing spell from business adversity.[37]

The payment of the redemption option value is designed to reflect the possibility that within a period of three years, the value of a restructured company might be such that enables the senior creditors to be paid in full and provides incremental value to the immediately junior class of stakeholders. The detailed rules are quite complex, however, and there seems little prospect of their immediate implementation.

The European Commission's Recommendation on a new approach to business failure and insolvency does not explicitly incorporate the 'absolute priority' principle. Recommendation 17, however, provides that creditors with different interests should be treated in separate classes which reflect those interests. The 'absolute priority' principle does not appear to be expressly incorporated in the laws of many, if any, EU Member States. No doubt, however, this issue would be considered in many states where courts have to address the overall fairness of a plan, whether any creditor has received an unfair advantage, and whether a reasonable creditor and a member of the class concerned could have voted in favour of the plan.

3.9 SUPER-PRIORITY NEW FINANCING

The general philosophy of the European Commission's Recommendation on a new approach to business failure and insolvency is to facilitate new money financing with a view to promoting corporate restructuring and rescue.[38] This approach conforms very much to that taken in the UNCITRAL *Legislative Guide on Insolvency*, where the provisions on new money finance are said to have a threefold purpose.[39] The first is to facilitate the flow of finance for the continued operation or survival of the debtor's business or the preservation or enhancement of the value of

---

[37] *Ibid.* 207.
[38] C(2014)1500, final recommendations 27–29.
[39] See UNCITRAL, *Legislative Guide on Insolvency*, p. 118.

the assets of the estate. The second is to ensure appropriate protection for the providers of new finance, and the third is to ensure appropriate protection for those parties whose rights may be affected by the provision of such finance.

It is provided in the UNCITRAL *Legislative Guide* that new finance can be secured on unencumbered assets or the subject of lower-ranking or equal-ranking security on already encumbered assets. It is also provided that it should rank ahead of existing unsecured creditors. Special provision in this regard is made in a number of EU Member States, including France, Germany, Greece and Lithuania. Portugal may go a little further in that any constraints faced by the debtor in relation to new finance are removed and priority is granted not only over existing unsecured debts but also over certain types of preferential debt. The available evidence, however, suggests that the formal new finance provisions have not, thus far at least, been extensively availed of in practice.[40]

Other EU countries may have no special rules, although new finance is a likely part of any restructuring and is usually given priority over certain existing debts by agreement between the relevant creditors. This reflects the UK position.

The UNCITRAL *Legislative Guide* goes further than the European mainstream and closely mirrors the US position. It stipulates that new finance may trump existing security interests if certain conditions are met including: (a) existing security interest holders were given the opportunity of being heard; (b) the debtor can show that it cannot obtain the finance in any other way; and (c) the interests of existing secured creditors will be protected. Super-priority new financing is often seen as necessary to resolve 'debt overhang', that is existing assets being fully secured, and to cure 'under-investment' problems, that is lack of incentives to finance value-generating projects.[41] Finland appears, though, to be the only EU Member State with provisions along these lines. It has special rules to encourage new finance, including rules that permit the trumping of exist-

---

[40]   See in particular the comments from the German, Greece and Lithuanian reporters. The Greek reporter (at p. 20) points to the fact that the new financing provisions are relatively new and points to more general liquidity and financing issues affecting banks.

[41]   Recommendation 67. See generally G. McCormack, 'Super-Priority, New Financing and Corporate Rescue' [2007] *Journal of Business Law* 701; G. Triantis, 'A Theory of the Regulation of Debtor-in-Possession Financing' (1993) 46 *Vanderbilt Law Review* 901; S. Dahiya, K. John, M. Puri and G. Ramirez, 'Debtor-in-Possession Financing and Bankruptcy Resolution: Empirical Evidence' (2003) 69 *Journal of Financial Economics* 259.

ing debt if the court is satisfied that the new debt does not significantly increase the risk of those creditors whose priority position would be weakened as a result of the provision of super-priority new finance.[42]

In the United States, new financing is dealt with in section 364 of the Bankruptcy Code, which lays down that credit extended during the restructuring process has priority over existing unsecured claims. If the extension of credit is in the ordinary course of business, then priority is automatic, whereas if the extension of credit is outside of the ordinary course, then the priority must be authorized by the court prior to the granting of credit. If the lender does not agree to the contrary, a company can get a restructuring plan confirmed only by ensuring that the new lender is paid in full at the confirmation stage and even if the plan fails, 'new' debts have priority over existing unsecured debts in the ensuing liquidation. There may be a lot of cases where a company's assets are secured to such an extent that mere priority over existing unsecured creditors offers new lenders little chance of recovery in any subsequent liquidation. In these circumstances, meaningful priority means priority over existing secured creditors, and section 364(d) provides that the court may authorize this in narrowly defined circumstances. The existing secured creditor is safeguarded by the fact that the company must prove that it cannot obtain the loan without granting such a security interest and that the secured creditor is adequately protected against loss. The case law suggests that the statutory requirements are strictly applied and that the 'priming' of prior secured lending is permitted only in infrequent and exceptional instances.

3.10 CONCLUSIONS ON RANKING OF CLAIMS AND ORDER OF PRIORITIES

As pointed out at the outset of the chapter, this study has indeed revealed very different approaches in Member States on the priorities enjoyed by the holders of security interests (secured creditors) and preferential (priority) claimants in an insolvency. This may cause creditors to assess credit risk by reference to individual countries rather than on a Europe-wide basis. Undoubtedly, however, a number of other factors enter into

---

[42] It may be noted, however, that apparently under the World Bank *Doing Business* 'getting credit' methodology indicator, the highest mark is awarded where new financing merely receives priority over ordinary, unsecured creditors and this solution is seen as preferable to a situation where new financing is given super-priority over all creditors, both secured and unsecured.

the assessment of credit risk and not just the insolvency or collateral law in a particular country. The factors include the overall shape of the economy in a particular country, including the state of the public finances.

Nevertheless, this chapter on the ranking of claims and the order of priorities has raised a number of issues that are appropriate for consideration by the European legislator, although some of them may be rather controversial and it may be difficult to secure agreement. These issues include the following:

- whether the relatively poor position of EU countries on the 'getting credit' indicator of the World Bank *Doing Business* project is down primarily to the way in which these rankings are composed rather than due to any fundamental deficiencies in the relevant laws and practices of EU Member States;
- whether a minimum set of EU rules on the ranking of claims in the event of insolvency might impact favourably on the availability and cost of credit in some or all EU Member States;
- whether a EU-wide norm should be enacted that puts tax and other public law claims in the category of general unsecured claims rather than such claims having any special priority status;
- whether claims by unpaid employees should be given any special status at EU level, whether such priority status should be subject to monetary and/or other limits, and whether such priority should apply also in respect of secured as well as general creditors;
- whether the financial position of employees in the context of insolvency proceedings might be more appropriately protected by enhancing the protections available under employment law Directives and, in particular, by strengthening the safeguards available under national wage guarantee funds and other employee safeguarding measures;
- whether the insolvency and more general insolvency related protections available to employees should be extended to self-employed persons and how self-employed persons might be defined for this purpose;
- whether a general EU norm should be enacted subordinating shareholder loans and/or other amounts due to shareholders to general creditor claims;
- whether a portion of the amounts secured by security rights (rights *in rem*) should be set aside for the satisfaction of general unsecured creditor claims and how this portion should be calculated;
- whether the general priority rules that apply in liquidation proceedings, including the priority of debt claims over shareholder (equity)

claims should also apply in restructuring proceedings and whether any exceptions should be made to this principle;

- whether any special rules are appropriate giving 'new money' advanced during the course of, or in anticipation of, restructuring and/or liquidation proceedings priority over other creditors; how 'new money' should be defined for this purpose; what should be the extent of this priority and, in particular, whether existing creditors should have 'veto' rights in respect of super-priority new finance; and what safeguards should be in place to prevent improper advantage-gaining by the new money financier.

4.   Avoidance and adjustment actions

4.1   INTRODUCTION

In many formal insolvency regimes, a most important aspect of administering the affairs of an insolvent company or individual is for the person
appointed to administer the affairs and property of the debtor, the insolvency practitioner (IP), to accumulate as many assets as possible that are
owned by the insolvent or to which the insolvent has rights, in order to
augment the size of the insolvent's estate. This process sometimes includes
seeking to take advantage of rules that permit the avoidance of transactions that occurred prior to the insolvent's entry into insolvency proceedings ('pre-insolvency transactions'). If a transaction can be avoided then
this might mean that additional assets or funds will become available to
the IP and can be distributed to the creditors in general and boost their
recovery from the insolvent.

As is patent from the following discussion, while legal systems in the
various jurisdictions of the European Union differ, the solutions which
these systems provide for in relation to transactions involving loss of assets
for debtors, and especially due to fraud, have many commonalities,[1] and
one can see the similarities in addressing problematic transactions entered
into prior to the advent of insolvency proceedings, either at a time when
the debtor was insolvent or solvent. But, after saying that, there are also
a fair amount of variations of approach and a range of time periods that
are used to define when a transaction might be able to be challenged.
There are normally several conditions that usually have to be fulfilled and
proven before a transaction can be successfully set aside and while many
are common throughout the EU, there are some differences.

Perhaps the most notable and unusual feature of avoidance rules is that
they provide for the setting aside of transactions that were, at the time
that they were made, generally valid and not vulnerable to challenge. For
the most part they were not illegal or in breach of any legal rules, and not

---

[1]   C-339/07 *Seagon* v. *Deko Marty Belgium NV* [2009] BCC 347, para. [26].

even tainted in any way.[2] Outside of insolvency (and outside of specific maintenance of capital rules) a company is usually permitted to deal with property in the way that it deems appropriate.

There does not appear to be any standard theory which has been developed in Europe as to the reason for the existence of provisions that permit IPs (and, sometimes, others) to avoid transactions entered into prior to the opening of insolvency proceedings, but there are clear policies that underpin the provisions. First, the property of an insolvent is to be distributed fairly and rateably among its creditors,[3] subject to any statutory exceptions.[4] The underlying aim of the inclusion of avoidance provisions for reasons of equality is to produce fairness.[5] But, fairness does not mean absolute equality in many cases because any distribution of funds recovered in avoidance proceedings is undertaken subject to any statutory requirements, such as those giving priority to certain creditors, such as employees. So, avoidance provisions exist so as to enable the general body of creditors to be protected from an unfair reduction in the value of the insolvent's estate which can be the consequence of the debtor giving an advantage to one party prior to the opening of insolvency proceedings. In this respect, provisions are formulated so as to prohibit the unjustified enrichment of one party (whether he or she is a creditor or not) to the detriment of all creditors and to ensure that one or more creditors (or any third party) do not get an advantage over the general body of creditors. Their objective is to address the situation where insolvents transfer assets, prior to entry into insolvency proceedings, at a price that is below market value, which often is done to give an advantage to an

---

[2] An example of an avoidance action that can operate outside of insolvency and that usually involves a tainted transaction is provided for in the *actio pauliana*. This is an action that was developed in Roman times to allow for attacking fraudulent conveyances, namely transfers of property to third parties with fraudulent intent (to prejudice creditors).

[3] E. Warren, 'Bankruptcy Policymaking in an Imperfect World' (1993) 92 *Michigan Law Review* 336, 353; J. McCoid, 'Bankruptcy Preferences and Efficiency: An Expression of Doubt' (1981) 67 *Virginia Law Review* 249, 260; A. Keay, 'In Pursuit of the Rationale Behind the Avoidance of Pre-Liquidation Transactions' (1996) 18 *Sydney Law Review* 56.

[4] The most prevalent exception that is found is that the employees of the insolvent are entitled to be paid a part or all of outstanding wages owed to them before other creditors are paid.

[5] J. McCoid, 'Bankruptcy Preferences and Efficiency: An Expression of Doubt' (1981) 67 *Virginia Law Review* 249, 271; T.M. Ward and J.A. Shulman, 'In Defence of the Bankruptcy Code: Radical Integration of the Preference Rules Affecting Commercial Financing' (1983) 61 *Washington University Law Quarterly* 1, 16.

associate or connected party (often referred to as 'an insider'), and also the situation where some creditors are paid by the company while other creditors are not. These situations will produce a loss for the general body of creditors.[6] In some Member States, such as the Czech Republic, Germany and the Netherlands, it is articulated in legislation providing that the critical issue that has to be established is that transactions against which avoidance actions are taken are detrimental to the interests of the creditors. Certain types of transactions, such as transactions at an undervalue, are presumed to be detrimental,[7] as they take the whole, or part, of the value of property away from the company and hence the creditors, and gives it to someone else who is not entitled to it and does not deserve to receive it.

A second policy that arguably has only become prominent in the past 30 years at most is that voidable transaction provisions aim to prevent the dismemberment of the insolvent's estate,[8] which can occur as a result of certain pre-insolvency transactions. It is noted that one of the World Bank's principles on effective insolvency rules is to prevent the dismemberment prematurely of a debtor's property.[9] The reason for this being an aim of insolvency is that a loss of assets might reduce the chances of the insolvent being able to continue doing business efficiently or at all, and reduces the possibility of the insolvent being able to be restructured effectively, or at all.[10] The value of the assets of the debtor might be greater when employed in a business that is a going concern than when disposed of independently.[11] It is a moot point as to whether the existence of avoidance rules is likely to stop dismemberment, as such rules only apply *ex post* and parties are likely to take from a debtor what they can when a debtor is insolvent or close to it and hope that, if the company enters insolvency within the requisite time period, the IP does not seek to avoid the transaction in later recovery proceedings.

---

[6]   Briefing Note, *Harmonisation of Insolvency Law at EU Level: Avoidance Actions and Rules on Contracts* (2011), p. 11.

[7]   For instance, see Greece.

[8]   J. Westbrook, 'Two Thoughts About Insider Preferences' (1991) 76 *Minnesota Law Review* 73, 77; A. Keay, 'In Pursuit of the Rationale Behind the Avoidance of Pre-Liquidation Transactions' (n. 3 above).

[9]   World Bank, *Principles for Effective Insolvency and Creditor Rights Systems* (2005), p. 6.

[10]   Briefing Note, *Harmonisation of Insolvency Law at EU Level* (n. 6 above) 11.

[11]   If this is the case then the outcome is clearly inefficient: F. Mucciarelli, 'Not Just Efficiency: Insolvency Law in the EU and Its Political Dimension' (2013) 14 *European Business Organization Law Review* 175, 179.

Thirdly, it might be argued that policy dictates that avoidance rules are designed to deter the entry into transactions that could be avoided if a company becomes subject to insolvency proceedings,[12] but this is debatable given the fact that many parties will take the benefit of such transactions because the company might not enter insolvency proceedings, and even if it does, the IP appointed might decide not to initiate avoidance actions for a number of reasons, such as lack of funding. And even if the IP does commence proceedings and succeeds, there is no penalty imposed on the party who benefited from the impugned transaction save for having to return the benefit received. In fact, if a creditor has to return a benefit that is regarded as a preference he or she is entitled to claim in the insolvent estate for what is owed.

The various Member States obviously have different approaches to a number of the kinds of transactions that are subject to possible avoidance. The states differ in the complexity of their avoidance regimes. Some, like Germany, have an elaborate regime, while others provide a somewhat less elaborate scheme. Our comparator jurisdictions, Norway and the United States, also provide for significant avoidance rules. They differ markedly from one another and the United States' rules are substantially different from many Member States.

4.2 POSITION UNDER EUROPEAN INSOLVENCY REGULATION

Article 4 of the Regulation on Insolvency Proceedings[13] (article 7 in the recast) provides that the *lex concursus* will apply to administering the affairs of the insolvent. If the IP (referred to as 'a liquidator' in the Regulation, but as an IP in the recast Insolvency Regulation) of an insolvent company against whom insolvency proceedings have been opened, is minded to attack a pre-insolvency transaction and seeks to avoid it, whether or not he or she can do so will be determined, according to article 4(2)(m) (article 7(2)(m) in the recast), by the law of the Member State where the proceedings were opened. *Prima facie*, if the law of this state permits the transaction to be avoided, the IP can apply to the courts for an order of avoidance. It was indicated in the recent decision of the Court of

---

[12] D. Milman and R. Parry, 'Challenging Transactional Integrity on Insolvency: An Evaluation of the New Law' (1997) 48 *Northern Ireland Legal Quarterly* 24, 26.

[13] Council Regulation on Insolvency Proceedings (EC) (1346/2000), 29 May 2000.

Justice of the European Union (CJEU) in *Lutz* v. *Bauerle*[14] that the scope of article 4(2)(m) is not limited to actions commenced in court, because the provision refers to avoidance rules and not avoidance actions. It has also been held by the CJEU in *Seagon* v. *Deko Mary Belgium NV*[15] that courts in the place where insolvency proceedings were opened are able to decide an action to avoid because of insolvency that is taken against a company whose registered office is in another Member State.

There is an exception to the operation of article 4(2)(m) in the form of article 13 (article 16 in the recast). The latter provides that an avoidance action permitted by the law of the place of the opening of insolvency proceedings is not able to be taken in relation to pre-insolvency transactions in certain situations. The rationale for the inclusion of article 13 is found in recital 24 of the Preamble, namely to protect legitimate expectations and certainty of transactions in other Member States. In particular, there is concern to protect the expectations of creditors or third parties of the validity of transactions and other acts as provided for under national law from being prejudiced by the rules of a different *lex concursus*.[16]

Article 13 states that:

> Article 4(2)(m) shall not apply where the person who benefited from an act detrimental to all the creditors provides proof that:
> * the said act is subject to the law of a Member State other than that of the State of the opening of proceedings, and
> * that law does not allow any means of challenging that act in the relevant case.

Thus, article 13 provides that the rules set out in the law of the Member State where proceedings were opened are not to apply when the person who has benefited from the impugned act is able to prove the two points referred to in the article. The existence of article 13 seems to militate

---

[14]   C-557/13 *Lutz* v. *Bauerle* [2015], para. [30].

[15]   C-339/07 *Seagon* v. *Deko Mary Belgium NV* [2009] ECR 1-767, [2009] BCC 347. This approach has been affirmed recently in C-328/12 *Schmid* v. *Hertel* [2014] BPIR 504, insofar as the defendant is an individual residing in another Member State. This is also made clear in Preamble, recital 35 of the recast Insolvency Regulation: Regulation (EU) 2015/848 of the European Parliament and of the Council of 20 May 2015 on insolvency proceedings (recast) [2015] OJ L141/19, 5 June 2015.

[16]   *Report on the Convention of Insolvency Proceedings* ('Virgos-Schmit Report'), para. 138.

against the effect of article 4(2)(m) and makes it difficult for avoidance to be obtained in cross-border insolvencies.[17]

The avoidance provisions are one of those areas of insolvency law that a report of INSOL Europe[18] in 2010, examining the need for and the feasibility of harmonization of European insolvency law, concluded were apt for harmonization and that harmonization in relation to this area was desirable and achievable.[19] Some of the reasons supporting this view are considered at the end of this chapter when it is considered whether the divergence of approach in Member States as far as avoidance rules are concerned has created problems.

4.3 PRESUMPTIONS

In order to assist IPs or others to establish the conditions that need to be proved before a transaction can be set aside, legislation specifies some presumptions, most of which are rebuttable by the person against whom the avoidance action has been instituted.

The existence of presumptions is an implicit acknowledgement by legislators that IPs would find it exceedingly difficult to prove some conditions if they were not helped by presumptions. It is an element in the recognition that the IP comes to an insolvent's estate with very limited knowledge about the debtor's affairs and he or she can only obtain a restricted amount of information, often because the directors and other officers fail to co-operate with the IP as much as they should. A presumption that is often included in legislation is that the defendant to the avoidance action was aware or ought to have been aware of the debtor's insolvency when entering into the transaction that is impugned.

4.4 TIME

For the most part, avoidance provisions specify a period of time in which a transaction must have been entered into for it to be subject to successful

---

[17] See generally G. McCormack, 'Conflicts, Avoidance and International Insolvency 20 Years On: A Triple Cocktail' [2013] *Journal of Business Law* 141.
[18] European Association of Insolvency Practitioners and Scholars.
[19] INSOL Europe, *Harmonisation of Insolvency Law at EU Level* (April 2010), p. 20, available at www.europarl.europa.eu/meetdocs/2009_2014/documents/empl/dv/empl_study_insolvencyproceedings_/empl_study_insolvencyproceedings_en.pdf.

challenge. This period, often known as 'the suspect period', should, according to the World Bank,[20] be reasonably short in respect to general creditors to avoid disrupting normal commercial and credit relations, although the World Bank acknowledges in its principles on effective insolvency rules that the period may well be longer in the case of gifts or where the person receiving the transfer is closely related to the debtor.

Different periods are specified for the avoidance of different transactions under the laws of the various Member States. The time periods can be quite diverse, and a number of time periods might be used in any one jurisdiction's avoidance rules, depending on the kind of transaction that is subject to action. This can make the application of the avoidance rules quite complicated. Interestingly, in Lithuania there are no specific time periods prescribed by law. An IP can challenge a transaction entered into at any time before insolvency proceedings were opened. The IP is obliged to review all transactions that occurred in the three years prior to insolvency proceedings commencing, but he or she can go back further if minded to do so. This appears to be contrary to the approach favoured by the World Bank, and mentioned above, that there should be time periods and they should be reasonably short.

Where time periods are established it is important to know from what point one goes back in time to ascertain whether transactions are able to be avoided. The point is usually the time when insolvency proceedings are opened. What opening means can be different in each Member State, and that has caused some problems in the application of the European Insolvency Regulation.

4.5   WHAT CIRCUMSTANCES MUST EXIST FOR AVOIDANCE?

Besides a transaction occurring within a set time period prior to the advent of insolvency proceedings, legislation usually prescribes that certain conditions must exist at the time of the transaction. This might involve some subjective criteria which we have already mentioned, namely the party dealing with the company knew that the company was insolvent. Often there will be some requirement that the debtor was insolvent at the time of the transaction or it became so as a result of entering into the transaction, probably because the debtor has paid out a sum of money or transferred property to a third party. For example, in France and Luxembourg (and

---

[20]   *Principles for Effective Insolvency and Creditor Rights System*, C.11.3 (p. 18).

other Member States) it is the cessation of payments by the debtor, and in Germany and Austria (and elsewhere) it is the illiquidity or over-indebtedness of the debtor. This is generally interpreted to mean that the debtor is insolvent. In other Member States, such as the United Kingdom, it is actually stated that the insolvency of the debtor, whether based on cash flow or balance sheet grounds, is the critical issue.[21]

As noted already, another condition that is required in some states is that the debtor and, sometimes, the other party to the transaction were aware that the transaction that is impugned would harm the creditors in general.

4.6 CONNECTED/RELATED PERSONS

Nearly all Member States provide, in their avoidance rules, a different approach to transactions where the persons entering into transactions with the debtor company are connected or related to the debtor company in some way,[22] sometimes known as 'insiders'. Special provision is made when such persons are involved in a transaction with the debtor company. Primarily this means that the company will be presumed to be insolvent when the transactions occurred, a requirement found in the avoidance rules of most Member States, or it involves permitting avoidance to take place in relation to a longer period of time before the opening of insolvency proceedings,[23] and the difference between time periods for non-connected compared with connected persons can be substantial.[24] The reason why a longer suspect period is usually provided for where there is a connected party involved in a transaction is that a connected party might either directly or indirectly cause the business of the debtor to continue for a term before it enters insolvency proceedings so that any transaction entered into falls outside of the suspect period that is provided for in the avoidance rules. Alternatively, the connected person could influence the

---

[21]   See Insolvency Act 1986, ss. 240, 341.

[22]   France, Malta and Luxembourg are examples of exceptions. But in the first nation personal links between the parties might be taken into account in determining whether the party dealing with the debtor was aware of the debtor's insolvency.

[23]   Croatia is an exception.

[24]   For instance, in Estonia, with gratuitous contracts which can be set aside in the period of one year before the commencement of insolvency proceedings normally, which goes up to five years where connected persons are involved unless the connected person can establish that the debtor was not insolvent at the time of the transaction: Bankruptcy Act, s. 111.

directors of the company in the decisions they make, particularly as to whether the company enters insolvency proceedings.

The existence of a connected party can also mean that any required mental elements that have to be established by the IP to avoid a transaction, such as knowledge of the inability of the debtor to pay its debts, is presumed, as is the case, for instance, in Germany[25] and the United Kingdom.[26] How this works out around the EU will be disclosed later in the discussion.

The scope of the definition of connected persons varies between jurisdictions. The definition in the Netherlands is particularly broad and includes foster children of a director of the debtor company.[27] Other states that provide a fairly comprehensive list of connected persons are Poland and Spain. Persons who are usually regarded as connected in the context of corporate insolvency are directors of the debtor company and their close relatives, such as spouses, children and siblings, shareholders of the debtor company, guarantors of the debts of the debtor company, and companies in the same group as the debtor company.

4.7   KINDS OF TRANSACTIONS

Although there is a clear corpus of transactions that are generally invalidated in nearly all Member States, the laws around the EU provide for the avoidance of various and different types of transactions. The transactions most frequently subject to some form of avoidance rule are preferences and transactions that might be classified as transactions at an undervalue/gifts.

4.7.1   Preferences

Preferences involve the debtor (who subsequently enters insolvency proceedings because of insolvency) giving some benefit, perhaps payment of a debt owed to, or the creation of security in favour of, one of the debtor's creditors within a certain time period prior to the commencement of insolvency proceedings against the debtor, and this is to the detriment of the other creditors who do not get paid or receive any security in relation to the debts owed to them. The general body of creditors suffer detriment in that they will have to share *pari passu* in a company's liquidation with

---

[25]   But there are no extended time periods in Germany where connected persons are involved in the transaction.

[26]   Insolvency Code (Insolvenzordnung), ss. 130(3), 131(2), 133(2).

[27]   Bankruptcy Act, art. 43.

one another from what is left in the insolvent's estate and this is not likely to benefit them as much as the creditor who was paid or granted security prior to the opening of insolvency proceedings. The World Bank has indicated that the kind of transactions that we are considering here should be set aside if they are entered into within a certain period prior to the opening of insolvency proceedings.[28]

A condition for the proving of a preference that is found in most Member States is that the debtor must have been insolvent at the time of the granting of the preference, and some, such as the Czech Republic, the United Kingdom, and the United States also provide an alternative, namely that the giving of the preference caused the insolvency of the company. In some Member States, such as Austria, the Czech Republic, Estonia, Latvia, Slovakia and the United Kingdom, the existence of insolvency at the time of the transaction is presumed where the one benefiting from the preferences is a party connected to the debtor company.

As mentioned earlier, time is a critical issue in relation to claims for avoidance. All Member States except for the Netherlands set some time period in which a transaction must have occurred if it is to be avoided as a preference.

The ease of proving preferential transfers varies. Generally, where the creditor is a person who is connected with the debtor, such as close relatives of a director of the debtor, it is much easier to establish that there has been a preference. The existence of a connected person means, in the vast majority of jurisdictions, that the time period as to when the transaction was entered into is much longer than where a non-connected party is involved, that is, the suspect period is longer. For instance, in Italy and Sweden preferences in favour of a connected person as far back as five years prior to the opening of proceedings can be challenged, while payments made to non-connected persons can only be attacked if they occurred within one year and three months respectively preceding the opening of proceedings. A popular period for avoidance of a preference in favour of connected persons is two years, as demonstrated by the legislation in Bulgaria, Denmark, Ireland and the United Kingdom. Other states have different time periods. The Czech Republic has one year for non-connected parties and three years for connected parties. Also, in Austria, where there is a tradition of a bank being intimately involved with a company, and known as a '*haus bank*' (house bank), it is any payment to it by the company in the six months prior to the opening of bankruptcy proceedings that will be able to be challenged successfully.

---

[28] *Principles for Effective Insolvency and Creditor Rights System*, C.11.3 (p. 18).

Most Member States tend to have both objective and subjective elements included in their preference avoidance provisions. A good example of a subjective element is found in Irish[29] and UK[30] (other than that applying in Scotland) law, which specifically requires the liquidator to establish that when the debtor was making the transfer in favour of a creditor, the debtor was influenced by a desire to produce an advantage for the creditor who benefits from the transfer over other creditors. This requirement makes it very difficult for an IP to succeed with a claim for avoidance. The intention is, however, presumed where the creditor is a connected person, so in the United Kingdom most preference claims tend to be brought against connected persons.

Bearing in mind that the general aim of the avoidance rules is to protect the collective scheme of insolvency, it may be said that it makes more sense to provide rules that are totally objective.[31] But if it is felt that subjective criteria has to operate then it makes more sense that the subjectivity relates to the beneficiary/creditor and not to the debtor.[32] This is the case in Germany[33] and Italy,[34] where the creditor has to have knowledge of the insolvency of the debtor for there to be avoidance. Similarly, in Greece, in order to succeed to avoid a preference the creditor who is granted the preference must know that the payment is detrimental to the creditors.[35] In Germany[36] and Greece,[37] knowledge that is required of the creditor is (as in the United Kingdom) presumed where the creditor is a connected person. If objectivity alone is to be implemented then there must be a time constraint placed on the right to avoid or else it will create a substantial amount of uncertainty.[38]

While some Member States, such as Ireland and the United Kingdom, do not distinguish in their preference law between payments that are made to creditors when payment is due, on the one hand, and payments made when the debt was not due (in other words the latter payments were

---

[29]   Companies Act 2014, s. 604.
[30]   Insolvency Act 1986, s. 239(5).
[31]   See A. Keay, 'Preferences in Liquidation Law: A Time for a Change' (1998) 2 *Company Financial and Insolvency Law Review* 198.
[32]   R.J. de Weijs, *Harmonisation of European Insolvency Law and the Need to Tackle Two Common Problems: Common Pool and Anticommons* (19 October 2011), p. 5, available at http://ssrn.com/abstract=1950100.
[33]   Insolvency Code (Insolvenzordnung), s. 130.
[34]   Bankruptcy Law (Legge Fallimentare), art. 67.
[35]   Insolvency Code, art. 43(1).
[36]   Insolvency Code, s. 130(3).
[37]   Insolvency Code, art. 43(2).
[38]   R.J. de Weijs, 'Towards an Objective European Rule on Transaction Avoidance in Insolvencies' (2011) 20 *International Insolvency Review* 219, 226.

made earlier than necessary at law, sometimes referred to as payment of immature debts) on the other hand, others, such as Bulgaria, Croatia, Greece, Denmark, Luxembourg, Slovenia and Slovakia, as well as one of our comparator states, Norway, do so. In Bulgaria, a preference involving the discharge of a due debt can be avoided if occurring in the six months prior to the opening of insolvency proceedings, but the time period is extended to one year if the payment was made when it was not due.

Other Member States distinguish between preferences that involve the payment of debts that are paid in the normal course of commerce and those that are not.[39] In France, payments made in the normal course of commerce will only be set aside if the creditor knew that the debtor was insolvent (ceased paying debts) at the time of the payment.[40] But payments not in the normal course of commerce are able to be set aside without any knowledge factor involved.[41] In Germany, a payment will only be avoided if the debtor was insolvent at the time of the transaction, but where a payment is made when the creditor is not entitled to being paid then insolvency is presumed.[42]

Some Member States, such as Croatia and Germany, provide for special conditions where a preferential type transaction involves the repayment of loans made to the company by a shareholder.

Many Member States provide that security is to be avoided on the basis of being a preference if it was granted in order to convert a debt from being unsecured to being secured and this was done within a certain time before the advent of insolvency proceedings.[43] For example, X, an unsecured creditor of Y company who is owed a substantial amount, agrees to refrain from taking legal proceedings against Y company if the company agrees to give security for the existing debt that is owed to X. This involves both X's debt being converted from unsecured to secured, and it leaves the company in no better position financially than it was before granting the security. And creditors in general will, if the company enters insolvency proceedings, be worse off as the creditor who is now secured will get more than the unsecured creditors.

There is no open-ended period in which preferences can have occurred. All states prescribe a particular point of time, apart from the Netherlands,

---

[39] An instance is Denmark, although the distinction is not critical as far as time period and knowledge of insolvency is concerned.

[40] Commercial Code, art. L632-1.

[41] *Ibid.* art. L632-2.

[42] Insolvency Code (Insolvenzordnung), s. 131.

[43] For example, see Bulgaria, Croatia, Estonia, France, Greece, Italy, Portugal, Romania, Sweden and the United Kingdom.

and it usually runs back from the time when insolvency proceedings were opened. As mentioned above, the time period provided for the avoidance of preferences is increased substantially where the creditor is a connected person. In Bulgaria, the time is doubled, but in other Member States, such as Ireland and the United Kingdom, the time period is quadrupled from six months to two years, and in Denmark and Italy, the increase in time period is even greater, with the time going from three months to two years for the former, and from six months to three years for the latter.

In the United States, preferential transfers can be avoided when they are made in the 90 days before the commencement of bankruptcy.[44] There are no subjective elements in the proving of a successful claim. An important element is that the company is insolvent when making the transaction that is said to be a preference and it is presumed that the debtor was insolvent if the preference was made in the aforementioned time period.[45] A number of countries around the world only have objective factors as part of their preference laws.[46] In the United States, where a connected person (referred to as 'an insider' in the US legislation[47]) is the creditor then the time period is extended, as it is in most jurisdictions studied for this Report, to one year. A critical defence against a claim that a transaction is a preference in the United States is that the transaction involved a transfer that was in payment of a debt incurred by the debtor in the ordinary course of business or financial affairs of the debtor and the transferee, and the transfer was made in the ordinary course of business or financial affairs of the debtor and the transferee, or made according to ordinary business terms.[48] Table 4.1 summarizes the position with regard to preferences.

Transactions that constitute preferences can be challenged in both our comparator jurisdictions. In both Norway and the United States, preferences granted in the three months (90 days) before the opening of proceedings can be set aside. Preferences that were given earlier may be challenged in Norway if payment was made with unusual means of payment; was made before the debt which it sought to discharge was due; or the payment substantially reduced the debtor's ability to satisfy its obligations. As noted above, in the United States, the time period is extended to one year where the creditor is an insider (connected person).

---

[44]   Bankruptcy Code, s. 547.
[45]   *Ibid.* s. 547(f).
[46]   For instance, Australia.
[47]   Bankruptcy Code, s. 101(3) defines 'insiders' as directors, officers and controllers of a company.
[48]   *Ibid.* s. 547(c)(2).

Table 4.1   The position with regard to preferences

Country	Provisions avoiding preferences	Time when transaction must have occurred	Situation where there are connected parties	Presumption(s)
Austria	√	Up to one year before the opening of insolvency proceedings (but limited to transfers made after insolvency and within 60 days of insolvency)		Connected parties are presumed to know of insolvency or disadvantageous nature of transaction
Belgium	√	6 months prior to the bankruptcy date		
Bulgaria	√	6 months before the opening of insolvency proceedings for payments relating to due debts	2-year time period applies	
		1 year before the opening of insolvency proceedings where the payment related to debts not due and where security was given in relation to an unsecured debt		
Croatia	√	3 months prior to the filing of the request to open bankruptcy proceedings	Presumed that they knew that the company was insolvent at the time of the transaction	Creditor knew or should have known of the circumstances from which it would be necessary to conclude that insolvency exists
		5 years in relation to payment of shareholders' loans	No change in time period	

Table 4.1 (continued)

Country	Provisions avoiding preferences	Time when transaction must have occurred	Situation where there are connected parties	Presumption(s)
Cyprus	√	6 months before the commencement of insolvency proceedings		None
Czech Republic	√	1 year before the commencement of insolvency proceedings	3 years before the commencement of insolvency proceedings	Insolvency is presumed where connected parties are involved
Denmark	√	3 months before the filing for insolvency proceedings	2-year period applies	
Estonia	√	3 months before the opening of proceedings	2-year period applies where a connected party is involved unless the connected person can establish that the company was not insolvent at the time of the transaction	A connected person is presumed to be aware of the company's insolvency
Finland	√	In the 3 months before the opening of insolvency proceedings where there is non-conventional payment, or where there is premature payment, or the amount is significant in relation to estate's resources	In the 2 years before the opening of insolvency proceedings	Transaction in favour of connected parties within 2 years before the petition for bankruptcy, the transaction is avoided, unless it is shown that

France	√	From the point when there is a cessation of payments until the opening of proceedings (but up to a maximum of 18 months before the opening of proceedings)	the debtor was not insolvent and payment did not cause the company to become insolvent Commercial Code legislation lists acts deemed to be against an equal treatment of creditors (e.g. gifts, non-balanced contracts, securities granted for former debts)
Germany	√	3 months prior to the opening of the insolvency proceedings for securities or debt satisfaction; 10 years where the debtor acted with the intention to disadvantage their creditors; creditor needs to know of the insolvency/debtor's intent	Knowledge of insolvency is not necessary if the creditor receives something to which he or she is not entitled. It is presumed if the creditor is a connected person
Greece	√	From the point of the cessation of the payment of debts until the company is declared insolvent	Connected persons presumed to know of the debtor's cessation of payments and that the transaction will be detrimental for creditors

Table 4.1 (continued)

Country	Provisions avoiding preferences	Time when transaction must have occurred	Situation where there are connected parties	Presumption(s)
Hungary	√	90 days before the request for the opening of insolvency proceedings		If a contract was concluded with the member or director of a company, or where the company majority shareholder is the debtor himself, it is to be presumed that such contracts were concluded in bad faith or at no value
Ireland	√	6 months before the opening of proceedings	2 years before the opening of proceedings	
Italy	√	6 months preceding the opening of insolvency proceedings where the transaction was in the normal course of commerce and 1 year when it was not	3 years and 5 years, respectively	With abnormal transactions the creditor's knowledge of the debtor's insolvency is presumed
Latvia	√	6 months before the commencement of insolvency proceedings		If connected persons are involved they are presumed to know of the company's insolvency
Lithuania	√	3 years before the commencement of bankruptcy proceedings		

Luxembourg	√	10 days prior to the cessation of payment of its debts[a] (applies to the payment of debts before due date)	
Malta	√	6 months before the date of (deemed) dissolution[b]	
Netherlands	√	Not limited in time	Time not limited, presumption that debtor and creditor were aware that the transaction would harm the debtor's creditors where it was entered into during one year before bankruptcy Multiple presumptions in respect of knowledge that creditors would be prejudiced as a result of the transaction, for example in respect of transactions performed with related parties within one year prior to bankruptcy and debtor and creditor were aware that the transaction would harm the debtor's creditors (where the debt paid is not due)

Table 4.1 (continued)

Country	Provisions avoiding preferences	Time when transaction must have occurred	Situation where there are connected parties	Presumption(s)
Poland	√	6 months[c] prior to the filing of insolvency petition (for securing or paying debts not due)	6 months prior to filing of insolvency petition	
Portugal	√	60 days before the opening of insolvency proceedings (creation of a security for existing debts)		The transaction is detrimental to creditors The creditor acted in bad faith
		6 months before the opening of insolvency proceedings (payment of debts not due until after the opening of insolvency proceedings)		
Portugal		6 months before the opening of insolvency proceedings (payment of debts not due or payment was uncommon in commercial terms)		
		1 year prior to the opening of insolvency proceedings (payment of shareholder loans)		
Romania	√	2 years before the opening of insolvency proceedings, but with certain transactions (such as payments of debts not due) it is only 6 months	2 years	A rebuttable presumption of fraud to the detriment of the creditors in case of voidable transfers which applies even where the debtor has delayed

Country				
Slovakia	√	1 year prior to the opening of insolvency proceedings	3 years prior to the opening of insolvency proceedings	the opening of the procedure to ensure that the suspect period expires Presumption of knowledge that a transfer was avoidable where the beneficiary of the transfer passes it to a connected person It is presumed that the debtor was insolvent where there are preferences in favour of a connected person
Slovenia	√	(1) 3 months before the opening of insolvency proceedings if the debt was due (2) 1 year before the opening of insolvency proceedings if payment was not performed in accordance with normal business practice (3) 1 year before the opening of insolvency proceedings if the debt was not due to be paid	Related parties' transactions are not avoidable if performed on arm's length basis. Therefore, general 1-year time period applicable In personal bankruptcy 3-year time period for avoidance of transactions among connected persons	Presumption that all elements needed to prove a preference are met if: (1) the transaction was in the 3 months before the opening of insolvency proceedings (2) payment was not performed in accordance with normal business practice (3) the debt was not due to be paid

Table 4.1 (continued)

Country	Provisions avoiding preferences	Time when transaction must have occurred	Situation where there are connected parties	Presumption(s)
Spain	√	2 years before the opening of insolvency proceedings	Presumed that there was a detriment to the creditors	(1) Non-rebuttable in case of not-for-profit acts and payments or other acts that terminate obligations that will mature after insolvency proceedings are opened (2) Rebuttable when the debtor concludes a for-profit transaction in favour of a person closely related to him; creates a security right *in rem* in favour of pre-existing obligations or new ones concluded to replace them; or pays or otherwise terminates obligations secured by a security right *in rem* and which mature after the opening of the insolvency proceeding

Sweden	√	3 months before the filing of insolvency proceeding and where the payment was made before the debt was due or paid in an abnormal way. The period is extended to 5 years where the creditor knows of the debtor's financial difficulties	At any time before the opening of proceedings where a close relative (in personal or corporate terms) is involved	Where the creditor is a connected person then knowledge of the insolvency of the debtor is presumed
United Kingdom	√	6 months before the opening of insolvency proceedings	2 years before the opening of insolvency proceedings	Debtor presumed to be insolvent at time of giving of preference if a connected person was the creditor

Notes:

a This is set by the court dealing with the insolvency proceedings involving the company, but it cannot be later than six months before the date that the court decides the opening of insolvency proceedings.

b Deemed dissolution occurs on the making of a liquidation order.

c This was two months until 1 January 2016.

4.7.2   Transactions at an Undervalue

Transactions at an undervalue involve a debtor providing some benefit to a third party, often someone associated with the debtor (who is able to be categorized as a connected person), that enriches the third party to the detriment of the debtor and eventually, if the debtor enters insolvency proceedings, the debtor's creditors. An example would be where X company sells an asset valued at 100,000 euros to Y (the spouse of one of X company's directors) for 50,000 euros. The end result is that the company has lost 50,000 euros. The transaction is partially gratuitous.

Gifts can be regarded as a form of a transaction at an undervalue as a gift obviously involves the debtor company transferring property or funds and getting nothing in return. A gift is a totally gratuitous transaction as far as the debtor is concerned. Gifts are generally able to be set aside in most Member States, subject to certain conditions.[49] They are usually specifically referred to in legislation. For instance, in Austria they may be challenged if made within the two years before the opening of insolvency proceedings.[50]

The World Bank's *Doing Business* index relating to insolvency issues considers it desirable that undervalue pre-insolvency transactions should be subject to the possibility of avoidance in insolvency proceedings.

As with preferences, it is a condition for the proving of a transaction at an undervalue, in most Member States, that the debtor must have been insolvent at the time of the transaction being made, and some, such as the Czech Republic, Denmark and the United Kingdom, also provide an alternative condition, namely that the entering into of the transaction caused the insolvency of the company.

As with provisions that allow for the avoidance of preferences provisions dealing with transactions at an undervalue, conditions will generally include the time period in which the transaction must have occurred for it to be able to be set aside. Again, as with preferences, the time period will sometimes be extended if a connected person was the beneficiary of the transaction or certain presumptions will apply as far as the proving of the conditions are concerned. Generally speaking, the time period is longer for transactions at an undervalue compared with preferences. As one would expect the time period is variable across the EU. The longest suspect period is to be found in Germany and Croatia where transactions entered into within the

---

[49]   For example, as in Germany: German Insolvency Code (Insolvenzordnung), s. 134 and in Spain: Clifford Chance, *European Insolvency Procedures* (London, Clifford Chance LLP, 2012), p. 54.

[50]   Insolvency Code, s. 29.

four years prior to the opening of proceedings may be challenged. Several states, such as Belgium, Denmark, France, Romania and Sweden, have a relatively short period of six months, while several other states have more of a medium term, such as two years in Austria, Hungary and the United Kingdom (see Table 4.2).

Norway, in common with most jurisdictions, provides that gifts can be avoided. All gifts that have been made in the year before the opening of insolvency proceedings can be set aside and there is no need to establish any bad faith on the part of the debtor or the beneficiary of the gift. If there is such bad faith, however, gifts that have been made ten years before the opening of the proceedings may be avoided. Other Norwegian provisions would also permit the avoidance of transactions that are at an undervalue. In the United States, if a transfer is deemed to be a constructively fraudulent transfer then it can be avoided if it occurred in the two years before the commencement of bankruptcy.[51] Such transfers can only be set aside if the company was insolvent at the time that they were entered into or they caused the company to become insolvent. These transfers are to be contrasted with actual fraudulent transfers where it must be proved that the debtor intended, in entering into the transaction, to delay or defeat creditors (see below).

4.7.3 Invalidation of Security

Most Member States also have some avoidance rule(s) that especially provide for the invalidation of security (rights *in rem*) in certain conditions. Security interests are subject to some protection under the Insolvency Regulation.[52] Article 5(1) of the Regulation (article 8 in the recast) states that:

> The opening of insolvency proceedings shall not affect the rights in rem of creditors or third parties in respect of tangible or intangible, moveable or immoveable assets – both specific assets and collections of indefinite assets as a whole which change from time to time – belonging to the debtor which are situated within the territory of another Member State at the time of the opening of proceedings.

The rationale for this protection is demonstrated in Preamble, recital 25 to the Regulation which states that there is a particular need to diverge from the law of the Member State where proceedings were opened in relation to rights *in rem*, as they are of considerable importance for the granting of credit. Recital 25 goes on to say that:

---

[51]   Bankruptcy Code, s. 548.
[52]   See A. Keay, 'Security Rights, the European Insolvency Regulation and Concerns about the Non-application of Avoidance Rules' (2016) 41 *European Law Review* 72.

Table 4.2   Transactions at an undervalue/gifts

Country	Provisions exist	Time period	Time period where connected party involved	Presumptions
Austria	√	2 years		
Belgium	√	6 months		
Bulgaria	√	3 years		
Croatia	√	4 years		Knowledge that insolvency exists
Cyprus				
Czech Republic	√	1 year	3 years	Debtor presumed to be insolvent at time of making of transaction if other party is connected
Denmark	√	6 months	2 years	
Estonia	√	1 year	5 years	A gratuitous contract is assumed to damage the interests of the creditors
Finland	√	12 months	3 years	Presumed that the debtor was insolvent at the time of the transaction where connected person is the beneficiary
France	√	6 months before the point when there is a cessation of payments (only for gifts)		
Germany	√	4 years before the insolvency proceedings are opened		
Greece	√	From the point of the cessation of payments until the company is declared insolvent		Connected persons presumed to know of the debtor's cessation of payments and that the transaction will be detrimental for creditors
Hungary	√	2 years before the request for		

Table 4.2 (continued)

Country	Provisions exist	Time period	Time period where connected party involved	Presumptions
		the opening of insolvency proceedings		
Ireland	√	No limit		Must show effect was to perpetrate a fraud on the company, creditors or members
Italy	√	1 year preceding the opening of insolvency proceedings		
Latvia	√	3 years before the commencement of insolvency proceedings		If connected persons are involved they are presumed to know of the company's insolvency
Lithuania	√	3 years before the commencement of bankruptcy proceedings		
Luxembourg	√	10 days prior to the cessation of payment of its debts		
Malta	√	6 months before the deemed date of dissolution		
Netherlands	√	No time limit	No time limit	Presumptions apply in respect of knowledge of debtors and the beneficiaries to the transactions that creditors would be prejudiced as a result of transactions performed within

Table 4.2 (continued)

Country	Provisions exist	Time period	Time period where connected party involved	Presumptions
Netherlands				one year prior to the bankruptcy, for example in relation to acts performed by a debtor for no consideration or in respect of transactions where the value of the debtor's obligation considerably exceeds that of the counterparty's obligation
Poland	√	1 year prior to the filing of the insolvency petition		
Portugal	√	1 year prior to the opening of insolvency proceedings		The transaction is detrimental to creditors The creditor acted in bad faith
Romania	√	6 months before the opening of insolvency proceedings for transactions at an undervalue 2 years for gifts		Presumption of fraud where there is a transaction at an undervalue or a gift
Slovakia	√	1 year prior to the opening of insolvency proceedings	3 years prior to the opening of insolvency proceedings	Presumed that the debtor was insolvent at the time of the transaction if a connected party is involved
Slovenia	√	3 years before the opening of insolvency proceedings		

Table 4.2 (continued)

Country	Provisions exist	Time period	Time period where connected party involved	Presumptions
Spain	√	2 years before the opening of insolvency proceedings		Transaction causes a detriment to the creditors if a connected person is involved
Sweden	√	6 months before the filing of insolvency proceedings	1 year before the filing of insolvency proceedings where the beneficiary is a connected person and the debtor retained property after the transaction and was such that it could be the subject of execution and fulfilled its debts or else 3 years before the filing of insolvency proceedings	
United Kingdom	√	12 months before the filing of insolvency proceedings	2 years before the filing of insolvency proceedings	Debtor presumed to be insolvent at time of making of transaction if other party is connected

The basis, validity and extent of such a right in rem should therefore normally be determined according to the *lex situs* and not be affected by the opening of insolvency proceedings. The proprietor of the right in rem should therefore be able to continue to assert his right to segregation or separate settlement of the collateral security.[53]

---

[53] Recast Insolvency Regulation, Preamble, recital 68 also provides for this.

Nevertheless, article 5(4) provides that what is said in paragraph (1) of article 5 can be overridden as far as the avoidance actions referred to in article 4(2)(m) are concerned.[54]

In some Member States, such as Cyprus, Denmark, Ireland and the United Kingdom, floating charges are particularly susceptible to invalidation. Usually, the charge is only invalidated if the debtor granting the charge was insolvent at the time of the granting of the charge. In the United Kingdom, floating charges may be invalidated when they are granted by companies that are on their last legs,[55] and the creation of which will be to the detriment of the unsecured creditors. In the United Kingdom, the charge can be set aside if it was entered into 12 months before the opening of insolvency proceedings. This is extended to two years if the secured creditor is a connected party. The same position exists in Ireland.[56] Denmark has a similar approach but its time zones are three months and two years, respectively. Another instance of invalidation, although not in relation to floating charges, is to be found in Germany[57] where any security that is created by a debtor within the three months before an insolvency filing and at a time when the debtor is in a position of illiquidity can be avoided if at the time of the granting of security the creditor who became secured as a result of the creation of the security knew of the illiquidity.[58]

Usually, the critical point of time in determining whether a transaction should be set aside is either when the charge was created, as in the United Kingdom, or perfected (normally this will involve execution and registration), as in Denmark.

As mentioned above, the legislation in many states provides that security is to be avoided if it was granted in order to convert a debt from being unsecured to being secured.[59] Also, Norway allows for security to be set aside in such circumstances. In the United States, security by way of liens can be invalidated if they are not perfected properly.

---

[54]   See *Lutz* v. *Bauerle* (n. 14 above) para. [26].
[55]   Insolvency Act 1986, s. 245. For a discussion, see A. Keay, *McPherson's Law of Company Liquidation* (3rd edn, London, Sweet and Maxwell, 2013), pp. 721–9.
[56]   Companies Act 2014, s. 597.
[57]   Other Member States have similar provisions. For example, see Italy (Clifford Chance, *European Insolvency Procedures* (London, Clifford Chance LLP, 2012), p. 34).
[58]   German Insolvency Code (Insolvenzordnung), s. 132; Clifford Chance, *European Insolvency Procedures* (London, Clifford Chance LLP, 2012), p. 49.
[59]   For example, see Bulgaria, France, Greece, Italy.

4.7.4 Transactions Intended to Prejudice Creditors

Any transaction that was entered into by a debtor who subsequently becomes subject to formal insolvency proceedings can be set aside if there was some intention to put creditors at a detriment as a result of the transaction. This derives from the *actio pauliana*. In many civil law jurisdictions in the EU, the *actio pauliana* can still be relied on and it exists alongside specific avoidance rules contained in insolvency legislation. In jurisdictions where the *actio pauliana* is not operative, the avoidance rules that are provided for almost equate to the *actio pauliana*.

The kinds of transactions that are regarded as being entered into with the intention of prejudicing creditors usually involve the transfer of property to associates of the debtor who benefit from it at the expense of the creditors. This is often done when the debtor can foresee that liquidation/ bankruptcy is likely or even inevitable and the idea is to transfer property to related persons and out of the hands of the creditors. In some Member States, an action against a person to whom a debtor transferred property is not limited by a time period and so this means that it might be a better option than claiming that the transaction was a transaction at an undervalue. In other words, IPs may go back in the past as far as they like to locate transactions that can be attacked. This is the case, for instance, in Belgium,[60] Luxembourg,[61] Poland and the United Kingdom.[62] However, in other Member States there is a time period, in much the same way as one exists with the avoidance rules relating to other kinds of transactions that may be challenged, such as preferences. The only difference is that often the time period is significantly longer than where other transactions are involved. The reason for the extended time period is that there is a fraudulent element to the transaction. In Austria,[63] Croatia,[64] Germany[65] and Norway, the period in which transactions can be challenged is ten years. It is somewhat shorter in places like the Czech Republic,[66] Greece,[67] Slovakia and Hungary,[68] where the period is five years. It is shorter still in Estonia, where it is three years (five years if the beneficiary was a

---

[60] Bankruptcy Law, art. 20.
[61] Commercial Code, art. 448.
[62] Insolvency Act 1986, s. 423.
[63] Insolvency Code, s. 28.
[64] Bankruptcy Act, art. 202.
[65] Insolvency Code (Insolvenzordnung), s. 133.
[66] Insolvency Act 2006, s. 242.
[67] Insolvency Code, art. 44.
[68] Insolvency Act, s. 40(1)(a).

connected person),[69] and in Portugal and Romania[70] it is two years. In Poland, the time period is not calculated, as in most states, back from the opening of insolvency proceedings. Here action can only be taken up to five years after the transaction was entered into, so the longer a debtor can stay out of formal insolvency proceedings the more likely it is that the transaction will not be attacked. Malta has a time period of only six months, but this is stretched to 12 months where officers of the company are involved in the transaction.

All of the Member States that provide for the avoidance of the transactions covered by this section of Chapter 4 provide for some subjective factors. Transactions are set aside when the debtor intends to prejudice the creditors. An intention to prejudice is presumed and does not have to be proved in some states where the beneficiary of the transaction is a person connected to the debtor.[71] While it is necessary for the debtor to intend to damage creditors, some Member States provide that transactions are only set aside where, as well as the debtor intending to damage creditor interests, the person benefiting from the transaction also knew or should have known that the transaction damaged or would damage the interests of creditors.[72] In Germany,[73] Croatia,[74] Slovakia and Greece,[75] for instance, it must be established that the party benefiting from the transfer was aware, at the time of the transaction, of the debtor's intention to prejudice his or her creditors. In Germany, this is presumed if the beneficiary knew of the debtor's imminent insolvency and knew that the transaction constituted a disadvantage for the creditors.[76] It is also presumed in Croatia if the other party knew that the debtor was threatened with insolvency and that this transaction would cause damage to the creditors.[77] In the Netherlands[78] and Poland,[79] an action is only available if the beneficiary of the transaction knew or ought to have known that the transaction would harm the rights of the creditors of the debtor. Polish law provides that knowledge of the effect

---

[69]   Bankruptcy Act, s. 110.
[70]   Insolvency Law, art. 117(2)(c)(g).
[71]   For instance, see Hungary: Insolvency Act, s. 40(1)(3).
[72]   Such as in the Czech Republic, Portugal and Poland. In relation to the first, if the beneficiary is a connected person it is assumed that he or she knew that the debtor sought to prejudice the interests of the creditors: Bankruptcy Act, s. 117.
[73]   Insolvency Code (Insolvenzordnung), s. 133.
[74]   Bankruptcy Act, art. 202.
[75]   Insolvency Code, art. 44.
[76]   Insolvency Code (Insolvenzordnung), s. 133.
[77]   Bankruptcy Act, art. 202.
[78]   *Ibid.* art. 42.
[79]   Civil Code, arts 527–34.

of the transaction is presumed if the beneficiary is a connected person, and in Slovakian law it is presumed that the beneficiary was aware of the debtor's intention to prejudice creditors if the beneficiary is a connected person. In Italy, the IP need only prove that the debtor was aware of the fact that the transaction would be detrimental to the creditors if no consideration were given in the transaction to the debtor, but if consideration were given then the IP must establish also that the third party who received the benefit from the debtor was aware that the transaction would disadvantage the creditors. In Malta, where a transaction involves the passing of consideration between the parties, it must be proved that there was fraud on the part of both contracting parties, whilst if the transaction was gratuitous, fraud on the part of the debtor only is sufficient for avoidance.

The position in many Member States, such as the Czech Republic[80] and the United Kingdom,[81] is that there is no need to prove that at the time of the entry of the company into the relevant transaction the company was in fact insolvent. However, in Norway it must be proved that the beneficiary of the transaction knew or should have known that the debtor was in financial difficulty and the circumstances that made the transaction improper.

If the benefit of the transaction is passed to some other party by the immediate beneficiary, then in some Member States, such as Poland,[82] the IP may take proceedings against that other party if the transaction was gratuitous or the party knew of the circumstances that would enable the transaction to be set aside, namely the transaction was intended to hurt the interests of creditors.

In the United States, fraudulent transfers/conveyances are able to be avoided if they were effected in the two years before the commencement of bankruptcy.[83]

4.7.5 Transactions Made After the Opening of Insolvency Proceedings

Usually, there will be a period of time, which may be considerable in some cases, between the point where insolvency proceedings are opened and a court order is made to bankrupt/liquidate the debtor company (or declare the company to be insolvent). During this period of time, transactions might be entered into by the debtor company. Some Member States specifically provide that such transactions are able to be avoided.

---

[80] Insolvency Act 2006, s. 242.
[81] Insolvency Act 1986, s. 423.
[82] Civil Code, art. 531(2).
[83] Bankruptcy Code, s. 548.

Examples are Austria,[84] Belgium,[85] Denmark,[86] Estonia, Ireland[87] and the United Kingdom.[88] The relevant transactions might be able to stand if they were part of the necessary carrying on of the company's business or the party dealing with the insolvent assumed, reasonably, that the transaction was necessary for the continuation of the company's business and he or she did not know or should not have known that insolvency proceedings had been opened in relation to the company debtor.

The United States also provides for avoidance in the way that is set out above. It grants power to the trustee of a bankrupt company to avoid any transactions involving the transfer of company property after the filing of bankruptcy proceedings in the court and before a formal bankruptcy order (known as post-petition transfers).[89] It is potentially a problem for creditors in those Member States that do not have any provision for the avoidance of transactions after the commencement of insolvency proceedings unless an independent person, such as an IP or a government officer, takes control of the company's affairs.

4.7.6 Other Transactions

Some Member States allow for the setting aside of transactions that might be somewhat different from those avoided elsewhere and not included in the kind of transactions that have been discussed hitherto. The following provides some examples. Some Member States, such as Bulgaria, which allow set-off,[90] do not do so when a transaction leads to a right of set-off within a certain time period before the opening of insolvency proceedings. Denmark permits the avoidance of any execution that is levied against the debtor's property in the three months prior to the opening of insolvency proceedings.[91] The United Kingdom provides for the avoidance of what are known as extortionate transactions.[92] Under this provision, a court may make an order in relation to an extortionate credit transaction entered into within the three years before the opening of insolvency proceedings. It

---

[84]   Insolvency Code, s. 31.
[85]   Bankruptcy Law, art. 16.
[86]   Bankruptcy Act, s. 72.
[87]   Companies Act, s. 602.
[88]   Insolvency Act, s. 127.
[89]   Bankruptcy Code, s. 549.
[90]   Set-off involves one party, X, against which another party, Y, has a claim, seeking to claim that it can set off against Y's claim what Y owes to X.
[91]   Bankruptcy Act, s. 71.
[92]   Insolvency Act, s. 244. For an analysis see Keay, *McPherson's Law of Company Liquidation* (n. 55 above), pp. 718–21.

must be established that the company entered into a credit transaction that involved extortionate terms, namely loans which no reasonable company in normal circumstances would enter into save where there was some underlying rationale, such as where there is a sham agreement designed to confer an undue benefit on the lender. The relevant provision has not been employed in any known case.

To complete the consideration of transactions themselves, Table 4.3 summarizes the major kinds of transactions that are able to be avoided.

4.8 SUBJECTIVE AND OBJECTIVE ELEMENTS

One important matter that is provided for in avoidance provisions (and it often tends to be a highly controversial issue) is either that avoidance can occur if certain facts and conditions are merely established, which involves an objective test, or that avoidance will only be ordered if it can be proved that there was some subjective element(s) on the part of the debtor or the third party (who received a benefit from the debtor) in the making of the transaction that is sought to be impugned. This issue was raised earlier in relation to preferences. Subjective tests are concerned with the state of mind of one or more parties while objective tests are not. Objective elements of a preference provision comprise: establishing that the general body of creditors receive less as a result of the transaction; the transaction placed the creditor recipient in a better position than he or she would have been in a liquidation; the debtor is insolvent; the time period when the transaction occurred; the recipient of the preference was an existing creditor of the debtor. Subjective elements include: a knowledge or deemed knowledge on the part of the recipient that the debtor was insolvent at the time when the preference was given, and the debtor intended to give the recipient a benefit over all of the other creditors.

Many jurisdictions, such as the United Kingdom, have a mixture of objective and subjective tests, but the Netherlands only employs subjective tests.[93] German law allows for an order invalidating security if the creditor benefiting from the creation of the security knows of the illiquidity of the debtor that bestows the security. This requires a subjective element, namely the knowledge of the creditor. In contrast to the German position, while the UK law (excluding Scotland) on preferential transfers includes a subjective test, it actually requires the liquidator to establish, on the part

---

[93]   R. Vriesendorp and F. van Koppen, 'Transactional Avoidance in the Netherlands' (2000) 9 *International Insolvency Review* 47, 51–4.

Table 4.3 Transactions able to be avoided

Country	Prefer-ences	Transactions at an undervalue	Gifts	Transactions to defraud creditors	Invalidate security	Transactions entered into after insolvency proceedings
Austria	√		√	√	√	√
Belgium	√	√	√			√
Bulgaria	√	√	√		√	
Croatia	√	√	√	√	√	√
Cyprus	√				√	
Czech Republic	√	√	√	√		√
Denmark	√	√	√		√	√
Estonia	√	√	√	√	√	√
Finland	√	√	√	√	√	
France	√	√	√		√	
Germany	√	√	√	√	√	√
Greece	√	√	√	√	√	
Hungary	√	√	√	√		
Ireland	√	√	√	√	√	√
Italy	√	√	√		√	
Latvia	√	√	√		√	√
Lithuania	√	√	√	√	√	√
Luxembourg	√	√	√		√	
Malta	√	√	√	√		
Netherlands	√	√	√	√	√	
Poland	√	√	√	√	√	
Portugal	√	√	√	√	√	
Romania	√	√	√	√	√	
Slovakia	√	√	√	√		√
Slovenia	√	√	√	√	√	√
Spain	√	√	√	√	√	
Sweden	√	√	√		√	
United Kingdom	√	√	√	√	√	√

of the debtor when making the transfer in favour of a creditor, that the debtor was influenced by a desire to produce an advantage for the creditor who benefits from the transfer over and above other creditors.[94]

---

[94] Insolvency Act 1986, s. 239(5). This does not apply to part of the United Kingdom, namely Scotland. See Insolvency Act 1986, s. 243. This latter provision applies an objective test.

4.9   WHO CAN TAKE ACTION?

Generally speaking, no transactions are void in the sense that no action has to be taken in the courts in relation to them. An application has to be made to the courts for them to declare the transactions void and they are to be set aside. Some other order might possibly have to be made, such as ordering the return of property to the insolvent company.

As INSOL Europe noted in its report on harmonization of EU law on insolvency, different positions exist in Member States as to who is entitled to initiate proceedings.[95] The candidates are the IP, a government official, a court supervisor and possibly a creditor. If a creditor is able to do so, it may only be once the approval of one of the following has been secured: the IP, the court, or some other independent body. Proceedings normally have to be brought by the IP, as is the case in many Member States, such as the Czech Republic, Germany, Greece, Ireland and the United Kingdom, but on occasions he or she might choose not to do so for some reason (perhaps due to the obstacles that exist to the bringing of a successful action, as discussed in Chapter 1, see Table 1.3), and, hence, creditors in some states, such as Greece[96] and Spain,[97] might be able to do so, with or without a court order approving them taking such action. In the United Kingdom, the way to proceed would be for a creditor to apply to the court for the court to review the decision of the IP not to bring proceedings.[98] It would seem to be unwise to permit creditors to bring proceedings without them obtaining permission, as the institution of avoidance actions would ordinarily be part of the role of the IP, and a creditor should have to establish a good reason why he or she believes that proceedings should be instituted when the IP did not. If creditors are able to bring proceedings to obtain an order that will benefit them personally then this could offend the *pari passu* principle (creditors should share the assets of an insolvent collectively on an equal and rateable basis) which runs through insolvency law.

---

[95]   INSOL Europe, *Harmonisation of Insolvency Law at EU Level* (n. 19 above) 20, available at www.europarl.europa.eu/meetdocs/2009_2014/documents/empl/ dv/empl_study_insolvencyproceedings_/empl_study_insolvencyproceedings_en. pdf.
[96]   Insolvency Code, s. 48.
[97]   Insolvency Act, art. 72.
[98]   Insolvency Act 1986, s. 168(5).

4.10   INSTITUTION OF PROCEEDINGS

The legislation in nearly all Member States provides a limitation period as far as the institution of avoidance proceedings is concerned, that is, a period in which proceedings to avoid transactions must be instituted or else the right to avoid is lost.[99] The period varies. It is two years in Poland,[100] three years in Germany, the Netherlands and Italy, and in the United Kingdom it depends on the type of claim and is either six or twelve years.[101]

The limitation period starts to run from different points in different states. In Croatia, Germany and Italy,[102] it begins from the point when the insolvency proceedings are opened. This is also the case in the United States[103] and Hungary,[104] although the time period is only two years and one year, respectively. In the United Kingdom, the date from which the date runs is the date on which the cause of action accrued, which will normally be the date of the appointment of the IP. In other states, such as Poland and Portugal, it is from the date of the declaration of bankruptcy and elsewhere it will begin from the time when the IP becomes aware of the relevant facts that indicate a transaction can be avoided. This is the case in Greece, where the IP has one year to bring the proceedings.[105] The period may be extended by a further six months if the court approves. Slovenia has a six month period from the time of the publication of the notice of the opening of insolvency proceedings.[106] Short limitation periods do place a significant burden on IPs to ascertain whether there appears to be an avoidance action, to seek advice, obtain funding, and to accumulate the necessary evidence. But they do at least serve to focus the mind of IPs on such actions early on in their administration. The danger is that IPs will either just not get to the point of considering whether avoidance actions are possible or not even bother. Also, with a short time period, an IP might launch proceedings without having really assessed the evidence and this could leave the estate of the insolvent vulnerable to the payment of costs to

---

[99]   Latvia and Malta are examples of Member States that do not have a limitation period.

[100]   Although it is five years for actions that are classified as *actio pauliana* claims.

[101]   Limitation Act 1980, ss. 8 and 9.

[102]   It cannot be more than five years after the transaction was carried out.

[103]   Bankruptcy Code, s. 546.

[104]   Insolvency Act, s. 41.

[105]   Insolvency Code, art. 51.

[106]   Insolvency Act (ZFPPIPP) (Slovenia), art. 277.

the person against whom proceedings were initiated. The benefit of a long limitation period is that it enables IPs to be meticulous in their investigations and evidence gathering, but the danger is that they can procrastinate or even be slovenly in ascertaining whether proceedings can be instituted and then taking the necessary action if proceedings are a possibility.

In a Note, titled *Harmonisation of Insolvency Law at EU Level: Avoidance Actions and Rules on Contract*, the European Parliament's Policy Section felt that harmonization in respect of this issue did not seem necessary given the fact that IPs act under the supervision of one body or another and are subject to the discipline of these bodies.[107] But the case of *Lutz* v. *Bauerle*[108] (discussed below) suggests that if time limits are not harmonized this can cause uncertainty and even injustice.

4.11 ORDERS

Obviously, it is the order of a court with which an IP and the creditors are most concerned. What is actually ordered is critical. In some states, in relation to some or all of the transactions that can be challenged the courts have no discretion; the courts of the jurisdiction (France is an example) must make a specific order if the required conditions are proved. Thus, while certain transactions are said to be null and void, an application does have to be made to the courts, but once it is brought and the relevant conditions satisfied the court has no discretion but must set aside the transaction. In other states, what a court orders is left entirely within the discretion of the court hearing the matter. A good example of the latter is UK Insolvency Act 1986, section 241, which, while it indicates that UK courts have a wide discretion as to what order they see fit, sets out a broad range of orders that might be made by a court.[109] The advantage of the former approach is that the IP knows what order he or she will obtain, if the proceedings are successful. The advantage of the latter approach is that it means that a court can tailor an order to reflect the circumstances and also take into account the good faith of those dealing with the debtor.

The primary order that is required to be made by courts where a transaction is successfully challenged is that the party who received property or funds from the debtor company is ordered to return the property or

---

[107] Briefing Note, *Harmonisation of Insolvency Law at EU Level* (n. 6 above) 16.

[108] *Lutz* v. *Bauerle* (n. 14 above).

[109] For a discussion of this, see A. Keay, 'The Recovery of Voidable Preferences: Aspects of Restoration' [2000] *Company Financial and Insolvency Law Review* 1.

funds. If the impugned transaction involved the transfer of property and it
cannot be re-transferred, then the recipient of the benefit must usually pay
compensation instead. Sometimes courts are permitted to make orders
that require the recipient of the benefit from the transaction to disgorge
any gains from using the property or the funds. It is provided in some
jurisdictions that the recipient of any property from the debtor company
who improves the property should receive some sort of allowance for the
costs entailed in doing that. Failure to allow for this enables the creditors
to be unjustly enriched.

4.12   NEW FINANCING

In most Member States, such as the Czech Republic, Estonia, Germany,
Hungary, Lithuania, Luxembourg, Malta, the Netherlands, Slovakia and
the United Kingdom, as well as Norway, there is no special protection
provided in relation to parties who provide new financing, and avoidance
rules that are generally applicable will apply to new financing, but it will
mean that any security that is granted in exchange for new financing,
and in order to support restructuring, will usually be safe from attack;
the financier is giving something new to the company and the company
is, therefore, benefiting. In Poland, new financing involving a connected
person and provided within the six months prior to the filing of bankruptcy
proceedings can be set aside. In some states, such as France, new financing
cannot be challenged if the lender supplied funds and it was in relation to a
settlement that had been approved of by the court.[110] In Bulgaria, the provider of new financing is safe if the insolvent enters bankruptcy provided
that the new financing was provided pursuant to a bona fide attempt to
rehabilitate the insolvent and any restructuring provisions were adhered
to. Somewhat similarly, new financing cannot be challenged in Greece,
where no new financing arrangements can be attacked subsequently by
an IP provided that the new financing occurred during the execution of a
restructuring plan;[111] in Romania, where the bankruptcy judge approves
of the reorganization arrangement;[112] and in Spain, if certain specified
conditions have occurred.[113]

In Latvia, new financing of a restructuring arrangement will not be able

---

[110]   Commercial Code, L631-8, at 3.
[111]   Insolvency Code, art. 45(c).
[112]   Insolvency Law, art. 117.
[113]   For example, the scheme is recorded in a public document.

to be challenged if the arrangement envisaged favourable treatment being bestowed on the financing,[114] and in Slovenia new financing arrangements cannot be avoided in a subsequent liquidation if the action was designed to fulfil obligations under the restructuring scheme and the scheme was approved of by the court.[115] In Germany, any transaction involving new financing is deemed not to have been entered into with the intention of harming creditors if it has been entered into pursuant to a serious effort to restructure. In Austria, the lender in a new financing initiative is deemed to know of the debtor's financial difficulties if any restructuring plan is found to be inadequate, so it will be easier for an IP to have the financing transaction avoided.

The general rule in the United States is new financing cannot be impugned under the avoidance rules, but if the financing is highly leveraged it might be possible to challenge the arrangements as preferences or fraudulent transfers. Effectively, this is very similar in approach to that extant in many Member States and Norway, as indicated at the beginning of this section.

4.13   DIVERGENCE PROBLEMS

Many of the national reporters whose reports were commissioned in connection with this study indicated that they had not detected any perceivable problems emanating from the divergence of approach in different Member States as far as it affected their own jurisdiction. But, of course, they are limited to their own knowledge, what information is available and their inquiries. But the reason why there have not been many, or even any, publicized problems could be due to the fact that IPs are not considering avoidance actions where there is a cross-border element, a matter that is referred to below. Other national reporters have reported problems, although not detailed them. These reporters were followed up with a request for more details, but most have not been able to provide any. It was stated by the German reporter that, from what he could glean, IPs tend to refrain from instituting proceedings to avoid transactions in cross-border insolvencies because 'neither the courts nor legal practitioners have any idea of the avoidance rules in other Member States. Thus, ascertaining the foreign law is expensive and time-consuming and the

---

[114]   Insolvency Law, s. 40(5).
[115]   Insolvency Act (ZFPPIPP) (Slovenia), arts 44 and 273.

outcome of litigation is unpredictable'.[116] This was supported by the Croatian report, which suggested that it would be far easier if IPs only had to consider the law of the place where proceedings were opened. Also, as the Croatian report indicated, where there is a combination of the *lex concursus* and the *lex causae* applying, there are opportunities for parties to engage in manipulation to ensure that the best law from their point of view applies.[117] Even if the foreign law is able to be ascertained, it is not always certain or clear to the IP which elements of the law are operative.

It is felt by several reporters that article 13 of the European Regulation on Insolvency Proceedings (article 16 in the recast Insolvency Regulation) is an obstacle to the enforcement of avoidance rules in the EU. This provision might be seen by some as possibly responsible for the wrong result, from a policy perspective, in a recent CJEU decision,[118] even though the result appeared quite correct in law. The report from Spain indicates that the divergence in avoidance rules discourages IPs from challenging transactions, something with which the French report agrees, and especially when another law other than the *lex concursus* is relevant. It is asserted that this is a reason for the absence of case law. The Netherlands report suggests that besides any divergence issues, there are issues surrounding the interpretation and application of article 13. As we will see shortly, it was only in 2015 that the CJEU was actually able to consider the whole issue for the first time. This is very surprising, given that the Regulation has been in operation since 2002 and avoidance issues are frequently matters that need to be considered in insolvencies. Perhaps this indicates the reluctance hitherto of IPs to consider avoidance actions in cross-border insolvencies because of uncertainty as to which law applies and/or the uncertainty of defendants concerning the applicable law to mount a defence to any avoidance actions.

It was indicated by the Estonian reporter that it appears that divergence in the rules on avoidance has created problems in practice, especially regarding specific substantive and procedural aspects in litigation; localization of claims; identification of claims; use of different languages; interpretation of different terms; use of litigation lawyers in another Member State; length of litigation in another Member State; transparency and predictability of litigation in different courts in another Member State, etc.

---

[116]   German National Report, p. 13.
[117]   See Keay, 'Security Rights, the European Insolvency Regulation and Concerns about the Non-application of Avoidance Rules' (n. 52 above).
[118]   *Lutz* v. *Bauerle* (n. 14 above).

> ### BOX 4.1 JUDGMENT NO. I CPG 1313/2013, HIGHER COURT OF LJUBLJANA, 22 JANUARY 2014
>
> Two claimants sued a Slovenian company in the Slovenian courts seeking the setting aside of a transaction which involved the first of the claimants disposing of 47,000 shares in a Romanian company in favour of the defendant. The first claimant was the subject of insolvency proceedings (bankruptcy) in Slovenia. Slovenian law was the *lex concursus*. The exact nature of the disposition is not clear. The claimants challenged the transaction based on the special provisions of Slovenia's Insolvency Law which provided rules governing transactions entered into one year before the opening of insolvency proceedings. The first instance court rejected the action on procedural grounds without going into the merits of the case. The claimants appealed to the Higher Court of Ljubljana which eventually upheld the judgment of the first instance court and refused the setting aside of the disposition. While the first instance court only considered the national conflict of laws rules, the appellate court considered the European Insolvency Regulation. The Higher Court, referring to article 5(3) of the Regulation, took the view that the rights entered into the register were to be considered as rights *in rem*, within article 5, and therefore constituted security. Article 5(3) provides that a right recorded in a public register and enforceable against third parties under which a right *in rem* can be obtained is able to be considered as a right *in rem*. The court did not consider article 5(4) of the Regulation which provides that 'Paragraph 1 shall not preclude the actions for voidness, voidability or enforceability as referred to in Article 4(2)(m)'. Also, the court did not refer to the relationship between articles 5(3) and 5(4) of the Regulation. Further, the court did not consider article 13 of the Regulation and the need for the defendant to demonstrate that there was law in a Member State that stopped the avoidance rule in the *lex concursus* operating. The court's failure to consider article 5(4), the relationship between articles 5(3) and 5(4), and the need to show that there was a law of a Member State that prevented the avoidance rule of Slovenia operating, is not easily explicable. However, it might be a manifestation of the difficulty that courts have, as well as the parties and IPs, in dealing with avoidance where there is a cross-border issue involved.

A case in Slovenia set out in Box 4.1 manifests this to some degree,[119] as well as, perhaps, indicating that courts might be struggling with assessing avoidance actions when they are subject to the Insolvency Regulation.

The concerns mentioned above in relation to divergence mirror what was said in INSOL Europe's report in 2010, *Harmonisation of Insolvency Law at EU Level*,[120] where it reported that differences between national

---

[119] Judgment No. I Cpg 1313/2013, Higher Court of Ljubljana, 22 January 2014.

[120] April 2010, available at www.europarl.europa.eu/meetdocs/2009_2014/documents/empl/dv/empl_study_insolvencyproceedings_/empl_study_insolvencyproceedings_en.pdf.

laws did create obstacles and problems for companies to engage in cross-border activities within the EU.

The best and first reported example from the CJEU of problems emanating from divergence in rules is considered in Box 4.2.

More recently, the CJEU had cause to consider articles 4(2)(m) and 13 again (see Box 4.3).

In the opinion that the CJEU delivered, it made several helpful points. First, the Court said that in an avoidance action, the application of article 13 requires all of the circumstances of the case to be taken into account.[121] Second, it was up to the defendant to an avoidance action to provide proof that the act impugned by the applicant was not able to be challenged.[122] Thus, a burden was imposed on the defendant to prove 'both the facts from which the conclusion can be drawn that the act is unchallengeable and the absence of any evidence that would militate against that conclusion'.[123] Third, the Court held that while article 13 indicates where the burden lies as far as showing that an act that is complained of is not able to be challenged, it does not provide for procedural matters, such as how the evidence relied on by the defendant is elicited, what evidence is actually admissible before a domestic court or the principles that govern the domestic court's evaluation of the probative value of the evidence that is adduced.[124] However, the Court did say that if a domestic court's rules of evidence were not sufficiently rigorous, which led, effectively, to a shifting of the burden of proof, it would not be regarded as being in line with the principle of effectiveness,[125] for this principle, together with the principle of equivalence, must be taken into account in any case.[126] This means that a Member State must not make it more difficult for a foreign person or company to exercise rights than for a domestic person or company which makes a similar claim.[127] Fourth, it is necessary for a defendant to establish that the impugned act is not able to be challenged on the basis of the insolvency law of the *lex causae* or the *lex causae* taken as a whole,[128]

---

[121] C-557/13 *Lutz* v. *Bauerle* [2015] EUECJ, [20].
[122] *Ibid.* [25], [31], [38], [42].
[123] *Ibid.* [25].
[124] *Ibid.* [27], [43].
[125] *Ibid.* [43].
[126] *Ibid.* [44].
[127] VAT Directive, 'Effectiveness and Equivalence', available at www.vatdirective.com/EU-domestic-VAT-Manual/1-9-effectiveness-and-equivalence; D.J. Rhee, 'The Principle of Effective Protection: Reaching Those Parts Other [Principles] Cannot Reach?', BEG/ALBA Conference, Athens, 29–30 May 2011, available at www.adminlaw.org.uk/docs/sc%2012%20Deok%20Joo%20Rhee.pdf.
[128] *Lutz* v. *Bauerle* (n. 121 above) [34], [39].

BOX 4.2   C-557/13 *LUTZ* V. *BAUERLE* [2015]

This case was decided in April 2015. In this case ECZ, a company which was registered in Germany, was in the business of selling cars and it operated in Austria by way of a subsidiary, X, which was registered in Austria. Lutz purchased a car from X. X failed to deliver the car and so Lutz initiated legal proceedings against X in Austria, seeking the return of the amount that he had paid out. On 17 March 2008, the court hearing the proceedings handed down an enforceable payment order against X and in favour of Lutz. On 13 April 2008, X filed an application in a German court seeking the opening of insolvency proceedings. Proceedings were opened on 4 August 2008. Meanwhile on 20 May 2008, the Austrian court had granted leave to Lutz to enforce the payment order and three bank accounts of X at an Austrian bank were attached. The bank was notified of the attachment on 23 May 2008. On 17 March 2009, the bank paid Lutz the sum of 11,778 euros from X's accounts. Earlier, the liquidator of X had in a letter of 10 March 2009 notified the bank that he reserved the right to challenge any payment made in favour of X's creditors. On 3 June 2009, the liquidator informed Lutz that he was going to attack the enforcement of Lutz's rights which had been authorized on 20 May 2008 by the Austrian court as well as the payment that had been made to him on 17 March 2009, relying on Regulation on Insolvency Proceedings, article 4(2)(m). On 23 October 2009, a new liquidator of X instigated proceedings against Lutz in Germany. She sought to have the transaction (the payment of the money) set aside and to recover the amount paid. At first instance and on appeal, the courts found for the liquidator. Lutz then asked the German Federal Court to determine a matter of law in relation to the interpretation of article 13. German law, the *lex concursus* in this case, provided that the right to attach the credit balance on X's bank accounts became invalid on the date when the insolvency proceedings against that company were opened. This was because the attachment was not authorized and put into effect until after the application to open the insolvency proceedings, and so the payment made to Lutz was invalid. But Austrian law provided that a liquidator only has a period of one year from the date when the insolvency proceedings were opened to commence an action to set aside a transaction. This was in contrast with the period in Germany, which was three years. So, the liquidator had fulfilled the German requirement but she had not complied with the Austrian requirement as the action to set aside was not instituted within one year of the opening of the insolvency proceedings. So, under article 4(2)(m), German law would permit the transaction to be avoided. However, Lutz argued that article 13 applied, as Austrian law did not permit the transaction to be avoided on the basis that proceedings to avoid had not been instituted within a year of the opening of insolvency proceedings. The matter was referred to the CJEU (First Chamber). The upshot of the Court's response to the questions posed to it was that Lutz succeeded.

According to the Court, article 13 makes no distinction between substantive and procedural provisions,[a] and thus the article applies to limitation periods or other time-bars relating to actions to set aside transactions pursuant to the law governing the transactions.[b] Thus, in this case, the Austrian time-bar was applicable and article 13 prevented the operation of the German avoidance rule.

Notes:
[a]   C-557/13 *Lutz* v. *Bauerle* [2015] EUECJ, [47], [53].
[b]   *Ibid*. [49].

**BOX 4.3   C-310/14 *NIKE EUROPEAN OPERATIONS
NETHERLANDS BV V. SPORTLAND OY***

In this case, Sportland (S), a Finnish company, purchased goods from Nike (N), a
Dutch company. S paid N 195,000 euros for the goods by way of a number of payments between 10 February 2009 and 20 May 2009. Subsequently, on 26 May
2009, insolvency proceedings were opened against S. Following this S brought
proceedings against N seeking recovery of the amounts it had paid to N. The basis
for this was that under Finnish law, payments of debts within the three months of
the opening of insolvency proceedings may be challenged if the payment is made
by way of an unusual means, is paid prematurely or is in amounts which, given the
debtor's estate, are significant. In defence, N relied on article 13 and claimed that
payments were governed by Dutch law and this did not require the payments to be
avoided. Dutch law provided that payments of debts may be challenged only if it is
proven that when they were received the recipient was aware that the application
for insolvency proceedings had already commenced or that the payment was
agreed between the debtor and the creditor in order to give the latter priority over
all of the other creditors of the debtor. While the Finnish courts at first instance
found that N had not established that, for the purposes of article 13, the transactions could not be challenged, an appellate court deemed it appropriate to refer the
matter to the CJEU, posing several questions concerning the interpretation and
application of article 13. The CJEU answered the questions and the matter has now
gone back to the domestic courts for a decision on the application, and with the
CJEU opinion in mind.

---

as article 13 provides that a defendant must prove that the act cannot be
challenged 'by any means'.[129] Thus, non-insolvency law provisions are
potentially relevant, as was subsequently demonstrated in the later case of
Kornhaas v. *Dithmer*[130] (discussed in Chapter 1).

While article 13 does appear to provide substantial scope for a defendant to an avoidance action to rely on the *lex causae*, it must be noted that
in both the *Lutz* and *Nike* cases the CJEU emphasized that article 13 must
be interpreted strictly as it provides for an exception to the general rule in
article 4 that the *lex concursus* is to be the law that applies in relation to the
insolvency proceedings.[131] In *Nike European Operations Netherlands BV* v.
Sportland Oy,[132] the CJEU said that:

---

[129]   *Ibid.* [35].
[130]   C-594/14 *Kornhaas* v. *Dithmer* (2015).
[131]   *Lutz* v. *Bauerle* (n. 121 above) [34]; C-310/14 *Nike European Operations
Netherlands BV* v. *Sportland Oy* (2015) [18], [40].
[132]   *Nike* v. *Sportland* (n. 131 above).

Article 13 of the Regulation precludes a broad interpretation of the scope of that article which would allow a person who has benefited from an act detrimental to all the creditors to avoid the application of the lex fori concursus by relying solely, in a purely abstract manner, on the unchallengeable character of the act at issue on the basis of a provision of the lex causae.[133]

Thus, the *Nike* decision might be seen to reduce the scope for questioning the application of article 4(2)(m) in certain situations, but clearly there still remains room for divergence in avoidance rules to lead to uncertainty and possible injustice.

So, to summarize, article 13 seems to be able to lead too easily to the negating of avoidance rules in many circumstances; it effectively acts as a veto. The article relates to both the main proceedings and any secondary proceedings commenced, with the result being that the law of the Member State in which main or secondary proceedings were opened will be affected.[134] The fact that article 13 might be interpreted in such a way that any law, insolvency or non-insolvency, might be relied on to challenge any application for avoidance exacerbates the problems for IPs in seeking to impugn, successfully, a pre-insolvency transaction. It might be thought that it is not equitable that a limitation of action provision, as in *Lutz* v. *Bauerle*,[135] should be able to stymie an avoidance action. As indicated above, there are considerable differences in the limitation of action provisions (effectively time-bar provisions) applying across Member States, and it might be argued that it is unfair that what is essentially a procedural provision should lead to the non-enforceability of an avoidance rule. While certainty for parties and the fulfilment of their expectations in entering into transactions is critical, as acknowledged in Preamble, recital 24 to the Regulation, it is likely that some parties will, in some inappropriate circumstances, exploit the fact that there is divergence.

There are probably at least two options to address the issue identified.[136] First, there could be provision for the exclusive application of the law of the Member State where proceedings have been opened.[137] This appeared

---

[133]   *Ibid.* [21].

[134]   Virgos-Schmit Report (n. 16 above).

[135]   *Lutz* v. *Bauerle* (n. 121 above).

[136]   See Keay, 'Security Rights, the European Insolvency Regulation and Concerns about the Non-application of Avoidance Rules' (n. 52 above).

[137]   L. Carballo Piñeiro, 'Towards the Reform of the European Insolvency Regulation: Codification Rather than Modification' (2014) 2 *Nederland Internationaal Privaatrecht* 207, 212.

to be favoured by the *Report on the Convention of Insolvency Proceedings*[138] on the basis that the main proceedings are only able to be opened if the debtor's centre of main interest (COMI) is in the Member State where proceedings are opened.[139] Such an approach would necessarily involve the abolition of article 13. This action might be said to be attractive as it would be easier for liquidators to pursue avoidance proceedings, as only the *lex concursus* would have to be taken into account, and there would not have to be an interpretation of the laws of other Member States, such as the *lex situs*, to assess whether they do in fact prevent the challenging of transactions creating security interests, or the *lex causae*.

A second option is to provide in article 13 that not only can a defendant to an avoidance action rely on that part of the *lex causae* which is able to be invoked to prevent any avoidance that is permitted under the *lex concursus*, but also a liquidator could rely on any part of the *lex causae* that might justify avoidance where the *lex concursus* did not.[140] This would mean that neither the *lex concursus* nor the *lex situs* would be able to be relied on in order to veto the avoidance action. If that were the case then it would not affect any expectations of the parties with regard to the nature of the parties' legal relationship.[141]

It could well be that the cases documented above are the 'tip of the iceberg' and that there are many other instances where divergence is causing problems but the relevant IPs have not instituted proceedings because of little direction on the interpretation and application of article 13, and the uncertainty that surrounds the article, as well as other matters referred to earlier, such as the uncertainty of what the foreign law is and how it will be interpreted and applied.

Several reporters from Member States, including the reporter from Norway, have expressed support for harmonization of avoidance provisions to alleviate some of the problems that they perceive to exist. The Slovakian reporter was of the view that divergence allows for differences

---

[138]   It has also been supported more recently by the Group for International and European Studies at the University of Barcelona, 'Proposals on the Reform of the Council Regulation No. 1346/2000 of 29 May 2000 on Insolvency Proceedings', at 160, presented at the Conference on the Future of the European Insolvency Regulation, Amsterdam, 28 April 2011, see www.eir-reform.eu/ and in S. Kolmann, 'Thoughts on the Governing Insolvency Law', also presented at the Conference.

[139]   Virgos-Schmit Report (n. 16 above) para. 148.

[140]   P. Pfeiffer, 'Article 13 EIR: Avoidance, Avoidability and Voidness' in *External Evaluations of Regulation No. 1346/2000/EC on Insolvency Proceedings*, JUST/2011/JVC/PR/0049/A4 (2011), para. 6.10.3.

[141]   *Ibid.*

in burdens of proof to cause problems. For instance, differences can motivate parties to open proceedings in a jurisdiction where a particular transaction will not be able to be challenged, and it will not matter that the *lex causae* does allow for avoidance.

While it has not been proven empirically in the work done by this study, and it might not be possible to do so in any event, that the divergence of approach has caused problems in insolvency practice involving cross-border issues, it is likely that it has and will do so increasingly as commerce develops and there is even greater trade across borders within the European Community.

There might be several ways of addressing the problems created by divergence. One might be to harmonize the avoidance rules across the EU. It might be thought that such an approach would bring certainty to a difficult area of insolvency law. However, such an approach might attract some criticism from those believing that domestic laws are necessary for dealing with domestic insolvencies as the domestic rules take into account the special needs of the local jurisdiction, as well as its history, culture and politics,[142] which might well differ from the position in other jurisdictions. But the South Square/Grant Thornton 2015 report, *From Discord to Harmony: The Future of Cross-Border Insolvency*, has stated that harmonizing processes can help increase the efficiency and timeliness of insolvency proceedings.[143]

4.14 CONCLUSION

When insolvency proceedings have been commenced an IP might well consider challenging transactions entered into by the insolvent company before those proceedings were opened, and have them avoided. There are various kinds of transactions occurring at different points before the advent of insolvency proceedings that can be challenged. These transactions may be impugned under avoidance rules that are enacted in each of the Member States; all states have avoidance rules in one form or another. While there is a variation across the EU, many states have rules that address the same or similar types of transactions. However, the conditions

---

[142] D. Mindel and S. Harris, *The Pursuit of Harmony Can Easily Lead to Discord: Why Local Insolvency Laws are Best Developed Locally* (Ernst and Young, April 2015), p. 1.

[143] South Square and Grant Thornton, *From Discord to Harmony: The Future of Cross-Border Insolvency* (2015), p. 12, available at www.southsquare.com/files/SouthSquare_GT_Report_From_discord_to_harmony.pdf.

that have to be fulfilled for an avoidance order to be obtained do differ to varying degrees. The differences primarily relate to the kind of presumptions that an IP can rely on in an avoidance action, in order to assist him or her discharge the burden of proving the conditions that must be fulfilled for avoidance, the time period (the suspect period) before the opening of insolvency proceedings in which a transaction must have been entered into for it to be avoidable, and in the determination of whether a transaction was avoidable whether a subjective or objective test is employed or even whether a combined subjective/objective test applies. In nearly all jurisdictions rules make it easier for an IP in establishing the need to avoid a transaction where a person connected to the company in some way benefits from a transaction with the company. This is a manifestation of the view that connected persons are insiders who may be benefited at a time when the company directors know that their company is insolvent or likely to become so, and it is unfair if such persons do benefit in these circumstances.

As discussed above, and demonstrated by the case studies, divergence between the rules applying in different Member States clearly does cause problems sometimes.

Apart from the possible action at the conflict-of-law rules level described in the previous section, an alternative approach, and the most far-reaching, would be to seek to harmonize the avoidance rules across the EU. As noted earlier, a report of INSOL Europe[144] in 2010, examining the need for and the feasibility of harmonization of European insolvency law, concluded that avoidance rules were apt for harmonization and that harmonization in relation to this area was desirable and achievable.[145] Certainly, some reporters, although not referring to this Report, expressed agreement with this general approach.

Total harmonization has many advantages. First, it would produce uniformity and consistency. It has been said that the tests on avoidance remain burdensome and not completely predictable 'and it is arguable that some kind of harmonisation of the avoidance remedies, at least in the context of business insolvency, might be advantageous to further integration and development of the European common market'.[146] Creditors might be more ready to extend loans and give credit to companies if

---

[144]   European Association of Insolvency Practitioners and Scholars.
[145]   INSOL Europe, *Harmonisation of Insolvency Law at EU Level* (n. 19 above) 20.
[146]   J. Alexander, *Avoid the Choice or Choose to Avoid? The European Framework for Choice of Avoidance Law and the Quest to Make it Sensible* (15 March 2009), p. 38, available at http://ssrn.com/abstract=1410157.

they know which law will apply if the company was to become subject to insolvency proceedings. The harmonization could lower costs and increase trade because of greater certainty. The Commission Communication of December 2012 to the European Parliament on a new European approach to business failure and insolvency[147] highlighted certain areas where differences between domestic insolvency laws may hamper the establishment of an efficient internal market. Those differences affect the principle of free movement, in particular free movement of capital, competitiveness and overall economic stability. The INSOL Europe study commissioned by the European Parliament had shown that disparities between national insolvency laws can create obstacles, competitive advantages and/or disadvantages and difficulties for companies with cross-border activities or ownership within the EU.[148]

Perhaps a major benefit of total harmonization is that it fosters equality in that the same rules of avoidance will apply to all insolvencies that occur in the EU. Thus, like cases will be treated in the same manner no matter where the proceedings were opened or what is said to be the law of the contract that led to the voidable transaction. This should provide uniform benefits to creditors across the EU.

One of the primary quibbles of liquidators with the existing law is that it causes uncertainty for them as to what law will apply and makes the winding up of the affairs of insolvents complicated. Harmonization provides those affected by it, namely liquidators and creditors, with certainty as to when and how rules are applied to specific situations. It could well reduce the possibility of lenders escaping the effect of any avoidance rules applied by the *lex concursus* and might well foster the more equal treatment of creditors and generally provide for a level playing field. The creation of a level playing field of national insolvency laws should lead to greater confidence of companies, entrepreneurs and private individuals willing to operate in the internal market.[149] It has been asserted that total harmonization is the instrument that is best able to achieve the internal market.[150]

---

[147] COM(2012)742 final, available at http://ec.europa.eu/justice/civil/files/insolvency-comm_en.pdf.

[148] INSOL Europe, *Harmonisation of Insolvency Law at EU Level* (n. 19 above).

[149] COM(2012)742 final, 3.

[150] H. Micklitz, 'The Targeted Full Harmonisation Approach: Looking Behind the Curtain' in G. Howells and R. Schultze (eds), *Modernising and Harmonising Modern Consumer Contract Law* (Sellier European Law Publishers, 2009), pp. 51–2.

A harmonized avoidance regime could have specific efficiency benefits. It might well provide a remedy against negative externalities produced by the provisions in the national legislation of Member States.[151] In addition, it has been said that harmonizing processes can help increase the efficiency of insolvency proceedings and ensure that they are dealt with in a more timely fashion.[152] Parties to impugned transactions might be less ready to fight proceedings to avoid when they know that they are unable to point to other rules which will defeat the application of avoidance provisions. The provision of harmonized rules could reduce transaction costs in that liquidators will only need to be aware of one set of avoidance rules and they would become proficient in understanding their application. To a degree it might mean that liquidators do not need to seek as much legal advice as in the past. Also, law firms that advise on insolvency matters would not need to become conversant with more than one series of rules. Harmonization is able to reduce legal risk and as a consequence it enhances the stability and efficiency of the financial markets as a whole.[153]

The employment of the same avoidance rules might act to deter the making of transactions that might be challenged on an insolvency under the rules, as it will be known to all parties which rules will definitely apply if the liquidator takes proceedings to avoid.

Finally, if there were harmonized avoidance rules, this might deter a person or company from moving his, her or its COMI, as the same law would apply across the EU. A debtor might seek to change the COMI because a transaction that might come under the scrutiny of a liquidator benefits a person connected with the debtor, such as the spouse of an individual debtor or the relative of a director of a corporate debtor.

While not a drawback, but a fact that is associated with any harmonization, there might well be some teething problems before we could be assured of a degree of uniformity in approach and practice across the EU. There will undoubtedly be an important role to be played by the CJEU at certain points, just as it has played a critical part in assisting the smoother operation of the Insolvency Regulation, because it has the authority to provide the ultimate determination of how the rules are to be interpreted

---

[151]   F. Mucciarelli, 'Not Just Efficiency: Insolvency Law in the EU and Its Political Dimension' (2013) 14 *EBOR* 175, 197.
[152]   South Square and Grant Thornton, *From Discord to Harmony* (n. 143 above) 12.
[153]   M. Haentjens, *Harmonisation of Securities Law: Custody and Transfer of Securities in European Private Law* (unpublished PhD thesis submitted to the University of Amsterdam, 2007), p. 235.

and applied. In doing this it undertakes a significant role in European integration.[154]

Providing for total harmonization of the avoidance rules is a bold move and while there are arguments in favour of harmonization of avoidance rules, there may well be problems.

(1) As this study has demonstrated, there exists significant divergence in relation to the nature of the avoidance provisions and this divergence is characterized in a number of ways; while there are similarities in the rules applying to two or more regimes, there are no two avoidance regimes in these legal systems that are identical. Most legal systems have several provisions dealing with avoidance as well as providing for differently structured avoidance regimes that reflect the large number of transactions that are able to be avoided and the different kinds of attempts to prevent the benefiting of third parties and the concomitant prejudicing of creditors. All of these provisions, with their individual nuances, cannot be contained in a harmonized set of rules, and all of the kinds of transactions that are presently subject to challenge are unlikely to be covered in any EU provisions. So there might be difficult decisions in determining what would remain and what would be omitted. Drafting harmonized rules is difficult given the fact that there is often controversy within Member States over some or all of the avoidance rules applying therein. Furthermore, most states classify prejudicial transactions in different categories, which can cause difficulties,[155] as the categories employed will differ from country to country.

(2) There are significant differences between states in how to address particular problems. For instance, there is significant divergence in Member States in relation to whether a rule imposes a subjective or an objective test in determining whether a transaction should be avoided or not.[156] Even where Member States apply the same kind of test, the content of the test differs or it is imposed on different people. Take, for instance, a comparison of German and English law as far as preferences are concerned. A preference, in general terms, involves the granting of some benefit to a creditor of the insolvent by the insolvent before the opening of insolvency proceedings such that the creditor gains an advantage over

---

[154] L. Del Duca, 'Developing Global Transnational Harmonization Procedures for the Twenty-First Century: The Accelerating Pace of Common and Civil Law Convergence' (2007) 42 *Texas International Law Journal* 625, 647.

[155] See de Weijs, 'Towards an Objective European Rule on Transaction Avoidance in Insolvencies' (n. 38 above) 220–21.

[156] Carballo Piñeiro, 'Towards the Reform of the European Insolvency Regulation' (n. 137 above), 212.

other creditors of the insolvent. Both German and English law include subjective tests. But they apply very differently. The German law provides[157] that in determining whether or not a preference can be avoided one has to consider the mind of the creditor/beneficiary of the preferential transfer, whereas in England and Wales it is the insolvent debtor's intention, and not the creditor's, that is one of the critical issues.[158]

(3) In deciding upon the content of such harmonized rules, there will need to be a common understanding about the goals of these rules and therefore there is likely to be a need for some form of European debate on bankruptcy theory.[159]

(4) We might witness creditors protecting themselves further either through the inclusion of (more) restrictive covenants in credit contracts or increasing the cost of credit by raising interest and costs associated with the granting of loans.

(5) Total harmonization prevents national governments enacting fresh avoidance rules to deal with particular concerns or abuses, or amending any that are currently in place in order to address perceived problems. Thus, it might be said that a harmonized approach might damage local interests which can be best catered for by domestic legislation.[160]

(6) It is more difficult to amend rules if they are made at the EU level when compared with national laws in many jurisdictions, so if certain rules appear to be functioning poorly or are not drafted effectively, it could be some time before the problems can be remedied.

(7) It might be argued that applying a harmonized law to avoid transactions rather than a domestic law produces a 'one size fits all' approach that is not appropriate in all national situations. Allied to this is the fact that the purpose of avoidance rules is to redistribute the insolvent's property according to statutory priorities and these will differ between jurisdictions.[161] It is true that there are differences between Member States as far as the priority rules go, although they are not generally that diverse. The main difference tends to be between states, such as Germany and the United Kingdom, which do not give priority to tax authorities, and others, such as Spain and Italy, that do. It has been said that harmonization or

---

[157] German Insolvency Code (Insolvenzordnung), s. 132.
[158] Insolvency Act 1986, s. 239(5). But not in Scotland. The issue of desire is not relevant in England and Wales where the creditor who received the benefit is a connected person.
[159] De Weijs, *Harmonisation of European Insolvency Law* (n. 32 above) 1.
[160] Mucciarelli, 'Not Just Efficiency' (n. 151 above) 198.
[161] J. Westbrook, 'Avoidance of Pre-Bankruptcy Transactions in Multinational Bankruptcy Cases' (2007) 42 *Texas International Law Journal* 899, 903.

unification of the law in the area of determining priority among creditors is extremely unlikely to happen.[162] The rules on priorities are far closer to matters of national policy than are the avoidance rules. The essential reasons for having avoidance rules were discussed earlier and the existence of them is generally seen across the EU as beneficial. What individual Member States do as far as the prioritizing of the payment of creditors might affect several areas of insolvency law but that does not really affect the avoidance rules. The only way that priority issues come into play is on a distribution of recoveries. It is unlikely that a state will include a particular rule to ensure that its priority system benefits. Clearly, those with priority debts will benefit as they will be paid first out of any recovery obtained by a liquidator, but that is not a reason for declining to harmonize. Successful employment of avoidance rules will generally produce a larger amount of property which is able to be distributed to creditors. There is going to be divergence across Member States as far as the likely beneficiaries of the fruit of avoidance. Such an approach might attract some criticism from those believing that domestic laws are necessary for dealing with domestic insolvencies as the domestic rules take into account the special needs of the local jurisdiction as well as its history, culture and politics,[163] which might well differ from the position in other jurisdictions. Nevertheless, it might be argued that avoidance rules, unlike rules in other areas of life, do not really impinge on such matters as history or culture. Furthermore, if there are agreed rationales for the existence of avoidance rules, then again these matters should not be an issue.

(8) When there is total harmonization of substantive rules as opposed to procedural ones there is more room for divergence of opinion and that could lead to uncertainty, as courts in different states take different approaches in interpreting and applying the rules. This occurred in the early days of the Insolvency Regulation, but gradually things started to become more balanced. It might take some decisive judgments of the CJEU, as it has done in other areas of insolvency, such as on the nature and application of the concept of the COMI.

(9) While several insolvency regimes apply in each Member State, there are different kinds of regime, including liquidation/bankruptcy regimes and restructuring/ reorganization regimes, and the nature of liquidation or restructuring regimes do differ across the EU. There might be opposition

---

[162]   J. Garrido, 'Two Snowflakes the Same: The Distributional Question in International Bankruptcies' (2011) 46 *Texas International Law Journal* 459, 460.
[163]   Mindel and Harris, *The Pursuit of Harmony Can Easily Lead to Discord* (n. 142 above) 1.

to having standard avoidance rules applying to all forms of insolvency regimes given the differences. If avoidance rules did not apply across the board then this could, one would think, produce some uncertainty. Perhaps harmonized avoidance rules could be restricted to applying to liquidation/bankruptcy. But if that were the case what avoidance rules, if any, would apply to other regimes? Some Member States might not have avoidance rules for some regimes, such as restructuring regimes, while others might. For instance, some of the UK avoidance rules are able to be invoked in relation to administration as well as liquidation.

(10) It is likely that there would be some divergence in interpretation of any harmonized rules. This might be a result of the way that the rules are translated. In a recent decision of the CJEU,[164] the Court noted that the Finnish version of article 13 was different from the versions in other language versions and this had led to divergence.

Thus, in summary, harmonization could encounter a number of problems, but it would have the clear advantage of producing greater certainty (especially for IPs) and would contribute to the prevention of forum shopping. It would also induce a feeling of fairness in that one rule would apply to all insolvencies no matter where assets were located, what law is said to govern the contract and where the insolvency proceedings were opened. It would also provide for greater transparency, so that all parties are able to know what will happen on the insolvency of a debtor.[165]

---

[164]   C-310/14 *Nike European Operations Netherlands BV* v. *Sportland Oy*, para. [17].
[165]   B. Wessels, 'Harmonization of Insolvency Law in Europe' (2011) 8 *European Company Law* 27, 30.

5. Procedural issues relating to formal insolvency proceedings

5.1 INTRODUCTION

There are various kinds of formal insolvency proceedings that exist around the world. But they generally tend to be divided up into liquidation/bankruptcy proceedings, on the one hand, and restructuring/rescue/reorganization proceedings, on the other hand. The former essentially involves, for the most part, the process that leads to the end of a company's life after its assets are sold off and its creditors paid out of the proceeds of the assets. Creditors will only be paid a portion of what they are owed, if they receive anything at all after the payment of the costs of the liquidation. An order of the court will usually be required for the liquidation/bankruptcy to commence.[1] The latter kind of proceeding is designed to facilitate the continuation of the company or its businesses by way of a restructuring process. This can involve a multitude of strategies, such as the infusion of new finance, the sale of parts of the company's business and the settlement of some or all of the debts of the company. Often courts will be involved in some way in the process, but a number of jurisdictions have reorganization proceedings that do not require, necessarily, any court involvement.

This chapter of the report addresses the most important procedural issues that are related to companies entering formal insolvency proceedings.

5.2 OPENING OF INSOLVENCY PROCEEDINGS

5.2.1 Basis for Opening

At some point there will need to be some process that will lead to the opening or commencement of formal proceedings where companies

---

[1] A clear exception is voluntary liquidation in the United Kingdom where the members can initiate liquidation.

are near to being, or are actually, insolvent. This section of the report considers what circumstances must exist before proceedings are opened and whether directors of insolvent companies are obliged to open such proceedings.

Before formal insolvency proceedings are opened the debtor company must usually be in some significant financial distress. For the most part the legislation of Member States require a company to be insolvent, but they have different ways of expressing it and also different ways of defining/ interpreting similar concepts related to insolvency, and this is discussed below briefly. Before examining these it must be noted that some Member States permit the opening of restructuring procedures when a company is not insolvent but is likely to become so or where its insolvency is imminent. A good example of proceedings that can be opened where the company is not insolvent or likely to become so is the United Kingdom's administration procedure,[2] although this is not necessarily going to lead to a restructuring of the company.[3] The United States' Chapter 11 procedure, a classic reorganization proceeding, actually permits companies to enter proceedings when they are not insolvent or not even likely to become insolvent, but are seeking to reorganize their affairs because they are experiencing some difficulties. The only major requirement is that companies are acting in good faith.

Many Member States, such as the Czech Republic, Estonia, Greece, Ireland, Malta, Poland, Portugal and the United Kingdom, allow for the opening of insolvency proceedings when companies are unable to pay their debts based on either a cash flow test or a balance sheet test. The former essentially means that a company cannot pay their debts as they become due and the latter is defined as the position where the value of a company's liabilities outweigh the value of its assets. These explanations of the tests might seem fairly straightforward, but often in practice it is not always easy to determine that either or both of these tests are satisfied. What often causes difficulties is how contingent and prospective liabilities and assets are dealt with.

There are several Member States, such as Austria, Bulgaria, Germany and Slovenia, which provide that proceedings may be opened when a company is illiquid or over-indebted and these generally correspond with cash flow and balance sheet insolvency, respectively. In Germany a debtor is regarded

---

[2]   Examples of other Member States which also allow the filing of proceedings for restructuring of one kind or another are Croatia, Germany, Greece, Hungary, the Netherlands, Portugal, Romania and Spain.

[3]   It could be a precursor to liquidation or straight dissolution.

as illiquid if it is not able to pay its debts that are due. Other states, such as Belgium, Denmark, France, Luxembourg,[4] Spain and the Netherlands, have a different way of expressing insolvency. They set out the requirement that the debtor must have ceased or suspended paying its debts before proceedings can be opened. Again, this is reminiscent of cash flow insolvency.

In one or two Member States, insolvency is defined more precisely than in the ways adverted to above. In Slovakia, for example, insolvency means that a debtor is unable to pay at least two debt obligations to more than one creditor after they have been due for 30 days.

The failure to obtain any benefit from some form of execution levied against a debtor might, in some Member States, constitute the basis for the opening of insolvency proceedings (Lithuania, Sweden), or, as in Ireland, Malta and the United Kingdom, deem the debtor to be unable to pay its debts and thus this will fulfil the requirement to prove that the debtor is insolvent. In Croatia, the fact that a debtor has paid, or is able to pay, partially or in full, claims of certain creditors does not of itself mean that the debtor is solvent if certain other circumstances exist, such as the fact that the debtor has not paid three consecutive salary payments that are owed to an employee under the contract of employment.[5]

There are indications from a large number of Member States that if a company's ability to pay debts is temporary, or at least not permanent,[6] then the company will not be regarded as cash flow insolvent/illiquid provided that the temporary delay is not overly long, such as three months in Austria. In Bulgaria, experts have to be appointed to determine if a debtor is irreversibly insolvent before a company is said to be insolvent. In Slovenia, the debtor must be suffering long-term illiquidity before being regarded as insolvent.

In a number of Member States, the balance sheet approach used to be applied mechanistically, that is a snapshot of the company's affairs being taken when the courts considered the position of the debtor, but this appears to have been replaced by a more 'dynamic approach'. *Inter alia*, this approach involves consideration of ability to pay debts in the future, say up to two years (Austria), and if events can be foreseen even further into the future, for example the maturity of a loan in ten years' time. In Denmark, the courts must consider whether it is realistic that the company could continue in business. In Germany when considering over-indebtedness the

---

[4]　In addition in Luxembourg the debtor must be unable to raise any credit.

[5]　Bankruptcy Act, s. 6(1).

[6]　Such as Austria, Belgium, Bulgaria, Denmark, Estonia, Finland, Slovenia and Sweden.

courts can consider whether the debtor company is likely to continue to exist and meet its debts as they fall due during the current and next year, and they will take into account all liabilities and not just existing ones. In Ireland and the UK courts are now able to take a more global view of the state of a company's finances and this could involve a consideration of a combination of both the cash flow and balance sheet tests.[7]

Norway is similar in approach to many Member States in that cash flow and balance sheet tests apply.

5.2.2 Obligation to Open

There is a mixed approach across the EU as to whether directors are required to open insolvency proceedings at a particular point, usually this being when they realize that the company is insolvent. This was discussed to some extent in Part 1 of the Report when considering the duties that are imposed on directors and thus it will not be considered in detail. Table 5.1 provides an indication of the approach taken in all States. Just a little over half of EU States require directors to file insolvency proceedings on their company becoming insolvent, and when they do so they usually set out a time period in which action must be taken. Our comparator states of the US and Norway reflect this mixed approach as the former does not require directors to take action when a company is insolvent while in Norway directors are obliged to do so. Where it is provided in legislation that proceedings must be opened it is usually a reference to bankruptcy/ liquidation proceedings. Many Member States, such as Belgium, which require proceedings for bankruptcy to be instituted, do not require debtors to file proceedings for reorganization.

Several States do not have an obligation imposed on the directors to open proceedings as this, it is argued, will not always be in the interests of the creditors. One reason is that opening proceedings could stymie the recovery of a company and a recovery, if possible, would benefit the creditors (and others).

---

[7] See *BNY Corporate Trustee Services Ltd* v. *Eurosail UK 2007-3JBL plc* [2013] UKSC 28.

Table 5.1 Publication of opening of proceedings

Country	Publication in a register(s) or database(s)	Published in journal/ gazette/ newspaper[a]	Notification of individual creditors who are known
Austria	√	√	√
Belgium		√	
Bulgaria	√		
Croatia	√		
Cyprus	√		
Czech Republic	√		
Denmark		√[b]	
Estonia	√	√	√
Finland	√	√	√
France	√	√	√
Germany	√	√	√
Greece	√		
Hungary		√	
Ireland		√	
Italy	√	√[c]	√[c]
Latvia	√		
Lithuania	√		√
Luxembourg		√	
Malta	√		
Netherlands	√	√	
Poland		√	
Portugal	√		√[d]
Romania	√	√	
Slovakia		√	Creditors who are known by the debtor and have their seats in other Member States
Slovenia	√		
Spain	√	√	√
Sweden		√	
United Kingdom		√	

Notes:
a   It might be obligatory to place notice in more than one of these.
b   For restructuring and bankruptcy proceedings.
c   This is only in certain cases.
d   Certain creditors are advised by registered letter.

5.3   CREDITOR INVOLVEMENT IN PROCEEDINGS

5.3.1   Opening of Proceedings

While debtors themselves will often open insolvency proceedings, creditors are generally entitled to do so in all Member States if certain conditions exist. These conditions vary across Member States, although there are several that are common. Usually applicants must establish that they are creditors (and a debt is due to be paid to them[8]) and that the debtor is insolvent/illiquid/over-indebted/ceased to pay its debts. Sometimes the insolvency requirement is presumed, and of particular importance when a creditor is seeking to open insolvency proceedings against the debtor, or the debtor is deemed to be insolvent because of something that the debtor has done or not done. This latter situation might result from the debtor failing to pay within a prescribed period a formal demand served on it by a creditor.[9] In the Czech Republic, a debtor is presumed insolvent, *inter alia*, if it has debts that are overdue for more than three months and in Romania the presumption applies where a debt is not paid for 60 days after the due date for payment.[10]

In some Member States, such as Cyprus,[11] Hungary,[12] Latvia,[13] Romania[14] and the United Kingdom,[15] in order to succeed with insolvency proceedings creditors must be able to demonstrate that they are owed a minimum amount by the debtor, with the consequence that creditors with relatively small debts are not able to use the insolvency process. It is a requirement in some states that the debt due must have been owed for a particular period of time. In Slovenia it is two months. Debtors can usually oppose the making of any bankruptcy order. One frequently used defence, in some states such as the Czech Republic, Estonia, Finland, Ireland and the United Kingdom, is that the debtor disputes the debt(s) that it is said are owed to the creditor who is seeking to open proceedings. Another option available to a debtor is to establish that it is not in fact insolvent.

---

[8]   Although the debt does not have to be due in Denmark.
[9]   The time period is three weeks in Cyprus, Ireland, Latvia and the United Kingdom. In Sweden it is one week.
[10]   Insolvency Law, art. 5, point 29.
[11]   Cyprus: 5,000 euros.
[12]   Hungary: 200,000 Hungarian Forints.
[13]   Latvia: 4,268 euros.
[14]   Romania: 40,000 lei.
[15]   In the United Kingdom, it was £750 until October 2015, but currently it is £5,000.

In support of doing this in some states, such as Sweden and the United Kingdom, a debtor can rely either on funds that could be obtained from the sale of assets effected within a reasonable period of time or loans that would not increase the overall liability of the debtor, such as those secured against totally or partly unencumbered company property. The approach in Slovenia is, if the company is insolvent, to permit the debtor to agree to restructuring on the basis that that will address the insolvency situation.

In the United States, creditors are able to open proceedings, but it is rare for this to happen. For a bankruptcy action to be instituted by creditors there must be three or more of them holding non-contingent claims of an aggregate of at least US$15,325, unless there are fewer than 12 creditors owed money by the debtor, and then one creditor with a non-contingent claim of at least US$15,325 may file.

Generally speaking, creditors do not have power to open insolvency proceedings that are designed to provide for a restructuring process. This is usually a matter for the directors of the debtor company alone. Poland, for instance, was an exception to this but reforms that came into effect on 1 January 2016 effectively mean that the debtor is the only one who can apply for restructuring proceedings. In Croatia and Slovakia, a creditor is entitled to file for restructuring proceedings but only with the debtor's consent. Creditors are entitled to apply to a court for administration in the United Kingdom, but while administration may lead to restructuring it does not always do so as it often leads to the end of the life of the company.

5.3.2 Advice to Creditors of Opening

There is some kind of advice given or available to creditors concerning the opening of proceedings in all Member States. It seems that there are three general approaches evident in Member States. First, the opening of proceedings is noted in a register and creditors are not advised individually or by any notices. Second, the opening has to be inserted in some official journal or gazette and/or local newspapers. Third, the court notifies creditors who are known at the time.[16] Some Member States, such as Austria, France, Lithuania, Portugal and Romania, employ more than one of these approaches. Other jurisdictions give discretion to courts to direct additional or alternative ways of publicizing the opening of proceedings.

In some Member States, such as Denmark, creditors are not advised at all about the opening of proceedings, but once a court has made an order then they are advised. In Portugal creditors are informed about the

---

[16] Examples of the last kind are Austria and Portugal.

opening of reorganization proceedings by the debtor. The danger with this is that it can lead to only those creditors who are likely to be 'friendly' to the debtor being advised. In the United States, a list of creditors must be provided if a debtor files for bankruptcy and when proceedings are opened the court notifies the creditors on the list.

The court, where proceedings are opened, or an IP which it has appointed, is obliged to inform creditors in other Member States that proceedings have been opened, where those creditors are known (article 40(1) of the European Regulation on Insolvency Proceedings and article 54(1) of the recast Insolvency Regulation).

Norway provides that the opening of proceedings has to be noted in the Norwegian Business Registry which can be accessed by the public. The proceedings will also be published in the *Norwegian Gazette* and all known creditors will be notified.

5.3.3   Limits on Filing Claims

Critically the insolvency practitioner (IP) who is administering the affairs of the debtor company needs to know what claims there are against the debtor. IPs will be aware of many creditors, but need to be advised of any that are unknown because of, for example, the poor record-keeping of the debtor. If IPs are aware of creditors they usually are required to notify them that they need to make a claim if they wish to take part in the proceedings. To ensure that their claims are acknowledged and taken into account in the calculation of creditors' pay-out in liquidation and in the voting for arrangements for restructuring, creditors will need to file their claims with the IP. The time allowed for the filing of claims varies significantly across the European Union. In some Member States there are specific times set by legislation whereas elsewhere the time is flexible and will be determined by a court or the IP.

Most Member States allow for the late filing of claims, but in some cases that might lead to some kind of penalty, such as the payment of a fee in Austria, and in Germany and Norway the payment of the costs caused by the creditor's delay. In Slovakia, a creditor filing late is not granted any voting rights and in Spain late creditors are subordinated, forfeiting any voting rights.

In the United States, in Chapter 11 bankruptcy proceedings, creditors whose names are listed in the debtor's petition filing for bankruptcy and whose debts are not disputed, not contingent or not unliquidated do not need to file a claim. Otherwise it is left to the court to fix a date by which claims must be filed.

In Norway, there is no specific date for the filing of claims. It is up to

Table 5.2   Times for the filing of claims by creditors

Country	Time limit for filing claims	Allows late filing
Austria	60–90 days after the opening of proceedings	Yes
Belgium	30 days from the time of the judgment of the court concerning insolvency	Up to 1 year from judgment concerning insolvency
Bulgaria	Within 1 month of the publication of the decision of the court to open proceedings in the Commercial Register	Within 3 months of the publication of the decision of the court to open proceedings in the Commercial Register
Croatia	Within 60 days of the publication of the decision to open proceedings	No
Cyprus	None stated	
Czech Republic	Within 2 months of the making of an order in the insolvency proceedings	
Denmark	Within 4 weeks of the making of a bankruptcy order	Yes, until the ratification of the statement of receipts and payments
Estonia	Within 2 months of the date of the publication of the bankruptcy of the debtor in the official publication	
Finland	In bankruptcy proceedings no earlier than 1 month and no later than 2 months from the date set by the IP. In restructuring proceedings, until the approval of a restructuring arrangement	Until the approval of a restructuring arrangement
France	Within 2 months of the publication of the opening of insolvency proceedings in the *Official Journal of Legal Publications* (foreign creditors have an extra 2 months)	
Germany	No longer than 3 months after the court requires filing	
Greece	None stated	
Hungary	40 days from the time of the publication of the opening of liquidation proceedings 30 days from the publication of the opening of restructuring proceedings	
Ireland	The time is fixed by the IP, and advised by written notice (the time set cannot be shorter than 28 days from the date of the notice)	At the discretion of the court

Table 5.2　　(continued)

Country	Time limit for filing claims	Allows late filing
Italy	No later than 30 days before the date provided for the meeting for examining the total of indebtedness In Liquidazione coatta amministrativa proceedings, it is to be within 60 days of publication in the *Official Gazette* of the opening of the proceedings; in Amministrazione straordinaria proceedings, it is to be within 90–120 days (depending on the decision of the court) from entry in the Register of Firms of the declaration of the state of insolvency	Claims may be filed up until the completion of the distribution of the assets to the creditors
Latvia	Within 1 month of the entry in the register of the opening of insolvency proceedings	Within 6 months of the entry in the register of the opening of insolvency proceedings but not later than the time when the plan for the settling of creditor claims has been formulated
Lithuania	Bankruptcy judge establishes a date for filing and it must not be later than 45 days from the decision on bankruptcy	
Luxembourg	Bankruptcy judge establishes a date for filing and it must not be later than 20 days from the day of the judgment that opens proceedings	
Malta	Within the time fixed by the courts	Only with the special leave of the court and subject to any terms the court may impose
Netherlands	Determined by the court and communicated to all known creditors	Yes, claims filed after expiry of the determined period may, under certain circumstances, be admitted
Poland	30 days from the publication of the decision on declaration of bankruptcy[a]	Yes, but only until approval of the final distribution plan. Any actions already taken in proceedings (including earlier distribution plans) are effective with

Table 5.2   (continued)

Country	Time limit for filing claims	Allows late filing
		respect to creditors filing late, and late filing creditors' claims are taken into account only in the bankruptcy estate distribution plans made after that claim has been approved
Portugal	The time is determined by the court order made in the insolvency proceedings, but it cannot exceed 30 days from the time of the order	Lodged up to 6 months after the making of the court order or within the period of 3 months following the discovery of the debt
Romania	Within 45 days of the opening of proceedings	At the bankruptcy judge's discretion, up to 75 days of the opening of proceedings
Slovakia	Within 30 days from the time that restructuring is permitted. Within 45 days from the date of declaration of bankruptcy	Up until completion of the administration
Slovenia	Within 1 month of the opening of compulsory settlement proceedings. Within 3 months of the opening of bankruptcy proceedings	
Spain	1 month from the day after the publication of the opening of insolvency proceedings in the *Official Journal*	Until the final list of creditors is prepared
Sweden	Between 4 and 10 weeks after the commencement of the lodging of proof process	
United Kingdom	IPs will, by giving notice, prescribe a date by which claims must be lodged, but it cannot be for a date that is earlier than 21 days from the time of the notice	Until the end of the formal regime

Note: a   This was the position from 1 January 2016.

the court/IP to announce a date by which claims must be filed, which must be set as between three and six weeks after the proceedings are opened. Claims filed after this period, but before the closing of the proceedings, will also be considered. In this case, the estate may demand that the creditor reimburses the estate for the additional costs incurred due to the delay in filing the claim.

It should be noted that article 39 of the Insolvency Regulation (article 53 of the recast) preserves the right of a creditor who does not reside in the Member State where insolvency proceedings have been opened to lodge a claim. In the notice that is sent to foreign creditors by the court where proceedings are opened the creditors will be advised of the time limit for the lodging of claims (article 40(2)). The recast Regulation tries to facilitate the lodging of claims by foreign creditors.[17] For instance, in the context of the discussion on time limits, irrespective of shorter periods under national law, foreign creditors are given at least 30 days following publication of the notice of opening of proceedings in the insolvency register to lodge their claims.

5.3.4   Creditors' Committees

All of the creditors of a debtor company are not able, especially where there are a large number of them, to be involved in the administration of the debtor's affairs. Hence, in the vast majority of jurisdictions a creditors' committee may/must be appointed and its general role is to safeguard the interests of creditors. The amount of input that committees have in the administration of the insolvency varies. In Denmark, they are merely carrying out an advisory role. But elsewhere the functions of the committee are, principally, to support and supervise the IP (and even control the IP) and give consent for some actions to be taken by the IP, such as the continuation of the running of the company's business, the selling of certain assets, and especially the company's business, initiating the removal of the IP, approving the remuneration of the IP, and the institution of legal proceedings on behalf of the debtor. In restructuring proceedings the committee often has to be given a copy of any proposed plan or even has to give its approval to any reorganization or distribution plan.[18] In proceedings in general, an IP might seek advice from the committee before taking any particular action.

---

[17]   Recast Insolvency Regulation, arts. 53–55.
[18]   Such as in Greece. In Italy, the committee must be asked its view but that is not generally binding on the IP.

The composition of the committee varies from state to state, and in most states there are not a set number of members, but a range of members allowed. The majority of jurisdictions seem to have around three to five members as the required number. Several Member States permit an employee representative to be a member of the committee. This is consistent with a stakeholder approach and the fact that in many nations employees are regarded as major stakeholders of companies. This is particularly so if there is any chance of a company being rescued because obviously employees' jobs are at stake.

The power of committees seems to vary between Member States. In some cases, the committee's views are binding on the IP and in others they are merely treated as advisory, although in the latter case, as is the situation in the Netherlands, for instance, the committee might apply to the court for it to determine a matter of dispute.

The creditors' committee is an essential element of Chapter 11 proceedings in the United States and it has wide-ranging powers to consult and obtain information from the directors, as well as investigating the debtor's conduct and the operation of its business.

As is manifested in Table 5.3, the composition of the committee varies between Member States.

In Norway, the bankruptcy court will usually appoint a committee which will consist of 1–3 persons; normally these are individuals representing creditor interests. The committee may also include an additional person who is an employee representative.

5.3.5   Classes of Creditors

For the most part Member States do not provide for classes of creditors for the purposes of voting in relation to bankruptcy/liquidation proceedings. All creditors vote together. Where there are reorganization proceedings then classes often exist for voting purposes. In Italy, creditors are divided into four classes: preferential, secured, unsecured and subordinated. They are accorded different rights. However, Italian law also provides for the possibility that the proposal for reorganization divides creditors into classes according to the nature of their claims (e.g. preferential/secured/unsecured/subordinated claims) or the homogeneity of their economic interests (e.g. employees, suppliers, customers and banks). Classes will often consist of secured creditors, on the one hand, and unsecured creditors, on the other. Some jurisdictions, such as Finland, even have unsecured creditors divided into different classes. Creditors with special interests might constitute particular classes, separate from the general body of unsecured creditors, as is the case, for

Table 5.3   Creditors' committees and their composition

Country	Creditors' committees able to be appointed	Committees not generally appointed	Number of members	Can appoint non-creditors
Austria	√		3–7	√
Belgium				
Bulgaria	√		3–9	
Croatia	√		Must be an odd number but not more than 9	
Cyprus	√		Up to 5	
Czech Republic	√		3–7	
Denmark	√		Up to 3	
Estonia	√		3–7 usually	
Finland	√		At least 3	
France	√[a]			
Germany	√		3–7	Yes, especially (but not exclusively) a representative of the debtor's employees
Greece				
Hungary	√		3–7	
Ireland	√		Not more than 5 (up to 3 additional members can be appointed later)	
Italy	√		3–5	
Latvia				
Lithuania	√		At least 5	An employee representative when there are employment-related claims
Luxembourg	√	√		
Malta	√		Not more than 5	No more than 5 contributories
Netherlands	√	As far as bankruptcy is concerned	At least 9 persons representing the most important categories of creditors	

Table 5.3 (continued)

Country	Creditors' committees able to be appointed	Committees not generally appointed	Number of members	Can appoint non-creditors
Poland	√		5 members and two assistants (deputies)[b]	
Portugal	√		3–5 (plus 2 alternates)	A representative of the employees
Romania	√		3–5	
Slovakia			3–11 (depending on the number of creditors) but it should be an odd number. The number is determined by the court	
Slovenia			3–11 (depending on the number of creditors) but it should be an odd number. The number is determined by the court	
Spain				
Sweden	Only in reorganizations and not bankruptcies		2–3 (in special cases limited to one creditor)	An additional member, who represents the employees, can be appointed if the debtor has more than 25 employees
United Kingdom	√		3–5	

Notes:
a   This is in respect of large companies with more than 150 employees and a turnover exceeding 20 million euros.
b   This was the position from 1 January 2016.

instance, in Poland. Classes will often consist of types of priority creditors, such as employees. Whether there are to be classes and what they are to be might not be determined by legislation, but might be decided by judges.

Classes are an important element of Chapter 11 proceedings in the United States, and creditors are only able to be included in the same class if they are 'substantially similar'.[19] This issue is discussed further in Chapter 6.

5.3.6 Voting Rules

In the creditors' committee voting is on a one person, one vote basis in all Member States save for France and Slovakia where there is consideration of the value of the claims of the creditors who are members of the committee and the view of the creditors representing a majority of claims will hold sway. Generally, if there is a tie in voting the chairperson has a casting vote, although in Croatia the court makes the final decision. Norway has no rules on the voting at committee meetings. Likewise, the United States has no hard and fast rules and it allows committees to determine their own voting procedures.

When it comes to voting by creditors at a creditors' meeting, there are generally three approaches employed. First, voting involves looking at both the number of creditors in favour and the value of creditors' claims. Thus a decision could not be made unless there was a majority of creditors in favour of it and these creditors hold more than half of the value of claims represented by the creditors who attend the meeting and vote.[20] Second, the majority of the value of claims held by creditors attending the meeting is in favour,[21] an approach adopted in Norway. Third, the number of creditors is in favour of the motion. Table 5.4 sets out the approach in each Member State. Clearly the majority of Member States rely on value of claims alone, although there is a healthy number that also require a majority in number.

Belgium is something of a mixture of the first and the last approaches mentioned above. In reorganization proceedings the first approach is adopted, but in bankruptcy/liquidation proceedings it is the last.

A few Member States, such as Poland, disqualify some creditors, and

---

[19] Bankruptcy Code, s. 1122(a).
[20] Such as in Austria and Luxembourg.
[21] Such as in Bulgaria.

Table 5.4 *Voting in creditors' meetings*

Country	Majority based on both the number of creditors and the value of claims	Majority based on the value of claims	Majority based on the number of creditors
Austria	√		
Belgium	√		
Bulgaria		√	
Croatia		√	
Cyprus		√	
Czech Republic	√a		
Denmark		√	
Estonia	√		
Finland	√b	√c	
France		√	
Germany	√		
Greece		√	
Hungary		√	
Ireland			√
Italy		√	
Latvia		√	
Lithuania		√	
Luxembourg	√d		√
Malta		√	√
Netherlands	√		
Poland	√		
Portugal		√	
Romania	√		
Slovakia		√	
Slovenia^e	√		
Spain		√	
Sweden	√e		
United Kingdom		√	

Notes:
a   Where the approval of a reorganization plan is subject to the vote.
b   In restructuring proceedings.
c   In bankruptcy proceedings.
d   This is for reorganization proceedings.
e   There are no creditors' meetings.

particularly those who are related to the company in some way, from voting. Other examples of those who are disqualified are subordinated creditors.[22]

In some states different motions require different majorities. That is, normally a simple majority suffices, but in some cases a special majority, often 66.66 per cent or 75 per cent, is needed. For instance, in Latvia creditors holding two-thirds of claims must support the removal of the IP. In Poland, an arrangement is adopted if two-thirds of creditors holding two-thirds of the amount of claims approve it, whereas in Sweden a proposal for composition must be accepted by the creditors if three-fifths of those voting have accepted the proposal and their claims amount to three-fifths of the total amount of the claims,[23] and this also applies to any arrangement proposed in reorganization proceedings. In Hungary, creditors holding two-thirds of the value of claims must vote in favour of a reorganization plan. A greater majority is required in the United Kingdom where there is a vote in relation to whether a proposal for an arrangement in a company voluntary arrangement will be accepted. This process of restructuring is only passed if there is a majority of three-quarters or more in value (of claims) in favour. It is interesting to note that in Italy creditors who do not register a vote in relation to a motion that is put to the creditors are counted as supporting the motion. There is more discussion on majorities in Chapter 6.

Voting rules might differ between bankruptcy and restructuring proceedings. This is the case, for instance, in Italy.

There are no creditors' meetings in Slovenia, and none in US bankruptcies except for an initial meeting, and so there are no rules governing voting.

5.4   LIQUIDATION OF THE INSOLVENT ESTATE

Liquidation of a company involves the cessation of its business, the realization of its assets, the admission and proof of claims, the payment of its debts and liabilities, and the distribution of any remaining assets to the shareholders in the company. At the end of the liquidation process, a

---

[22]   As in Portugal.

[23]   This is modified to requiring three-quarters of those voting to agree on the proposal with their claims amounting to three-quarters of the amount of the claims where the composition will lead to less than 50 per cent of the amounts claimed being paid out.

company is wound up and ceases to exist (also in some cases after a dissolution process).

The UNCITRAL *Legislative Guide on Insolvency Law* makes the point that around the world liquidation proceedings tend to follow a similar pattern, including the appointment of an IP to conduct and administer the liquidation and ceasing the business activities of the debtor if the business cannot be sold as a going concern.[24] Provision will also be made for the sale or realization of the debtor's assets on a piecemeal basis if sale on a going concern basis is not possible; for adjudicating the claims of creditors; for distributing available funds to creditors on the basis of a priority scheme and dissolving the debtor if it is a corporation or some other form of legal person.

Going concern sales may result in a much higher price being paid by a purchaser than sales on a break-up or piecemeal basis. A US Congressional report on the measures that led to the US Bankruptcy Code makes the common-sense point that 'assets that are used for production in the industry for which they were designed are more valuable than those same assets sold for scrap'.[25] It is therefore an understandable legislative objective to promote going concern sales, whether by means of a 'pre-pack' or otherwise.

5.4.1   Pre-packs: General Context and Background

Pre-packs build on the insight that there is likely to be a substantial saving of cost and convenience if a debtor minimizes the time that it spends in formal insolvency procedures. The longer and more drawn out the procedure, the greater the costs and expenses that are likely to be incurred. Moreover, a debtor may suffer a loss of goodwill and a defection of valuable customers upon the commencement of formal insolvency procedures.

There are, however, substantial differences in the use of the expression 'pre-packs' and what is meant by the expression. In some contexts, the expression refers to expedited restructuring procedures and, in another context, to expedited procedures that may lead to a going-concern sale of all, or part, of an ailing company's assets.

For instance, the UNCITRAL *Legislative Guide on Insolvency* acclaims the general advantages of expedited restructuring procedures. It refers to preserving the benefits of voluntary restructuring negotiations where

---

[24]   UNCITRAL, *Legislative Guide on Insolvency Law*, pp. 30–31.
[25]   HR Rep. No. 595, 95th Congress, 1st Sess. 220 (1977).

BOX 5.1   *EVERYWARE GLOBAL INC.*

Everyware Global Inc. was a leading global marketer of food preparation products and in April 2015, along with 12 affiliated companies, it filed a pre-packaged bankruptcy case in the US State of Delaware for judicial approval. A final decree closing the case was handed down on 19 August 2015 (see https://cases.primeclerk.com/everyware/Home-Index).

At the time of the bankruptcy filing, the company had a US$248.7 million term loan facility and a US$60 million asset backed loan. Under the pre-packaged plan, the debtors intended to pay general unsecured creditors (whose continued support was crucial to the carrying on of the company's business) 100 per cent in cash. The US$248.7 million term loan facility was to be converted to approximately 96 per cent of new equity with the remaining 4 per cent allocated to existing shareholders in return for their support of the plan. In order to continue operations while the Chapter 11 case was pending, the debtors received commitments for a US$40 million debtor-in-possession loan facility and continued access to their asset backed loan facility.

---

a majority of each affected class of creditors agree to a plan; binding minority members; minimizing time delays and expense; and ensuring that the plan negotiated and agreed in voluntary restructuring negotiations is not lost.[26] UNCITRAL appears to envisage expedited restructurings as the main vehicle for preserving value. Nevertheless, it acknowledges the possibility of going-concern sales of all or part of the debtor's assets on an expedited basis though it does not do much to regulate the practice.[27]

Pre-packs have long been a feature of the corporate restructuring landscape in the United States. In a pre-packaged Chapter 11, substantial negotiations are held with creditors prior to the commencement of the formal process. In some cases the creditors actually vote on the proposed restructuring beforehand, whereas in other cases the contours of the plan are merely worked out. But, in both scenarios, the formal Chapter 11 process is activated as a means of binding dissenting individuals or groups to the plan. While some of the standard procedural safeguards do not operate, a Chapter 11 pre-pack will still come before the court for approval.

The case study in Box 5.1 highlights some of the standard features of a US Chapter 11 pre-pack, including a debt for equity exchange; some continued participation by 'old' equity in the restructured entity so as to ensure their co-operation during the restructuring process; payment of

---

[26]   Recommendations 160–168.
[27]   Recommendations 52 and 55–57.

essential suppliers; and debtor-in-possession financing during the Chapter 11 case.

Despite their perceived advantages, there have been substantial criticisms of pre-packs in the United States. For example, it has been suggested in some empirical studies that companies with pre-packaged Chapter 11s[28] are more likely to go forum-shopping, that is to file for bankruptcy in what is perceived to be the most advantageous jurisdiction rather than the centre of the company's operations, and that such companies have a greater propensity to refile for Chapter 11 protection at some later stage.[29]

Notwithstanding this, however, market practice in the United States has developed so as to combine the advantages of expedited restructuring procedures with expedited procedures that lead to a going-concern sale of all, or part, of an ailing company's assets. This was the situation with the General Motors (GM) and Chrysler restructurings.[30] In the GM and Chrysler cases, huge auto manufacturers and distributors were effectively reorganized through a sale of the potentially profitable part of the company's businesses to newly created shell companies. The shell companies paid a certain amount for the assets of the 'old' car companies and also agreed to assume certain workforce-related liabilities. The detailed structure and funding arrangement in respect of the shell companies had been

---

[28] See T. Eisenberg and L.M. LoPucki, 'Shopping for Judges: An Empirical Analysis of Venue Choice in Large Chapter 11 Reorganizations' (1999) 84 *Cornell Law Review* 967, 976–7.

[29] *Ibid.* and see also L. LoPucki and S. Kalin, 'The Failure of Public Company Bankruptcies in Delaware and New York: Empirical Evidence of a "Race to the Bottom"' (2001) 54 *Vanderbilt Law Review* 231. But for different perspectives see R. Rasmussen and R. Thomas, 'Timing Matters: Promoting Forum-shopping by Insolvent Corporations' (2000) 94 *Northwestern University Law Review* 135, arguing that the US Bankruptcy Code would be more efficient if the law facilitated more forum shopping for bankruptcy venues; D. Skeel, 'What's So Bad about Delaware?' (2001) 54 *Vanderbilt Law Review* 309; H. Miller, 'Chapter 11 Reorganization Cases and the Delaware Myth' (2002) 55 *Vanderbilt Law Review* 1987; T. Zywicki, 'Is Forum-Shopping Corrupting America's Bankruptcy Courts?' (2006) 94 *Georgetown Law Journal* 1141.

[30] On the Chrysler and General Motors restructurings see the report on the same by US Congressional Oversight Panel, *The Use of TARP Funds in the Support and Reorganization of the Domestic Automotive Industry* (September 2009), available at http://cop.senate.gov/documents/cop-090909-report.pdf. This report contains a perceptive analysis of US bankruptcy law and attached papers that are both supportive and critical of the GM/Chrysler de facto rescues.

hammered out in advance of the bankruptcy filings, and essentially the US government provided most of the funding.[31]

It was argued by certain creditors that the purported 'business sales' amounted to de facto reorganization plans and also upset the normal scheme of bankruptcy priorities. The Bankruptcy Court would have none of this, stating that section 363 of the US Bankruptcy Code permitted sales of corporate assets outside the normal course of business if there was a business justification for the sale.[32] A speedy sale was considered to be justified because business and customers would melt away if there were continued uncertainty about the fate of the car companies.[33]

A major advantage of section 363 sales also is that buyers take free of security interests and other encumbrances and claims against the insolvency estate. But there have been some concerns about the GM and Chrysler decisions and section 363 sales generally. The concerns are that quick sales lack the safeguards of the Chapter 11 plan confirmation process and may benefit some stakeholders (notably secured lenders and debtor in possession lenders) to the disadvantage of unsecured creditors.

5.4.2 Pre-packs in the EU

In Europe, the practice of pre-packs has been largely confined to the United Kingdom, France, the Netherlands and, to a certain extent, Greece, Ireland and Slovenia. Moreover, pre-packs have tended to take the form of pre-packaged asset sales rather than pre-packaged restructurings. While responding to market pressure and developed informally by practitioners, there have been concerns in the United Kingdom and the Netherlands about a lack of procedural protection for unsecured and outside creditors. In both countries, the legislature has responded by regulating the practice of pre-packs.

In the United Kingdom, pre-pack sales are quite common in the context of administration though not in liquidation. The primary objective of liquidation is the orderly winding-up of a company and the distribution of its assets to its creditors rather than rescue and rehabilitation.[34]

---

[31]   It appears that this was done for political reasons as the US government otherwise feared the collapse of the domestic auto industry with unpredictable economic and social consequences.

[32]   On the 'business justification' test for s. 363 sales see *In re Lionel Corp.*, 722 F.2d 1063 (1983).

[33]   See *In re Chrysler LLC*, 405 BR 84 (2009).

[34]   See A. Keay, *McPherson's Law of Company Liquidation* (3rd edn, London, Sweet and Maxwell, 2013), ch. 1.

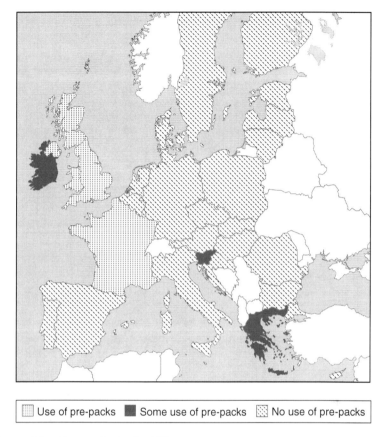

| Use of pre-packs | ■ Some use of pre-packs | No use of pre-packs |

Figure 5.1   Pre-packs in the EU

Administration, on the other hand, is intended as a rescue procedure aimed at facilitating the survival of the company's business either in whole or in part.

UK insolvency legislation does not make any reference to pre-packaged administrations but the pre-pack has emerged as a result of developments in insolvency practice:[35]

---

[35] See generally, P. Walton, 'Pre-Packaged Administrations: Trick or Treat' [2006] *Insolvency Intelligence* 113 and see also V. Finch, 'Pre-packaged Administrations: Bargains in the Shadow of Insolvency or Shadowy Bargains?' [2006] *Journal of Business Law* 568.

> A pre-pack . . . administration is one where a deal has already been agreed prior to the company entering administration. The company's business will commonly be sold to the incumbent management team immediately the company is placed into administration. The business survives intact but will have managed to jettison some or all of the unsecured debt. The business is saved and jobs are saved. The pre-pack will usually require the support of the company's bankers or the injection of new venture capital.

In the wake of the economic recession there have been continuing concerns about the lack of transparency in pre-packs which are seen to involve a 'sweetheart' deal for company management at the expense of general creditors. The secured creditors are paid out of the sale proceeds and/or agree to transfer lending facilities in favour of the new corporate entity that has taken over the company assets. To many observers, the old company appears to be trading on but having shed its unsecured debt and the pre-pack functions as a means 'by which powerful players can bypass carefully constructed statutory protections'.[36] Moreover, if the outcome is a 'done deal' before the company enters administration, it is hard to see how the administrator has properly addressed the statutory objectives of administration.

The main concerns are about sales of company assets to connected parties where there has been no open marketing of the assets. These concerns led to the formulation in the United Kingdom of Statement of Insolvency Practice (SIP) 16 by the IP representative bodies. SIP 16 requires that creditors be provided with a detailed explanation and justification of why a pre-pack was undertaken within seven days of the transaction. The administrator must disclose information about the terms of the sale; marketing activities undertaken; alternative courses of action that the administrator considered, with an explanation of what their possible financial outcomes would have been; why it was not possible to trade the business and offer it for sale as a going concern during administration; and any connection between the purchaser and the directors or others involved in the company. An administrator should also keep a detailed record of the reasoning behind the decision to undertake a pre-pack.

In June 2014, the UK government announced the results of a new round of consultations on pre-packs, the 'Graham review'.[37] The review suggested the strengthening of SIP 16 and a raft of voluntary measures,

---

[36] See Finch, 'Pre-packaged Administrations' (n. 35 above) 568.
[37] *Graham Review into Pre-pack Administration: Report to The Rt Hon Vince Cable MP* (June 2014).

with the government taking a reserve power to legislate if there was not sufficient voluntary compliance.[38]

In the Netherlands, the sale of the business as a going concern has long been facilitated and is increasingly promoted. To this end, a legislative programme 'Recalibration of Bankruptcy Law' was recently launched of which the first pillar relates to strengthening the possibilities for corporate restructuring. The first pillar includes a legislative proposal (Continuity of Enterprises Act) that aims to facilitate pre-packaged asset sale. The proposed Act puts on a statutory footing a practice in some District Courts in the Netherlands of effectively recognizing the appointment of a so-called silent bankruptcy administrator who has the task, *inter alia*, of facilitating the preparation of an asset sale in the impending bankruptcy. The proposed legislation will regularize the practice and also introduce some safeguards in that the debtor will have to show that the appointment of a 'silent bankruptcy administrator' serves the collective interests of creditors or societal interests such as public order and safety, the continuity of the entrepreneurial activities of the debtor and preservation of jobs.

In France, pre-pack sales may be prepared and organized before formal insolvency proceedings within the framework of the confidential pre-insolvency 'conciliation' procedure. The conciliator appointed by the President of the court prepares an amicable settlement ('accord amiable') under which a pre-packed sale may be proposed to main creditors. An expedited collective procedure (*sauvegarde accélérée*) gives the court power to approve the pre-pack.

In many other EU countries, pre-packs, while not strictly speaking prohibited, are rarely, if at all, encountered in practice. The lesson however, from the experience in the United Kingdom and the Netherlands, as well as also the United States, where the practice originated, is that pre-packs are potentially a valuable tool for preserving going concern value and maximizing returns from the debtor's estate. Nevertheless, pre-packs need to be hedged about with sufficient safeguards so as to prevent abuse of the insolvency procedure including connected parties and other favoured parties benefiting at the expense of the general body of creditors.

---

[38] See Small Business, Enterprise and Employment Act 2015, s. 129 (inserting a new provision in Insolvency Act 1986, Sch. B1, para. 60) which allows regulations to be made that prohibit or impose requirements or conditions in relation to the disposal, hiring out or sale of property of a company by an administrator to a connected person of the company. No such regulations have been made yet.

5.4.3 Measures to Facilitate Sales: Valuations and Public Auctions

Liquidation procedures throughout the EU have the common general objective of producing the most advantageous returns from the debtor's estate. Nevertheless, states adopt a number of different rules and practices in trying to facilitate achievement of this objective. There are a variety of approaches that are used. These range from a free hand for the IP in choosing the most advantageous mode of disposing of assets, to:

- requirement of a court approved sale;
- requirement of approval by a creditors' committee or meeting;
- mandatory valuations;
- mandatory auctions;
- default procedures if auctions fail to produce certain outcomes.

The above methods of disposals may be required either individually or in combination. If both court and creditor approval as well as a valuation plus public auction are all required, then the process of liquidating assets is likely to be a long drawn out and complicated process.

The divergence of approach is also to an extent reflected in the comparator countries, the United States and Norway. In the United States, court approval is required for substantial asset sales (sales outside the ordinary course of business) by a bankruptcy trustee or debtor in possession and the courts apply a 'business justification' test in deciding whether or not to approve the sale. In Norway, the law provides that assets must be realized in the way in which, given the circumstances, it is likely to yield the highest return for the estate and its creditors. There are no provisions which specifically regulate 'pre-pack sales' or sale of the estate as a running business, but it is accepted that a sale as a going concern is allowed as long as it is considered to yield the highest return for the estate and its creditors. This means that the IP has a wide discretion on how to structure realizations of assets and these can also be carried out on a piecemeal basis if this is considered to yield the highest return.

The same approach is exhibited in Finland with the IP empowered to sell assets in the manner he or she considers most advantageous for the insolvency estate. Nevertheless, it has been suggested that to protect himself or herself against unnecessary claims or challenges, an IP should consult creditors and seek creditor approval where appropriate. The same fundamental approach is followed in the United Kingdom, where IPs may dispose of assets in a way that they consider most advantageous to the insolvency estate and this may consist of piecemeal sales as well as a going-concern sale. There are no special requirements on the valuation of assets or on whether such sales should take place by means of a public auction. The overriding criterion is the most advantageous realization of assets. Again, it is desirable for an IP to consult creditors on the manner of disposal of assets but this is not mandatory.

The German approach is also generally quite flexible but the approval of creditors is generally required. The sale of the business as a going concern is a very important restructuring tool in Germany though asset sales are not explicitly mentioned within the German insolvency legal framework. German Insolvency Code (Insolvenzordnung) (InsO), s. 1, states however, that the 'insolvency proceeding(s) shall serve the purpose of collective satisfaction of a debtor's creditors by liquidation of the debtor's assets and by distribution of the proceeds, or by reaching an arrangement in an insolvency plan, particularly in order to maintain the enterprise'. An asset sale fits this purpose as it is intended to liquidate debtor assets.

In practice, many IPs make use of their powers to carry out an asset-deal restructuring, meaning that they separate the business from the debtor, transfer it to a buyer (a newly established 'shell' company or a third party already conducting business operations), and distribute the proceeds from the sale among the creditors via the insolvency procedure. Asset deals are heavily favoured in practice, as they are meant to be quick, enable the IP to effectively separate the assets from the liabilities of the debtor, and ultimately rescue the business and the employment it provides.

In Hungary, however, providing the IP with a free hand in liquidating and disposing of assets has led to abuses. The Hungarian reporter comments that '[w]hile until 1997 the system was too liberal and left basically everything to the liquidator, because of the many abuses detailed technical rules have been added to the Insolvency Act. Additionally, a special decree was passed that adds further requirements.'

5.4.4   Disposing of Low Value or Onerous Property

Member States invariably have provisions in their insolvency laws allowing an IP to disclaim or surrender low vale or onerous property where either the property will produce no meaningful returns for the insolvency estate or else unduly prolong the process of realization and distribution of assets of the estate. The evidence from the study suggests that there do not appear to be any significant practical problems with this issue.

In Austria, low value assets can be given away by the administrator to the debtor with the approval of the creditors' committee and the court. This is done if the asset is of low value per se, or, more importantly, if the asset is valuable but encumbered to a degree as to make it unlikely that the estate will receive any money from its sale. In the Czech Republic, the IP, subject to approval from the creditors' committee and the court, has power to disclaim onerous assets. In the Netherlands, in a provision designed to speed up the sale of assets, the IP may require the holders of a valid pledge or mortgage to enforce their collateral within a reasonable period though this period may be extended one or more times by the supervisory judge in bankruptcy. After the expiration of the relevant period, the IP is entitled to claim the collateral and sell it for the benefit of the insolvency estate. Although the holders of a valid pledge or mortgage maintain their right of priority over the sale proceeds, they will then have to pay part of the costs of the insolvency proceedings. Setting a reasonable period is therefore an effective action for the IP to speed up the enforcement of the collateral since there are serious consequences of expiration of this period for the holders of a valid pledge or mortgage.

An IP also has powers in the comparator countries (Norway and the United States) to abandon low value assets. In the United States, bankruptcy trustees can abandon assets that have no value to the estate or that are of such low value that the costs of sale outweigh the economic benefits. In Norway, an IP also has the right to abandon assets that are considered to be worthless or disproportionately difficult to dispose of. This will typically be the situation when the IP chooses not to terminate the debtor's rental agreement for storage or office space and leaves behind things without any value.

In other countries, including Spain, Poland and Romania, the standard procedures governing disposals of assets by an IP are relaxed in relation to wasting or deteriorating assets.

5.4.5   Recent Controversies

In some countries, concerns have been raised about the sale of assets by IPs at low prices to connected parties or more generally about lack of transparency in relation to such sales. The underlying basis for the concern is a perception that privileged insiders may be benefiting from the insolvency process at the expense of the general body of creditors. It is difficult to substantiate these claims, however, in concrete cases but nevertheless in the United Kingdom and the Netherlands the regulatory apparatus has been strengthened in response in particular to concerns about pre-packs.

In other countries such as Slovenia the concern is more about 'rigged' auctions either by the exclusion of certain parties from the bidding process, by inducements offered to certain parties or by collusion among prospective buyers. Perhaps the best way to combat such abuses is by bolstering the professionalism of the IP profession and introducing measures to ensure rigorous enforcement of existing prohibitions against conflicts of interest and dishonest profit-taking. In Hungary, however, a World Bank ICSID arbitral tribunal[39] has recently found that the rights of foreign investors (Portuguese investors in this case) had been flagrantly violated by the way in which liquidation proceedings had been conducted by the court (see the case study in Box 5.2).

BOX 5.2   *DAN CAKE (PORTUGAL) SA V. HUNGARY*, ICSID
CASE NO. ARB/12/9, DECISION ON JURISDICTION
AND LIABILITY, 24 AUGUST 2015

A Portuguese investor had acquired a majority shareholding in a Hungarian subsidiary company. The subsidiary experienced liquidity issues and creditors initiated liquidation proceedings against it in Hungary, leading the Hungarian Bankruptcy Court to declare the company insolvent and appoint an IP (liquidator). The Bankruptcy Court ordered a public auction of the company's assets within 120 days of the liquidation order notwithstanding the company's attempt to settle its debts with the creditors by agreement.

The investor claimed a breach of the Portugal-Hungary Bilateral Investment Treaty and the ICSID arbitral tribunal found in its favour. The tribunal found that the Hungarian court had frustrated the company's attempts to reach an agreement with its creditors. It found that the Hungarian Court's conduct of the liquidation proceedings amounted to a breach of Hungary's obligations under the bilateral investment treaty in respect of the fair and equitable treatment of the foreign investor. The court's conduct was described as 'shocking' and in 'flagrant violation' of Hungarian law, constituting a clear denial of justice and a breach of the treaty.

The Bankruptcy Court, acting as an organ of the Hungarian state, had made the sale of the company's assets inevitable. Under international law its conduct was attributable to Hungary which was considered to have violated its obligation to treat the foreign investor in a fair and equitable manner. The Bankruptcy Court's decision was 'tainted by unfairness' and therefore Hungary had also failed to ensure that the foreign investment was not impaired 'by unfair or discriminatory measures'.

The arbitral tribunal did not consider why the Hungarian Bankruptcy Court had acted in the way that it did but it was considered to have removed any possibility for the foreign investor to have a fair chance at saving its investment. It should also be noted that the foreign investor did not bid for the company's assets at the auction. There may have been factors which rendered such a course of action unrealistic or impracticable but the arbitral tribunal did not speculate on the reasons for this.

---

[39]   International Convention for the Settlement of Investment Disputes, available at https://icsid.worldbank.org/; *Dan Cake (Portugal) SA* v. *Hungary*, ICSID Case No. ARB/12/9, Decision on Jurisdiction and Liability, 24 August 2015.

5.5   INSOLVENCY PROCEEDINGS FOR SMEs

Question 5(d) of the questionnaire raises the issue of special insolvency procedures for small and medium-sized enterprises (SMEs) and in particular, special procedures intended to encourage the speedy rescue of small businesses.

It could be argued that a 'one size fits all' paradigm may not produce efficient results when applied to small businesses. Long drawn out complex procedures are likely to be disproportionately expensive in small business cases and to eat up a correspondingly greater share of recoveries. Large cases may need greater procedural protections to accommodate more diverse investor and creditor interests. 'Large' cases are likely to involve companies with more complex capital structures including different layers of debt. Large public companies and small businesses may not be as far apart as apples and oranges but what is appropriate in the case of a small company with simple structures may not be appropriate in the case of a larger company with sophisticated structures.

Having said that, it may not be easy to determine what counts as a 'small' business for the purpose of a special restructuring regime. In general terms, there are a number of factors that one could use in measuring the size of a business.[40] For example, the revenues generated by the business, the number of its employees, the volume of transactions, the extent of its operations and the amount of its assets or liabilities might all be taken into account depending on the particular circumstances.[41] The exercise of distinguishing between different cases is largely a matter of policy and depends on the nature of the regime that is intended to be created. The concept of small business is a fluid one and selecting the appropriate definition requires a series of trade-offs between accuracy and precision in the light of the quality of information that is available at the outset of the procedure.

In the United States, there is a small business restructuring regime in

---

[40]   See generally, Brian A. Blum, 'The Goals and Process of Reorganizing Small Business in Bankruptcy' (2000) 4 *Journal of Small and Emerging Business Law* 181, 193: 'there is no standard, widely accepted definition of small business . . . [but] it seems fair to say that the most readily identifiable attributes of smallness are the limited scale of business operations, resources, and personnel – both management and workers'.

[41]   For a definition of 'small companies' see UK Companies Act 2006, s. 382. To come within this category a company must satisfy two out of the following three criteria: (1) annual turnover does not exceed £6.5 million; (2) balance sheet total not to exceed £3.26 million; and (3) no more than 50 employees.

the sense that the Chapter 11 process is streamlined for 'small business debtors'. These are defined as persons engaged in commercial or business activities that have aggregate non-contingent liquidated secured and unsecured debts as of the date of the filing of the bankruptcy petition in an amount not more than around US$2.5m. In other words, a simple bright line, liabilities-based test is considered to be the most cost-effective for accurately categorizing a business as large or small for Chapter 11 purposes.

An obvious point that emerges from this study, however, is that a substantial majority of EU countries do not have such small business rescue procedures. The results of the study are set out in Table 5.5.

The absence of small business rescue procedures includes countries with mature, sophisticated economies such as Germany, Austria, the Netherlands and the Scandinavian countries (Denmark, Sweden, Finland, and the comparator, Norway).

The German reporter observes that German insolvency law provides for one single and unitary insolvency procedure and this principle applies irrespective of whether a restructuring or liquidation objective is being pursued and no matter whether the debtor is a natural or legal person or large or small company.

The Dutch reporters remark that a characteristic feature of insolvency proceedings under Dutch law is the expedient and flexible manner in which proceedings can be conducted. This flexibility includes prompt commencement of the proceedings following a basic insolvency test and the short periods applicable to certain formal processes. There is limited but effective court supervision and the fact that the IP has extensive powers to manage and realize the insolvent estate has further minimized procedural delays while maintaining a sufficient degree of checks and balances. The Austrian reporter comments that Austrian insolvency law dates from 1914 when most businesses were small. The entire procedure is considered to be well-suited for SMEs with cases in excess of generally accepted SME thresholds being very much the exception rather than the norm.

Even in countries such as Spain and the United Kingdom which have such procedures, the procedures are either considered not to work particularly well in practice or not to be widely used. In Spain, for example, the privileged position that state creditors enjoy in the procedures appears to work against their effectiveness, especially since public debts make up a large component of the debt profile for small businesses. In Italy, on the other hand, there are simplified insolvency procedures, including liquidation and composition procedures that may be applied to SMEs but as yet there is no evidence to suggest that the simplified procedures are particularly successful.

Table 5.5   Special insolvency arrangements for SMEs

Country	Special insolvency arrangements for SMEs and their effectiveness
Austria	No. But Austrian Insolvency law dates from 1914 when most businesses were small. Entire procedure is well-suited for SMEs, proceedings are considered big if the claims total more than 10 million euros. Current procedures considered sufficient
Belgium	No
Bulgaria	No
Croatia	No
Cyprus	No
Czech Republic	Streamlined liquidation proceedings are available for small business debtors. Indeed, the majority of business insolvencies seem to take this form
Denmark	No
Estonia	No, about 95% of existing companies in Estonia are SMEs
Finland	No, but the Restructuring Act enables simplified restructuring proceedings that are, in practice, more suitable for SMEs
France	Yes, for companies and individual debtors submitted to rescue proceedings, court appoints only IP for checking of claims and representing the collective interests of creditors; limits no more than 20 million euros turnover or less than 20 employees. Simplified liquidation procedure for SMEs, no more than 750,000 euros turnover, 5 employees and no immovable assets. Procedures considered to be a convenient tool for many debtors, i.e. individuals with few assets, by giving them a very efficient tool for a rescue through discharge
Germany	No. German insolvency law provides for one single and unitary insolvency procedure, no matter whether the debtor pursues restructuring or liquidation and no matter whether the debtor is a natural or legal person or large or small company. No special forms or templates
Greece	Simplified liquidation procedure for SMEs but only for companies with assets of less than 100,000 euros
Hungary	Some special rules for small businesses but no special procedures. Standard forms and templates. The rules were introduced not for encouraging the quick rescue of small businesses but rather to minimize opportunities for committing fraud
Ireland	Special procedure in that a small company is enabled to apply to the Circuit Court rather than the High Court to access the recovery procedure; promoted as a more cost efficient process but questionable since the working capital required to fund the company during the process and the dividends for creditors will not change and High Court continues to hear cases that could have been heard in the Circuit Court. Changes not having a visible effect in practice
Italy	No special insolvency arrangements applicable only to SMEs but simplified insolvency procedures, including liquidation and

Table 5.5   (continued)

Country	Special insolvency arrangements for SMEs and their effectiveness
	composition procedures that may be applied to SMEs. No special forms or templates and as yet no evidence to suggest that the simplified procedures are particularly successful
Latvia	No
Lithuania	Simplified and more expeditious bankruptcy procedure available when the court or IP established during the case that the enterprise has no assets or that its assets are insufficient to cover the legal and administrative expenses. Considered useful generally to have provisions specifically tailored for SMEs
Luxembourg	No
Malta	No and the provisions on corporate recovery do not expressly apply to small companies as such term is defined in the Act. Considered that provisions allowing for a more expeditious and cost-effective mode of insolvency for small and often family run enterprises would be a welcome development
Netherlands	No, but a characteristic feature of insolvency proceedings under Dutch law is the expedient and flexible manner in which proceedings can be conducted. Examples include prompt commencement of the proceedings following a basic insolvency test and the short periods applicable to certain formal processes. Limited court supervision and extensive powers of the IP to manage and realize the insolvent estate have further minimized procedural delays whilst maintaining a sufficient degree of checks and balances
Norway	No
Poland	No special procedures though size and nature of debtor's enterprise is recognized as an important factor in certain provisions of the insolvency law
Portugal	No
Romania	Simplified liquidation with special forms and templates but the procedure is not designed at all for business rescue
Slovakia	Simplified liquidation procedure with modified rules but no special templates. A special restructuring procedure for SMEs not considered to be realistic since the 'restructuring process requires experienced experts with strong integrity, who are generally very few and the costs of their services are high'
Slovenia	Simplified composition rather than liquidation procedures but a greater role for creditors in the procedure considered to be useful
Spain	Speedy insolvency procedure for debtors with liabilities of less than 5 million euros. Also procedure with standard forms for an out-of-court restructuring plan specifically tailored for debtors with liabilities of less than 5 million euros. But the fact that state claimants have a privileged position in the procedure appears to militate against its effectiveness
Sweden	No

Table 5.5   (continued)

Country	Special insolvency arrangements for SMEs and their effectiveness
United Kingdom	Special arrangement introduced for SMEs but not widely used and not considered to be a great success
United States	Chapter 11 process is streamlined for 'small business debtors', which are defined as persons engaged in commercial or business activities that have aggregate non-contingent liquidated secured and unsecured debts as of the date of the filing of the bankruptcy petition in an amount not more than (currently) US$2,490,925. The requirement for an official creditors' committee can be relaxed by the court in small business cases. Other onerous disclosure requirements are substantially reduced. Otherwise, small business cases are subject to usual Chapter 11 procedures
	The small business provisions are not thought to work well in practice because of their inflexibility and associated process costs. As a consequence, small businesses often seek recourse to alternative procedures outside of the bankruptcy system
	At present, it appears that the small business provisions of the Bankruptcy Code are not effective for encouraging quick rescues. However, US experience suggests that it can be very difficult to strike a balance between streamlined process and effective protection for creditors. One concern that led to the tightening of the small business provisions in 2005 was that too many non-viable small businesses were using them to delay their inevitable failure, thus prolonging their demise at increased administrative cost, when an immediate orderly liquidation would have provided a better return to creditors

More countries, however, have simplified liquidation procedures for small enterprises or at least special provisions of insolvency law that apply to the liquidation of debtors with relatively small liabilities, for example, France, Greece and Hungary. The threshold for the application of the special provisions varies, however, ranging from liabilities of 100,000 euros in Greece, 750,000 euros in France to 5 million euros in Spain.

5.5.1   Merits of a Small Business Restructuring Regime

It is appropriate to consider the merits of a small business restructuring regime as well as any possible demerits. In this connection, it is instructive to consider the US experience and how the Chapter 11 restructuring regime was streamlined for small business debtors.

In short, the 'standard' Chapter 11 case was potentially long drawn out and complex with many court hearings necessary, including a hearing to determine whether there was adequate disclosure of information to investors prior to voting on the restructuring plan. Its use in small business cases was criticized as being too cumbersome, expensive and slow, with the quintessential family enterprises required to follow the same restructuring steps as large conglomerates.

Many Chapter 11 small business cases failed. The Chapter attracted many small businesses that had no realistic hope of confirming a restructuring plan but, typically, they died a lingering death and when finally converted to Chapter 7 liquidation, unsecured creditors rarely received a dividend.[42] In many of these cases, an expeditious liquidation from the outset might have been the best way forward. In 1994, special elective provisions designed to speed up small business Chapter 11 bankruptcies were introduced but few debtors availed themselves of these procedures. Few debtors were inclined to self-administer the treatment that the small business regime prescribed.

The National Bankruptcy Review Commission addressed the perceived shortcomings of Chapter 11 in the small business arena[43] and its report led to the enactment of the Bankruptcy Abuse Prevention and Consumer Protection Act (BAPCPA) 2005. This Act amended the US Bankruptcy Code and established mandatory provisions for small business cases, including deadlines for the filing and confirmation of a restructuring plan. The new regime has two main goals. The first being to filter out early cases where there was little hope of a successful restructuring thereby preventing 'dead on arrival' debtors from languishing in Chapter 11 to no good end. The second goal was to expedite the administration of cases and achieve more effective case management by cutting out unnecessary delay.

---

[42] For information on the number of Chapter 11 filings and other bankruptcy filings, see www.uscourts.gov; and see generally E. Warren and J.L. Westbrook, 'Financial Characteristics of Businesses in Bankruptcy' (1999) 73 *American Bankruptcy Law Journal* 499, 543–4 and notes 80–82.

[43] National Bankruptcy Review Commission, *Bankruptcy: The Next Twenty Years* (E. Warren, Reporter, 1997), pp. 609–0. The report is available at http://govinfo.library.unt.edu/nbrc/. The report acknowledged, however, that reasonable people differ about how to define 'success' in Chapter 11 cases (see p. 611): 'Some argue that a Chapter 11 case in which no plan is confirmed should be considered successful where the case produces an orderly sale of assets or a negotiated solution without a formal plan. Creditors may define success in terms of distribution amounts or in terms of preserving future dealings with the debtor. The debtor, on the other hand, may define success in terms of job preservation, enhancement of going-concern value, or future returns to equity. The public may define success in terms of overall fairness.'

There is now an expanded role for the United States Trustee whose office is heavily relied upon to provide close oversight of the debtor in a way that has not typically been provided by creditors' committees.[44] Before the first meeting of creditors, the US Trustee is required to hold an 'initial debtor interview' which aims at investigating the debtor's viability.[45] The US Trustee monitors the debtor's activities; identifies cases where there is unlikely to be a confirmed plan, and generally expedites the administration of cases. Perhaps the most important role of the US Trustee is to move, where appropriate, for: dismissal of the case; conversion of the case into a Chapter 7 liquidation; or the appointment of an outside trustee or examiner to displace existing management.

The 2005 Act tries to improve techniques for the early identification of those businesses that have a reasonable probability of succeeding in Chapter 11 and those that do not. Fulfilling this objective is sometimes difficult because basic data about the business is often not available. The statute endeavours to rectify this state of affairs by imposing on the small business debtor a requirement to increase the amount of financial information made available. According to the amended section 308 of the Bankruptcy Code, such debtors are now obliged to file periodic financial and other reports containing financially sensitive information as prescribed.

There is, however, something of a contradiction at the heart of the legislation. The additional procedures provided for the court to weed out hopeless cases increase the administrative burden on the debtor and the system and may hamper the goal of reducing cost and complexity.[46] But the feeling was that, since the US Trustee and the court need reliable information, the quality of debtor reporting had to be improved to enable the system to operate effectively. The additional reporting, while expensive and burdensome, especially for the very small business, was seen as imposing a discipline that could assist rehabilitation efforts.

The US small business provisions are not thought to work well in practice, however. Certainly, they have not met with universal support[47]

---

[44]   On the role of the United States Trustee, see www.usdoj.gov/ust.

[45]   US Bankruptcy Code, s.586.

[46]   B.A. Blum, 'The Goals and Process of Reorganizing Small Business in Bankruptcy' (2000) 4 *Journal of Small and Emerging Business Law* 181, 215.

[47]   For strong criticism see J.B. Haines and P.J. Hendel, 'No Easy Answers: Small Business Bankruptcies after BAPCPA' (2005) 47 *Boston College Law Review* 71; R.M. Lawless, 'Small Business and the 2005 Bankruptcy Law: Should Mom and Apple Pie be Worried?' (2007) 31 *Southern Illinois University Law Journal* 585.

and small businesses often seek recourse to alternative procedures outside of the bankruptcy system. The detailed record keeping required by the procedure increases the cost for small businesses seeking bankruptcy protection. The value of the reforms may be outweighed by the procedural burdens that the statute imposes on small business debtors. Certainly, the American Bankruptcy Institute (ABI) 2014 Chapter 11 Commission study[48] indicated widespread dissatisfaction with the small business bankruptcy provisions introduced into Chapter 11 in 2005. The ABI report was based on two years of field studies and evidence gathering:

> Witnesses before the Commission generally testified that chapter 11 is not working for small and middle-market debtors, and several of these witnesses suggested that certain of the deadlines imposed by the BAPCPA amendments were particularly challenging and counterproductive.[49]

5.5.2 Designing a Small Business Restructuring Regime

The US experience demonstrates that designing an appropriate small business restructuring regime is not likely to be easy.[50] Such a regime may, however, involve a 'debtor in possession' norm with light touch monitoring of management, either by an official agency or by licensed private sector IPs. Debtors are more likely to make use of the procedures at an appropriately early stage if there is a debtor in possession presumption and such a policy should also limit costs. Management displacement adds another layer of costs to the process as the new controller(s) takes time to become familiar with the debtor and its operations.

At the same time, there is a widespread view that a debtor needs to be effectively monitored during the restructuring period. In Hungary, for example, the motivation behind the introduction of special insolvency provisions in small business cases, it seems, has been to prevent dishonest debtors abusing the insolvency procedures and bringing them into disrepute. In Slovenia, the watchful eye of an experienced IP is considered important in the large number of cases where managerial faults have led to the debtor's difficulties.

Creditors are likely to be involved in the approval of a restructuring

---

[48] See ABI, *Commission to Study the Reform of Chapter 11, 2012–2014, Final Report and Recommendations* (2014), ch. VII, available at http://digitalcommons. law.umaryland.edu/cgi/viewcontent.cgi?article=1096&context=books.

[49] *Ibid*. 281.

[50] See generally, G. McCormack, 'Rescuing Small Businesses: Designing an "Efficient" Legal Regime' [2009] *Journal of Business Law* 299.

plan. Appropriate information should be provided to them in advance but disclosure mechanisms should be easy to comply with and straightforward. Routine and regular court involvement in the restructuring process is likely to increase costs and thereby reduce the prospects of the procedure being realistic and feasible for use in the majority of cases. Nevertheless, formal court approval of a restructuring plan may reassure dissenting creditors who are 'crammed down' and reinforce public confidence in the integrity of the process. It may also make the plan more easily 'saleable' internationally since it has a judicial stamp of fairness.

5.6 COSTS OF FORMAL INSOLVENCY PROCEEDINGS

This issue overlaps with Question 2(g) on the remuneration of IPs. The fees and expenses of IPs invariably make up the bulk of the costs of formal insolvency proceedings and are determined more or less in the same way with controls by the court and creditors. There are fees payable to the court in many countries for the institution and hearing of formal proceedings and these are invariably borne by the debtor and are payable out of the insolvency estate. But these fees are likely to be relatively modest compared with the fees of the IP.

Legal fees incurred by an IP in the course of the insolvency proceedings are payable as part of the expenses of the proceedings. In many cases the IP is a lawyer but may instruct another lawyer to represent the insolvency estate in litigation in which case he or she is entitled to be reimbursed for these expenses separately. Austria is a case in point.

Supervision over the level of expenses in the insolvency proceedings is generally exercised by the court and creditors but there are concerns in some countries that these checks are not sufficiently robust and that abusive behaviour may go unpunished. In Bulgaria, for example, the suspicion has been voiced that some IPs may contract for services ostensibly for the benefit of the insolvency estate at above market rates. There is a perception that the contractor is in some way 'linked' to the IP or that the IP is rewarded for putting business in the way of the contractor. Abuses of this nature will only be stamped out by a rigorous licensing system for IPs, as well as adequate levels of remuneration, high standards of personal integrity and strong disciplinary and enforcement mechanisms.

Issues about the level of IP fees and expenses are not unique to the EU. In the United States, the manner of dealing with these issues is also superficially similar though the controls may work more effectively in practice than in some EU countries. The national reporter comments that in the United States, professional fees are controlled by the court and in large cases courts can and do appoint fee examiners or fee auditors to assist the court in fulfilling its statutory duty to review the reasonableness of fees and expenses.

5.7 CONCLUSIONS ON PROCEDURAL ISSUES RELATING TO INSOLVENCY PROCEEDINGS

This chapter has highlighted the fact that there is a considerable degree of variation between the laws of Member States on procedural issues relating to insolvency proceedings. These divergences may affect the assessment of credit risk (more likely to be done on a country-by-country basis rather than a pan-European basis) and hinder the financing of businesses at a cross-border level. On some issues, however, there is a fair degree of consensus between Member States.

For instance, in most jurisdictions either the insolvent debtor itself or creditors are able to open insolvency proceedings that lead to liquidation/ bankruptcy. In fact in the majority of Member States, directors are obliged to open some form of insolvency proceedings if their company is insolvent or else they might be penalized. In a large majority of Member States the opening of proceedings is published in a gazette or journal to which the public has access or in a newspaper. Proceedings that are designed to lead to a restructuring can usually only be opened by the insolvent company itself. Once proceedings have been opened it is important that the IP is aware of all creditors who have a claim against the company. Rules in Member States provide that creditors must make claims within specified periods of time.

It is important that creditors are involved in the resolution of a company's insolvency and to this end they are, besides being able to file insolvency proceedings, entitled to be involved in insolvency proceedings by voting at creditors' meetings and being represented by a group of creditors in creditors' committees that have various functions, including overseeing the work of the IP.

There is a general understanding that insolvency law exists, in part at least, to preserve the 'going concern' value of an ailing enterprise and to reduce or eliminate frictions in making the most effective use of assets. Generally, assets are worth more if they are kept together as part of an enterprise – a network of relationships – than if they are scattered far and wide. The analysis in this chapter suggests that in considering how to frame an insolvency law it is necessary to address the following:

- Whether the law should provide for a uniform obligation on directors to file insolvency proceedings when they are aware, or should be aware, that their company is unable to pay its debts, and if so, what time period should be specified.
- Whether there should be a standardized way for the notification of the opening of insolvency proceedings.
- Whether there should be a prescribed minimum amount that must be owed by a debtor before a creditor is able to open insolvency proceedings against the debtor.
- Whether the rules as to the kind of majority vote that is required of creditor meetings should be made more uniform.
- Whether there should be any standardized time period in which creditors are to file claims in insolvency proceedings.
- Whether the law should facilitate expedited liquidation and/ or restructuring proceedings as an appropriate mechanism for preserving 'going concern' value.
- What provisions should be put in place with a view to ensuring that expedited procedures do not unfairly advantage certain creditors and other 'insider' parties at the expense of others.
- How can the participation rights of creditors and other stakeholders be protected during the course of expedited procedures.
- Whether the law should contain particular provisions for use in small business cases, in particular small business restructurings.
- How should small business restructuring provisions be designed and in particular what companies should be eligible to make use of any special tailored procedure.
- With a view to saving on costs, whether a 'debtor in possession' norm is appropriate in a small business restructuring regime.
- In view of the possible costs, whether the approval of the court should be necessary in the context of a small business restructuring.
- Whether it would be more appropriate to 'think small first', that is to design a set of provisions that are appropriate for use in all insolvency cases and then supplement these provisions with other provisions specifically tailored for use in respect of small businesses.

6. Commission Recommendation on a new approach to business failure and insolvency

6.1 INTRODUCTION

This chapter considers the issue of Member State compliance with the EC Recommendation of 12 March 2014 on a new approach to business failure and insolvency.[1] The Recommendation encourages Member States to 'put in place a framework that enables the efficient restructuring of viable enterprises in financial difficulty' and to provide for 'minimum standards on ... preventive restructuring frameworks'.[2] The Recommendation also encourages Member States to put in place a framework to 'give honest Entrepreneurs a second chance' and to provide for 'minimum standards' on the 'discharge of debts of bankrupt Entrepreneurs'.[3] These provisions are considered in Chapter 7 of our report.

The Recommendation is fully in line with international developments

---

[1] C(2014)1500 final and see also Commission Communication, *A New European Approach to Business Failure and Insolvency*, COM(2012)742.

[2] For background see the accompanying Impact Assessment, SWD(2014)6; the INSOL Europe study done for the European Commission, *Study on a New Approach to Business Failure and Insolvency: Comparative Legal Analysis of the Member States' Relevant Provisions and Practices*, TENDER NO. JUST/2012/JCIV/CT/0194/A4 and more generally H. Eidenmuller, 'A New Framework for Business Restructuring in Europe: The EU Commission's Proposals for a Reform of the European Insolvency Regulation and Beyond' (2013) 20 *Maastricht Journal* 133.

[3] For analysis of the Recommendation see, *inter alia*, S. Madaus, 'The EU Recommendation on Business Rescue: Only Another Statement or a Cause for Legislative Action Across Europe?' [2014] *Insolvency Intelligence* 81; K. Van Zwieten, *Restructuring Law: Recommendations from the European Commission* (2015), available at www.ebrd.com/downloads/research/law/lit114e.pdf; H. Eidenmuller and K. Van Zweiten, *Restructuring the European Business Enterprise: The EU Commission Recommendation on a New Approach to Business Failure and Insolvency*, European Corporate Governance Institute (ECGI) Law Working Paper No. 301/2015, Oxford Legal Studies Research Paper No. 52/2015.

in the business restructuring and recovery spheres and more generally with international insolvency initiatives. UNCITRAL has stated clearly that modern and efficient insolvency laws are critical in enabling a state to achieve the benefits of integration with the international financial system. In its view, such laws and institutions should 'promote restructuring of viable business and efficient closure and transfer of assets of failed businesses, facilitate the provision of finance for start-up and reorganization of businesses and enable assessment of credit risk, both domestically and internationally'.[4]

Many of these initiatives build upon Chapter 11 of the US Bankruptcy Code on the restructuring of ailing businesses. As one US court put it, 'the purpose of [Chapter 11] is to provide a debtor with the legal protection necessary to give it the opportunity to reorganize, and thereby to provide creditors with going-concern value rather than the possibility of a more meagre satisfaction of outstanding debts through liquidation'.[5]

Influential US commentators[6] suggest that Chapter 11 deserves a prominent place in 'the pantheon of extraordinary laws that have shaped the American economy and society and then echoed throughout the world'. Chapter 11 has been cited as a great success by its proponents and the model to which European restructuring laws should aspire.[7]

But the available statistics may be interpreted in different ways and this is acknowledged in a recent study on 'Bankruptcy Survival' which suggests that about 70 per cent of large, public companies in the United States which seek to remain in business through Chapter 11 succeed whereas the assets of the other 30 per cent are absorbed into other businesses.[8] The study acknowledges, however, that it is difficult to define the concept of

---

[4] See UNCITRAL *Legislative Guide on Insolvency Law*, p. 10.

[5] *Canadian Pacific Forest Products Ltd* v. *JD Irving Ltd*, 66 F.3d 1436, 1442 (1995).

[6] See E. Warren and J.L. Westbrook, 'The Success of Chapter 11: A Challenge to the Critics' (2009) 107 *Michigan Law Review* 603, 604.

[7] See M. Brouwer, 'Reorganization in US and European Bankruptcy Law' (2006) 22 *European Journal of Law and Economics* 5; A. Tilley, 'European Restructuring: Clarifying Trans-Atlantic Misconceptions' (2005) *Journal of Private Equity* 99; C. Pochet, 'Institutional Complementarities within Corporate Governance Systems: A Comparative Study of Bankruptcy Rules' (2002) 6 *Journal of Management and Governance* 343.

[8] See L.M. Lopucki and J.W. Doherty, 'Bankruptcy Survival' (2015) 62 *UCLA Law Review* 970. For a somewhat different analysis of the data see, e.g., K. Ayotte and D. Skeel, 'Bankruptcy or Bailouts' (2010) 35 *Journal of Corporate Law* 469, 477: '[R]oughly two-thirds of all large bankruptcy outcomes involve a sale of the firm, rather than a traditional negotiated reorganization in which debt is converted to equity through the reorganization plan.'

bankruptcy survival since companies may undergo tumultuous changes during bankruptcy:

> They may shrink in size, be split into multiple businesses, sell their businesses to new owners, discharge their managers, change their names, and fundamentally change the nature of their businesses. One or more businesses may survive after a bankruptcy, but it may nevertheless be difficult to say whether that survivor is the bankrupt company, a company that acquired the bankrupt company, or a company that acquired elements of the bankrupt company.[9]

The study tries to navigate around these difficulties by regarding the company as the web of relationships among employees and with outsiders and firm assets. According to the study, if the structure of those relationships survives and remains distinguishable from the company's owner, then the company is taken as surviving. The well-known General Motors bankruptcy case is given as an example because after the bankruptcy filing, the valuable part of the company's business including its name, its managers and employees, were transferred to a new company formed to purchase them. The old company remained in bankruptcy but did not carry on any business and changed its name to Motors Liquidation Company. In the study, General Motors is regarded as surviving bankruptcy because the sale of the web of relationships constituting the company is regarded as the sale of the company.

The economic context of insolvency and bankruptcy law has been hotly contested in the United States, particularly in relation to the General Motors and Chrysler motor manufacturing restructurings. On one side of the coin are those who argue that 'once all stakeholders' interests are taken into account, if survival is achievable, survival is virtually always economically preferable to liquidation'.[10] These commentators point to the large economic and social costs that company failure places on employees, suppliers, customers and communities. On the other hand, it has been suggested that the 'paradigmatic firm is a restaurant in a large city. When the restaurant closes, workers lose their jobs, but they can find work elsewhere. A new restaurant or another firm can move into the space, and life goes on.'[11] On this side of the theoretical divide, it is argued that if employment preservation is seen as an independent policy of bankruptcy

---

[9] *Ibid.* 979.

[10] See L.M. Lopucki and J.W. Doherty, 'Bankruptcy Survival' (2015) 62 *University of California Law Review* 970.

[11] D.G. Baird, 'Bankruptcy's Uncontested Axioms' (1998) 108 *Yale Law Journal* 573, 580.

law, then it has the potential of undermining the key role of bankruptcy law in facilitating economic growth. In a free market or entrepreneurial economy, there have to be consequences associated with unsuccessful risk taking and bankruptcy law should not distort incentives and interfere with market mechanisms for monitoring and disciplining.[12]

Notwithstanding this, and while the US government may have exited its investments in the restructured General Motors and Chrysler entities at a net financial loss, an overall cost benefit assessment has to take into account the enormous social cost and dislocation associated with the closure of these entities.[13] This would have caused an asymmetric shock in a particular region of the United States, with devastation of the local tax base and a perceived need to provide unemployment relief, training, assistance and relocation packages as well as other transfer payments. The leading bankruptcy law Professor and influential US Senator Elizabeth Warren has commented in an analogous context:

> Business closings affect employees who will lose jobs, taxing authorities that will lose rateable property, suppliers that will lose customers, nearby property owners who will lose beneficial neighbours, and current customers who must go elsewhere.[14]

Some of the main features of Chapter 11 which may have contributed to its 'success' are as follows:

- The management of the company is not displaced in favour of an outside insolvency practitioner (IP) and the management itself can prepare a restructuring plan and submit the plan to the creditors.
- A court-appointed trustee may be appointed to monitor the rehabilitation process, but such trustee's powers are not as far-reaching as those under a management-displacement regime.
- A moratorium exists to protect the company from its creditors.
- There is also a mechanism for the approval of a restructuring plan, including 'cram-down' provisions under which a class of creditors,

---

[12]   See generally, T. Jackson and D. Skeel, 'Bankruptcy and Economic Recovery' in M.N. Baily, R.J. Herring and Y. Seki (eds), *Financial Restructuring to Sustain Recovery* (Washington, DC, Brookings Institution Press, 2013).

[13]   See CAR (Centre for Automotive Research) Research Memorandum by Sean P. McAlinden and Debra Maranger Menk, *The Effect on the U.S. Economy of the Successful Restructuring of General Motors* (2013), available at www.car group.org/assets/files/the_effect_final.pdf.

[14]   'Bankruptcy Policymaking in an Imperfect World' (1993) 92 *Michigan Law Review* 336, 355.

including secured creditors, can be forced to accept a restructuring plan against their wishes if the court determines that there is at least one class of creditors who have accepted the plan and it is of the view that the restructuring plan is feasible.

● There is provision for debtor-in-possession financing under which the company can obtain new funds either to continue its operations or to further the restructuring process. The providers of these new funds may enjoy 'super-priority' ahead of other creditors if existing creditors are deemed by the court to be adequately protected.

All of these elements are found to a greater or lesser extent in the EC Recommendation and might be thought to form the basis of possible future legislative initiatives in this area. Nevertheless, it is worth sounding a cautionary note for, as far as particular countries are concerned, different detailed solutions may be appropriate given the differences in history, culture, national economies, as well as in the state of economic development. For instance, the importance of the local in the global context has been acknowledged recently by the Insolvency Law Review Committee in Singapore.[15] The Committee recognized that Chapter 11 had proved durable and successful in the United States, but nevertheless considered that it would be inappropriate to attempt to replicate it in Singapore where the local economic and social conditions were very different.

The EC Recommendation contains a central underlying philosophy of promoting business rescue but is also committed to the balancing of the interests of the different economic actors within the insolvency process. The concept of balance is fundamentally important.[16] UNCITRAL, for instance, has stressed that a desirable legal framework should:

> (a) Provide certainty in the market to promote economic stability and growth; (b) Maximize value of assets; (c) Strike a balance between liquidation and reorganization; (d) Ensure equitable treatment of similarly situated creditors.[17]

The notion of 'balance' between different actors in the insolvency process will be revisited in the concluding section of this chapter.

---

[15] *Report of the Insolvency Law Review Committee, Final Report* (2013), pp. 106–7, available at www.mlaw.gov.sg/content/dam/minlaw/corp/News/Revised%20Report %20of%20the%20Insolvency%20Law%20Review%20Committee.pdf.

[16] A. Keay, 'Balancing Interests in Bankruptcy Law' (2001) 30 *Common Law World Review* 206.

[17] See UNCITRAL *Legislative Guide on Insolvency*, Recommendation 1.

From the study it appears that modern restructuring procedures already exist in most, if not all, Member States[18] and that European insolvency law has gone through a significant transformation over the past decade or so. Until recently, restructuring of financial obligations took place through negotiation of restructuring agreements between the debtor and its financial creditors. If no consensual solution was reached, then the alternative was a liquidation process with a major loss of enterprise value.

France is an example of a jurisdiction that has undergone major reforms in the insolvency and corporate restructuring sphere with the introduction of Sauvegarde, Accelerated Financial Sauvegarde and Accelerated Sauvegarde.[19] Cyprus has also reformed its laws with the introduction of a new examinership procedure that is closely modelled on an Irish example dating back to 1990.

But difficulties across the European Union remain:

(1)   There are still significant outliers where restructuring procedures are outdated at best or completely lacking.
(2)   In other cases, the procedures may be cumbersome and inefficient and have the effect of transferring wealth to out-of-the money creditors and shareholders.
(3)   Other inefficiencies include prolonging the life of financially unviable enterprises.[20] This has detrimental consequences for healthy competitors and the overall soundness of the economy. It hinders achievement of the objective of putting assets to their most effective use.[21]

---

[18]   For a brief outline of some of these developments see the European Commission evaluation of the implementation of the Recommendation, available at   http://ec.europa.eu/justice/civil/files/evaluation_recommendation_final. pdf; and see also B. Wessels, 'Themes of the Future: Rescue Businesses and Cross-Border Cooperation' [2014] *Insolvency Intelligence* 4.

[19]   For a brief account of the French reforms see A. Gallagher and A. Rousseau, 'French Insolvency Proceedings: La Revolution a Commence' (2014) *American Bankruptcy Institute Journal* 20.

[20]   See the Recommendation Impact Assessment SWD(2014)61, p. 2, stating that an 'effective insolvency law should be able to liquidate speedily and efficiently unviable firms and restructure viable ones'.

[21]   For a study suggesting that in Italy (a) a reform of the reorganization procedures that strengthened borrower rights to renegotiate outstanding financial contracts increases the cost of bank financing and reduced investment whereas (b) a reform of the liquidation procedures that strengthened creditor rights reduces the cost of bank financing and spurs investment, see G. Rodano, N. Serrano-Velarde and E. Tarantino, *Bankruptcy Law and Bank Financing*

(4)   There are other countries with a multiplicity of procedures that may lead to a restructuring outcome, for example France, Germany and the United Kingdom. The overall result may be complexity in the law and a number of potentially conflicting options for a financially ailing debtor to contemplate in a particular case. In the United Kingdom, not all these options are covered by the recast Insolvency Regulation (2015/848) and therefore entitled to the benefit of automatic EU-wide recognition under that Regulation.[22] The United Kingdom has a company voluntary arrangement (CVA) procedure in its insolvency legislation which is referenced in the impact assessment that accompanies the EC Recommendation.[23] But the United Kingdom also has the scheme of arrangement procedure which is based on company law rather than insolvency law[24] and this tool may also be used by companies of doubtful solvency to restructure their debts. The scheme of arrangement is outside the Regulation on Insolvency Proceedings (1346/2000) and the recast Insolvency Regulation since it is not listed

---

(2014), available at www.igier.unibocconi.it/files/547.pdf. See more generally S. Davydenko and J. Franks, 'Do Bankruptcy Codes Matter? A Study of Defaults in France, Germany and the UK' (2008) 63 *Journal of Finance* 565, 603–4 for the statement that many European restructuring frameworks are still inflexible, costly and value destructive.

[22]   Regulation (EU) 2015/848, arts 20 and 32 which are essentially the same as Regulation 1346/2000, arts 17 and 25. Lawyers and IPs in the United Kingdom lobbied hard for schemes to be kept outside the Regulation; see, e.g., the Insolvency Lawyers Association (ILA), City of London Law Society Insolvency Law Committee and Association of Business Recovery Professionals joint response of 25 February 2013 to the UK government consultation on the proposed changes to the Insolvency Regulation, p. 6, available at www.gov. uk/government/uploads/system/uploads/attachment_data/file/279289/insolvency-lawyers-association-evidence.pdf: 'We consider that the benefits derived from the different jurisdictional thresholds for sanctioning Schemes of Arrangement . . . are capable of providing a better outcome in terms of value to creditors. Additionally, we believe that Schemes provide the UK with an important commercial advisory opportunity as well as enhancing the reputation of the UK as a leading commercial centre.'

[23]   Recommendation Impact Assessment SWD(2014)61, pp. 15–16, though the reference does not acknowledge that most CVAs take place during the course of the insolvency administration procedure and will also have the costs associated with administration.

[24]   Schemes are dealt with in Part 26 of the Companies Act 2014 and see generally G. O'Dea, J. Long and A. Smyth, *Schemes of Arrangement Law and Practice* (Oxford, Oxford University Press, 2012); J. Payne, *Schemes of Arrangement: Theory, Structure and Operation* (Cambridge, Cambridge University Press, 2014).

in Annex A which sets out exhaustively the list of proceedings covered by the Regulation.[25]

In short there appears to be incomplete and inconsistent implementation of the Recommendation.[26] A Commission evaluation[27] concluded that while 'the Recommendation has provided useful focus for those Member States undertaking reforms in the area of insolvency, it has not succeeded in having the desired impact in facilitating the rescue of businesses in financial difficulty'.

The appendix to this chapter sets out the extent to which the laws, procedures and practices in Member States parallel the essential provisions in the EC Recommendation. The remainder of the chapter will address in narrative form the main features of the Recommendation and their implementation in Member States.

6.2   EARLY STAGE RESTRUCTURING PROCEEDINGS: INITIATION STAGE

The vast majority of Member States (Bulgaria being an obvious exception) have provisions in their national law that may be classed as early stage restructuring procedures:

- The procedures differ greatly between states in terms of detail, flexibility and sophistication.

---

[25]   In C-461/11 *Ulf Kazimierz Radziejewski* [2013] OJ C9/20, the Court of Justice of the European Union (CJEU) held that the Regulation on Insolvency Proceedings applied only to the proceedings listed in the annex. Recital 9 of the Preamble to the recast Insolvency Regulation states that where a procedure is not listed in Annex A it is not covered by the Regulation. For more on schemes see 6.12 below.

[26]   Capital Markets Action Plan, COM(2015)468, p.25 also relies on the World Bank *Doing Business Report* and rankings, available at www.doingbusiness.org/: 'The 2015 World Bank Doing Business Report ranks countries on the strength of their insolvency frameworks on a scale of 0–16. The EU simple average is 11.6, which is 5% below the OECD average for high income countries (12.2). Some Member States score below 8.' But for criticisms of these rankings see G. McCormack, 'World Bank Doing Business Project: Should Insolvency Lawyers Take it Seriously' [2015] *Insolvency Intelligence* 119.

[27]   At p.4, see http://ec.europa.eu/justice/civil/files/evaluation_recommendation_final.pdf. The evaluation was published on 30 September 2015, the same date as the Capital Markets Action Plan.

- In most cases, it is the debtors alone who may access such procedures though some Member States do give creditors a role in the initiation process.
- The conditions for access vary. Creditor involvement may signify support for a possible restructuring plan but if required in all cases it may stymie recourse to the procedure and hinder the objective of achieving early stage restructuring.
- In the majority of states, a formal court decision appears necessary to activate the procedures.[28]

The Recommendation contemplates the commencement of restructuring proceedings on application by the debtor.[29] It suggests that debtors should have access to a framework that allows them to restructure their business with the objective of preventing insolvency and that this restructuring possibility should become available as soon as it is apparent that there is a likelihood of insolvency.[30] The Recommendation itself does not formulate any test for determining insolvency but, as discussed in Chapter 5, two tests are generally international currency, that is the 'cash flow' test and the 'balance sheet' test. The 'cash flow' test of insolvency depends on it being established that the debtor is generally unable to pay its debts as they fall due for payment, while the 'balance sheet' test depends on it being established that the debtor's liabilities exceeds the value of its assets. Whether creditors in particular may be able to establish whether the 'cash flow' test is satisfied, debtors clearly are in the best position to judge the likelihood of insolvency. Hence, the presumption in the Recommendation is that debtors should initiate restructuring proceedings though creditor initiation of such proceedings is not necessarily precluded. This possibility is allowed in certain states, including Finland, where a creditor must show that its own significant financial interests are at risk if proceedings are not opened.

---

[28] The UK scheme of arrangement process is, however, set in train without any court decision as such and S. Madaus, 'The EU Recommendation on Business Rescue: Only Another Statement or a Cause for Legislative Action Across Europe?' [2014] *Insolvency Intelligence* 81, 84 suggests that the 'Commission obviously had this tool in mind when they designed the Recommendation'.

[29] See Recommendations 8–13.

[30] Recital 16 of the Preamble to Recommendation states that 'in order to avoid any potential risks of the procedure being misused, the financial difficulties of the debtor must be likely to lead to its insolvency and the restructuring plan must be capable of preventing the insolvency of the debtor and ensuring the viability of the business'.

6.3   EASE OF ACCESS TO PROCEDURES, INCLUDING COURT INVOLVEMENT

In respect of ease of access to the procedures there are considerable variations between the laws of the Member States. The standard situation requires a likely inability to pay debts. Germany exemplifies this approach, requiring a risk of illiquidity or over-indebtedness and the fact that the procedure envisaged is not obviously futile.

In some countries, there are more significant procedural obstacles to be overcome before the procedures can be accessed. For instance, in Slovakia the debtor is required to present a written statement from an IP that recommends adoption of the restructuring procedure in the light of the debtor's financial position, while in Italy the debtor, as a condition of accessing certain types of restructuring proceedings, must obtain the prior consent of creditors representing 60 per cent in value of the debts. In Portugal, the relevant restructuring procedures are designed to apply to companies which are in difficult financial situations but are not actually insolvent and for one type of procedure, commencement is predicated upon the debtor submitting a draft restructuring plan.

In the Netherlands, on the other hand, under a new procedure designed to come into force in 2017, there is no criterion of imminent insolvency and the procedure is designed to be used before the risk of insolvency materializes. In many respects, the procedure seems to be modelled on that of the UK scheme of arrangement which is a procedure based on company law rather than insolvency law. The scheme of arrangement can be used for various purposes, including as a takeover mechanism in relation to wholly solvent companies, but it may also be used as a restructuring mechanism for companies of doubtful solvency. In addition, it may be used within a formal liquidation process to achieve a less costly and more efficient realization and distribution of assets than the liquidation rules would normally allow.

The case study set out in Box 6.1 illustrates how the scheme of arrangement works in a relatively straightforward case.

In many Member States, while there is a hope or expectation that companies will avail themselves of the opportunities for restructuring at an earlier stage, the fact that actual insolvency is clear or established does not preclude recourse to the procedure. The restructuring mechanism may be used by both solvent and insolvent companies. In France, for example, the Accelerated Sauvegarde procedure may be used by a company that is actually insolvent provided that it is not in a situation of cessation of payments for more than 45 days, a situation that requires the directors to file for bankruptcy.

BOX 6.1   *IN THE MATTER OF MACQUARIE MOTORWAYS GROUP LTD* [2014] EWHC 4562 (CH)

The case concerned a scheme of arrangement in respect of a company that was part of a group of companies that operated a privately developed toll road. The scheme aimed to restructure the debts of the group by over £1 billion and also to place the group as a whole on a more sustainable footing for the future. The management of the company believed that in the absence of a scheme there was a significant prospect of formal insolvency proceedings with major losses for creditors and that the proposed restructuring presented the best opportunity for financial recovery.

There was a high creditor turnout at the relevant meetings and those creditors present unanimously approved the scheme arrangement. The court had no hesitation in adding its approval since there was no reason to differ from the views of those directly involved. The relevant test was whether the scheme was one that an intelligent and honest person acting in respect of its own interest might reasonably approve and the answer was a clear 'yes'.

The fact that reorganization may be used as an alternative to liquidation within a formal insolvency procedure is generally beneficial and positive provided that early stage restructuring possibilities are also available and encouraged. In the United States, under Chapter 11 of the Bankruptcy Code, applications for relief must be made in 'good faith' which means that the application must have been filed with the intention of achieving a corporate restructuring or to bring about a liquidation or sale of the company. If this is not the case, then creditors may apply to have the Chapter 11 petitions dismissed. *SGL Carbon Corp.*[31] is a case in point where a Chapter 11 petition was dismissed on the basis that the company had failed to manifest a genuine 'reorganizational purpose'. As certain commentators note:[32]

> [S]olvent firms have filed for Chapter 11 bankruptcy to take advantage of the considerable powers incumbent managers have to remake the corporation, undo its commitments, and reduce its obligations . . . In many cases, the reorganizing firm was not insolvent, and may in fact have been performing rather well.

This includes cases where a company was faced with large potential tort liabilities and attempts to reach a global settlement with plaintiffs have

---

[31]   200 F.3d 154 (1999).
[32]   B. Carruthers and T. Halliday, *Rescuing Business: The Making of Corporate Bankruptcy Law in England and the United States* (Oxford, Clarendon Press, 1998), p. 266.

broken down. Well-publicized examples include the *Johns-Manville* case involving asbestos-related liabilities where the court stated that a business foreseeing insolvency was not required to wait until actual inability to pay debts before entering Chapter 11.[33] Another example concerns the *AH Robins* corporate restructuring precipitated by the liability to women plaintiffs who had suffered injury as a result of using the Dalkon Shield birth control device.[34]

The EC Recommendation suggests that debtors should be able to enter a restructuring process without the need to formally open court proceedings.[35] It appears that the majority of national laws differ in this respect from the Commission Recommendation, though the level of court involvement is, in most states, difficult to gauge. The court hearing on the application to commence an early stage restructuring may range from a more or less cursory pro forma to a detailed examination on the merits of a possible restructuring. In Portugal, for the SIREVE restructuring procedure there is no court decision on the commencement process. Instead, an administrative entity for the restructuring of small and medium-sized enterprises (IAMPEI) exercises a filter mechanism. The debtor must make use of a mandatory electronic diagnostic made available by IAMPEI for the analysis of its financial affairs.

The UK scheme of arrangement and the putative new Dutch procedure are further outliers. The scheme process is activated by the filing of documents with the court and application to the court to convene meetings of relevant creditors and shareholders to approve the scheme, though the process is set in train without any court decision as such.

In the United States also, the Chapter 11 procedure begins with the mere filing of certain documents with the court. Normally, the debtor voluntarily files a petition with a bankruptcy court and the petition is accompanied by a list of creditors and also a summary of the debtor's assets and liabilities.

---

[33]   36 Bankruptcy Rep. 727 (1984).

[34]   For an account of this case see R.B. Sobol, *Bending the Law: The Story of the Dalkon Shield Bankruptcy* (Chicago, IL, University of Chicago Press, 1991) and see his comment at 326: 'Bankruptcy is the appropriate response when a business is unable, or can foresee that it will be unable, to pay the cost of mass tort liability. Novel and difficult questions are presented when the liabilities of a financially distressed business arise primarily out of personal injury claims, but no other mechanism is available and, with due regard for the exceptional context, these questions must be addressed and resolved within the bankruptcy system.'

[35]   See Recommendation 8.

6.4 DEBTOR IN POSSESSION

The Recommendation suggests that the debtor should keep control over the day-to-day operation of its business. It countenances the possible appointment of a mediator or supervisor by the court but stresses that this should not be compulsory, but rather done on a case by case basis where it was considered to be appropriate. The role of the mediator was envisaged to be one of assisting the debtor and creditors in negotiations on a restructuring plan, while that of a supervisor was overseeing the activities of the debtor and taking the necessary measures to safeguard the legitimate interests of creditors and other interested parties.

The fact that the management of the debtor will not be displaced in favour of an outside IP encourages timely use of the restructuring option. It has been said in a US context that:

> current management is generally best suited to orchestrate the process of rehabilitation for the benefit of creditors and other interests of the estate . . . The debtor-in-possession is a fiduciary of the creditors and, as a result, has an obligation to refrain from acting in a manner which could damage the estate, or hinder a successful reorganization. The strong presumption also finds its basis in the debtor-in-possession's usual familiarity with the business it had already been managing . . . often making it the best party to conduct operations during the reorganization.[36]

Like the Recommendation, the US Chapter 11 takes a debtor-in-possession approach to corporate restructuring. Under Chapter 11, however, an outside bankruptcy trustee can be appointed to take over management of a company for cause, though their appointment in Chapter 11 is exceptional. In *Re Marvel Entertainment Group*,[37] for instance, it was stressed that the appointment of an outside trustee should be the exception rather than the rule.

Alternatively, a US court may appoint an examiner instead of an outside trustee though, again, it seems that such an appointment is not the norm.[38] The examiner carries out the investigations that have been entrusted to it by the court that are appropriate in the particular circumstances of the case and often examiners are called upon to consider possible causes of action that a company may have. Unlike, however,

---

[36] *Re Marvel Entertainment Group*, 140 F.3d 463, 471 (1998).
[37] 140 F3d 463, 471 (1998).
[38] Section 1104(c)(2) at first glance, however, appears to require the appointment of an examiner where the company's unsecured, non-trade and non-insider debt exceeds US$5 million, i.e. in every medium to large case.

the appointment of a trustee, the appointment of an examiner does not displace the existing management, which may continue to conduct the day-to-day operations of the company in tandem with whatever functions the court assigns the examiner.

It should be noted, however, that the mediator or supervisor envisaged by the Recommendation is neither a bankruptcy trustee nor an examiner in the sense of the US Chapter 11 appointee.

For early stage restructuring proceedings it seems that there is a general debtor-in-possession European norm. In this respect, there is compliance with the Recommendation. The Recommendation states that the appointment of an IP is not compulsory but rather is at the discretion of the court on a case-by-case basis. Our study suggests, however, that debtor-in-possession in Europe normally also involves the appointment of an IP. There are exceptions, however, where no IP is appointed, including Slovenia. Moreover, in neither the new procedure intended in the Netherlands nor in the UK scheme of arrangement is there an IP appointed either to mediate or supervise the debtor. If negotiations break down or the debtor is perceived to be misbehaving in terms of its obligations, then the creditors would be likely to have recourse to formal insolvency procedures. The threat of creditor action in this regard forms a backdrop to the negotiations and may act as a powerful stimulus on the debtor.

Perhaps French law comes closest to the Recommendation in terms of debtor-in-possession and exceptions thereto. Under the French ad hoc mandate procedure, the court appoints an official who assists the company in trying to resolve its differences and come to an agreement with creditors but does not interfere with management. In the Sauvegarde procedures, one or more IPs are appointed who supervise the debtor, safeguard the interests of creditors and assist with the negotiations on the restructuring plan. Other Member States take a variety of different approaches on the issue and the roles of mediator and supervisor may be more or less combined. For instance, in Finland, the IP appointed by the court has a general monitoring and oversight role in relation to the debtor and also prepares a restructuring plan.

As these examples illustrate, the choice between debtor-in-possession and management displacement is not an 'all or nothing' one and there are in fact a plurality of possible approaches to this issue.[39] There may be certain risks, however, associated with what might be termed 'co-determination

---

[39] These approaches are discussed in INSOL Europe, *Study on a New Approach to Business Failure and Insolvency* (n. 2 above) 24–6.

models' like the Finnish one. The division of authority caused by the dual decision-making structure may create an arena for clashes of opposing interests. As one (non-European) commentator remarked:

> The flow of information between the various decision-makers is susceptible to errors, miscommunication and hence distortion. Secondly, between management and the trustee, the former enjoys superior access to information concerning the debtor. Because the two decision-makers represent different interest groups, management has an incentive to withhold information from the other representative (the trustee), undermine the latter's effective decision-making and thus tip the scale of power and risk taking in favour of its own constituency, the equity holders.[40]

6.5 STAYS ON ENFORCEMENT ACTIONS

The Recommendation suggests that debtors should have the right to request a court to grant a temporary stay of individual enforcement actions instituted by creditors, including secured and preferential creditors. The stay is intended to give the debtor a breathing space in order to negotiate a restructuring plan.[41] The stay is a prominent feature of international insolvency instruments, such as the UNCITRAL *Legislative Guide on Insolvency*.[42] The *Legislative Guide* reflects the view that to allow recovery procedures by creditors to operate without restraint could frustrate the overall socially desirable goal of restructuring and rescue. Since going-concern value may be a lot more than break-up value, restructuring proceedings are designed to keep a business alive so that this additional value can be captured. This goal will be compromised, however, if creditors are able to seize assets that are essential to the carrying on of the company's business. Therefore, we have a stay or moratorium on actions by creditors to collect debts or repossess property in the ailing debtor's possession and there are counter-balancing measures in place to protect those who may be affected by the stay.

---

[40] D. Hahn, 'Concentrated Ownership and Control of Corporate Reorganizations' (2004) 4 *Journal of Corporate Law Studies* 117, 152.

[41] This Report does not consider the performance of ongoing contracts during the period of the stay. For a detailed cross-country comparison of this issue see D. Faber, N. Vermunt, J. Kilborn and K. van der Linde, *Treatment of Contracts in Insolvency* (Oxford, Oxford University Press, 2013).

[42] See Recommendations 39–51.

The stay is also an intrinsic feature of Chapter 11 of the US Bankruptcy Code and has been described[43] as one of the:

> fundamental debtor protections provided by the bankruptcy laws. It gives the debtor a breathing spell from his creditors. It stops all collection efforts, all harassment, and all foreclosure actions. It permits the debtor to attempt a repayment or reorganisation plan, or simply to be relieved of the financial pressures that drove him into bankruptcy.

The approach taken in Member States varies considerably as to the types of creditor enforcement actions that may be stayed and whether these cover actions by secured and preferential creditors as well as by unsecured creditors. In Belgium, for instance, the stay covers generally asset seizures (so-called 'executions') in respect of the debtor's real and personal property but security over receivables and certain other types of secured claim may still be enforced. In Greece, it seems that the stay may potentially affect secured claims but not generally the enforcement of employee claims. In Slovenia, the stay appears to cover enforcement actions by both secured and unsecured debts but only in respect of financial debts rather than trade debts. There are some similarities between the position in Slovenia and that in France under the latter's Accelerated Financial Sauvegarde (AFS) where the stay does not operate against trade creditors because their rights may not be cut down or abridged by the AFS procedure. In Portugal likewise, if creditors have indicated their unwillingness to take part in the SIREVE restructuring procedure then they are not bound by any stay.

6.5.1   Stay: Automatic or Otherwise?

There is also considerable variation among states on the conditions necessary for the granting of a stay and whether the stay is more or less automatic upon the commencement of the restructuring procedure or whether it is granted by the court upon a full hearing on the merits of the application. It does not appear, however, that any Member State, with the possible exception of Lithuania, has a stay as far-reaching and comprehensive as the US Chapter 11 stay. This so-called 'automatic stay' imposes

---

[43]   HR Rep. No. 595, 95th Cong, 1st Session 340 (1977). The statement continued: 'The automatic stay also provides creditor protection. Without it, certain creditors would be able to pursue their own remedies against the debtor's property. Those who acted first would obtain payment of the claims in preference to and to the detriment of other creditors. Bankruptcy is designed to provide an orderly liquidation procedure under which all creditors are treated equally. A race of diligence by creditors for the debtor's assets prevents that.'

a freeze on proceedings or executions against the debtor and its assets and has worldwide effect.[44] The US courts have inferred extra-territorial effect from the language of the Bankruptcy Code provisions[45] and they have also held that the bankruptcy estate comprises property of the debtor wherever situated throughout the world.[46] The long arm of the US bankruptcy jurisdiction is illustrated by a recent series of Chapter 11 cases involving foreign shipping companies.[47] These debtors have recognized the benefits and advantages served by Chapter 11 proceedings, including the debtor in possession norm and the reach of the automatic stay but, in some cases, the US connections of the debtors have been rather tenuous.

On the other hand, typical of the discretionary approach in Europe is Germany, where the stay depends on a court order, and Poland, where under a proposed new regime, enforcement of security may be suspended if a judge considers that the secured property is necessary for the success-ful running of the enterprise. In France, by contrast, the nature of the stay depends on the type of procedure involved. In ad hoc mandate and conciliation proceedings, the stay is dependent on an application to the court, whereas in Sauvegarde proceedings it is automatic consequent on the opening of the proceedings. In the United Kingdom, it also depends on the nature of the proceedings. In the scheme of arrangement, as in the proposed new Dutch procedure, there is no automatic stay. Any stay is strictly short-term in duration and is intended to stop imminent executions against the debtor's property.[48]

Despite the differences in the Member States, it appears that, in line with the Recommendation, debtors in the Member States will generally be granted a stay where '(a) creditors representing a significant amount of the claims likely to be affected by the restructuring plan support the

---

[44] For a recent example see *In re Nortel Networks Inc.*, 669 F.3d 128 (2011).

[45] See *Nakash v. Zur (In re Nakash)*, 190 BR 763 (1996), where the automatic stay was enforced against a foreign receiver in respect of the foreign assets of a foreign debtor.

[46] See *Hong Kong & Shanghai Banking Corp. v. Simon (In re Simon)*, 153 F.3d 991, 996 (1998):
'Congress intended extraterritorial application of the Bankruptcy Code as it applies to property of the estate.'

[47] For an early example see *In re Global Ocean Carriers Ltd*, 251 BR 31 (2000), which concerned a shipping company headquartered in Greece and where it was held that the unearned portions of retainers provided to US counsel constituted property that was sufficient to form the basis for a US bankruptcy filing.

[48] The limited stay has been fashioned from the Civil Procedure Rules: *BlueCrest Mercantile BV v. Vietnam Shipbuilding Industry Group* [2013] EWHC 1146.

negotiations on the adoption of a restructuring plan; and (b) a restructuring plan has a reasonable prospect of being implemented and preventing the insolvency of the debtor'.[49]

6.5.2 Suspension of Liquidation Type Proceedings

The commencement of early stage restructuring proceedings generally suspends the operation of liquidation type proceedings.[50] This is the case in the majority of European countries though there are some exceptions, including Austria and the United Kingdom, where the fact that a scheme of arrangement is being considered does not preclude a winding-up petition being brought by a dissentient creditor, though it is conceivable that a judge, on a discretionary basis, would postpone a hearing on the petition until it was known whether the proposed scheme of arrangement was likely to be accepted. It appears that this is also the case in the Netherlands under the proposed new procedure that closely models the UK scheme of arrangement.

In Poland, it seems that to the extent that creditors are not affected by the stay they may still petition for the opening of liquidation proceedings. Under a proposed new regime, however, liquidation cannot be declared while the restructuring proceedings are pending. In France, the picture is more nuanced and depends on the nature of the restructuring proceedings that have been opened. In respect of the ad hoc mandate and conciliation proceedings, there is no suspension of insolvency proceedings though a court might postpone the hearing of liquidation proceedings until it is known whether a restructuring plan is likely to meet with approval. In the case of standard Sauvegarde proceedings, if cessation of payments occurs during the observation period, then the proceedings may be converted into insolvency proceedings.

6.5.3 Duration of the Stay and Lifting the Stay

The Recommendation suggests that the stay, in terms of duration, should strike a fair balance between the interests of debtor and creditors, including in particular secured creditors. It goes on to say that the length of the stay should depend on the complexity of the case, and the anticipated restructuring. In the first instance, it should not exceed four months but,

---

[49] Recommendation 11.
[50] A distinction should be drawn between the stay on liquidation type proceedings and the stay on individual enforcement actions.

depending on progress in the negotiations, it might be extended, though the total duration should not exceed 12 months. Linked with duration is the question of lifting the stay and the Recommendation provides that where the stay is no longer necessary for facilitating the adoption of a restructuring plan, it should be lifted.[51]

Long drawn out restructuring proceedings, and in particular those involving restrictions or a stay on the enforcement of collateral, have the effect of transferring wealth to managers and shareholders at the expense of creditors. Creditors are kept out of their money while managers may keep their jobs. Shareholders may also benefit from the restructuring efforts in that, if the company is kept afloat, the value of their shareholdings can be preserved.

In respect of duration and lifting the stay, it seems that the 'early stage' restructuring proceedings in Member States comply with the spirit of the Recommendation though there are divergences in relation to time limits. The Hungarian law, however, falls exactly in line with the Recommendation in that the stay lasts for an initial period of 120 days but may be extended subject to a one year total. The Swedish position is somewhat similar, for the stay lasts initially for three months but exceptionally may be extended for up to a year. Some countries have tighter timeframes, such as Portugal where the stay may be for up to three months in SIREVE procedures and two months in PER procedures, but in both cases the stay may be extended for an additional month. Other countries offer greater flexibility: in Italy it depends on the nature of the proceedings but there appears to be an outer limit of 11 months on the duration of the stay. French law also differs depending on the type of restructuring procedure employed in the particular case. In a standard Sauvegarde, the initial stay is for six months but this period is renewable twice up to 18 months in total. The specialized forms of Sauvegarde are more expedited. For Accelerated Sauvegarde there is a three-month stay that is not renewable, whereas for Accelerated Financial Sauvegarde, there is a stay for a one month period that is renewable once.

The fact that stay time limits are tight in many Member States may mean that the possibility of applying for the lifting of the time limit before the expiry of this time limit is denied or at least heavily restricted. In Greece, a creditor may seek the lifting of the stay and the court will accede to the application if satisfied that there is no reasonable prospect of the restructuring procedure being successful. In Member States generally, if the restructuring proceedings are terminated, this signifies the end of the

---

[51]   Recommendation 14.

stay but in Germany the stay may be lifted if the prerequisites for its existence are no longer met. In Latvia also, a secured creditor may request the
sale of secured property if the stay causes significant harm to the interests
of the creditor. Moreover in Sweden, if there is probable cause to believe
the debtor will seriously jeopardize a creditor's rights, the court may lift
the stay and open insolvency proceedings.

In stressing the importance of safeguarding creditor rights during the
period of any stay, and, in particular, the rights of secured creditors,
the Recommendation is in keeping with international precedents. These
international precedents also illustrate, however, how the precise manner
of protection may vary across countries and legal regimes. Under the
UNCITRAL *Legislative Guide on Insolvency*, a secured creditor is entitled to relief from the stay if the encumbered asset is not necessary to a
prospective restructuring or sale of the debtor's business. Moreover, while
the stay lasts, a secured creditor is entitled to the protection of the value
of the asset in which it has a security interest.[52] Appropriate measures
of protection are stated to include cash payments by the debtor's estate,
provision of additional security interests, or such other means as the court
determines.

In the US Chapter 11 procedure, a secured creditor, along with anybody
else affected by the statutory stay, can apply to have it lifted and there is
a specific requirement of 'adequate protection' for the holders of property
rights who are adversely affected by the stay.[53] Examples of 'adequate
protection' are provided by the statute, although the concept itself is not
defined.[54] It should be said, however, that it is only the value of the collateral that is entitled to adequate protection.[55] An under-secured creditor
may find itself footing the bill for an unsuccessful restructuring attempt.
It is prevented from enforcing the collateral by the automatic stay yet it is
not entitled to interest during what may be a long drawn out Chapter 11
process. An over-secured creditor is, however, entitled to be paid interest

---

[52]   UNCITRAL *Legislative Guide*, Recommendation 50.
[53]   US Bankruptcy Code, s. 361.
[54]   The examples given are cash payments, additional or replacement security
interests on other property and, unusually expressed, something that will give the
creditor the 'indubitable equivalent' of its security interest.
[55]   See *Re Alyucan*, 12 BR 803 (1981), where the court rejected the view that the
preservation of a certain collateral-to-debt ratio was part of the creditor's property
interest that warranted protection. See also *United Savings Association of Texas* v.
Timbers of Inwood Forest Associates Ltd, 484 US 365 (1988), where the Supreme
Court held that the adequate protection provision did not entitle an under-secured
creditor to compensation for the delay caused by the stay in enforcing the security.

out of the security 'cushion' at the plan confirmation stage as a condition of the court approving the plan.

6.6 RESTRUCTURING PLANS

The EC Recommendation in points 15–29 contains clear and fairly explicit provisions on the contents of restructuring plans. It is provided that creditors with different interests should be dealt with in separate classes which reflect those interests and, as a minimum, there should be separate classes for secured and unsecured creditors. Point 19 states that creditors should enjoy a level playing field irrespective of where they are located and this includes being allowed to vote by distance means of communication, such as registered letter or secure electronic technologies.[56]

The Recommendation does not prescribe detailed rules on the majorities required before a majority of creditors in a particular class is deemed to have accepted a plan and whether all classes of affected or impaired creditors are required to give their consent. It does, however, lay down that it should be possible to adopt restructuring plans even though non-affected creditors have not been consulted or given their consent.

The Recommendation suggests that court confirmation of a restructuring plan is appropriate, with the court ensuring that the legitimate interests of creditors have been respected; the restructuring plan does not reduce the rights of dissenting creditors below what they would reasonably be expected to receive in alternative scenarios such as a liquidation or going-concern sale of the debtor's business; and that any new financing envisaged in the plan is necessary and does not unfairly prejudice the interests of dissenting creditors.[57]

There seems to be some variation in Member States about the necessary content of restructuring plans. It is probably fair to say that while there is compliance with the general spirit of point 15 of the Recommendation, the exact letter of point 15 is not met in every respect. In Germany, there is a requirement that a plan should contain all relevant information about its rationale and its impact on the parties. In certain countries there is a requirement that the plan should specifically detail its effect on employees.

---

[56] It seems that most Member States permit voting by proxy but where there is a requirement of a physical meeting, creditors will have to be present either in person or by proxy if they want to have their vote recorded as being either for, or against, a restructuring plan.

[57] Recommendation 22.

This is, for example, the case in Estonia and under the French Sauvegarde procedure.

Point 15(c) of the Recommendation states that the plan should set out the position taken by affected creditors on the particular restructuring plan. The Slovakian and Polish reports state explicitly that, in their national law, this detail is not complied with to the letter and it seems that this is also the position in a number of other states. This may be because, while creditors have been consulted in general terms about the proposed restructuring, they are not necessarily acquainted with all its aspects. Another possibility is that last minute adjustments have been made to the plan to accommodate particular concerns and this may affect creditor attitudes. In the United Kingdom, for instance, there is considerable flexibility about the contents of any restructuring plan. While this depends partly on the nature of the particular restructuring procedure, in general, creditors must be given sufficient information to enable them to make an informed choice about whether or not to accept the proposal.

6.7   SEPARATE CLASSES

Recommendation 17 suggests that creditors with different interests should be treated in separate classes which reflect those interests and, as a minimum, there should be separate classes for secured and unsecured creditors.

To make the adoption of restructuring plans more effective, Member States should also ensure that it is possible for restructuring plans to be adopted by certain creditors or certain types or classes of creditors only, provided that other creditors are not affected.

Creditor classification and division is very important in a corporate restructuring context. Creditor classification may facilitate negotiations over the division of the 'going concern surplus' since different creditors may have different views on the value of the restructured enterprise and the risks that may be presented by extending the maturity of debts. There are several practical justifications for classifying creditors differently. For example, creditors with alternative forms of payment, such as third party guarantees, have different incentives vis-à-vis the debtor, and creditors who view the ailing company as a valuable vendor or customer have more of an interest in its survival than do the company's one-off tort victims.[58]

---

[58]   See the comment made by the US Bankruptcy Court in *Re Greystone 111 Joint Venture*, 995 F.2d 1274 (1991): '[I]f the expectation of trade creditors is

On the other hand, certain creditors may have extraneous interests that run contrary to the goal of corporate rescue. These creditors, for example, may be debt traders or hedge funds who have bought all or part of the company's debt at a steep discount. They may have a 'loan-to-own' strategy. Alternatively, they may wish to preserve a reputation for toughness and this reputation is seen as more important than their private stake in the particular case. The individual interests of these creditors is at odds with the goal of restructuring the particular debtor.

In many cases, it makes clear commercial sense to group creditors into separate categories and deal with them somewhat differently. For instance, tort creditors could be paid out of a newly established fund while trade creditors are paid off directly in cash and unsecured lenders in short-term commercial paper.[59] Trade creditors receive cash but unsecured debt held by financial institutions is paid over a longer period or is exchanged for an equity stake in the business. The ability to place creditors into separate classes is a powerful one.[60] While facilitating negotiations on a restructuring plan, it may in some cases hinder the goal of debtor rehabilitation and rescue. A multiplicity of creditor classes may make it more difficult to achieve creditor consensus, especially if the legislative framework in place in a particular country requires that all creditor groups should approve a restructuring plan before it becomes binding. The issue still exists, albeit not to the same degree, if there is a requirement of near unanimity among creditor groups.

In Europe, while there may be general compliance with the spirit of Recommendation 17, a number of different approaches are exhibited on creditor classification and division. In Germany, for example, there is provision for separate classes and equal treatment of creditors within the class. In Luxembourg, there are detailed requirements in respect of how a plan may treat different classes of creditors: the face value of a secured claim may not be reduced and payment may not be suspended generally for a period of more than 24 months. In Hungary, there are separate classes for secured and unsecured claims and also for the claims of creditors who are

---

frustrated . . . [they] have little recourse but to refrain from doing business with the enterprise. The resulting negative reputation quickly spreads in the trade community, making it difficult to obtain services in the future on any but the most onerous terms.'

[59]   See National Bankruptcy Review Commission Report, *Bankruptcy: The Next Twenty Years* (1997), p. 568.

[60]   See Bruce A. Markell, 'Clueless on Classification: Toward Removing Artificial Limits on Chapter 11 Claim Classification' (1994) 11 *Bankruptcy Developments Journal* 1, 16.

in some way connected with the debtor. Finland adopts the approach of grouping creditors in separate classes according to the priority status of their claims. In France, the classification is done more on the nature of the claim rather than its priority status. Generally in Sauvegarde proceedings, financial creditors and trade creditors are represented by separate committees and bondholders also vote differently. The Accelerated Financial Sauvegarde procedure affects only financial creditors and so trade creditors do not vote.

The fact that creditors do not vote on a restructuring plan if they are not affected is also found in other EU countries. In Finland, for example, creditors who are not affected by the plan do not have a right to vote. In the United Kingdom, the position is slightly different and depends on the nature of the restructuring procedure. The company voluntary arrangement (CVA) does not involve the division of creditors into classes but does not affect secured creditors unless they consent to their inclusion in the procedure. The scheme of arrangement, however, does involve the division of creditors into classes and each affected class must accept the scheme for it to become binding. A class of secured creditors can be included in the procedure and become bound by it. The proposed new restructuring regime in the Netherlands is similar in that only those whose rights are amended will be involved in the procedure.

This approach is perfectly compatible with the EU's new approach to business failure and insolvency, which in Recommendation 20 states that to 'make the adoption of restructuring plans more effective, Member States should also ensure that it is possible for restructuring plans to be adopted by certain creditors or certain types or classes of creditors only, provided that other creditors are not affected'.

The UNCITRAL *Legislative Guide* also accepts the approach of treating secured creditors differently depending on whether they are, or are not, bound or affected by a restructuring plan. It states that 'where the insolvency law does not affect secured creditors and, in particular, does not preclude them from enforcing their rights against the encumbered assets, there is no need to give these creditors the right to vote since their security interests will not be affected by the plan'.[61]

Moreover, under the US Chapter 11, creditors whose rights are not impaired are deemed to have accepted a restructuring plan. The notion of 'impairment' is fundamental to Chapter 11 because only the holders of 'impaired' claims or interests are entitled to vote on the restructuring plan. Section 1124 provides that a claim or interest is impaired unless the plan

---

[61]   UNCITRAL, *Legislative Guide on Insolvency Law*, p. 220.

leaves unaltered the rights outside bankruptcy that are associated with that claim or interest. The plan divides claims (indebtedness) and interests (equity shares) into separate and distinct classes for voting purposes and also for purposes of treatment and payment. Each class of claims or interests should be designated as either impaired or not impaired and in accordance with section 1126(f), the holders of claims or interests that are not impaired are deemed to have voted to accept the plan since their rights against the debtor outside bankruptcy are preserved and protected in full.

On the other hand, if secured creditors are excluded from the plan for this reason, this necessarily reduces the scope of the plan and reduces the chances of the plan restoring the financial health of the debtor. Inclusion of the secured assets may be essential to the success of the plan and modification of the rights of the secured creditors is crucial in this regard.

6.8 CONDITIONS FOR ACCEPTANCE OF THE PLAN: VOTING AND COURT APPROVAL

Recommendation 22 provides:

> The conditions under which a restructuring plan can be confirmed by a court should be clearly specified in the laws of the Member States and should include at least the following: (a) the restructuring plan has been adopted in conditions which ensure the protection of the legitimate interests of creditors; (b) the restructuring plan has been notified to all creditors likely to be affected by it; (c) the restructuring plan does not reduce the rights of dissenting creditors below what they would reasonably be expected to receive in the absence of the restructuring, if the debtor's business was liquidated or sold as a going concern, as the case may be; (d) any new financing foreseen in the restructuring plan is necessary to implement the plan and does not unfairly prejudice the interests of dissenting creditors.

This is a complex issue and the UNCITRAL *Legislative Guide on Insolvency Law* recognizes the possibility of a wide variety of different approaches in determining whether a restructuring plan is approved. But it suggests that the approach adopted is set out clearly in the insolvency law so that parties to the restructuring proceedings are provided with clarity and transparency.[62]

There is in fact considerable variation in the conditions necessary

---

[62] But *ibid.* 210 suggests that 'priorities afforded to creditors in liquidation should be maintained in reorganization, that creditors receive in reorganization as much as they would have received in liquidation, that the effect of the plan should

for approval of a restructuring plan in the EU Member States. The Recommendation sets out the general parameters and most, if not all, states would meet these general parameters, though the detailed conditions for approval vary widely.

6.9 NO CREDITORS WORSE OFF

Creditors may, in particular, be concerned with Recommendation 22(c), the 'no creditor worse off' principle, and whether the valuation mechanism in a particular insolvency regime and the delays associated with the procedure means that in practice a creditor is worse off.

This Recommendation embodies what in US Chapter 11 terms would be referred to as the 'liquidation' or 'best interests' test which requires that a creditor should receive at least as much under the plan as it would in liquidation.[63] The UNCITRAL *Legislative Guide* refers, in particular, to protecting the position of the secured creditor during restructuring proceedings by ensuring that payments of future interest will be made and that the value of encumbered assets is not affected.[64]

In some respects, the principle that no creditors should be left worse off is a formal requirement of the restructuring law, whereas in other countries if the necessary majorities are obtained the restructuring plan is approved and the court does not formally consider alternative values of the debtor's assets, such as liquidation value. The legislative assumption may be that if the restructuring value is likely to be less than the value obtained on a liquidation, then creditors would not support a restructuring. Romania is an example of a country in the first category. There, in a judicial reorganization, the plan has to provide fair and equitable treatment; respect the priority of claims; and provide a dissenting creditor with at least as much as they would receive in a bankruptcy. Germany also considers liquidation values but only in the context of cross-class creditor cram-down, that is where not all creditor groups have approved a restructuring plan but it is proposed to approve the plan regardless. In Germany, even if all the creditor groups have not agreed, court approval is possible if a majority of groups agree and the court is satisfied that the dissenting group receive at least as much under

---

not be such that the debtor remains insolvent and is returned to the marketplace in that condition'.

[63]   Section 1129(a)(7)(A)(ii).
[64]   See the discussion at UNCITRAL *Legislative Guide*, pp. 220–21.

the plan as they would do otherwise. The court also considers the overall fairness of the plan.

The United Kingdom takes even more of a 'creditor democracy' approach. CVAs do not necessarily go before the court for approval. Once the necessary 75 per cent in value of creditors voting threshold has been met, the arrangement becomes binding on dissenting creditors. A dissenting creditor may challenge the arrangement in court, subject to tight time limits, if he can establish that the arrangement is unfairly prejudicial or there is some procedural irregularity which led to acceptance of the arrangement.

UK schemes of arrangement do have to be approved by the court but, in deciding whether or not to give approval, the court will accord considerable latitude to the scheme proponents. The court must be satisfied that it is a fair scheme – one that 'an intelligent and honest man, a member of the class concerned and acting in respect of his interest, might reasonably approve'.[65] On the other hand, the scheme proposed need not be the only fair scheme or even, in the court's view, the best scheme. There is room for reasonable differences of view on these issues and in commercial matters creditors are considered to be much better judges of their own interests than the courts. The court in *Re British Aviation Insurance Co. Ltd*[66] pointed out that the test is not whether the opposing creditors have reasonable objections to the scheme. A creditor may be equally reasonable in voting for or against the scheme and in these circumstances creditor democracy should prevail.

The overall flexibility of the UK scheme of arrangement has proved attractive to foreign incorporated companies and to international creditors, as the case study in Box 6.2 illustrates.

6.10 'ABSOLUTE PRIORITY' RULE: RESPECTING PRE-INSOLVENCY ENTITLEMENTS

Recommendation 22 does not explicitly refer to the so-called 'absolute priority' rule requiring that insolvency priorities should be respected; in other words, that creditors should be paid in the same order as they would in liquidation with creditors paid out before shareholders and senior creditors before junior creditors, and so on. Recommendation 17 does,

---

[65] See *Anglo-Continental Supply Co. Ltd* [1922] 2 Ch. 723, 736.
[66] [2005] EWHC 1621, para. 75.

BOX 6.2 *RE DTEK FINANCE BV* [2015] EWHC 1164 (CH)

In this case a company applied for the court to sanction a proposed scheme of arrangement between it and the holders of loan notes that it had issued. The company was incorporated in the Netherlands and was part of a group that carried on an energy business, primarily in the Ukraine. Finance for the company was raised by issuing loan notes in capital markets which were guaranteed by other group companies. At the time of issue these notes were governed by New York law and with a maturity date of April 2015. The group, however, encountered financial difficulties as a result of the political situation in Ukraine and was unable to meet its obligations under the notes.

A scheme of arrangement was proposed under which, in return for the old notes the noteholders would get new notes at 80 per cent of the par value of the existing notes with an extended 2018 maturity date and at the same interest rate as well as cash for the remaining 20 per cent of the par value. The noteholders agreed to change the governing law to English law and at a meeting to approve the scheme of arrangement, over 90 per cent of noteholders by value voted in favour of the scheme. The English court decided that it had jurisdiction to sanction the scheme; that the statutory requirements had been satisfied; and that the scheme should be approved in the exercise of the court's discretion.

It was held that the change in the governing law to English law created sufficient connection with the United Kingdom so as to give a UK court the authority to approve the scheme. All the creditors had been placed in a single class even though some noteholders had received a small additional payment as an incentive to indicate early acceptance of the scheme. But the court said that this was not enough to necessitate the creation of separate classes. The existing rights of the creditors that were to be discharged by the scheme were the same for all creditors and all creditors were being conferred with the same rights under the scheme. The court was satisfied that the large majority of creditors voting in favour of the scheme fairly represented the interests of the creditors as a whole. There was nothing to suggest that they were acting *mala fide* or for some collateral purpose that was adverse to the interests of the creditors as a whole.

---

however, provide that creditors with different interests should be treated in separate classes which reflect those interests.

The UNCITRAL *Legislative Guide* states that the normal ranking of claims under insolvency law should be respected by the plan and that similarly ranked creditors should be treated equally.[67] The 'absolute priority' principle is also a fundamental part of the US Chapter 11. The principle requires that unless creditors are to be paid in full, or unless each class of creditors consents, the company's old shareholders are not entitled to receive or retain any property through the restructuring

---

[67]   See UNCITRAL *Legislative Guide*, Recommendations 148, 149 and 152(e).

process on account of their old shares. Effectively, it provides the senior creditors with the right to appropriate the entire going concern surplus. The principle was originally applied to prevent senior creditors and shareholders from colluding to squeeze out junior creditors[68] and, more recently, law and economics scholars have argued that deviations from the priority rules that apply outside insolvency are too costly and will result in increases in the cost of borrowing: lenders adjust their rates to reflect the fact that shareholders retain some value that would otherwise have gone to the lenders. Put another way, the failure to enforce the absolute priority rule will affect investment decisions, drive up the cost of capital and distort allocations between equity and debt. On the other hand, it may be that these propositions are based on perfect market theories that are not necessarily sound in practice.[69]

It does not appear that the 'absolute priority' principle is expressly incorporated in the laws of many, if any, EU Member States, though no doubt this issue would be considered in many states where courts have to address the overall fairness of a plan, whether any creditor has received an unfair advantage and whether a reasonable creditor and a member of the class concerned could have voted in favour of the plan.

6.11   NECESSARY MAJORITIES

Apart from respecting or not respecting pre-insolvency entitlements, EU Member States also differ on the relevant majorities in respect of obtaining approval of a restructuring plan. Estonia requires a majority in number plus two-thirds in value of each affected class. For Finland, the requirements are more than 50 per cent in number and value of creditors participating in the voting. French conciliation agreements are only binding on those who agree to them, whereas with Sauvegarde procedures, a two-thirds majority is required in respect of those who vote in each committee plus two-thirds of bondholders. Germany requires a majority in number plus a majority in value of creditors in the group. Greece requires

---

[68]   National Bankruptcy Review Commission Report, *Bankruptcy: The Next Twenty Years* (1997), p. 547.

[69]   See generally M.J. Roe and F. Tung, 'Breaking Bankruptcy Priority: How Rent-Seeking Upends the Creditors' Bargain' (2013) 99 *Virginia Law Review* 1235, and the comment at 1237: 'The bankruptcy process is in fact rife with rent-seeking, as creditors and their professionals contest existing distribution rules and seek categorical changes to improve their private bankruptcy returns. Priority is not in fact absolute. It is often up for grabs.'

the consent of the holders of at least 60 per cent in value of claims against the debtor, including at least 40 per cent of secured claims. For Latvia, the requirement is that of consent from the holders of more than two-thirds in value of secured claims and more than half in value of unsecured claims.

Part of the complexity and variation in Member States is accounted for by the fact that is some cases majorities are determined by reference only to those creditors actually voting and in others to the total number of creditors, whether voting or not. There are three possible approaches. One is to say that creditors not voting are deemed to have voted in favour of the plan; another approach is to say that those not voting are deemed to have voted against the plan; where the third approach, a *via media*, in effect disregards the votes of those not voting. Italy appears to illustrate the first approach in that it seems that the relevant majority is that of a majority in value of affected creditors eligible to vote but if an eligible creditor does not actually vote his vote is deemed to be in favour of the plan. In Lithuania, on the other hand, at least two-thirds in value of creditor claims must be voted in favour of the plan. The new procedure in Luxembourg is symptomatic of the third approach in that there is a requirement for a majority in number and a majority in value of the total claims but in both cases only among those voting.

Other countries may distinguish between 'connected' and 'non-connected' creditors. For instance, in the UK CVA scheme, the require-ment is that of 75 per cent by value of those voting, including at least 50 per cent of those with debts not connected with the company. In Romania, debt arrangement procedures require a 75 per cent majority in value of all claims; connected creditors may only vote if they would receive less than they would do in bankruptcy proceedings.

Other countries may have majority requirements that vary depending on either the percentage of creditors voting, or the extent of the 'haircut' that creditors will suffer as a result of the proceedings. In Portugal, the requirement is either two-thirds in value of creditors provided that at least one-third in value of creditors vote or more than 50 per cent in value of total debt. In Sweden, it is necessary to distinguish for this purpose between restructuring and composition proceedings. For the former, an IP should attest that at least 40 per cent of affected creditors who hold at least 40 per cent in value of claims accept the restructuring proposal. For composition proceedings, thresholds are higher: at least 60 per cent in numbers voting and total value of claims must approve if the payment is 50 per cent or more. For steeper discounts on the debt, the threshold for acceptance increases to 75 per cent.

6.12 ROLE OF THE COURT, INCLUDING CONSIDERATION OF FINANCIAL VIABILITY OF RESTRUCTURING PLAN

Recommendation 21 provides that in the interests of legal certainty, restructuring plans which affect the interests of dissenting creditors should be confirmed by a court in order to become binding. This appears to be the norm in nearly all EU Member States, though the United Kingdom is a partial exception in that company voluntary arrangements (CVAs) do not have to be approved by a court. In fact, they only come to court if challenged by a dissenting creditor on procedural grounds or on grounds of unfair prejudice.[70] The majority of large scale corporate restructurings in the United Kingdom, however, are accomplished by means of schemes of arrangement which are considered and approved by the court. The scheme of arrangement is outside Regulation 1346/2000 and the recast Insolvency Regulation since it is not listed in Annex A. Insolvency proceedings covered by either Regulation are those listed in Annex A. Nevertheless, it has proved extremely attractive as a restructuring vehicle of choice for companies incorporated outside the United Kingom, since the UK courts have jurisdiction to sanction a scheme if the company is deemed to have 'sufficient connection' with the United Kingdom irrespective of where it was incorporated. In practice, a loan facility governed by English law will be enough to pass the sufficient connection test.[71]

According to Recommendation 23, Member States should ensure that courts can reject restructuring plans which clearly do not have any prospect of preventing the insolvency of the debtor and ensuring the viability of the business, for example because new financing needed to continue its activity is not foreseen. Financial viability of the debtor is a matter that is addressed in some states but not in others. For instance, Finland considers viability in some circumstances. Creditors vote in separate classes according to the priority status of their claims but, under certain strict conditions, approval may be granted if not all groups of affected creditors vote in favour of the plan. In this circumstance, there must be sufficient evidence that the restructuring is likely to succeed. On the other hand, in Italy, Luxembourg and Lithuania, financial viability is not a matter that is within the purview of the court.

In many countries, financial viability might be considered indirectly perhaps as part of overall fairness; whether a restructuring plan is likely

---

[70] Insolvency Act 1986, s. 6.
[71] *In Re Magyar Telecom BV* [2013] EWHC 3800 (Ch).

to be carried or whether the debtor is reasonably likely to fulfil the promises it made in the plan. Examples in this regard include Austria, where the court will consider whether the restructuring plan is likely to be implemented, and Hungary, where a debt restructuring agreement must have been concluded in good faith and not contain provisions which are clearly and manifestly unfavourable or unreasonable from the point of view of creditors as a whole, or certain groups of creditors. Sweden also typifies this approach in that the court may consider special reasons for not approving the composition, such as the fact that there is no likelihood that its terms will be fulfilled. Under the proposed new procedure in the Netherlands, the court will also assess whether the composition is necessary and not unfairly prejudicial towards one or more creditors or that the debtor is not reasonably likely to fulfil the promises made in the plan.

In the United States, a 'feasibility' review is a strongly entrenched part of Chapter 11. Section 1129(a)(11) says that for a plan to be confirmed it must be feasible. This involves the court in finding that plan confirmation is not likely to be followed by liquidation or the need for further financial restructuring of the company or any successor to the company under the plan, unless the plan itself proposes liquidation. To see whether the feasibility standard has been achieved, the courts may look at a number of matters or factors affecting a company, including (1) adequacy of the capital structure; (2) earning power; (3) general economic conditions and the identity and abilities of the firm's management.[72]

The feasibility standard may help to ensure that companies come out of Chapter 11 with adequate capital structures. On the other hand, there is a view that conducting a financial viability review is more a matter for investment bankers than for judges. One leading bankruptcy judge has commented:[73]

> A judge is bound by the record that is presented. If you have good lawyers, they will present a record that establishes feasibility. If the judge reviews the disclosure statement and things leap out, I think the judge will ask questions. But if you have good lawyers and they're doing their job right, the likelihood

---

[72] See *Consolidated Rock Products Co.* v. *Du Bois*, 312 US 510, 525 (1941): 'Findings as to the earning capacity of an enterprise are essential to a determination of the feasibility as well as the fairness of a plan of reorganization. Whether or not the earnings may reasonably be expected to meet the interest and dividend requirements of the new securities is a sine qua non to a determination of the integrity and practicality of the new capital structure.'

[73] See L.M. LoPucki, *Courting Failure: How Competition for Big Cases is Corrupting the Bankruptcy Courts* (Ann Arbor, MI, University of Michigan Press, 2005), p.105.

of things jumping out is pretty slim. Lawyers may disclose assumption, but in the absence of discovery or something being flagrant on its face, it's hard for a judge to know what's wild assumption and what's not.

The UNCITRAL *Legislative Guide* takes on board these concerns. It states (at 228–9) that it is:

> highly desirable that the law not require or permit the court to review the eco-nomic and commercial basis of the decision of creditors . . . nor that it be asked to review particular aspects of the plan in terms of their economic feasibility, unless the circumstances in which this power can be exercised are narrowly defined or the court has the competence and experience to exercise the neces-sary level of commercial and economic judgement.

6.13   CREDITOR CRAM-DOWN

Recommendation 26 provides that a restructuring plan which is confirmed by a court should be binding upon each creditor affected by and identified in the plan.

This Recommendation raises the issue of creditor 'cram-down', that is the extent to which a restructuring plan can be made binding on dissent-ing creditors. The term 'cram-down' can be understood in two senses. In one sense, it simply means that if the necessary majority within a class approve a plan then the plan becomes binding on the other class members. But it can also be used in the sense of cramming down a dissenting class in its entirety, that is forcing a majority of the class to accept a scheme against their wishes. Cross-class creditor cram-down is a notable feature of Chapter 11 of the US Bankruptcy Code. A class of creditors, including secured creditors in exceptional circumstances, can be crammed down in the United States, that is forced to accept a restructuring plan against its wishes provided that at least one other class of impaired creditors has accepted the plan.

Before an objecting class of creditors can be crammed down, however, an onerous list of requirements must be met. To cram down a secured class, the requirements of sections 1129(b)(1) and 1129(b)(2)(A) must be satisfied. Under section 1129(b)(1), the plan must not discriminate unfairly and must be fair and equitable. This requires that creditors who are similarly situated should be treated in a comparable fashion. *A fortiori*, it would, for example, be unfair discrimination for a junior creditor to receive a higher interest rate than that imposed on a senior creditor on the same property. The fair and equitable standard means that an unrea-sonable risk of the plan's failure should not be imposed on the secured creditor. It also includes the section 1129(b)(2)(A) requirement such that a secured creditor must receive one of three alternatives:

(a) retention of its secured interest plus sufficient deferred payments to equal the present value of the collateral;
(b) sale of the collateral with the creditor's security interest attaching to the proceeds of sale;
(c) the creditor's receipt of the 'indubitable equivalent' of its security interest.

Restructuring laws in some EU Member States require that all classes of creditors support a plan for it to be approved by the court. France and the United Kingdom are typical in this regard. A few laws, however, allow support by some classes to make the plan binding on other classes that do not support the plan. For example, a simple majority of the classes may be required. Italy exemplifies this approach with approval from a majority of classes binding the remainder. Ireland goes even further, with cram-down rules that are modelled on the US Chapter 11.

Other states adopt an approach whereby a restructuring plan may nevertheless be made binding on dissenting classes that do not support the plan, provided that certain more general conditions are met. For instance, in Finland under certain strict conditions, including sufficient evidence that the restructuring is likely to succeed, court sanction may be given to a restructuring plan notwithstanding the disapproval of certain creditor groups. In Germany, if all classes have not agreed, the court may still approve a restructuring plan if a majority of classes agree; the 'liquidation' or 'best interests of creditors' test is considered to be satisfied and the plan generally is considered to be fair. In the Netherlands, under the proposed new regime, the court may approve a restructuring plan against the objections of dissenting classes if it considers that these classes could not reasonably have voted the way they did. The court will also assess whether the plan is necessary and not unfairly prejudicial towards one or more creditors. In Poland, the court may override a dissenting class if at least two-thirds in value of total creditors approve the plan and the dissenting groups receive at least as much under the plan as they would do in a liquidation. In Romania, there are somewhat different requirements for cross-class creditor cram-down to become permissible. At least 30 per cent of creditors by value must accept the plan and the plan has to provide fair and equitable treatment; respect the priority of claims; and provide a dissenting creditor with at least as much as they would receive in a liquidation.

6.14 DISSENTING CREDITORS (REMEDIES)

Generally, throughout the EU Member States, creditors may challenge confirmation of a restructuring plan at the confirmation hearing, though Lithuania may be an exception in this respect. They may argue that the statutory grounds set out in the law for the approval of a restructuring plan have not been met and therefore the plan should be rejected. In the Netherlands, for example, creditors may object on the basis that the plan is being put forward for improper reasons or that it is unfairly prejudicial towards certain groups, or in general on the basis that the conditions for court approval of the restructuring plan are not satisfied.

In many cases, however, including in Latvia, the right to object is hedged about with tight procedural restrictions. For instance, in Germany creditors may contest the fairness of the plan before the court and argue that the plan provides them with less favourable treatment than they would otherwise receive. Nevertheless, these objections will not hold up confirmation of a plan and instead the court will compensate creditors for the violation of their rights. In Italy, where creditors have not been divided into classes, then only 20 per cent in value of creditors may raise an objection. If there are classes, then only creditors within a dissenting class may object.

6.15 ENCOURAGING NEW FINANCE

There are certain provisions in the new approach to business failure and insolvency to encourage new financing in respect of ailing businesses. It is provided in Recommendations 27 and 28 that new financing which forms part of a restructuring plan that is confirmed by a court should be exempted from civil and criminal liability and not be rendered invalid as an act detrimental to the general body of creditors.

Most insolvency laws contain transactional avoidance provisions that strike at advantage gaining by creditors in the period immediately prior to the commencement of formal insolvency proceedings, though the length of this 'suspect' or 'vulnerability' period may vary greatly depending on the state, the nature of the transaction, whether it is in favour of a person connected with the debtor, and the type of avoidance action. Transactions in favour of 'connected' parties generally attract a longer vulnerability period. In principle, transactional avoidance mechanisms are capable of being used to attack the provision of new finance that forms part of a 'pre-insolvency' restructuring process. In the vast majority of cases, however, even if there are no formal legal provisions, new finance is likely in practice to be safe from attack under these transactional avoidance or claw-back provisions. The conditions for avoidance will not have been made out because the provisions generally catch what might be termed incongruent transactions where the creditor is receiving disproportionate benefits, such as security for an existing unsecured debt or repayment of an existing loan facility. In a new finance situation, there is no disproportionate benefit but rather a reciprocal flow of benefits and obligations from creditor to debtor and vice versa. The creditor is providing new finance and in return gets the benefit of the debtor's promise to repay and possibly security or a guarantee from a third party reinforcing the debtor's commitment to repay the advance. Only a few states, such as Romania, Slovakia and Slovenia, go further and specifically protect new finance provision from clawback actions. Generally, see the discussion in Chapter 4 and particularly 4.12 ('New Financing').

6.16   CONCLUSIONS ON A NEW APPROACH TO BUSINESS FAILURE AND INSOLVENCY

Recital 1 of the Preamble to the EC Recommendation on a new approach to business failure states that the objective of the Recommendation is to ensure that viable enterprises in financial difficulties, wherever they are located in the Union, have access to national insolvency frameworks which enable them to restructure at an early stage with a view to preventing their insolvency. This is designed to 'maximise the total value to creditors, employees, owners and the economy as a whole'. Recital 12 states that 'removing the barriers to effective restructuring of viable companies in financial difficulties contributes to saving jobs and also benefits the wider economy'.

It is important to note, however, the limitations of business restructuring law. The law can create an environment that facilitates negotiations on financial deleveraging, the adjustment of debts and other ongoing obligations. It cannot, however, mend a bad business model. If a particular company is exclusively committed to the manufacture or supply of a product for which there is no market, then the law cannot fix this. The owners of the company may, for whatever reason, be obliged to prop up the company and preserve jobs indefinitely but nevertheless, it is likely that more productive use of the assets may be made elsewhere. Having a liquidation law that facilitates the move of assets away from inefficient enterprises may contribute significantly to the overall health of the economy.

In a business restructuring context, parties bargain in the shadow of the framework provided by liquidation law.[74] The law may create a context that is conducive to business restructuring, *inter alia*, by allowing majority decisions and also by facilitating the continuation of the enterprise during a period of ongoing negotiations. Nevertheless, the parties must consider the alternatives if the negotiations fail. Liquidation and debt enforcement law provides these alternatives and liquidation law is ultimately a distributional exercise: 'who gets paid what'. Liquidation law reflects distributional norms and interest group politics rather than being purely an exercise in abstract economic efficiency.[75] Provisions in national insolvency law giving priority to certain categories of claim express the political bargains that have been reached in that particular country.

The global financial crisis has brought about shocks of an asymmetric nature in the European Union. These have produced political instability and exacerbated difficulties in particular countries. The potential implications of restructuring law for employment therefore cannot be ignored in a European Union context. Promoting restructuring law reform at the EU level that fosters growth and, even indirectly, facilitates employment, seems not only to be worthwhile but also a political imperative.[76]

An efficient business restructuring law should enhance the overall value of an enterprise and thereby maximize the potential for growth and employment. These ideas are at the core of the EC Recommendation. This study has shown that some Member States have either not implemented the Recommendation at all or implemented it in a divergent way and this points to the case for legislative action. In short, gaps and inconsistencies in the implementation of the Recommendation suggest the need for a mandatory measure of legislative harmonization. In 'firming up' the Recommendation, and making it part of the formal legislative landscape, there are, however, a number of issues to be considered. These include the following:

(1) What is the relationship between any 'mandatory' Europe-wide

---

[74] See generally, S. Paterson, 'Bargaining in Financial Restructuring: Market Norms, Legal Rights and Regulatory Standards' (2014) 14 *Journal of Corporate Law Studies* 333; *Rethinking the Role of the Law of Corporate Distress in the Twenty-First Century*, Law Society and Economy Working Paper Series, WPS 27-2014 (December 2014).

[75] See generally, A.J. Levitin, 'Bankrupt Politics and the Politics of Bankruptcy' (2012) 97 *Cornell Law Review* 1399.

[76] But see Eidenmuller and Van Zweiten, *Restructuring the European Business Enterprise* (n. 3 above) 26, suggesting that the Recommendation in its focus on restructuring financially distressed firms 'appears to overlook economic reality'.

restructuring regime as implemented in national law and existing national law provisions?

(2) If existing national law sits side by side with a new EU wide regime, what incentives should be in place to ensure that the EU regime is not effectively supplanted in practice by the national regime; in other words, that the EU regime is not 'crowded out' by national law?

(3) Particular attention needs to be paid to the design of particular aspects of any EU scheme, including whether voting of creditors in classes should be required.

(4) To facilitate participation by foreign creditors, should any EU regime go beyond requiring voting either in person or by proxy, where a formal voting process is envisaged; in other words, whether express 'authorization' should be given for 'virtual' meetings or is such a provision more appropriately to be considered in the context of general corporate law?

(5) It is also important to consider the majorities required for creditor cram-down, that is the percentage approval level when a plan is deemed to have been accepted notwithstanding the fact that some creditors still object.

(6) The issue of cross-class creditor cram-down is particularly controversial as it strips creditors of many of the advantages entailed by debts being assigned to a particular class.

(7) If legislative authorization for super-priority new finance is to be given, then the circumstances, if any, under which such new finance gains priority over existing creditors without their consent needs to be carefully considered and worked out.

APPENDIX: DATA TABLES

Table 6A.1   Review of Commission Recommendation of 12 March 2014 on a new approach to business failure and insolvency

Country	1.1 Early stage restructuring proceedings	1.2 Access to procedure	1.3 Conditions for access	1.4 Court decision necessary?
Austria	Yes, procedures under the Corporate Reorganization Law which came into force in 1997 Under amendments to the Bankruptcy Act in 2010 it is also possible to attempt a restructuring through the bankruptcy process	Debtor	A need for restructuring and the fact that the debtor is not actually insolvent	Yes
Belgium	Yes, since 1997 and new law since 2009	Debtor	Once the debtor believes that the continuity of its business is threatened in the short or long term, it may submit an application. A number of documents have to be filed with the court application, including proposals to restore the profitability of the company	Yes
Bulgaria	No such procedure			

Table 6A.1 (continued)

Country	1.1 Early stage restructuring proceedings	1.2 Access to procedure	1.3 Conditions for access	1.4 Court decision necessary?
Croatia	Yes, new pre-bankruptcy procedure	Debtor or creditor if debtor gives its consents	Need to establish imminent insolvency and certain documents, including those containing financial information, have to be filed with the court	Yes
Cyprus	Yes, under new examinership procedure which is very much modelled on the Irish examinership procedure	Debtor and creditors	Court may appoint examiner where there is reasonable prospect of survival of both the company and the whole or part of its undertaking as a going concern	Yes
Czech Republic	Yes, but the statutory possibilities are tied to formal insolvency proceedings New Insolvency Code came into force in 2008	Debtor	Debtor is required to provide certain financial information, a list of creditors and the written agreement of the majority of creditors to a stay/moratorium	Yes
Denmark				
Estonia	Yes, Reorganization Act since 26 December 2008	Debtor	Undertaking is likely to become insolvent; sustainable management is likely after the restructuring	Yes
Finland	Yes, under the Restructuring of Enterprises Act where the debtor is at risk of insolvency	Both	When the debtor is at risk of insolvency, normally opened on debtor's application but creditor can also initiate proceedings	Yes

France	Five procedures: ad hoc mandate, conciliation, Safeguard, Accelerated Safeguard and Accelerated Financial Safeguard, as well as administration (*redressement judiciare*) Liquidation Safeguard (Sauvegarde) was introduced in 2005: Accelerated Financial Safeguard (AFS) in 2010 and Accelerated Safeguard (AS) in 2014	Debtor	Ad hoc mandate; any solvent company that is likely to face financial difficulties Debtor may request opening of conciliation proceedings even if it is insolvent provided it has not been so for more than 45 days Safeguard: proceedings accessible by solvent debtors with material financial difficulties; same for AFS but where debt is essentially financial AS: debtor may be insolvent but not for more than 45 days Financial thresholds for all Sauvegarde proceedings but lower for AS	In all cases yes Ad hoc mandate and conciliation are confidential proceedings, whereas all forms of Sauvegarde are public
Germany	There are such procedures under German law	Debtor	A risk of illiquidity or over-indebtedness and the procedure envisaged is not obviously futile	Yes
Greece	Different legal possibilities but the most general one is that of 'recovery procedure' under a law of 2011	In general, only by the debtor but special liquidation procedures can also be accessed by creditors	In general, the debtor must foresee upcoming liquidity problems and potential default in payments	Yes for all types of proceedings

Table 6A.1 (continued)

Country	1.1 Early stage restructuring proceedings	1.2 Access to procedure	1.3 Conditions for access	1.4 Court decision necessary?
Hungary	Procedure dating from 1991 under which debtor may seek a composition with its creditors, but referred to as 'bankruptcy proceedings'	Debtor	At least a situation of imminent insolvency	Yes
Ireland	Yes, since 1990 through the examinership procedure. Schemes of arrangement are also available under company law rules similar to that in the United Kingdom but examinership is the preferred restructuring tool	Normally the debtor	Available when the company 'is, or is likely to be unable to pay its debts' (now Companies Act 2014, s. 509). Therefore the examinership can commence as a preventative insolvency measure, even where the company is insolvent, but most likely when the company is on the brink of insolvency	Yes
Italy	There are a number of potentially overlapping procedures that facilitate a composition or restructuring but it is questionable the extent to which these procedures may apply at the pre-insolvency stage	Debtor	Financial crisis: in the case of restructuring proceedings the debtor must first obtain the consent of creditors representing 60% in value of debts and then seek court approval for the restructuring agreement	Yes

Latvia	There are so-called legal protection proceedings designed to enable a debtor to settle debt obligations in the event of financial difficulties	Debtor	If the debtor is facing financial difficulties or expects them	Yes
Lithuania	There are procedures for restructuring of enterprises that entered into force in 2001	Generally, the debtor	Enterprise is in financial difficulties	Yes
Luxembourg	Existing procedures that allow a debtor to restructure its debt with the consent of a majority of its creditors outside of insolvency proceedings; allows limited suspension of payments; to be replaced by a new preventive procedure in the process of enactment	Debtor	New procedures may be accessed as soon as the continuity of the business is threatened	Yes
Malta	Company rescue procedure since 2015	Debtor or more than half in value of debtor's creditors	Possibility available for a company which is unable to pay its debts or imminently likely to become unable to pay its debts'	Yes
Netherlands	Under current law, a restructuring agreement outside of insolvency proceedings in principle requires the consent of all affected creditors A legislative proposal for a new	Debtor and creditors	New proposal provides no criterion of imminent insolvency where the debtor presents the reorganization plan. A creditor may only present a reorganization plan, however, if it is foreseeable that the debtor	No court decision necessary for initiating proceedings leading to a restructuring

Table 6A.1 (continued)

Country	1.1 Early stage restructuring proceedings	1.2 Access to procedure	1.3 Conditions for access	1.4 Court decision necessary?
	procedure for the composition of debts outside bankruptcy, in line with the EC Recommendation, is expected to be presented to Parliament in 2016		will not be able to meet its due and payable debts, and the creditor has given the debtor a reasonable period to present a plan	agreement outside of insolvency
Poland	Possible to commence rehabilitation proceedings to restructure the debts of an entrepreneur who is at risk of insolvency Under the new regime four types of restructuring proceedings will be available	Debtor	Currently, application to commence rehabilitation proceedings must be accompanied by a rehabilitation plan Under the new regime, debtor must at least be threatened by insolvency	Opening of proceedings does not need to be formally approved by a court
Portugal	Two procedures: Out-of-court System for the Recovery of Companies (SIREVE) from 2012 Special Revitalization Proceeding (PER), also from 2012 but altered in 2015	SIREVE: debtor but must identify creditors willing to negotiate that represent at least one-third of the debtors' total liabilities PER: debtor	Both procedures are designed to apply to companies (SIREVE) and to both natural persons and companies (PER) that are in difficult financial situations but are not actually insolvent For SIREVE debtor must submit a draft restructuring plan and for PER must submit a statement	For SIREVE not a court decision but an administrative entity (IAMPEI) exercises a filter mechanism in that the debtor must make use

	with at least one creditor	whereby debtor and at least one creditor indicates their willingness to work towards restructuring		of a mandatory electronic diagnostic made available for the analysis of its financial affairs For **PER** yes, but it is just a formality
Romania	Yes, the ad hoc mandate and arrangement procedures introduced in 2009 and reformed in 2014. There is also a judicial reorganization procedure since 2014	Debtor for the preventative procedures. Judicial reorganization procedures can be initiated at the request of creditors holding at least 20% of total claims	Debtor is in financial difficulties; certain information is required to be filed with the court	Yes
Slovakia	Yes, a procedure in operation since 2006	Debtor and creditors	Debtor must get a written statement from an IP recommending adoption of the restructuring procedure in the light of the debtor's financial position	Yes
Slovenia	Yes, new preventive restructuring procedure in operation since end of 2013	Debtor	Strong probability that debtor will become insolvent within the next year	Yes

Table 6A.1 (continued)

Country	1.1 Early stage restructuring proceedings	1.2 Access to procedure	1.3 Conditions for access	1.4 Court decision necessary?
Spain	Yes, in particular under a 2013 law which amended the Bankruptcy Code and which was itself amended in 2015	Debtor it appears	Debtor is in the vicinity of insolvency	No
Sweden	Yes, since 1996	Debtors and creditors	Inability to pay debts within a short period	Yes
United Kingdom	Yes, there are a number of such procedures: schemes of arrangement, administration and company voluntary arrangements	Debtors and creditors	Schemes of arrangement are very flexible, they may be used by completely solvent companies. The other procedures generally require likely inability to pay debts	No

Table 6A.2 Debtor in possession (points 6(b) and 9)

Country	2.1 Type of transactions debtor may conclude during procedure	2.2 Is IP appointed by court? If so, powers of IP
Austria	Generally, debtor in possession	An auditor is appointed by the court who considers the financial position of the debtor
Belgium	Debtor in possession proceedings and so debtor has standard powers of management in relation to the business	No IP but a judge is appointed throughout the proceedings who makes reports to the court
Bulgaria	NA	NA
Croatia	Standard commercial transactions as debtor remains in control of its business	Yes, supervises the business activities of the debtor
Cyprus	Retains normal management powers	Yes, IP appointed to examine the affairs of the company and to prepare restructuring/exit plan. May apply to the court to assume management powers
Czech Republic	Debtor in possession except in liquidation	IP, but in debtor in possession phases, the IP does not have the power to deal in assets of the estate. IP always in charge of listing assets, registering and verifying claims, and conducting resulting litigation
Denmark		
Estonia	May carry on business in the ordinary way in respect of 'normal' commercial transactions	Yes, examines the financial situation of the debtor and generally monitors its activities; prepares restructuring plan
Finland	May carry out standard commercial transactions in ordinary course of business	Yes, general monitoring and oversight role and prepares restructuring plan
France	For ad hoc mandate and conciliation debtor in possession, but in Sauvegarde the debtor is subject to supervision by an IP	In ad hoc mandate the court appoints an official who assists the company in trying to resolve its differences and come to an agreement with creditors but does not interfere with management

Table 6A.2 (continued)

Country	2.1 Type of transactions debtor may conclude during procedure	2.2 Is IP appointed by court? If so, powers of IP
France		In Sauvegarde, one or more IPs are appointed who supervise the debtor, safeguard the interests of creditors and assist with the negotiations on the restructuring plan
Germany	Standard commercial transactions, subject to the general supervision of an IP	Yes, an IP is appointed who supervises and monitors the debtor's activities
Greece	In recovery procedures, debtor remains in control of its property though exceptionally the court may impose special measures	No IPs as such in Greece but exceptionally a special administrator may be appointed by the courts to take full or partial control of the management of the debtor's business
Hungary	In general, may carry on its business in the ordinary way subject to monitoring and supervision by special administrator appointed by the court	Yes, with general monitoring and supervisory role
Ireland	Debtor in possession and so standard commercial transactions	Yes, duty to prepare to restructuring/exit plan but may apply to court to take over management powers of debtor in certain circumstances
Italy	It depends on the type of proceedings. In composition proceedings the debtor can continue to manage the business under the supervision of a court appointed officer	In composition proceedings, the court appoints an official to supervise the debtor and who also attempts to establish the causes of the financial difficulties
Latvia	Debtor in possession and so standard commercial transactions	Yes, but may (in out of court legal protection proceedings must) be chosen by a majority of creditors; generally supervises the debtor and may draw up a restructuring plan
Lithuania	Standard commercial transactions	Yes, supervision of the debtor and preparation of a restructuring plan

Luxembourg	New procedure is based on debtor in possession but in cases of serious misconduct or manifest bad faith of the debtor, the court may appoint an administrator	Generally, no IP is appointed unless requested by the debtor or where there is a transfer of undertakings to another legal entity
Malta	Management displacement procedure and so debtor loses essential powers	Yes, takes over powers of management
Netherlands	New proposal provides for a debtor in possession procedure	Under the new procedure no IP is appointed. Procedure seems to be modelled on the UK scheme of arrangement
Poland	Transactions within the ordinary course of management of the business	Yes, a court supervisor is appointed who monitors the activities of the debtor and under the new regime will prepare a restructuring plan
Portugal	Day-to-day operation of its business in both procedures	In SIREVE, no but in PER, yes. IP tries to safeguard the legitimate interests of creditors and ensure the parties do not delay the negotiation process
Romania	Generally, debtor in possession	This varies with the type of procedure and the degree of formality in the procedure but generally it is to draw up a restructuring plan or to assist in the formulation of such a plan; to settle a list of creditors; and in judicial reorganization to monitor the debtor and identify the causes of the business failure
Slovakia	Standard commercial transactions	IP appointed by the court but chosen by the debtor or creditors; IP supervises the debtor's activities
Slovenia	Debtor in possession	No IP appointed
Spain	Debtor in possession procedure	Bankruptcy mediator is appointed who draws up a payment proposal
Sweden	Standard commercial transactions but subject to monitoring and control by an insolvency administrator	Yes, an IP is appointed who supervises the debtor

Table 6A.2 (continued)

Country	2.1 Type of transactions debtor may conclude during procedure	2.2 Is IP appointed by court? If so, powers of IP
United Kingdom	Schemes of arrangement are debtor in possession procedures but administration is a management displacement procedure In a CVA the debtor has control over day-to-day operations unless the procedure is combined with an administration	It depends on the type of procedure: in a scheme of arrangement there is no provision for an IP but if a scheme is being proposed with creditors they may exercise a degree of de facto control Administration involves management displacement in favour of an IP In a standalone CVA, an IP maintains surveillance over the debtor and later ensures that it complies with the terms of the CVA

Table 6A.3   Stay of individual enforcement actions (points 10 to 14)

Country	3.1 Types of enforcement action stayed	3.2 Automatic or discretionary on application to court?	3.4 Opening of insolvency proceedings suspended?	3.5 Duration of stay	3.6 May the stay be lifted? Under what conditions?
Austria	No stay	Not applicable	No	Not applicable	Not applicable
Belgium	Stay covers generally executions against the debtor's real and personal property but security over receivables and certain types of secured claim may still be enforced	Automatic	Yes	For the duration of the procedure	No unless the procedure is terminated prematurely
Bulgaria	NA	NA	NA	NA	NA
Croatia	Stay covers lawsuits and enforcement actions but does not bar actions by secured creditors and employees	Yes, automatic	Yes	Generally, for 120 days but this period may be extended for a further 90 days	The stay lasts as long as the restructuring proceedings last
Cyprus	All enforcement action but secured creditor has limited window to enforce security	An inherent part of the application being granted	Yes	Initial period of 4 months and maximum 6 months	Yes

Table 6A.3 (continued)

Country	3.1 Types of enforcement action stayed	3.2 Automatic or discretionary on application to court?	3.4 Opening of insolvency proceedings suspended?	3.5 Duration of stay	3.6 May the stay be lifted? Under what conditions?
Czech Republic	Stay of most collection efforts by the creditors and also set-off is prohibited, but a majority of creditors must have supported the proposal for a moratorium	Automatic	Yes, it seems for the duration of the moratorium	4 months	It seems that creditors may apply for the lifting of the stay if their position is jeopardized
Denmark					
Estonia	Seems to cover both secured and unsecured creditors but not claims arising from an employment relationship	Automatic	Yes, but court can decide to terminate restructuring proceedings on the basis of bankruptcy petition	Continues until restructuring plan is approved or proceedings are terminated	No
Finland	Enforcement of both secured and unsecured claims	Automatic	Yes, court must order suspension of bankruptcy proceedings while a restructuring plan is being considered	Continues until restructuring plan is approved or proceedings are terminated	Generally, no, but special provisions apply to secured debts

Country					
France	Ad hoc mandate and conciliation are confidential procedures but the debtor may request a stay from the court In principle, the Sauvegarde stay covers enforcement of both unsecured and secured claims	In ad hoc mandate and conciliation a stay is dependent on an application to the court whereas in Sauvegarde it is automatic consequent on the opening of the proceedings AFS does not operate against trade creditors because they are not affected by the procedure	Ad hoc mandate and conciliation: no general suspension. In general, there is a suspension but in the case of a standard Sauvegarde if cessation of payments occurs during the observation period, the proceedings may be converted into insolvency proceedings	Ad hoc mandate and conciliation: no automatic stay, however directors may apply to the court for a grace period of up to 2 years on obligations to creditors (deferral/rescheduling of payment obligations) For Sauvegarde, the initial stay is for 6 months renewable twice up to 18 months in total AS: 3 months non-renewable AFS: one month renewable once	Conciliation grace periods are unusually accompanied by conditions and breach of the conditions will result in any restrictions on recovery being lifted The stay in Sauvegarde proceedings lasts until the end of those proceedings
Germany	May cover actions by both secured and unsecured creditors	Depends on a court order	Yes, for the period ordered by the court	No longer than 3 months	Yes, if the prerequisites are no longer met
Greece	Stay discretionary but potentially may affect secured claims but not generally enforcement of employee claims	No automatic stay but court ordered	Upon initiation of recovery procedure, applications by creditors to open bankruptcy proceedings are suspended	Generally, for 2 months or until approval of restructuring plan	Yes, a creditor may apply for lifting of the stay and court will lift the stay if satisfied that there is no reasonable prospect of the procedure being successful

Table 6A.3 (continued)

Country	3.1 Types of enforcement action stayed	3.2 Automatic or discretionary on application to court?	3.4 Opening of insolvency proceedings suspended?	3.5 Duration of stay	3.6 May the stay be lifted? Under what conditions?
Hungary	In general, enforcement of both secured and unsecured claims	Automatic	Yes	For an initial period of 120 days subject to a one year total	No
Ireland	Yes, stays on enforcement of secured and unsecured claims but secured creditor has a small window in which to take enforcement action	Interim stay when application made to court for appointment of examiner and then once application granted inherent part of procedure	Yes	Generally, so long as the debtor is in examinership, up to 4 months. Initially 70 days but may be extended up to 100 days	Yes, but court has a discretion and may lift the stay in accordance with the justice of the case before it
Italy	The stay applies to both secured and unsecured claims	Generally, automatic	Yes	It depends on the type of the proceedings; for example, in Concordato preventivo this stay may not be longer than 11 months	No, unless the restructuring procedure itself is brought to a premature end
Latvia	Covers secured as well as unsecured creditors	Generally, automatic	Yes	For the duration of the proceedings	Secured creditor may request the sale of secured property if the stay causes significant harm to the interests of this creditor

Lithuania	Covers secured as well as unsecured creditors	Automatic	Yes	Until court approval of a restructuring plan; must be filed with the court within 6 months	May be lifted in limited circumstances
Luxembourg	Under new procedure stay on both unsecured and creditors	Automatic, once all the procedures have been opened	Yes	New procedure: 6 months but may be extended up to a maximum of 12 months Old procedures: until whenever they terminate	Only when the procedure is terminated
Malta	Actions by secured and unsecured creditors	Automatic on commencement of the procedure	Yes	12 months and may be extended for two further periods of up to 2 months each	Not contemplated
Netherlands	No automatic stay under new proposal though the court may be asked to take action to protect interests of debtor and creditors	Under proposal stay is discretionary	Court may order suspension of bankruptcy proceedings while a restructuring plan is being considered	No specific duration but court may suspend the consideration of a bankruptcy petition for a reasonable period	Any unpaid creditor has a *prima facie* right to have the stay lifted. Moreover, the court should lift the stay where the restructuring plan has been rejected or is no longer likely to be accepted
Poland	The stay does not extend to secured claims and certain other claims Under the proposed changes, enforcement of security may be	Automatic	It seems that to the extent creditors are not affected by the stay they may still petition for the opening of bankruptcy proceedings	For the duration of the rehabilitation proceedings which are generally subject to a 4-month limit	Only when the proceedings are concluded

Table 6A.3 (continued)

Country	3.1 Types of enforcement action stayed	3.2 Automatic or discretionary on application to court?	3.4 Opening of insolvency proceedings suspended?	3.5 Duration of stay	3.6 May the stay be lifted? Under what conditions?
Poland	suspended if a judge considers that the secured property is necessary for the operation of the enterprise		Under the proposed new regime, bankruptcy cannot be declared while the restructuring proceedings are pending		
Portugal	Actions by both secured and unsecured creditors can in principle be stayed	Automatic upon commencement of the respective procedures but if creditors have indicated their unwillingness to take part in the SIREVE they are not bound by the stay	Yes, for the duration of the stay	Up to 3 months in SIREVE and 2 months in PER. In both cases may be extended for an additional month	Lifted when no longer necessary for facilitating the adoption of a restructuring plan and when the respective procedures are terminated
Romania	In the ad hoc mandate which is a confidential procedure there is no stay In the other	Generally discretionary on application to the court Judicial reorganization is regarded as a	For arrangement proceedings, yes Judicial reorganization proceedings are regarded	For up to 3 years	In the judicial reorganization procedure a secured creditor may seek the lifting of the stay on the basis that

	procedures any type of individual enforcement action may be stayed	formal insolvency procedure and the opening of this procedure brings about a stay	as insolvency proceedings		its security is not being adequately protected or is being impaired
Slovakia	Covers both secured and unsecured debts	Automatic	Yes	As long as the restructuring proceedings are taking place there is no fixed duration	No, except when the restructuring proceedings are terminated
Slovenia	Covers both secured and unsecured debts but it seems only financial debts	For enforcement of collateral the stay is dependent on application to the court	Yes	So long as the restructuring proceedings last but an application to confirm a restructuring plan must be filed at the latest within 7 months of the commencement of the procedure	It lasts as long as the restructuring proceedings last but creditors whose total financial claims account for at least 30% of all financial claims can request termination of the proceedings at any time
Spain	No judicial or extra-judicial executions	Automatic after communication to the court of the opening of the restructuring procedure	Yes, so it appears	3 months	Yes, the stay may be lifted in respect of assets that are not necessary for the continuity of the debtor's business

Table 6A.3 (continued)

Country	3.1 Types of enforcement action stayed	3.2 Automatic or discretionary on application to court?	3.4 Opening of insolvency proceedings suspended?	3.5 Duration of stay	3.6 May the stay be lifted? Under what conditions?
Sweden	The stay covers unsecured creditors and, in reorganization proceedings, secured creditors with the exception generally of those creditors with possessory security interests	Automatic upon the court's decision to open the restructuring proceedings	Yes	Initially for 3 months but exceptionally the stay may be extended for up to a year	If there is probable cause to believe the debtor will seriously jeopardize a creditor's rights, the court may lift the stay and open insolvency proceedings
United Kingdom	For schemes there is no stay but the other procedures generally involve a stay on actions by both secured and unsecured creditors	Apart from schemes automatic upon commencement of the procedure	Yes, except for schemes	In an administration may be up to a year in the first instance but this can be extended In a standalone CVA up to 3 months	Yes, if undue loss is being caused to a creditor by the administration stay or in the case of a CVA where the IP no longer believes that the purposes can be achieved

Table 6A.4 Restructuring plans (points 15 to 26)

Country	4.1 Rules on restructuring plans	4.2 Creditors in separate classes?	4.3 Voting: majority required?	4.4 Plan confined to affected creditors?	4.5 Conditions for court approval	4.6 Can dissenting creditors raise objections before a court?
Austria	General financial information about the debtor and how its financial health may be restored	There are no classes of creditors	A majority in number and a majority in value of those voting	Secured creditors are excluded from the restructuring plan unless they consent	Creditors must receive at least 30% of the value of their claims. The court will consider whether the restructuring plan is likely to be implemented and whether any creditor has received an unfair advantage	Yes, any creditors who did not consent to the plan may raise objections
Belgium	In general, the requirements of Recommendation 15 have to be met in the restructuring plan Creditors must receive under the plan at least 15% of what is due to them though differential treatment of creditors is allowed	No separate classes	A majority in number representing at least half in value of non-contested claims	Yes, only creditors whose rights are affected may vote	The statute lays down a number of detailed requirements It seems that the courts do not address financial viability as such but they will verify compliance with the statutory conditions and ensure there is no violation of public policy	Creditors may appeal against confirmation of a restructuring plan under strict conditions

Table 6A.4 (continued)

Country	4.1 Rules on restructuring plans	4.2 Creditors in separate classes?	4.3 Voting: majority required?	4.4 Plan confined to affected creditors?	4.5 Conditions for court approval	4.6 Can dissenting creditors raise objections before a court?
Bulgaria	May be restructuring plan in context of liquidation proceedings	Secured and unsecured creditors grouped separately	Each class has to approve by a majority of claims in the class; plan not approved where creditors holding more than half of admitted claims vote against, regardless of the classes	Such a distinction cannot be made	Requirements of the law observed; all creditors of the same class to be treated equally unless prejudiced creditors give their consent in writing	Yes, proceedings heard in camera but court may summon party who has raised the objection
Croatia	Plan must aim to improve the position of creditors and leave debtor in a position that it is able to meet its financial obligations as they fall due	Yes	Majority in number plus two-thirds in value of creditors	Secured creditors are not affected by the plan	Creditor must receive at least as much under the plan as he would reasonably expect to receive in the absence of a restructuring	Creditors may contest the plan on the basis that the statutory conditions have not been fulfilled

Cyprus	Plan must be designed to achieve purpose of procedure, i.e. rescue of both the company and the whole or any part of its undertaking as a going concern	Yes	Majority in number and majority in value of each class	Yes	Court must be satisfied that there is a reasonable viability prospect for the company on the basis of an independent expert report; takes into account the prospects of continuity of the business, employment positions and assesses whether the creditors of the company would be in a less favourable position if the company underwent winding-up	Yes, on the basis, *inter alia*, that their interests are being unfairly prejudiced or that the plan is not fair and equitable
Czech Republic	There are a number of detailed requirements and in general the objectives specified in point 15 of the European Commission Recommendation are met	Yes	Restructuring plan must be approved by a majority of the creditors and the court	No	Court must be satisfied that the plan complies with the law and the good faith test; creditor classes have either approved it or the lack of approval can be overcome by court decision; and post-commencement claims have been paid	Yes, objections may be raised before the court by creditors who objected to confirmation of the plan

Table 6A.4 (continued)

Country	4.1 Rules on restructuring plans	4.2 Creditors in separate classes?	4.3 Voting: majority required?	4.4 Plan confined to affected creditors?	4.5 Conditions for court approval	4.6 Can dissenting creditors raise objections before a court?
Denmark						
Estonia	Sets out expected economic position of enterprise after restructuring and impact of restructuring plan on employees	Creditors with the same rights form one class	Majority in number plus two-thirds in value of each affected class	Yes, creditors whose claims are not altered by the plan do not take part in the voting	In certain circumstances the court may accept a restructuring plan that has not been approved by creditors if less than one-half of creditors have voted and certain other conditions are fulfilled; opinion from 2 independent experts restructuring is likely to succeed; and no creditor is treated substantially less favourably or undertaking is an important employer	Yes, on the basis that there has been a procedural violation that affected the voting results or creditor is treated substantially less favourably

Finland	Generally, covers financial status of debtor and matters set out in Recommendation 15	Creditors in separate classes according to the priority status of their claims	More than 50% in number and value of creditors participating in the voting	Creditors not affected by the plan do not have a right to vote	General compliance with Recommendation 22; under certain strict conditions approval may be granted if not all groups of affected creditors vote in favour of the plan; must be sufficient evidence restructuring is likely to succeed	Yes
France	For conciliation agreements there should be provisions to ensure the continuation of the debtor's business and not to prejudice non-parties. In Sauvegarde, generally measures for alleviating the debtor's financial difficulties; the plan should also set out the consequences for employees. From 2014 any member of a	For conciliation no separate classes. For Sauvegarde proceedings, financial creditors and trade creditors are represented by separate committees and bondholders also vote differently	Conciliation agreements only binding on those who agree to them. For Sauvegarde two-thirds of those who vote in each committee and two-thirds of bondholders	Conciliation agreements do not affect those who are not parties to them. Sauvegarde proceedings in principle are confined to affected creditors, i.e. AFS binds only financial creditors and bondholders. But in the AS procedure, an approved plan binds all creditors	Conciliation agreement is a private agreement but may be endorsed by the court if certain conditions are fulfilled and this gives creditors certain advantages in respect of potential lender liability. If the plan involves a debt-equity swap then consent of two-thirds of shareholders is also required	Creditors may argue that their interests have not been adequately protected but there are strong incentives built into the Sauvegarde process to encourage sufficient agreement by creditors; the court

Table 6A.4 (continued)

Country	4.1 Rules on restructuring plans	4.2 Creditors in separate classes?	4.3 Voting: majority required?	4.4 Plan confined to affected creditors?	4.5 Conditions for court approval	4.6 Can dissenting creditors raise objections before a court?
	creditors' committee may put forward a restructuring plan					may impose uniform payment terms on creditors though not a 'haircut'
Germany	All relevant information about the rationale of the plan and its impact on the parties	Creditors divided into groups with all those in a group granted equal treatment unless all persons in the group agree otherwise	A majority in number plus a majority in value of creditors in the group plus the consent of all groups	Designed as a collective insolvency procedure so that in principle all stakeholders need to be involved; but subordinated creditors are not taken into account	Even if all the groups have not agreed, court approval is possible if a majority of groups agree and the court is satisfied that the dissenting group receive at least as much under the plan as they would do otherwise Court also considers overall fairness	Yes, they may contest the fairness of the plan and that the plan provides them with less favourable treatment than they would otherwise receive But these objections will not

288

Greece	In general, no limitation on the content of a restructuring plan but creditors in the same position must be equitably treated A restructuring through liquidation procedure requires that creditors receive at least 20% of the face value of their claims	No separate class	Holders of at least 60% in value of debtor's claims including at least 40% of secured claims	In principle, yes	Financial viability of debtor must be restored; dissenting creditors must receive at least as much as under enforcement or bankruptcy proceedings Creditors of the same class treated equally unless on the basis of important and justifiable business or social reasons	hold up confirmation of a plan and instead compensate creditors for violation of their rights Creditors who have not been duly notified of the proceeding may file an objection within 30 days of the publication of the court decision
Hungary	Essentially it is a plan for a composition with creditors and a meeting of creditors must be convened within 60 days of the opening of proceedings	Yes, including separate classes for secured and unsecured classes and for related party claims, etc.	It seems a majority in each separate class must approve the plan, probably a majority in value of those voting	It is explicitly stated that the restructuring plan will apply also to those creditors: (a) who have voted against the plan	Composition agreement must have been concluded in good faith and not contain provisions which are clearly and manifestly unfavourable or	Non-consenting creditors may object but their objections will be overruled if

Table 6A.4 (continued)

Country	4.1 Rules on restructuring plans	4.2 Creditors in separate classes?	4.3 Voting: majority required?	4.4 Plan confined to affected creditors?	4.5 Conditions for court approval	4.6 Can dissenting creditors raise objections before a court?
				or have failed to participate in voting (notwithstanding the fact they have been properly informed) and (b) to creditors for whom a reserve fund is established or security given	unreasonable from the point of view of creditors as a whole or certain groups of creditors Court does not assess viability of plan	they receive not less favourable treatment than consenting creditors
Ireland	Proposals should distinguish between classes of members and creditors whose claims and interests will or will not be impaired by the proposals; should also specify whatever changes are necessary in	Yes	Majority in value of class	Yes, in most cases but not necessarily	Equal treatment for each claim or interest of a particular class unless the holder agrees to less favourable treatment; cross-class cram-down possible if scheme not unfairly prejudicial and is fair and equitable towards any	Yes, on grounds of unfair prejudice, material irregularity or proposals put forward for an improper purpose

	the management and direction of the company for adequate supervision of the implementation of the proposals; also a description of the estimated financial outcome of a winding-up of the company for each class				impaired class; at least one impaired class must accept plan	
Italy	The plan must contain a list of creditors and indicate the effects of the proposed composition, etc. on claims or categories of claims	Division into separate classes is not necessary Creditors within the same class must be treated equally	Majority in value of affected creditors eligible to vote but in some proceedings, if an eligible creditor does not actually vote his vote is deemed to be in favour of the plan	Any creditor, even if secured, might be affected by the plan without his consent However, special safeguards are provided for non-consensual secured creditors	Court does not consider financial viability but in general compliance with the conditions laid down in Recommendation 22 is necessary If creditors are divided into classes, a majority of classes must approve the plan	Where creditors are not divided into classes only 20% in value of creditors may raise an objection If there are classes, then only creditors within a dissenting class

Table 6A.4 (continued)

Country	4.1 Rules on restructuring plans	4.2 Creditors in separate classes?	4.3 Voting: majority required?	4.4 Plan confined to affected creditors?	4.5 Conditions for court approval	4.6 Can dissenting creditors raise objections before a court?
Latvia	Must contain a list of creditors, comprehensive information on financial forecasts and how creditors will be affected by the plan	Division into secured and non-secured claims	Consent in writing from two-thirds in value of secured claims and more than half of unsecured claims	All creditors are affected by the plan	Verifies that the statutory conditions are fulfilled Protection of the legitimate interests of creditors; plan does not reduce rights of dissenting creditors below what they would receive in a liquidation or going-concern sale	Potentially may object to the court, although primarily objections as to the restructuring plan must be submitted to the debtor
Lithuania	Detailed information about the financial position of the debtor and the measures to restore it to profitability and a list of creditors	No	At least two-thirds in value of creditor claims must be voted in favour of the plan	No, all creditors (affected and not affected by the plan) are involved in the adoption of the plan	Verifies that the statutory conditions are fulfilled; does not assess financial viability of plan	No, and court decision approving plan is final and not subject to appeal

Luxembourg	No formal elements required but plan needs to be balanced	No, but under the new procedures there are detailed requirements in respect of how a plan may treat different classes of creditors: the face value of a secured claim may not be reduced and payment may not be suspended generally for a period of more than 24 months	Under new procedure, majority in number, majority in value of the total claims, in both cases among those voting	Yes, only participating creditors are bound by such a plan	Ensures that legal formalities are observed and that some creditors are not unfairly discriminated against. Court does not consider financial viability	Can argue that the statutory conditions for approval by the court of a plan have not been fulfilled
Malta	Company recovery application should give the full facts and circumstances and reasons which led to the company's inability together with a statement/business plan by the applicants as to how the financial and economic situation	Yes	Majority in number representing 75% in value of the creditors or class of creditors present and voting either in person or by proxy	The plan may be between the company and any class of creditors or members	No specific provision	No specific provision regulating objections raised by dissenting creditors

Table 6A.4 (continued)

Country	4.1 Rules on restructuring plans	4.2 Creditors in separate classes?	4.3 Voting: majority required?	4.4 Plan confined to affected creditors?	4.5 Conditions for court approval	4.6 Can dissenting creditors raise objections before a court?
	of the company can be improved and the company itself as a viable going concern					
Netherlands	Elements laid down in Recommendation 15 are required under new proposals	No system of predefined classes Creditors with claims and shareholders with rights that should reasonably be deemed to be similar should be placed in the same class	All affected classes must accept the plan Voting in each class is by simple majority in terms of value of those participating in the vote. Where shareholders are affected the majority must represent at least two-thirds of the issued capital	Only those creditors and shareholders whose rights are amended will be involved in the procedure	Court may approve a restructuring plan against the objections of dissenting classes if it considers that these classes could not reasonably have voted the way they did and they should receive at least as much as they would do in a liquidation Court will also assess whether the composition is necessary and not unfairly prejudicial towards one or more creditors or that	Dissenting creditors may object on the basis that the conditions for court approval are not satisfied

Poland	Should contain proposals to enable the entrepreneur to regain his market competitiveness; under proposals plan must contain the elements listed in Recommendation 15 with the exception of (e)	No specific requirements but the plan proposals should be identical for all the creditors falling within the same group	A majority in number representing at least two-thirds in value of each voting group	Yes, secured creditors are not included in a plan unless they consent to their inclusion; they may also object on the basis that the plan creates obstacles for them in making recoveries	the debtor is not reasonably likely to fulfil the promises made in the plan. The court may consider the financial viability of the enterprise and the debtor's capacity to fulfil the promises it made in the plan. It may also override a dissenting class if at least two-thirds in value of total creditors approve the plan and the dissenting groups receive at least as much under the plan as they would do in a liquidation	Creditors may argue that the statutory conditions have not been fulfilled and also creditors not subject to the plan may argue that the plan hampers recovery of their debts
Portugal	Compliance with Recommendation 15, with exception of (e), not required if plan contains detailed information on potential to prevent debtor's insolvency and ensure viability of	Only distinction is, for voting purposes, between the holders of subordinated and the holders of non-subordinated claims	Either two-thirds in value of creditors provided that at least one-third in value of creditors vote or more than 50% in value of total creditors	For the SIREVE it seems that creditors can opt out at the pre-plan stage; nevertheless a plan also becomes binding on these creditors if it has been	In SIREVE the plan may not go before the court at all unless it is intended to extend its effects to creditors who had previously opted out. In PER court verifies compliance with procedural conditions	Yes, creditor may argue that it receives less under the plan than would otherwise be the case

Table 6A.4 (continued)

Country	4.1 Rules on restructuring plans	4.2 Creditors in separate classes?	4.3 Voting: majority required?	4.4 Plan confined to affected creditors?	4.5 Conditions for court approval	4.6 Can dissenting creditors raise objections before a court?
	the business nor can court reject plan whenever it is clear that it has no prospect of preventing insolvency or ensuring viability of the business			endorsed by creditors representing at least one-third of total debts and it has been affirmed by the court A recovery plan approved in PER is binding on all creditors if affirmed by the court	In any case, court will only affirm the plan where creditors are treated equally unless there is clear justification for divergent treatment. In neither case does it consider financial viability	Creditor may also argue it is not being treated equally or that a certain creditor is being unduly favoured
Romania	A number of detailed requirements are laid down, including plans to restore the debtor to financial health	In arrangement procedures, no, but in judicial reorganization procedures, yes	In arrangement procedures 75% in value of all claims; connected creditors may only vote if they would receive less than they would do in bankruptcy proceedings	Not clear	In judicial reorganization there are detailed requirements depending on the number of classes and whether creditors have been disadvantaged Generally, a majority of creditor classes;	Dissatisfied creditors may argue before the court that the necessary procedures or statutory formalities have

	Elements contained in Recommendation 15 are referred to with the exception of (c)	Yes, including at least secured and unsecured creditors	In judicial reorganization procedures a majority in value in each class	Unaffected creditors are deemed to approve a plan. Each group of shareholders must also approve a plan by a simple majority of voting shareholders	an impaired class of creditors; and 30% of creditors by value must accept the plan. The plan has to provide fair and equitable treatment; respect the priority of claims; and provide a dissenting creditor with at least as much as they would receive in a bankruptcy Not clear whether the court addresses financial viability Must be satisfied that approval of the plan was not achieved by fraud or bribery and that the plan is not in substantial conflict with the common interest of creditors	not been observed
Slovakia			Generally, each class of creditors must approve a plan, including classes of secured creditors. For unsecured creditors it seems that a majority in number coupled with a majority in value of creditors is required			Yes, on the basis that the statutory conditions have not been fulfilled

Table 6A.4 (continued)

Country	4.1 Rules on restructuring plans	4.2 Creditors in separate classes?	4.3 Voting: majority required?	4.4 Plan confined to affected creditors?	4.5 Conditions for court approval	4.6 Can dissenting creditors raise objections before a court?
Slovenia	Elements referred to in the Recommendation must be in the restructuring plan	Plan only applies to financial claims and secured and unsecured claims are in separate categories. Creditors within the same class must be treated equally unless they agree to a difference in treatment	The holders of 75% of the class of affected financial claims must agree	Yes, secured financial claims need not be included	The court verifies that the statutory procedures have been observed, including an unqualified report from an auditor on the viability of the financial restructuring agreement	No
Spain	Depends on the nature of the procedure but generally creditors must be given sufficient information to enable them to make an informed	Yes, with classes depending on the nature of the creditor's claim, i.e. whether it is privileged, ordinary or subordinated;	Yes, the majorities required depend on the nature of the restructuring plan and also vary depending on the particular	No, subordinated claims cannot vote, but are also bound by the plan Creditor cram-down within a class is possible	The debtor, or any creditor voting in favour, may seek court approval of a restructuring plan provided that the plan has been agreed by at least 51% of the financial	Yes, creditors are entitled to challenge any plan but generally only on the grounds that the voting

	choice whether to accept the proposal	privileged claims are further sub-divided	class of creditors (60–75% in case of ordinary claims; 65–80% in case of secured creditors)	if the required class majority is obtained	creditors; otherwise the agreement is not eligible for court approval The court examines whether the plan meets the requirements legally established and declares it binding if the necessary majorities have been obtained	rules have not been respected
Sweden	No specific rules but the restructuring plan must describe how the objectives of the restructuring may be achieved	Creditors do not vote on the plan but any creditor may address the court that the restructuring purpose will not be achieved	It is necessary to distinguish for this purpose between restructuring and composition proceedings: IP should attest that at least 40% of affected creditors who hold at least 40% in value of claims accept the restructuring proposal For composition proceedings, thresholds are higher: at least 60% in numbers voting and total	All creditors are involved in the restructuring procedure but in practice only unsecured creditors are including in the composition proceedings	Court may consider special reasons for not approving the composition, such as there is no likelihood that its terms will be fulfilled	Any creditor may argue that the purpose of the restructuring will not be achieved and the court should refuse confirmation A creditor affected by a composition may also argue against it

Table 6A.4 (continued)

Country	4.1 Rules on restructuring plans	4.2 Creditors in separate classes?	4.3 Voting: majority required?	4.4 Plan confined to affected creditors?	4.5 Conditions for court approval	4.6 Can dissenting creditors raise objections before a court?
			value of claims must approve if payment is 50% or more; for lower payment amounts, threshold is 75%			
United Kingdom	Depends on the nature of the procedure but generally creditors must be given sufficient information to enable them to make an informed choice whether to accept the proposal	It depends on the nature of the procedure: in a scheme persons with dissimilar rights are in separate classes which would include secured creditors In a CVA no separate classes but secured creditors cannot be bound against their wishes	For a scheme a majority in number and 75% in value of those voting in the class; all classes must accept the scheme In a CVA, 75% by value including at least 50% if those with debts not connected with the company	Schemes can be made binding on certain classes leaving other classes unaffected A secured creditor is not bound by a CVA unless with its consent	CVAs do not necessarily go before the court for approval Schemes have to be approved by the court. It will ask whether a reasonably intelligent and honest member of the class concerned could have voted in favour of the scheme	A dissenting creditor may challenge a CVA on the basis of a procedural irregularity that is materially significant or that unfairly prejudices his interests

Table 6A.5 *Encouraging new finance (points 27 to 29)*

Country	5.1 Encouraging new money?	5.2 Protection from claw-back actions
Austria	No specific rules	No specific rules
Belgium	In principle new money financing is encouraged	Yes, in general protected from claw-back actions
Bulgaria	No such provision	Not applicable
Croatia	No special provisions in the law	No special protection but the conditions for avoidance may not be satisfied in practice
Cyprus	Yes	In practice protection
Czech Republic	Yes, within the framework of priority granted to post-commencement loans	No
Denmark		
Estonia	Law allows for these possibilities	No specific rules
Finland	Yes, special rules to encourage new finance	No specific rules
	Rules that permit priming of existing debt if court is satisfied that new debt does not significantly increase the risk of those creditors whose priority position would be weakened	
France	Yes, such finance is encouraged generally by special priorities over existing claims and protection from lender liability claims	Yes, protection from claw-back actions
Germany	Yes, it may be possible for new finance to take priority over existing unsecured debt	In principle, protected from claw-back actions
Greece	Yes, new finance ranked as preferential, i.e. payable ahead of general unsecured debts	Acts done by the debtor in the course of the special recovery procedure cannot be challenged in a subsequent bankruptcy
Hungary	Yes, law seeks to encourage new financing	No special provisions
Ireland	Yes, specific provisions to encourage new finance	In practice yes, but no specific provisions
Italy	Yes, new finance has super-priority, i.e. outranks existing claims, even the secured ones but subject to certain conditions that may be difficult to satisfy in the particular case	Yes

301

Table 6A.5 (continued)

Country	5.1 Encouraging new money?	5.2 Protection from claw-back actions
Latvia	Yes, new finance is allowed and will outrank existing unsecured claims in any subsequent insolvency proceedings	No special rules
Lithuania	Yes, new finance generally has priority over existing unsecured claims	Protection in practice though no specific measures in place
Luxembourg	No specific measures	No specific measures
Malta	No specific provisions	No specific provisions
Netherlands	New finance is envisaged under the legislative proposal	Specific protection is envisaged in the new proposal
Poland	No specific provisions	No specific provisions
Portugal	Yes, any constraints faced by the debtor in relation to new finance are removed and priority is granted over existing unsecured debts and certain types of preferential debt	Yes, protection is provided
Romania	Yes, the law encourages this	Yes, and it seems they are provided with a certain priority status in any ensuing bankruptcy
Slovakia	New finance is encouraged but there are no general legal measures save that it is protected from claw-back actions	See Chapter 5, 5.1
Slovenia	Yes, new finance is allowed and will outrank existing unsecured claims in any subsequent bankruptcy proceedings	Yes, specifically protected against claw-back actions
Spain	Not addressed	Not addressed
Sweden	No special rules encouraging new money	No special rules
United Kingdom	No special rules but a likely part of any restructuring and usually given priority over certain existing debts by agreement between the relevant creditors	In practice exempted from claw-back actions

7.   Second chance for entrepreneurs

7.1   INTRODUCTION

The implementation of the Commission Recommendation of 12 March 2014 on a new approach to business failure and insolvency includes the matter of rehabilitation of bankrupts and the provision of a second chance for honest entrepreneurs.[1] This has been an evolving concern since 2000,[2] which has, in part, informed the aims of the European Commission in its Recommendation. Encouragement of continuing entrepreneurship, even after failure, where failure is not due to dishonesty, is seen as essential to the health of Member States' economies and the efficient functioning of the internal market;[3] honesty here refers to failure that is not caused by fraudulent or irresponsible behaviour.[4] By the same token, the Small Business Act, Principle II advocates support for honest entrepreneurs who wish to try again.[5] Support for entrepreneurs second time around has shown to promote faster growth.[6] Yet fear of stigma and the consequences of bankruptcy not only disincentivizes re-start but affects would-be start-ups as well.[7] Furthermore, bankruptcy can be seen as the epitome of

---

[1]   Commission Recommendation of 12 March 2014 on a new approach to business failure and insolvency, C(2014)1500 final, Part IV, paras 30–33.

[2]   ECORYS, *Bankruptcy and Second Chance for Honest Bankrupt Entrepreneurs: Final Report* (October 2014), Executive Summary, available at www.eea.gr/system/uploads/asset/data/9042/Bankruptcy_and_second_chance_for_honest_bankrupt_Entrepreneurs_FINAL_REPORT.pdf.

[3]   Communication from the Commission to the European Parliament, the Council and the European Economic and Social Committee, *A New European Approach to Business Failure and Insolvency*, COM(2012)742 final, p. 2.

[4]   *Ibid.* 5.

[5]   *Ibid.* 4–5.

[6]   Report of the Expert Group, *A Second Chance for Entrepreneurs: Prevention of Bankruptcy, Simplification of Bankruptcy Procedures and Support for a Fresh Start* (2011), p. 3, available at http://ec.europa.eu/enterprise/policies/sme/business-environment/files/second_chance_final_report_en.pdf.

[7]   *Ibid.*; ECORYS Report (n. 2 above) 25.

failure, resulting in debtors' reluctance to access the system at the right time, or at all.[8]

Discharge from debt is integral to the goal of the promotion of a second chance for those who wish to learn from their mistakes and restart a business. It is an essential tool in the 'economic rehabilitation' of the debtor.[9] With this in mind, the Competitiveness Council called on Member States to limit the discharge time and 'debt settlement' for honest entrepreneurs after bankruptcy to a maximum of three years by 2013.[10] This was also reflected in the Entrepreneurship 2020 Action Plan.[11]

These aims are reflected in the Recommendation, which more specifically provides for the following:

- full discharge of debts subject of a bankruptcy within a maximum of three years starting from:
    - in the case of a procedure ending with the liquidation of the debtor's assets, the date on which the court decided on the application to open bankruptcy proceedings;
    - in the case of a procedure which includes a repayment plan, the date on which implementation of the repayment plan started;
- no need in principle for re-application to the court for discharge to have force;
- allowance for a longer period of discharge in specific circumstances, to discourage dishonesty, bad faith, non-compliance with obligations or behaviour that is detrimental to creditors;
- safeguarding of the livelihood of the entrepreneur.

There have been studies undertaken examining the need for the rehabilitation of the entrepreneur through second chance initiatives.[12] In 2011, the

---

[8] World Bank, Insolvency and Creditor/Debtor Regimes Task Force, Working Group on the Treatment of the Insolvency of Natural Persons. *Treatment of the Insolvency of Natural Persons* (2013), paras 120–121.

[9] *Ibid.*

[10] Council of the European Union, doc. 10975/11. See Communication from the Commission (n. 3 above).

[11] Communication from the Commission to the European Parliament, the Council, the European Economic and Social Committee and the Committee of the Regions, *Entrepreneurship 2020 Action Plan: Reigniting the Entrepreneurial Spirit in Europe*, COM(2012)795 final.

[12] Including academic and other commentary, e.g. K. Ayotte, 'Bankruptcy and Entrepreneurship: The Value of a Fresh Start' (2007) 23(1) *Journal of Law, Economics and Organisation* 161; M.W. Peng, Y. Yamakawa, S.-H. Lee,

World Bank's Insolvency and Creditor/Debtor Regimes Task Force was convened to consider a number of issues connected to insolvency and the global financial crisis, including the internationally diverse treatment of natural persons in this regard. The Working Group on the Treatment of the Insolvency of Natural Persons, set up as part of this initiative, published a Report in 2013 on personal insolvency ('World Bank Personal Insolvency Report').[13] This provides an overview of the issues, both in terms of policy and practicalities, that arise in relation to personal insolvency regimes and identifies potential solutions. The World Bank Personal Insolvency Report includes entrepreneurs, as natural persons, within its analysis. Most recently, in 2014, the consultancy and project management firm, ECORYS Netherlands BV, published a report on a study done for the Commission ('ECORYS Report'),[14] providing a review on the extent to which Member States had implemented the Competitiveness Council Recommendation in relation to the treatment of entrepreneurial insolvency and the provision of a second chance.

This chapter will consider the position of the entrepreneur, both in terms of procedures that are available and the extent to which such approaches reflect the Commission's goal of a second chance for honest entrepreneurs. Where procedures available are the same as for corporate entities, or where they are the same as for consumers, then the issues raised in Chapters 1 to 6 and 8, respectively will be relevant as appropriate. The purpose of this chapter is to address the main points covered in the Recommendation. These will be dealt with in turn, looking both at the approach of individual Member States and the comparator jurisdictions of the United States and Norway, drawing also, where appropriate, upon both the World Bank Personal Insolvency Report and the ECORYS Report. This will then allow observations to be drawn as to the extent to which second chance for entrepreneurs is being supported and advanced, as envisaged by the Commission. It should be noted here that whilst the Recommendation refers to 'bankruptcy', this chapter looks at all procedures that might result in discharge of debt for the entrepreneur, whether they be bankruptcy or debt settlement procedures. The Member States' reporters have used this terminology interchangeably.[15] However, in this

---

'Bankruptcy Laws and Entrepreneur-Friendliness' (2010) 34(3) *Entrepreneuership Theory and Practice* 517 (May 2010); Report of the Expert Group, *A Second Chance for Entrepreneurs* (n. 6 above).

[13] World Bank Personal Insolvency Report (n. 8 above).

[14] ECORYS Report (n. 2 above).

[15] Some reporters refer to procedures as 'bankruptcy' where both the liquidation of assets and some form of payment plan are involved in the process.

and the following chapter, references to bankruptcy and debt settlement procedures are as defined in the Glossary.

7.2   AVAILABLE PROCEDURES FOR THE ENTREPRENEUR

The Commission Recommendation of 12 March 2014 primarily envisages a new approach to *business* failure and insolvency. This goes beyond corporate insolvency and that of legal persons to the entrepreneur as a natural person, and the promotion of second chance. The World Bank Personal Insolvency Report, in its discussion of insolvency of natural persons, highlights the distinction between the all-encompassing economic concerns of a business insolvency, and that of a natural person, where there will be an 'element of humanitarian empathy'.[16] Fair treatment of the creditor and debtor, and the societal and community benefits, whether encouraging economic activity and productivity, or reducing the detriment caused by financial distress, such as health and exclusion issues, which can have wider societal impact, are all of equal concern in relation to individual entrepreneurs, particularly those that run small businesses. The approach of Member States, however, differs in terms of how they treat the entrepreneur.

Bankruptcy denotes a formal procedure with extensive court involvement and prescriptive rules, and may share similarity with corporate insolvency proceedings, the main aim being liquidation of assets. A debt settlement procedure will also involve the court to some degree, although this may vary, from relatively superficial involvement (for example approval of a payment plan) to a more detailed role including supervision of the debtor. An example is the Individual Voluntary Arrangement (IVA) in the United Kingdom (usually no court involvement with an insolvency practitioner (IP) conducting proceedings, and supervising the debtor). Other debt relief may also operate within a structured framework.

In current literature, the terminology used can denote a difference in approach. It has been observed that bankruptcy, favoured by the Anglo-Saxon countries, tends to be seen as an open access procedure, designed to bring forward discharge within a short time period, although historically the United States' approach has been more liberal than that, for example, in the United Kingdom or Ireland. A debt settlement procedure has a more

---

In this chapter, such procedures come under the definition of debt settlement procedures.

[16]   World Bank Personal Insolvency Report (n. 8 above) para. 50.

restrictive approach, and has been favoured by Continental Europe[17] and Scandinavian countries, where the role of debtor behaviour in the onset of the debtor's over-indebtedness may have more significance.[18]

The essence of bankruptcy is that the whole of the debtor's estate is subject to the proceedings, culminating, normally, in the discharge of pre-bankruptcy debt that has been proved. During the period of bankruptcy, the debtor is protected from claims by creditors, thus providing the debtor with a period of respite from the enforcement of outstanding debts. Once the estate and assets of the debtor have been realized, the funds are used to pay the creditors. The debtor is then released from his/her debts, so allowing a 'fresh start' and therefore 'second chance'. There are, however, often exceptions to this: debts such as maintenance payments for dependent children and fines, penalties, and so on incurred as a result of criminal activity are not dischargeable, and perhaps inevitably, the list is likely to be policy driven.

Certain assets may also be excluded from the liquidation process. These tend to be the assets required for everyday living, but often do not include the family home, beyond a temporary period. The dwelling place, if owned, will usually be the most valuable asset a debtor has, and the position is often complicated by joint ownership with a spouse. The balance between the secured creditor's interests and those of the debtor and his/her family therefore can be difficult to find. Whilst at first glance such exceptions may not seem relevant to a business insolvency, entrepreneurs are in effect individuals with unlimited liability, unable to hide behind a corporate structure. It is therefore important that tools of the trade are included in such exception (and indeed often are). The dwelling place may also be used as security for business debts, so threatening the family life of the entrepreneur in the event of liquidation. Indeed, the Cypriot law, for example, recognizes this, providing for a specific payment plan for such entrepreneurs; debtors whose house is subject to a charge as security for loan for a very small business[19] may be eligible to enter a debt settlement procedure known as a 'co-ordinated repayment plan'.

Procedures outside bankruptcy are also designed to give debtors some

---

[17] Cf. Jason Kilborn, who points to France as having developed a system as liberal as that of the United States: 'Reform, Counter Reform and Transatlantic Rapprochement in the Law of Personal Bankruptcy' (2015) 3(12) *Nottingham Insolvency and Business Law e-journal* 235.

[18] J. Niemi, 'Personal Insolvency' in G. Howells, I. Ramsay, T. Wilhelmsson, with D. Kraft (eds), *Handbook of Research on International Consumer Law* (Cheltenham and Northampton, MA, Edward Elgar Publishing, 2010), pp. 422–3.

[19] Less than ten employees.

form of relief from debt. A debt settlement procedure will include some form of agreed payment plan, again often culminating in the debtor being discharged from his or her debt. The idea here is to enable the debtor to avoid the stigma of being bankrupt, and allow a manageable scheme for meeting his/her obligations, from future income. The rationale behind the payment plan is often that the debtor 'earns' their fresh start. However, the payment plan can be controversial;[20] debtors have little extra over living expenses to offer as a monthly payment, and if the period set for the plan is too long it disincentivizes the debtor and reduces the likelihood of a return to productivity. Debt relief outside formal debt settlement procedures varies, and may, for example, be set up through arrangements, via an out of court settlement, and be run by an administrator with no involvement of the court at all – in other words, informal arrangements.

All Member States offer to the entrepreneur either some sort of bankruptcy or debt settlement procedure, or the availability of both, although these procedures may not include discharge of debt. Where debt settlement procedures are not available, the entrepreneur will normally still have access to bankruptcy procedures available to corporate debtors. Table 7.1 details the procedures available.

One important element to the treatment of entrepreneurs in terms of insolvency is whether they are regarded as any other business, whether they are regarded as a separate category, or whether they are treated the same as consumers. Here, there is some variety in approach, but many Member States group debtors on the basis of their business persona (i.e., legal entity or natural persons), such as the United Kingdom and Ireland. In such a case, entrepreneurs will only have access to proceedings designed for their relevant persona.

However within these groupings there can be either implicit or explicit differentiation of treatment, whether due to the appropriateness of procedures to particular types of debtor within the category (for example, no income, no assets debtors) or to some procedures being only available, for example, to consumers. An illustration is the Italian system. If a debtor qualifies for over-indebtedness procedures for natural persons, but has

---

[20]   Jason Kilborn points out that these plans are often illusory and have been criticized as inefficient: returns may not justify the administrative expense and simply delay the debtor's ability to regain financial initiative: J. Kilborn, *Expert Recommendations and the Evolution of European Best Practices for the Treatment of Over-indebtedness 1984–2010*, Law of Business and Finance Series (Deventer, Kluwer, 2011), p. 32. World Bank Personal Insolvency Report (n. 8 above) paras 263–264.

Table 7.1 Procedures available (shaded box indicates availability)

	AT	BE	BG	CY	CZ	DE	DK	EE	IE	EL	FI	ES	FR	HR	HU
Bankruptcy			▓										▓		
Debt settlement						▓						▓			▓
Bankruptcy and debt settlement*	▓	▓				▓	▓	▓	▓	▓	▓		▓		

	IT	LT	LU	LV	MT	NL	PL	PT	RO	SE	SK	SI	UK	US	NO
Bankruptcy			▓		▓		▓		▓						
Debt settlement		▓		▓							▓				
Bankruptcy and debt settlement*	▓					▓		▓		▓		▓	▓	▓	▓

Note: * Not all entrepreneurs may have access to both sets of proceedings where a Member State distinguishes between merchants and professionals or small-scale and larger entrepreneurial enterprises.

business debts, he or she can only access those procedures that are not reserved for consumers (i.e., an entrepreneur can access the Procedura di composizione della crisi da sovraindebitamento del consumatore through Accordo or the Liquidazione dei beni, but not the Procedura di composizione della crisi da sovraindebitamento del consumatore through Piano).

Alternatively, entrepreneurs may find they are, in effect, a group of their own. In Slovenia, the ZFPPIPP (Insolvency Act), has specific provisions for natural persons, but within this, it separates entrepreneurs in certain respects. Consumers and entrepreneurs are subject to a separate test of insolvency (entrepreneurs being treated as corporations in this respect). Entrepreneurs are then further split in relation to available procedures: an entrepreneur equated with the micro or small-sized company is subject to 'simplified' compulsory settlement proceedings, a procedure applicable to small corporate entities, as well as having access to bankruptcy specifically for the entrepreneur and professionals.

Where entrepreneurs are grouped with other business they may find that their only recourse is to bankruptcy, or business restructuring, such as in France, or in Croatia (where there is currently no consumer insolvency regime although there is ongoing detailed work and discussion

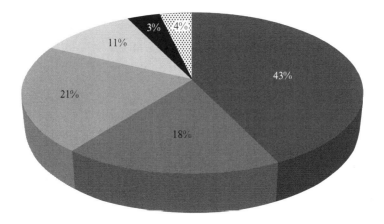

- ■ Access to consumer procedures as a natural person

- ■ Access to some consumer procedures but restrictions based either on size of enterprise or type of proceedings available

- ▨ Access to business insolvency proceedings only

- ☐ Access to separately defined procedures for entrepreneures, or light touch business insolvency proceedings

- ■ Access to business insolvency proceeding where no consumer proceedings exist

- ▨ No access to proceedings that allow discharge

Figure 7.1   Broad treatment of entrepreneurs in insolvency proceedings in the 28 EU Member States

on a draft Consumer Bankruptcy Act). On the other hand, where entrepreneurs are brought within general business regimes, there may be light touch or low cost procedures available or they may find that they have procedures designed specifically for them, such as in Slovenia, where there are separate bankruptcy and debt settlement procedures for entrepreneurs.[21]

As stated above, any special procedures provided for consumers may take place within a wider regime for all natural persons, or as discrete provision for consumers only. Consumer-only regimes exist in France, Latvia,

---

[21]   Although it should be noted that some procedural rules applicable to corporate bankruptcy and compulsory settlement proceedings are applicable *mutatis mutandis*.

BOX 7.1 CASE *U 1985.784 V* (DENMARK)

A chimney sweep had accumulated substantial debt to the tax and custom authorities. Debt rescheduling was not allowed as the debt was incurred through the business still run by the debtor. Therefore, to ensure the continued operation of the business, the matter was to be dealt with through the compulsory composition procedure or by agreement with creditors rather than the debt settlement procedure available to consumers.

Poland and Romania. Such procedures also exist in Belgium, Denmark and Luxembourg, but a former entrepreneur may also apply as long as he or she has not been in business in the last six months. This means that in these countries, it could be argued that the small business entrepreneur is in effect left with a procedure that is more appropriate for larger enterprises. The position of the sole trader and family business entrepreneur is more likely to reflect that of a consumer, and therefore procedures that are designed for corporate and/or larger business debtors may be inappropriate (see Box 7.1).

In some Member States, entrepreneurs may be further divided in other ways, and subject to different procedures. In Greece, entrepreneurs who are 'merchants' will be treated under the business/corporate regime, leaving only self-employed professionals access to the proceedings available for natural persons. Therefore, the special regime created for natural persons/consumers by Law No. 3869/2010 is only applicable to self-employed professionals, such as doctors and architects. Again, this can leave some types of sole trader exposed in terms of procedures that may be less appropriate. Alternatively, an entrepreneur may only access proceedings for natural persons after he or she has completed the process as a legal entity. This is the case in Latvia, where, if an entrepreneur is registered as an individual merchant with the commercial register, he or she must file as a legal person first. Only once the entrepreneur has been deleted from the Commercial Register can the individual then apply for procedures available to natural persons. This also applies to partnerships.

Individuals who run a small business in partnership may find they are exposed to the corporate/ business regime, and treated separately from the sole trader. For example, in Hungary, the Debt Consolidation of Natural Persons Act 2015 is not entirely clear as to who is covered by the natural person definition. It does provide special rules for entrepreneurs, however these rules, which relate to the exemption of certain assets from the debt settlement procedure, only apply to sole traders and professionals. In other Member States such as Slovenia, partnerships are clearly seen as a separate legal entity, and are excluded from the natural persons' regime. Yet it may be that a partnership represents a very small family business, such as husband and wife. Again, regimes designed for the natural person are arguably more appropriate for such a case.

For other Member States, the procedures for natural persons do apply to both entrepreneurs and consumers, although in some countries there may be restrictions or there may be differentiation made on the basis of the size of the business. For example, in Cyprus a particular debt settlement procedure is available for a natural person with business debt, but only if the business is small (employs less than ten people) and the home has been used as security for the business's borrowing. This idea is reflected in other Member States such as Finland, where if an entrepreneur has both personal debts and those in relation to an ongoing business, all debt can be adjusted at the same time if the business is small in scale, and in Sweden, where the debt settlement procedure aimed at severely indebted individuals is only available to a trader debtor with business debt if the business is 'easy to investigate'. In Italy, all debtors, whatever their status, can access the fast and low cost liquidation proceedings, but only if they are not eligible for the traditional insolvency proceedings designed for large enterprises. In Cyprus, Finland, Greece and Portugal, the relevant procedures can only apply to entrepreneurs when they are engaged in limited business activity, for example, self-employment or as a professional, and in Lithuania, a special regime that applies to natural persons includes farmers and those conducting individual business activities.

The way in which personal versus business debts are treated therefore primarily depends on whether there is a different procedure for entrepreneurs. Some states, as has been noted, simply allow any natural person to enter the procedures as long as they fulfil the other criteria, and here there is little difference in treatment between the entrepreneur and consumer. Alternatively, if a procedure is only available to a consumer, then an entrepreneur will not be able to access it. In terms of partnerships, the data that has been provided suggests that partnerships in some Member States are treated as 'hybrid' debtors, in that whilst the partnership is effectively treated as a legal entity (whether generally or for the purpose of the relevant procedure), individual partners can then access those procedures available to the individual (for example, as in Finland, Ireland and the United Kingdom).

The position in the comparator countries is that any natural person, as an entrepreneur, can enter the procedures as long as they fulfil relevant criteria, although this in some circumstances depends on the proportion of debt that is business related. In the United States, the Bankruptcy Code in Chapter 7 facilitates the immediate discharge of debt. This approach, however, has come under considerable pressure with concerns about abuse by debtors who can afford to repay some portion of their debts. This has resulted in access to this procedure being restricted through financial screening. However, where the debtor has more business than consumer debt he/she will not be subject to the screening process. Alternatively, the entrepreneur can use the debt settlement procedures under Chapter 11 or 13. In Norway, debt settlement procedures and bankruptcy under the Bankruptcy Act 1984 are applicable to both individuals and businesses/consumers. The debt settlement procedure under the Debt Settlement Act 1992 is primarily for personal debt. However, if the debtor's business related debt, incurred with regard to a sole proprietorship, represents an insignificant amount of overall liability, then the entrepreneur may use this route.

7.3 DISCHARGE OF DEBT

7.3.1 Full Discharge of Debts Subject of a Bankruptcy Within Three Years

The ECORYS Report had amongst its objectives an update on the extent to which Member States, together with certain other jurisdictions,[22] have introduced a maximum three-year period for debt settlement procedures and discharge, and a measurement of the extent to which Member States have complied with the Competitive Council's recommendation on the promotion of second chance. The Report found that, more generally, national rules differ greatly within Member States[23] in relation to discharge.

Nevertheless, it has been noted elsewhere that there is evidence of convergence in approaches to discharge, certainly in relation to personal insolvency.[24] In terms of debt settlement procedures in Europe, the mechanism of 'locking' a debtor into a payment plan over a period of time is

---

[22] Iceland, Norway, Turkey, Serbia and Montenegro.
[23] ECORYS Report (n. 2 above) 30.
[24] Niemi, 'Personal Insolvency' (n. 18 above) p. 423; J. Niemi, 'Consumer Insolvency in the European Legal Context' (2012) 35 *Journal of Consumer Policy* 443, 445; 'A Minimum Standard for Debt Discharge in Europe?' (2013) 26(7) *Insolvency Intelligence* 102 (paper resulting from Workshop 'As You Like It? (Minimum) Standards for Debt Discharge in Europe', Second European Insolvency and Restructuring Congress, Deutscher Anwaltsverein, Arebeitsgemeinschaft Insolvenzrecht und Sanierung, 15–17 May 2013.

also something adopted, although not always exclusively, by a majority of Member States. Nevertheless, the data analysed suggests there is considerable divergence in the detailed treatment of debt settlement procedures, whether in terms of legal basis and/or mechanisms, and the experiences of debtors across the EU may therefore differ.

The ECORYS Report also recommended that discharge be as automatic as possible, and this is addressed in the Commission's Recommendation. Discharge of debt can either be 'straight discharge' understood as 'fresh start',[25] where freedom from debt is given as a result of a bankruptcy, or conditional discharge in debt settlement procedures, where discharge is dependent upon some payment of debt, normally over a period of time.[26] In addition, or in the alternative, the discharge may be subject to a percentage of debts being able to be paid, or to a probation period.

Countries that allow full discharge as part of bankruptcy are Belgium, Cyprus, the Czech Republic, Estonia, France, Greece, Ireland, Luxembourg, Romania, Slovenia and the United Kingdom. However, of these countries there are a number where there is potential for discharge to take place beyond the three-year maximum recommended by the Commission. In Belgium, whilst a debtor may be able to obtain early discharge six months from the date of the bankruptcy order, the decision on discharge is taken on closure of proceedings, which in fact may last more than three years. In Estonia, the timeline for discharge can range from three to seven years, and in Slovenia, discharge can take place between two to five years from the debtor's proceedings to proposing discharge. In Greece, where an entrepreneur is subject to the Insolvency Code (merchant or trader professionals may access procedures as a consumer), discharge takes place over ten years (unless the debtor dies or creditors are paid in full with interest at an earlier date). Alternatively, there may be no maximum time limit as such; in Romania, whilst a simplified insolvency procedure under the general insolvency regime is available to entrepreneurs, no maximum period of three years is specified.

By contrast in the United Kingdom and Ireland, discharge automatically takes place after one year[27] (in that no further application is required), although even here discharge within this timeframe is not guaranteed. In Ireland, if a valid objection to the discharge is accepted by the court, the discharge can be postponed for up to eight years, or even

---

[25] World Bank Personal Insolvency Report (n. 8 above) para 335.
[26] *Ibid.*
[27] This changes to one year in Ireland as a result of the Bankruptcy (Amendment) Act 2015 in force 29 January 2016.

15 in limited circumstances.[28] Furthermore, even where there is automatic discharge, this does not necessarily mean the debtor is completely free to start again. The court can make an order requiring further payments from income over a period of time after the discharge (for a maximum of three years).[29] This reflects a similar model in the United Kingdom, although payments after discharge cannot extend beyond three years.

Other Member States provide for no discharge at all in relation to bankruptcy: for example, Austria, Bulgaria, Hungary, the Netherlands and Sweden. However, apart from Bulgaria, which appears to have no provision and no plans to make reforms, such Member States do offer relief from debts through debt settlement procedures, for example, the Netherlands, where discharge is available over three years, although this can be extended to five years.

The comparator jurisdictions of the United States and Norway both provide for procedures that may lead to discharge, but in relation to discharge on bankruptcy, only offer two extremes. Norway has no provision for discharge on liquidation of assets alone, whilst the United States has an automatic discharge procedure under Chapter 7 of the US Bankruptcy Code, where discharge may take place as soon as four months from the date the debtor files the petition for bankruptcy.

As stated above, a number of Member States offer a debt settlement procedure.[30] Payment plans, a feature of such procedures, may alternatively be part of an out of court arrangement. The countries which have debt settlement procedures that allow discharge are Austria, Cyprus, the Czech Republic, Denmark, Estonia, Finland,[31] Germany,[32] Greece, Hungary,[33] Ireland, Lithuania, Latvia, the Netherlands, Portugal,

---

[28] Bankruptcy Act 1988, s. 85A. The Bankruptcy (Amendment) Act 2015 amends s. 85A and increases this to 15 years where the debtor's failure to co-operate is particularly serious.

[29] Reduced from five years by the Bankruptcy (Amendment) Act 2015.

[30] The ECORYS Report found that of the Member States, only Belgium, Cyprus, France and Poland were found to not have a payment plan as part of bankruptcy proceedings; ECORYS Report (n. 2 above) 44–5.

[31] Until recently, in Finland discharge was only available for an entrepreneur if the business debts related to a former business. Otherwise, the Restructuring of Enterprises Act applied. However, since January 2015, entrepreneurs can apply for debt settlement, as private individuals, as long as the business is small and the debtor can demonstrate he or she will be able to pay at least some of the debt owed to creditors.

[32] From 2014, German entrepreneurs may opt for an insolvency plan, which allows them to settle with creditors during the insolvency proceedings and gain 'early' discharge.

[33] From September 2015.

Slovakia, Slovenia, Spain and the United Kingdom. In Sweden, the debt settlement procedure administered by the Enforcement Agency may be available to a trader in limited circumstance; this allows debt to be written off at the end of an administered payment plan. Otherwise, the only Member States that appear to offer no debt settlement procedures at all to entrepreneurs are Bulgaria, France, Luxembourg, Malta, Poland (due to change January 2016) and Romania.

However, the time-lines for discharge vary. For example, in Austria, discharge takes place once the court order approving the payment plan becomes final. The plan lasts for two years; in this way the normal discharge period is two years, as long as the plan is complied with. On the other hand, for example in Denmark, discharge may only take place within three years where the debtor owns the capital of a company going into bankruptcy and the debtor is applying for debt rescheduling, and cancellation of debt under the debt settlement procedure may take place *after* a five-year period. In the Czech Republic it can be up to five years (although it can be as little as 17 months).

In Germany, the discharge period of three years only applies if the debtor can repay 35 per cent of debts within this time, and meets the costs of the proceedings: a requirement reflected (though the percentage may differ) in a number of Member States. Otherwise, a German entrepreneur must assign any attachable earnings for six years, after which he or she will be discharged, unless an application is made for 'early' discharge after five years, but this is only allowed if the costs of the proceedings have been met. Similarly in Latvia, the debt settlement procedure may last between one to three years, dependent on certain criteria (primarily the percentage of debt obligations outstanding on completion of the proceedings). However, those that are registered as merchants or are farmers must go through insolvency proceedings as a legal person first, which may delay discharge by months or years.

In Lithuania, whilst discharge may take place within three years, this may extend to five, and in Slovakia, whilst discharge within three years is a possibility on the basis of a probationary period, it is not a maximum, and it should be noted that the three-year probationary period only runs once the debt settlement procedure is completed, which can take three years. Some other Member States do provide for discharge, but this will be over a longer period, for example, Portugal where, in certain circumstances discharge will normally take place over five years.

Other countries offer a payment plan via what is primarily an out of court procedure, for example, in Spain which allows a discharge period of five years, or the IVA in the United Kingdom, designed as an alternative to bankruptcy, which also, according to recent Insolvency Services statistics, usually lasts for approximately five to six years (although a percentage of arrangements do last longer than this).[34]

Again, the comparator jurisdictions represent different positions: in Norway, a debtor can obtain discharge by separate voluntary or compulsory debt settlement procedures under the Bankruptcy Act, or in limited circumstances under a debt settlement procedure allowed for individuals under the Debt Settlement Act 1992. Discharge is considered to have taken place when the debt settlement is granted, although this can be set aside in certain circumstances. In contrast, the US legislation offers not only discharge upon bankruptcy under Chapter 7 of the US Bankruptcy Code, but also allows for discharge conditional on debt settlement procedures under Chapter 11 or Chapter 13 (under Chapter 13, discharge is via payment plan only; the length of the plan depends on the median income of the debtor and will be three to five years).

Whilst the position is somewhat complicated in that in some Member States not *all* types of entrepreneur[35] will have access to *all* mechanisms otherwise available, Table 7.2 gives an initial broad view of whether discharge for an entrepreneur may be available within three years, either via bankruptcy (liquidation of assets only) or debt settlement procedures (which may include liquidation of assets as well as a payment plan in some form), as defined in the Glossary.

7.3.2 Discharge Without Re-application to the Court

The Recommendation at point 31 refers to *automatic* discharge within three years, meaning without the need in principle to re-apply to a court. This aspect to discharge is not present in a number of Member States, either due to a requirement for re-application by the debtor, or due to a final reconsideration by the court being required before discharge is granted. Such Member States include the Czech Republic, Estonia, Germany, Hungary, Italy, Latvia, Poland, Romania, Slovakia and Spain. Alternatively, the procedurally automatic nature of relief may be available for some procedures but not others, as for example in Sweden, where discharge is automatic in the debt settlement procedure available to natural persons, but not in bankruptcy, or Cyprus, where discharge is not automatic under the debt settlement procedure for natural persons, but is available for bankruptcy.

---

[34]   Insolvency Service, *Individual Voluntary Arrangements: Outcome Status of New Cases Registered Between 1990 and 2013, England & Wales* (November 2014).

[35]   Because e.g. entrepreneurs are split between those who are merchants and those who are professionals.

Table 7.2   Discharge in three years

	AT	BE	BG	CY	CZ	DE	DK	EE	IE	EL	FI	ES	FR	HR	HU
Full on bankruptcy	x	o	x	✓	o	x	x	o	✓	o	o	o	✓	o	x
Full under debt settlement procedure	✓	x	x	✓	o	o	o	x	o	o	o	o	x	o	o

	IT	LT	LU	LV	MT	NL	PL	PT	RO	SE	SK	SI	UK	US	NO
Full on bankruptcy	o	x	o	o	o	x	o	x	o	x	o	o	✓	✓	x
Full under debt settlement procedure	o	o	x	o	o	✓	x	o	x	o	✓	o	o	o	o

Key: ✓ = Yes, within three years
         x = No provision
         o = Discharge available but no maximum three-year period

It should be noted here that even where discharge is granted, the debtor may not be relieved of all debts. Whilst the most advantageous approach for an insolvent entrepreneur is for an insolvency procedure to relieve them of all debts, this does not always occur. Some debts may be non-provable in the bankruptcy, or alternatively not subject to discharge, either for policy reasons, or to avoid indirectly supporting irresponsible behaviour[36] (discussed below).

7.4   DISCOURAGEMENT OF DISHONESTY, BAD FAITH, NON-COMPLIANCE WITH OBLIGATIONS OR BEHAVIOUR DETRIMENTAL TO CREDITORS

The ECORYS Report's conclusions were, broadly, that where Member States provide no distinction between dishonest and honest entrepreneurs, they should do so, and that discharge should be made as fast as possible to save the resources of a failed entrepreneur.[37] Most Member States which

---

[36]   World Bank Personal Insolvency Report (n. 8 above) paras 367–374.
[37]   ECORYS Report (n. 2 above) 12.

allow discharge from debt also provide some form of sanction or restriction where the debtor is found to have acted dishonestly either before or during proceedings, or where obligations are not complied with.[38] Some sanctions are criminal, some prevent proceedings from being initiated from the outset, and others restrict the availability of discharge from debt, either by complete denial or delay.

Even where there may be no effect on discharge, there may still be criminal consequences for fraudulent behaviour; this, for example, is the position in Romania. In addition the remedy of *actio pauliana* may be employed here, where the creditor can intervene due to the bankrupt acting in such a way as to cause prejudice to the creditor. This, for example, is available in Malta, where a debtor must not enter contracts or act in a way that defrauds the creditor. The only intention required is the prejudicial nature of the conduct, intention to cause the creditor harm is not required.[39] Another example is the United Kingdom, where if the debtor enters a transaction defrauding creditors or there is a preferential transaction, the trustee in bankruptcy can apply to have these set aside.

In many jurisdictions, the data suggests acting in 'good faith' is a prerequisite to obtaining discharge and that availability of discharge is, *inter alia*, dependent on the debtor's due diligence. It should be noted, however, that 'good faith' is a fluid concept, and is a term that is used loosely by some reporters to include any negligent or intentional behaviour of the debtor that may lead either to his/her over-indebtedness or to the detriment of creditors. In its truest sense it is rarely defined, but rather left to court interpretation and therefore can result in uncertainty.

These various requirements, together with provisions that aim at swelling the debtor's estate (for example, requiring the debtor to seek employment), also reflect a desire to safeguard the creditors' interests. Slovakia provides an example of where the debtor must show commitment to meeting obligations of the creditors: not only must the debtor seek employment or otherwise increase his/her income, he/she must also make a statement expressing honest intent to make reasonable efforts to satisfy the creditors.

Such Member States' requirements that refer to honesty or good faith are in addition to the involvement of creditors in bankruptcy procedures or the requirement of creditors' consent to a payment plan within debt settlement procedures.

---

[38] Cf. the ECORYS Report, which found the majority of Member States treated honest and fraudulent bankrupts in the same way, *ibid.* 52.

[39] *Mario Camilleri* v. *Mario Borg ET*, Civil Court, First Hall, 21 October 2004. The onus of proof lies with the debtor: *HSBC Bank plc* v. *Fenech Estates Co. Ltd*, Civil Court, First Hall, 19 January 2000.

Further examples are as follows. In Austria, the payment plan under the debt settlement procedure is invalid if the debtor is convicted of fraudulent bankruptcy, or the consent from creditors was gained through fraudulent means. If creditors do not know about the plan due to an omission by/ fault of the debtor (for example, violation of reporting duties) then such creditors are not bound by the plan and are entitled to payment in full. In Belgium and Cyprus, debtors must have acted in 'good faith' prior to and during bankruptcy to obtain discharge, and with regard to the latter, there will be no discharge if the debtor fails to co-operate with the management of his or her estate or engages in misconduct (for example, concealment of income/rights over property or fraudulent transferring assets). Denmark does not allow debt settlement procedures where the debtor has either acted irresponsibly or has incurred debt through criminal activity or has disregarded obligations, for example, in relation to tax.

In Estonia, the restrictions are based on criminal conviction, non-compliance with obligations or gross negligence, for example, the concealment of information or hindrance of creditor satisfaction. In Finland, there is no debt settlement procedure allowed where there is a criminal investigation ongoing in relation to the debtor, where liabilities have been dealt with in a grossly improper manner, or where the debtor has made financial arrangements to the detriment of the creditor. French law does not allow debtors to access the debt settlement procedure if, *inter alia*, the debtor has acted in bad faith; and in Germany, discharge can be refused on the basis of a criminal conviction, or where there has been negligence, for example, in the provision of false information or in impairment of creditors' satisfaction, or if a debtor has during the discharge period favoured a particular creditor. In Greece, discharge is not available if the debtor has acted fraudulently or in bad faith and in Ireland, objections can be made if the debtor has failed to co-operate or has hidden income that could be used to the benefit of creditors.

In Lithuania, discharge proceedings can be discontinued if the debtor is subject to criminal penalties or has entered any transaction which violates creditor rights, or where there has been/is non-compliance with bankruptcy law. In the Netherlands, the debtor must have acted in 'good faith' for the last five years if he or she wishes to access debt settlement procedures, and to be allowed discharge the debtor must comply with all obligations during the three-year discharge period; in Portugal, there are provisions that require good faith, honesty and compliance with obligations. In Slovenia, reasons for the insolvency are taken into account, and an application can be rejected if the debtor has a criminal conviction or it is found he or she has provided false information. Finally, in the United Kingdom, bankruptcy proceedings can be suspended if it is discovered the debtor

Table 7.3   Provisions and protection

	AT	BE	BG	CY	CZ	DE	DK	EE	IE	EL	FI	ES	FR	HR	HU
Provisions to discourage dishonesty	✓	✓	✗	✓	✓	✓	✓	✓	✓	✓	✓	✓	✓	✓	✓
Protection against creditor detriment	✓	✓	✗	✓	✓	✓	✓	✓	✓	✓	✓	✓	✓	✓	✓

	IT	LT	LU	LV	MT	NL	PL	PT	RO	SE	SK	SI	UK	US	NO
Provisions to discourage dishonesty	✓	✓	✓	✓	✓	✓	✓	✓	✓	✓	✓	✓	✓	✓	✓
Protection against creditor detriment	✓	✓	✓	✓	✓	✓	✓	✓	✓	✓	✓	✓	✓	✓	✓

has not been complying with obligations, or has committed one or more of a number of criminal offences, for example, withholding information or fraudulent disposal of assets prior to the bankruptcy. There are also further restrictions where it is found that the bankrupt has acted dishonestly or has negligently or recklessly contributed to his/her insolvency.

Most Member States appear to have provisions that disallow certain debts from being discharged or from being provable in the bankruptcy or debt settlement procedures from the outset. The categories are very similar, consisting primarily of criminal fines, maintenance payments, student loans (where applicable), liability for tortious claims (intentional or negligence based), and in some Member States, tax obligations.

Table 7.3 shows where there is some provision for discouraging dishonesty and protecting against creditor detriment to at least some degree, that is across most Member States.

Norway has no regulation in relation to bankruptcy that specifically requires good faith before discharge can be obtained, as there is no facility for discharge in this respect. However, where the entrepreneur is entitled to access debt settlement procedures under the Debt Settlement Act for Individuals 1992,[40] relief will not be granted if it is clear the debtor has acted in bad faith or given false information, or alternatively where the debt is

---

[40]   Small-scale farmers/craftsmen, etc. with no employees.

related to criminal activity, unpaid tax, or where the majority of debt has been recently incurred (suggesting intentional or negligent accumulation of debt). The law in the United States broadly reflects the requirements of the Recommendation; for example, discharge can be denied where there is fraud.

7.5 SAFEGUARDING THE LIVELIHOOD OF THE ENTREPRENEUR

To facilitate a second chance, the debtor must not feel that he or she is being punished, and whilst contractual obligations should be respected, the debtor must be able to have the means to start again, if second chance is to be achieved. As part of this support mechanism, allowing the debtor sufficient income/assets to live and/or work is vital, not only for economic rehabilitation,[41] but also in recognition of welfare rights and protection of other vulnerable parties, such as the family of the debtor, particularly children.[42] In most Member States, personal and household effects needed by the debtor and family are excluded from any liquidation process, as are goods, including a vehicle in some cases where necessary to pursue a trade or profession or employment.

In relation to exemptions that specifically relate to safeguarding the debtor's livelihood, the following picture has emerged: Austria allows the debtor to retain a certain percentage of his or her earnings and certain items necessary for the business; Estonia allows payment of necessary support out of the debtor's estate for two months, or longer if the court extends this period; and in Finland, debtors are entitled to keep a living wage. Hungary has passed new laws, which from September 2015 allow entrepreneurs to keep the tools of their trade. Otherwise, for example, as in Malta, there are provisions but no details are given.

The debt settlement procedure in Portugal allows for the maintenance of debtors and their family and only disposable income is allocated to payment of debts, allowing the livelihood of the debtor to be catered for; this is also reflected in Slovakia's provisions. In Slovenia, a debtor may request the court to leave them with assets needed for the start of a new business, and in Spain the Spanish Insolvency Act allows a payment made

---

[41] The ECORYS Report identified the importance of exempting personal assets and housing from the bankruptcy provisions in order to support the honest bankrupt: ECORYS Report (n. 2 above) 48.

[42] World Bank Personal Insolvency Report (n. 8 above) para. 75.

Table 7.4 Safeguards

	AT	BE	BG	CY	CZ	DE	DK	EE	IE	EL	FI	ES	FR	HR	HU
Safeguard of debtor's livelihood	✓	✓	✗	✓	✓	✓	✓	✓	✓	✓	✓	✓	✓	✓	✓

	IT	LT	LU	LV	MT	NL	PL	PT	RO	SE	SK	SI	UK	US	NO
Safeguard of debtor's livelihood	✓	✓	✓	✓	✓	✓	✓	✓	✗	✓	✓	✓	✓	✓	✓

to the debtor equivalent to the minimum wage, if the debtor (including family) is in a state of necessity. In the United Kingdom, any payment agreement or order in bankruptcy must allow for living expenses and the entrepreneur to keep the tools of his trade. Pension rights are also excluded from the estate or from regular payments to be made to the trustee in bankruptcy. In terms of the IVA in the United Kingdom, an arrangement will only be allowed if there is a viable means of debt being able to be repaid; this will inevitably lead to allowance made for the debtor's living expenses. Some Member States, such as the United Kingdom and Latvia, also have specific rules that will in certain circumstances allow delay of the sale of the family home for up to a year. Extremes are represented across the EU, from the debtor being able to keep his or her home indefinitely to being unable to keep any assets at all (Poland).

Table 7.4 provides a broad illustration. It should be noted that individual Member States have differing ranges of exemptions and safeguarding the debtor's livelihood may only extend to retention of personal effects necessary for day-to-day living or to a basic income or receipt of state benefit.

In the comparator jurisdiction of the United States, the 'necessities of life' are excluded from the estate for realization purposes: such necessities include tools of the trade and pensions. In Norway, the debtor is entitled to retain some belongings such as clothes and other personal necessities, and equipment for his/her profession or education. This is regardless of whether the entrepreneur has accessed the debt settlement procedures available to individuals only (allowed in certain cases where business debt represents a very low percentage of overall commitment) or the debt settlement procedure or bankruptcy under the Bankruptcy Act (available to all).

7.6 FURTHER OBSERVATIONS: DIVERGENCE AND BEST PRACTICE

The Commission Recommendation targets greater coherence between national insolvency frameworks as a goal. As has been outlined, the aim is to foster early restructuring of viable companies in financial difficulties and promote a second chance for honest entrepreneurs, but with due support for the interests of creditors and investors, so encouraging cross-border investment. Efficient and consistent insolvency frameworks across the EU are also seen as allowing better assessment of credit risks and providing a reduction in cost in assisting over-indebted business.[43] This is further supported by the Action Plan on Building a Capital Markets Union,[44] which identifies divergent approaches to insolvency laws as a barrier to cross-border investment.[45]

7.6.1 Divergent Approaches and Exemplar Approaches

The data shows that there are a number of areas where there are divergent approaches to the insolvency of an entrepreneur, and even where there seem to be similarities, within procedures there are further disparities between Member States. Differences have emerged from the data in the following areas:

- basis upon which entrepreneurial debt is treated;
- availability of procedures;
- length of period before discharge of debt is granted;
- availability of discharge;
- safeguarding the livelihood of the debtor.

7.6.1.1 Basis upon which entrepreneurial debt is treated
The basis upon which entrepreneurial debt is treated primarily depends on how the entrepreneur is classed. There are three main categories in which the entrepreneur may be placed:

- with all debtors regardless of persona (less common);
- with business;

---

[43] Recommendation (n. 1 above) 3–4.
[44] Communication from the Commission to the European Parliament, the Council, the European Economic and Social Committee and the Committee of the Regions, *Action Plan on Building a Capital Markets Union*, COM(2015)468 final.
[45] *Ibid.* 24–5.

- with natural persons (i.e. grouped together with consumers).

Of itself, this may not create significant problems cross border, although potentially it produces uncertainty for creditors lending to entrepreneurs in terms of calculating costs of debtor default. These categorizations then dictate which procedures the debtor is entitled to access or is subject to, and in this aspect of the divergence may cause more concern (see further below) particularly where entrepreneurs do not have access to suitable procedures. This also leads to the situation where in one Member State an entrepreneur may have access to a range of procedures for both bankruptcy and debt settlement, yet in other Member States find he or she has only access to bankruptcy. As has been indicated, this does not therefore always guarantee discharge from debt.

7.6.1.2 Availability of procedures

Whilst the type of procedures to which the entrepreneur has access depends primarily upon how he/she is categorized, for example, debt settlement procedures and informal arrangements are more likely to be an option where entrepreneurs are treated as other natural persons, there are further differences in the procedures that are available:

- Where entrepreneurs are brought within the business insolvency framework, only some Member States provide fast track/low cost procedures for entrepreneurs.
- Some Member States only allow entrepreneurs with lower value business to access procedures available to natural persons.
- Some Member States only allow historical entrepreneurial debt to be included in procedures designed for natural persons, that is an entrepreneur in current difficulties will not have access to the procedures.
- Some Member States only allow professionals or the self-employed access to the procedures available for natural persons; sole traders may therefore be excluded, if not seen as 'self-employed'.
- Length of procedures vary.

Here, good examples of practices that support entrepreneurs include countries where entrepreneurs are either treated in the same way as natural persons, or are given access to lower cost or fast-track procedures. Whilst there is a balance to be achieved as far as creditors are concerned, in particular in relation to business debt, some entrepreneurs, particularly those who are sole traders with no or very few employees, suffer similar detriment to private individuals. This should be recognized.

The rationale for only treating smaller individual enterprises the same as natural persons is presumed to be that these debtors suffer the same detriments and vulnerabilities as an individual in a private capacity. As such this seems a valid approach: bigger business will have the resources and access to financial expertise, and the balance between debtor and creditor interests is served. By the same token it is important that sole traders with modest turnover be allowed full access to appropriate procedures and be treated as other individuals; the divergence across Member States in this regard may require further examination. This is also the case with the availability of low cost fast-track procedures where entrepreneurs are subject to the insolvency rules applicable to all businesses/corporations.

The final point to make here is that the divergence in approach may mean that in one Member State an entrepreneur will only have access to bankruptcy and face certain liquidation of assets, whereas in another debt settlement procedures will be available where liquidation may not be necessary. Whilst the debt settlement procedure model has its drawbacks, as is explored in further detail in Chapter 8, liquidation of a debtor's estate and business assets can also be a brutal experience for an individual.

7.6.1.3 Discharge from debt within three years

In the vast majority of Member States it is now possible for an entrepreneur to be discharged from debt; clearly where discharge is not yet available at all, reform is desirable. Beyond this, whilst incidence of no availability, or a discharge period of more than five years, is low, within the availability of discharge there are some observable differences:

- Discharge within three years is not guaranteed[46] (in fact this appears to be the case in only six of the Member States).
- Discharge may be available but is not always 'automatic' in that in some Member States the debtor may either have to re-apply or the order comes back before the court.
- Discharge does not guarantee a clean slate across all Member States (challenge/postponement or further payment requirements may be applied).
- Restriction is evident in that some Member States stipulate the debtor must be able to pay a percentage of debts in order to access the discharge procedure.

---

[46] The ECORYS Report concluded that the easiest states in which to obtain discharge were Romania, Portugal, Slovenia and Croatia; however, only Portugal guarantees discharge within three years.

- Discharge may only be available in bankruptcy or debt settlement procedures and not both.
- A number of Member States clearly refuse a ready 'third chance' in that they do not allow discharge if the debtor has already had one discharge in a previous period, for example ten years.
- Debts that may be excluded from discharge, or which may not be provable in the proceedings, vary.

Restrictions, such as not allowing a 'second bite of the cherry' in terms of having already accessed discharge procedures within a recent timescale, are perhaps an illustration of the balance that has to be achieved between the safeguarding of creditors as against the safeguarding of debtors. Constant recourse to discharge procedures may not only generate a danger of moral hazard but may also affect the availability of credit, in that creditors will see this as a negative risk factor. This period also potentially allows time for the debtor to receive advice, find sources of income and make a real attempt at rehabilitation, being given the necessary tools to help prevent further incidences of unmanageable debt.[47] The success of this will depend on an adequate support framework being in place.

However, it is clearly undesirable for there to be no availability of discharge at all, or for there to be a long period of time before a debtor can be discharged from debt: a period of over five years is most likely to be unsustainable for a debtor. This also flies in the face of the Commission's goal of a fresh start. Clearly here, examples of good practice are those Member States where discharge is guaranteed within three years, without further recourse to the court. However, it is important that any discharge can be revoked where it is apparent that the debtor has behaved in a manner clearly designed to disadvantage creditors. In this respect, the UK system provides an example of a system which encompasses these features.

The overall the picture is still relatively positive in that, although not necessarily available without further application to the court, discharge within three years is still *possible*, and in most cases can occur within five years. However, the data shows there is still work to be done before the goal of a maximum period of three years is realized. Furthermore, if some debts are excluded from discharge (for example, those incurred whilst

---

[47] Reifner *et al.* considered this period allows time for the debtor to receive advice, find sources of income and make a real attempt at rehabilitation, giving him/her the necessary tools to help prevent further incidences of unmanageable debt: U. Reifner, J. Niemi-Kiesilainen, N. Huls and H. Springeneer, *Over-indebtedness in European Consumer Law: Principles from 15 European States* (Books on Demand GmbH, 2010), p. 41.

pursuing a trade or those that relate to liability for a negligent act), the debtor and his/her family will not obtain a fresh start and will continue to be burdened by debts which have collectively pushed him or her into insolvency.

7.6.1.4   Safeguarding livelihood and support of the honest entrepreneur

The Recommendation makes it clear that potentially fraudulent or dishonest debtors should be discouraged from applying for discharge: prevention of re-application within a time period assists in this. However, provisions in the Member States also reflect a desire to restrict discharge where a debtor may have acted irresponsibly or not learnt from his or her mistakes. Certainly, the overall picture demonstrates that across most Member States criminal convictions, non-observance of bankruptcy obligations or other strategies that militate against creditors' interests will affect the availability of discharge. There is coherence in the existing provisions that restrict dishonest or fraudulent debtors, and discharge regimes across Member States contain provisions that safeguard creditors, whether by mechanisms for swelling the estate upon bankruptcy or delaying discharge.

Again, debtor protections in relation to safeguarding livelihood are present to some degree in most Member States. However, there are differing approaches beyond basic provision, and this in turn has the potential to militate against the debtor's rehabilitation and has a potential welfare cost:

- Whilst many Member States allow a living wage or a proportion of disposable income to be kept, there is no standard calculation across the EU.
- Not all Member States allow tools of the trade to be retained, or provisions differ in terms of which assets may be excluded from the liquidation.
- Protection against losing the home is not standard across the EU.

Here, the best examples of procedures clearly list those assets which can be retained, with a realistic calculation of what the debtor requires for a decent standard of living. Overall, it is interesting to note that there appears to be greater consistency in terms of restrictions for dishonest debtors rather than support for honest debtors; this arguably gives the impression that the emphasis is on exclusion of dishonesty rather than support for honesty.

BOX 7.2 *IRISH BANK RESOLUTION CORP. LTD V. QUINN* [2012] NI CH. 1

Sean Quinn was a property developer, resident in the Republic of Ireland, who filed for bankruptcy, North of the border, in the United Kingdom (Northern Ireland). This allowed him to take advantage of the much more generous UK system, which gives automatic discharge of debt after one year, once the bankruptcy order has been made. This is in contrast to 12 years, which applied in the Republic of Ireland at that time.

The creditor applied to have the bankruptcy order annulled, *inter alia*, on the basis that Quinn's real centre of main interest (COMI) was in the Republic of Ireland, and not the United Kingdom. The creditor succeeded. The court considered as relevant the facts that Quinn had an Irish passport, was registered as a voter in Ireland, and that although a UK taxpayer, 20 per cent of these taxes were transferred to the Republic of Ireland.

7.6.2 Remaining Observations

Council Regulation (EC) 1346/2000 on Insolvency Proceedings, and the recast Insolvency Regulation 2015/848 allow automatic recognition of bankruptcy and other proceedings across the EU (with the exception of Denmark). However, this is only where a procedure is listed by a country in Annex A of the Regulation, and this is left to the choice of Member States. This may therefore mean that whilst some procedures may be recognized in some Member States, others may not. Whilst procedures between Member States remain distinct, this situation leads to inconsistency, and ultimately the danger of insolvency tourism. Evidence of this lies in the experience of England and Wales, where the bankruptcy system is a particular choice of Irish and German nationals,[48] although this danger may be overstated.[49] On the other hand, favourable insolvency and over-indebtedness regimes may encourage individuals, particularly entrepreneurs, to move to such countries (see Box 7.2).

---

[48] See, e.g., *Official Receiver* v. *Eichler* [2007] BPIR 1636; *Official Receiver* v. *Mitterfellner* [2009] BPIR 1075, discussed in A. Walters and A. Smith, '"Bankruptcy Tourism" Under the EC Regulation on Insolvency Proceedings: A View from England and Wales' (2010) 19(3) *International Insolvency Review* 181, 182. Reasons for this are the automatic discharge provisions, the straightforward process and eligibility criteria: *ibid.* 191–3.

[49] H. Vallender, H. Allemand, S. Baister, P. Kuglarz, H. Mathijsen, B. O'Neill, E. Collins and S. Potamitis, 'A Minimum Standard for Debt Discharge in Europe' (2013) 26(7) *Insolvency Intelligence* 97.

It is disturbing to note more generally that the list of debts which are not discharged in an insolvency procedure appears to be increasing in many countries. The prospect here is that the stigma and legal and factual restrictions attached to an over-indebtedness procedure are present but the procedure itself does not in fact provide the conditions for a genuine fresh start.[50] The same point can be made about the continuing restrictions a debtor may face, even after discharge, and the continuing nature of debt settlement procedures. Here, the debtor may find him or herself tied to payment instalments over a long period of time, which prevent any meaningful accumulation of wealth that will allow an improvement in circumstances. However, even if bankruptcy and a clean slate is available, many debtors still seem to shun this procedure due to the heavy stigma that still attaches to it.

Nevertheless, there should be a balance between the protection of creditor and debtor interests. The effects of the recent financial crisis and credit crunch cannot be ignored, as this has resulted in the banks being more cautious in their approach to lending; this is particularly so in relation to small businesses[51] and therefore entrepreneurs. For example, in the period 2009–13, 25 per cent of small and medium-sized enterprises (SMEs) in the euro area encountered problems when applying for bank credit facilities.[52] A careful balance therefore has to be struck.

In conclusion, the 'spirit' of the principle of second chance is reflected across Member States at some level, although the aim of discharge within three years across the EU is not yet a reality. Some Member States, such as Hungary and Sweden, have or are bringing forward new legislation to better reflect the requirements of the Recommendation, but this is not across the board. Proposed new national legislation may assist further coherence in discharge regimes in terms of general approach, but divergences across Member States will perhaps inevitably still remain in the detail.

---

[50]   *Ibid.* 103.
[51]   ESRC Evidence Briefing, *The Effect of the Credit Crisis on UK SME Finance* (2009), available at www.esrc.ac.uk/files/publications/evidence-briefings/the-effect-of-the-credit-crisis-on-uk-sme-finance-pdf/.
[52]   G. Wehinger, 'SMEs and the Credit Crunch: Current Financing Difficulties, Policy Measures and a Review of Literature' (2013) 2 *OECD Journal, Financial Market Trends* 115.

8.   Consumer over-indebtedness

8.1   INTRODUCTION

Consumer over-indebtedness is a social circumstance that has grown in significance, in terms of policy both within Member States and at EU level. Policy approaches designed to address this circumstance have included not only insolvency laws, that allow bankruptcy, debt settlement procedures and discharge, but also other forms of protection and relief, such as regulation of the provision of credit, debt enforcement and collection[1] and the provision of state funded debt advice and financial education. Of course, any 'advice' or assistance to the consumer, whether provided through an insolvency practitioner (IP) (as commonly recognized), debt advisor or any other official or office holder involved in the insolvency procedure, must be completely impartial and in the best interests of the consumer. Any opportunity to exploit the role should be completely excluded. A debt advisor's aim is to help the over-indebted consumer find the best possible way to re-pay debt whilst maintaining an acceptable standard of life. This may differ from an IP whose primary focus is to obtain repayment of debt for the benefit of the creditor.

In this Report, we refer to consumer over-indebtedness. This is defined in the Glossary as indication of an inability or difficulty in meeting payment obligations. By this we mean ongoing difficulties in relation to financial obligations that have become due, such as monthly payments for rent or household bills and other payments, such as loan or other credit instalments. This reflects the definition adopted by the recent study into consumer over-indebtedness by Civic Consulting of the Consumer Policy Evaluation Consortium (in co-operation with the University of Bristol's Personal Finance Research Centre) ('Civic Consulting Report').[2]

---

[1]   U. Reifner, J. Niemi-Kiesilainen, N. Huls and H. Springeneer, *Over-indebtedness in European Consumer Law Principles from 15 European States* (Books on Demand GmbH, 2010), p. xi.

[2]   Civic Consulting, *The Over-Indebtedness of European Households: Updated Mapping of the Situation, Nature and Causes, Effects and Initiatives for Alleviating Its Impact, Final Report* (2014). The Report was commissioned by the Directorate General for Health and Consumers of the European Commission and was based

However, this does not include the overall amount due on large long-standing commitments such as a mortgage, where it is not envisaged the debt will be satisfied by a single payment. It should be noted at this stage, in any event, that secured debt on the home is often treated separately during bankruptcy.

There is plenty of information as to the causes of consumer over-indebtedness experienced by households. Reasons include a drop in income,[3] poor budget management, compulsive buying, and aggressive advertising.[4] Particular credit products, such as credit cards,[5] and high cost short-term credit,[6] have been associated with increasing the risk of consumer over-indebtedness. In the Civic Consulting Report, interviewed stakeholders[7] identified high interest rate credit, home loans and other forms of consumer credit as a cause of household financial difficulty.[8] However, one thing on which the research seems to agree is that such over-indebtedness normally results from an unexpected event, or from life-changing situations, and may be a combination of any or all of the above.

A connection has also been made between consumer over-

---

on interviews with stakeholders (in all Member States) and 'over-indebted households' (in France, Hungary, Germany, Slovenia, Spain and the United Kingdom), desk research, analysis of statistical data and country reports, and a survey of services connected to debt counselling and guidance.

[3]   *Ibid.* para. 1.1.4. Both stakeholders and consumers interviewed for the study indicated this as a reason for consumer over-indebtedness.

[4]   European Commission, *Towards a Common Operational European Definition of Over-Indebtedness*, OEE Etudes (2008), pp. 23–8.

[5]   E.g., revolving credit provided by credit cards: I. Ramsay, 'Regulation of Consumer Credit' in G. Howells, I. Ramsay, T. Wilhelmsson with David Kraft (eds), *Handbook of Research on International Consumer Law* (Cheltenham and Northampton, MA, Edward Elgar Publishing, 2010), p. 368; G. Trumbull, *Consumer Lending in France and America: Credit and Welfare* (Cambridge, Cambridge University Press, 2014), p. 191, or high cost credit such as home credit (doorstep loans).

[6]   T. Wilson, 'The Responsible Lending Response' in T. Wilson (ed.), *International Responses to Issues of Credit and Over-indebtedness in the Wake of Crisis* (Farnham, Ashgate, 2013), p. 120.

[7]   The study conducted 277 stakeholder interviews in all the Member States. This included independent experts and interviewees from the financial industry, civil society organizations, and public authorities.

[8]   Civic Consulting, *The Over-Indebtedness of European Households* (n. 2 above) 9.

indebtedness, poverty and exclusion, both social and financial.[9] As a result of a drive to combat poverty and social exclusion,[10] Member States adopted National Action Plans for social inclusion, the basic aim being to promote more effective policy in this regard. These plans were reviewed by the European Commission in 2003, where again the importance of fighting social exclusion and poverty was reiterated.[11] This was continued in the Europe 2020 strategy,[12] where tackling poverty and social exclusion is integral to the Flagship Initiative 'European Platform against Poverty'.[13]

Perhaps inevitably, more vulnerable members of society (e.g. those on low incomes, single parents) are more likely to be excluded.[14] Moreover, the vulnerable are more likely to experience financial difficulty.[15] Those on low incomes and the young are the most likely to become over-indebted should they suffer financial shock, whether through general economic conditions such as a rise in interest rates, or through personal circumstances (such as unemployment).[16] Those consumers who do not have access to the full range of credit facilities within the market place are left with no option but to turn to more expensive forms of credit. Such consumers are more likely to want short-term cash loans, a service not provided by mainstream lending. Higher interest rates (and other costs) will inevitably mean a greater risk of inability to cope should an unexpected event occur. However, it is not just those on low incomes that may be affected. Individuals across society can experience unmanageable debt and its consequences. In the comparator country, the United States, this is

---

[9] See, e.g., UK Government White Paper, *Fair Clear and Competitive: The Consumer Credit Market in the 21st Century* (Cm 6040, 2003), para. 5.1.

[10] Prompted by the aim of the Lisbon European Council (of March 2000) to eradicate poverty by 2010. Communication from the Commission to the Council, the European Parliament, the European Economic and Social Committee and the Committee of the Regions, Joint Report on social inclusion summarising the results of the examination of the National Action Plans for Social Inclusion (2003–2005), COM(2003)773 final, Executive Summary, p. 4.

[11] *Ibid.* 5.

[12] Communication from the Commission, *Europe 2020 A Strategy for Smart, Sustainable and Inclusive Growth*, COM(2010)2020 final, p. 18.

[13] *Ibid.* 19.

[14] HM Treasury (UK), *Promoting Financial Inclusion* (2004), ch. 2.

[15] Certainly this has been the case in the United Kingdom: E. Kempson, *Over-indebtedness in Britain, A Report to the Department of Trade and Industry* (Personal Finance Research Centre, 2002). The report lists young householders, those who experience key life events, low incomes or drop in income as most likely to be in financial difficulty (para. 3.3).

[16] *Ibid.* para. 1.46.

also an observable middle class problem,[17] and indeed this appears to be a developing trend across EU Member States.[18]

All of these issues are directly linked to the welfare of consumers and also touch on consumer spending and purchasing power. The Civic Consulting Report refers to reported reduced standards of living and a decline in health, particularly mental health (evidenced by depression and feelings of stress).[19] The impact of interest rates and lending practices on borrowers (particularly the more vulnerable) and the effect of unpaid debt on the economy are also relevant.[20] Consumer over-indebtedness procedures, however, are only one aspect of tackling these questions. Other controls, such as ensuring fair and responsible lending practices, are used, together with 'softer' options such as financial education. Interest rate caps are also utilized sporadically across the EU, in some countries this being more controversial than others.

The efficacy and validity of interest rate control by means of a legal ceiling is a question that has, for example, dogged UK policy. There have been many arguments for and against such control, and it is only very recently that a cap on rates for high cost credit (payday lending) has been imposed. Price is certainly seen as key in determining whether consumer credit is given on unfair terms.[21] This, however, is not something specifically addressed in the Consumer Credit Directive 2008/48/EC; the emphasis seems to be on ensuring transparency of cost rather than amount. It was recognized in the report for the D-G for Employment Social Affairs and Equal Opportunities in 2008, *Towards a Common Operational European Definition of Over-Indebtedness*, that the question of an interest rate cap is a complex issue; not only does it raise, for example, questions

---

[17]   E. Warren, T.A. Sullivan and J. Lawrence Westbrook, *The Fragile Middle Class American in Debt* (New Haven, CT, Yale University, 2000), ch. 1.

[18]   Civic Consulting, *The Over-Indebtedness of European Households* (n. 2 above) 6.

[19]   *Ibid.* 11.

[20]   *Ibid.* 11–12.

[21]   The EESC in particular saw price as a relevant factor. When considering the initial proposal for the Consumer Credit Directive, it advocated interest rate ceilings as a protection for those consumers who do not in reality have freedom of choice; setting interest rates at an EU level was the most effective way of ensuring there would be limited restriction on competition. Opinion of 16 and 17 July 2003 of the European Economic and Social Committee on the Proposal for a Directive of the European Parliament and of the Council on the harmonisation of the laws, regulations and administrative provisions of the Member States concerning credit for consumers [2003] OJ C234/1, para. 2.2.4.5.

of exclusion and market distortion (as referred to above), different rules as to the control of interest rates apply in different EU Member States.[22]

Some states do not employ a ceiling at all,[23] whilst others, although imposing a ceiling or ceilings, use varying methods of calculation and parameters. On this basis, the report concluded that the issue of interest rate caps was best dealt with at national level.[24] In 2011, a public consultation was published by the European Commission on interest rate restrictions in the EU. Some Member State authorities supported interest rate restrictions, some were less supportive, citing potential problems with illegal lending, distortion of competition and a drift of interest rates towards the imposed ceiling. The Commission was advised that the principle of subsidiarity was still most appropriate.[25]

The question as to how this detriment, particularly for consumers, can be prevented, or its impact reduced through law, is complex and is informing reform across the EU. For example, in the years leading up to the 2006 reforms of the Consumer Credit Act 1974, the UK government set up a Task Force to look into the reasons for and consequences of consumer over-indebtedness, since such over-indebtedness was seen as one of the 'main drivers' behind the consultation on legislative amendment.[26] Reforms have taken place in other EU Member States to address this issue, and are continuing, most notably in some of the newest Member States, such as Romania, Hungary, Lithuania and Slovenia.

The Commission Recommendation of 12 March 2014 aims to facilitate 'the efficient restructuring of viable enterprises in financial difficulty and give honest Entrepreneurs a second chance'. Whilst the consumer is not as such within the scope of the Recommendation, it is nevertheless indicated that some points of the Recommendation may also be relevant to the

---

[22] OEE Etudes, *Towards a Common Operational European Definition of Over-indebtedness* (2007), pp. 71–4; I. Ramsay, 'To Heap Distress upon Distress? Comparative Reflections on Interest Rate Ceilings' (2010) 60 *University of Toronto Law Journal* 713.

[23] *Towards a Common Operational European Definition of Over-indebtedness* (n. 22 above) 74.

[24] *Ibid.*

[25] European Commission, *Summary of Responses to the Public Consultation on the Study on Interest Rate Restrictions in the EU* (15 June 2011), p. 5, available at http://ec.europa.eu/internal_market/finservices-retail/docs/policy/irr_summary_en.pdf.

[26] DTI, *Tackling Loan Sharks and More: Consultation Document on Modernising the Consumer Credit Act 1974* (July 2001), para. 1.2.

treatment of consumer over-indebtedness,[27] where the aim is to help the consumer recover and allow a 'fresh' start.

Over-indebtedness legal procedures attract a varied terminology that is used interchangeably,[28] and indeed this is the case more generally in relation to the terms used to denote consumer insolvency or consumer inability to meet debt commitment.[29] Member States' approaches have been variously grouped by commentators. For example, a recent study conducted by Viavoice Research Institute[30] classifies EU insolvency procedures into 'model' systems:[31] the Market Model,[32] Rehabilitation Model[33] and Liability Model.[34] However, at a general level, as discussed in Chapter 7, they can be broadly identified as bankruptcy, debt settlement procedures or informal arrangements. Debtors subject to bankruptcy will necessarily have their assets sold, with payment of proceeds split between creditors according to a preordained list. In debt settlement procedures, liquidation of assets is not inevitable, and debtors will be expected to commit to regular payments to satisfy creditors, whether in full or in part, under a payment plan. Both categories of legal proceedings will normally culminate in discharge some time in the future, with a moratorium in place during the payment plan or other period whilst the legal proceedings are extant. The difference essentially lies in how quickly discharge will be achieved.

The conventional aim of a debt settlement procedure is to enable the debtor to avoid the stigma of bankruptcy, and allow a manageable scheme for meeting his/her obligations from future income. However, as outlined in Chapter 7, the payment plan presents problems if monthly or

---

[27]   Commission Recommendation of 12 March 2014 on a new approach to business failure and insolvency (COM(2014)1500 final), p. 4.

[28]   E.g., in the comparator jurisdiction of Norway, debt settlement procedures are distinct from bankruptcy, yet both may involve liquidation of the debtor's estate.

[29]   S. Viimsalu, 'The Over-Indebtedness Regulatory System in the Light of the Changing Economic Landscape' (2010) 17 *Juridica International* 217, p. 218. Bankruptcy and insolvency, although often seen as interchangeable, also have distinct connotations in law within the United Kingdom: D. Milman, *Personal Insolvency Law, Regulation and Policy (Markets and the Law)* (Abingdon, Routledge, 2005), p. 3.

[30]   Viavoice, *Introductory Report Towards a 'Second Chance' Legislation in Europe* (February 2015).

[31]   *Ibid.* 4.

[32]   Encourages responsible lenders.

[33]   Focuses on social consideration and deserving debtors.

[34]   Burden on debtor to show good conduct.

weekly payments by the consumer debtor are set at too high a level or the payment plan endures for many years. It should also be re-iterated here that whilst some assets may be excluded from a liquidation process, and a basic level of income is allowed to the debtor so that he/she and any dependants can enjoy a basic standard of living, the family home is often only subject to temporary reprieve from sale. Losing the home inevitably has a detrimental impact on the debtor and his/her family, both practically and psychologically.

The comparator jurisdictions of the United States and Norway both provide for procedures that may lead to discharge, although aspects of the US approach have come under considerable pressure with concerns about abuse by debtors, particularly consumer debtors, who can actually afford to repay some portion of their debts but are attempting to escape this obligation.[35] The payment plan (with discharge once the plan is completed) under Chapter 13 of the US Bankruptcy Code, is now seen as more appropriate for such debtors, rather than the immediate discharge from debt allowed by Chapter 7. Consumer debtors, therefore, but not those individual debtors with a set proportion of business debts, are screened financially before being allowed access to Chapter 7 proceedings. Interestingly then, this potentially excludes consumers rather than entre-preneurs from the benefits provided by Chapter 7. The 'new' US policy was implemented by amendments to the Bankruptcy Code provisions in the Bankruptcy Abuse Prevention and Consumer Protection Act 2005. Some commentators have, however, criticized both the rationale of this new policy and the manner of its implementation.[36]

Discharge in Norway is available through the debt settlement proce-dures under the Bankruptcy Act and Debt Settlement Act. Here, a vol-untary or compulsory debt settlement procedure can be filed either under the Bankruptcy Act 1988 or under the Debt Settlement for Individuals Act 1992. The aim is for the debtor to regain control of his or her affairs through an arrangement with creditors. Discharge is considered to have

---

[35] R.M. Lawless, A.K. Littwin, K.M. Porter, J.A.E. Pottow, D.K. Thorne and E. Warren, 'Did Bankruptcy Reform Fail? An Empirical Study of Consumer Debtors' (2008) 82 *American Bankruptcy Law Journal* 349, p. 351.

[36] J. Kilborn, 'La Responsibilisation de l'economie: What the United States Can Learn from the New French Law on Over-indebtedness' (2005) 26 *Michigan Journal of International Law* 619. See also, e.g., C.J. Tabb and C. Jordan, 'The Death of Consumer Bankruptcy in the US?' (Fall 2001) *Bankruptcy Developments Journal*; C.J. Tabb, 'Bankruptcy after the Fall. US Law under s 256' (2006) 43 *Canadian Business Law Journal* 28; M.J. White, *Bankruptcy Reform and Credit Cards*, NBER Working Paper No. 13265 (July 2007).

taken place when the debt settlement is granted, although this can be set aside in certain circumstances.

As noted in relation to entrepreneurs, there is evidence of convergence in general approaches to discharge.[37] Nevertheless, in relation to consumers the data gathered for this Report suggests there is considerable divergence in the detailed treatment of discharge and in the procedures that lead to it.[38] Experiences of debtors across the EU therefore differ and the same issues of insolvency tourism mentioned in Chapter 7 may be relevant, although the evidence is slight.

This chapter provides the comparative analysis on a number of aspects of Member States' approaches to consumer over-indebtedness procedures, and provides a basis for future consideration of legal change.

8.2   GENERAL ASPECTS OF CONSUMER OVER-INDEBTEDNESS

There are a number of legal and policy tools for tackling the problem of consumer over-indebtedness, such as ensuring fair treatment of the consumer, transparency, responsible lending,[39] and more controversially, the price of credit.[40] However, where consumer over-indebtedness cannot be avoided it is important to ensure the related circumstances of financial and social exclusion are mitigated. One way of delivering this is by putting in place mechanisms that support the debtor, including the opportunity for a second chance, or a 'fresh start', as outlined in the Commission Recommendation of 2014.

Consumer over-indebtedness has been recognized as a problem at EU

---

[37]   J. Niemi, 'Personal Insolvency' in G. Howells, I. Ramsay, T. Wilhelmsson with David Kraft (eds), *Handbook of Research on International Consumer Law* (Cheltenham and Northampton, MA, Edward Elgar Publishing, 2010), p. 423; J. Niemi, 'Consumer Insolvency in the European Legal Context' (2012) 35 *Journal of Consumer Policy* 443, 445.

[38]   As observed by Niemi, 'Consumer Insolvency in the European Legal Context' (n. 37) 445.

[39]   See, e.g., Reifner *et al.*, *Over-indebtedness in European Consumer Law* (n. 1 above) 91.

[40]   S. Brown, 'Using the Law as a Usury Law: Definitions of Usury and Recent Developments in the Regulation of Unfair Charges in Consumer Credit Transactions' (2011) 1 *Journal of Business Law* 91. See, e.g., the recent imposition of an interest rate cap on payday lending in the United Kingdom.

BOX 8.1 SWEDISH NATIONAL AUDIT OFFICE SUMMARY 2015

The Swedish National Audit Office published a report in May 2015 (*Audit Summary: Government Measures Against Over-indebtedness*, RiR 2015:14) stating that the number of over-indebted individuals was increasing:

- Recent figures suggested approximately 28,000 people in Sweden would be eligible for debt settlement procedures.
- 10,083 applications were received in 2014, the highest since the introduction of the Debt Relief Act.
- Costs to society were manifested in healthcare, unemployment benefit and other social security support mechanisms.

---

level,[41] and across Member States, particularly as a result of the global financial crisis from 2008 onwards,[42] and response to the crisis prompted reform, for example, in Greece.[43] The recent Hungarian reform, providing for specific insolvency proceedings for consumers, was introduced as a result of the financial crisis, which caused consumer inability to meet obligations in relation to loans, credit cards, and most significantly, foreign currency denominated mortgage-backed housing credits.[44]

Concern about consumer over-indebtedness continues, with the situation being monitored by some countries, for example in Sweden (see Box 8.1).[45]

Interestingly, however, the number of debtors *accessing* procedures in other Member States may be decreasing, as is demonstrated by the Insolvency Service of England and Wales in the United Kingdom (see Box 8.2).

---

[41] See, e.g., the report prepared for the European Commission, *Towards a Common Operational European Definition of Over-indebtedness* (n. 22 above); European Economic and Social Committee, Opinion of the European Economic and Social Committee on Credit and Social Exclusion in an Affluent Society [2008] OJ C44/19.

[42] Although individual Member States' experience varies, see Civic Consulting, *The Over-Indebtedness of European Households* (n. 2 above) 241.

[43] In Cyprus, where the recent reform to the Cypriot insolvency laws were introduced as emergency measures in response to the financial problems faced by Cyprus in 2011–12.

[44] Introduced in 2004.

[45] See www.responsible-credit.net/index.php?id=1980&viewid=48843.

BOX 8.2   INSOLVENCY SERVICE OF ENGLAND AND
WALES, KEY FINDINGS FOR Q2 2015

Insolvency Service, *Insolvency Statistics, January to March 2015* (Q2 2015), pp. 4,
12, 13, available at www.gov.uk/government/uploads/system/uploads/attachment_
data/file/448858/Q2_2015_statistics_release-web.pdf:

● Individual insolvencies were at their lowest level since Q3 2005: there were
a total of 18,866 individual insolvencies in Q2 2015, 9.1 per cent lower than
Q1 2015 and a decrease of 29.3 per cent compared to Q2 2014.
● The number of bankruptcies was at the lowest level since Q4 1990: there
were a total of 3,944 bankruptcy orders in Q2 2015, 6.3 per cent lower than
Q1 2015 and 27.9 per cent lower than Q2 2014. The number of bankruptcy
orders has been on a decreasing trend since 2009. However, the introduction of debt relief orders (DROs) in 2009 is likely to have affected the number
of bankruptcies.
● The number of DROs was at the lowest level since Q1 2010: there
were 5,832 DROs in Q2 2015, which was a 6.1 per cent decrease compared to Q1 2015 and 16.8 per cent lower compared to the same period in
2014.
● IVAs were at the lowest level since Q1 2006: there were 9,090 IVAs in Q2
2015, which was a 12.1 per cent decrease compared to Q1 2015 and 35.9
per cent lower than Q2 2014. IVAs have decreased for four consecutive
quarters having previously been on an increasing trend.
● The rate of insolvency decreased: in the 12 months ending Q2 2015, one in
523 adults (0.19 per cent of the adult population) became insolvent. This was
the lowest rate since the 12 months ending Q1 2006.

Evidence of debtors taking up procedures is referred to further below.

Research into the problem was seen as a priority as early as 1992[46] and
this issue has been regarded as extremely relevant to the aim of a harmonized European market, and social justice.[47] Yet in order to tackle this phe-
nomenon, some coherent understanding of consumer over-indebtedness is
needed. Historically, definitions have had some manifestation of financial

---

[46]   Within the development of consumer protection policy: Opinion of the
Economic and Social Committee on household over-indebtedness (own initiative
opinion), CES 511/2002.
[47]   The EESC Opinion on credit and social exclusion in an affluent society
2008/C44/19, highlighted once more concerns about over-indebtedness and its
consequences, in particular in relation to 'exclusion, social justice and the internal
market' (para. 1.2).

problems as their base.[48] For example, the European Economic and Social Committee in their Opinion on Credit and Social Exclusion in an Affluent Society identified 'failed attempts at self-employment [or the] collapse of a small family business' as possible culprits of consumer over-indebtedness, demonstrating it is not always easy to differentiate between entrepreneurial and consumer financial difficulty.

The study published in 2012 by London Economics used difficulty or impossibility to pay debts owed 'according to the schedule of payments. . . agreed in the debt agreement',[49] as a definition of consumer over-indebtedness. However, despite attempts to find a common definition across Europe,[50] no such definition at present exists[51] and there are calls for this to change.[52] Having said that, in the most recent study on causes of consumer over-indebtedness and potential solutions conducted by Civic Consulting in 2014, the conclusion was that a precise definition is, in reality, not that helpful, and that in fact a reliable set of common indicators of consumer over-indebtedness is what is required.[53]

8.2.1 Definitions

The term 'over-indebtedness' is used by a number of Member States to denote, not a consumer 'condition', but the situation where a business's assets are insufficient to cover its liabilities. Nevertheless, it is clear from the data gathered for this Report that whilst the term 'over-indebtedness' may not be applicable to consumers, various definitions are used by Member States to identify what is in effect consumer over-indebtedness, whether in the insolvency context, that is an inability to pay debts as a

---

[48] Whether focusing on arrears or simply difficulty in meeting current commitments, see European Commission, *Towards a Common Operational European Definition of Over-indebtedness* (n. 22 above).

[49] London Economics, *Study on Means to Protect Consumers in Financial Difficulty: Personal Bankruptcy, Datio in Solutum of Mortgages, and Restrictions on Debt Collection Abusive Practices, Final Report* (2012), p. vii.

[50] *Towards a Common Operational European Definition of Over-indebtedness* (n. 22 above).

[51] Civic Consulting, *The Over-Indebtedness of European Households* (n. 2 above) para. 1.1.1.

[52] Opinion of the European Economic and Social Committee on consumer protection and appropriate treatment of over-indebtedness to prevent social exclusion, Rapporteur-general: Reine-Claude Mader (2014).

[53] This was based on the interviews with stakeholders across Member States who showed little enthusiasm for a better definition, preferring clarity in terms of indicators of over-indebtedness: Civic Consulting, *The Over-Indebtedness of European Households* (n. 2 above) 4.

criteria for accessing legal procedures, or in a wider social context. In Austria, the Czech Republic, Denmark, Estonia, Finland, Germany, Latvia, Lithuania, Poland, Portugal, Romania, Slovakia and Slovenia, consumer over-indebtedness is described specifically as consumer insolvency or 'bankruptcy'. In other Member States, such as in Cyprus, Greece, Ireland, the Netherlands, Spain and the United Kingdom, it is recognized as a basis for relief from debt more generally.

A stand-alone definition may be used for policy purposes, such as is the case in the United Kingdom and Poland. However, very few Member States use a specific definition for legal purposes; France (*'surendettement'*) to the extent that consumer over-indebtedness attracts its own procedure (as opposed to insolvency), and Luxembourg (article 2 of the Law of 8 January 2013). Italian insolvency law provides a statutory definition of over-indebtedness, this being a condition for entering into debt settlement procedures.[54] Slovenia has a consumer 'insolvency' definition in the ZFPPIPP (Insolvency Act). Spain has a general insolvency definition for natural and legal persons. These definitions are all, in effect, stated statutory objective measurements for allowing a debtor access to a procedure.

Otherwise, Member States 'measure' consumer over-indebtedness through general legal preconditions for access to bankruptcy, debt settlement procedures and other mechanisms. These are primarily eligibility criteria by which a procedure may be available, and may therefore differ within a particular country's approach to a particular procedure. For example, there are different requirements for bankruptcy compared to other debt settlement procedures in Cyprus, Ireland and the United Kingdom.

The law in some countries is prescriptive, with baseline minimum amount of debts in certain situations, such as the United Kingdom (England), where a minimum of £5,000[55] must be owed before a creditor can petition for a debtor's bankruptcy (although this is not required if the debtor petitions him/herself); and in Slovenia, where the debtor must be in payment default of at least 1,000 euros if unemployed in order to access bankruptcy under the ZFPPIPP.[56] In Scotland, a debtor must owe at least £1,500; and in Latvia, the debtor must show his/her debt exceeds 5,000 euros before he or she can petition for bankruptcy, or alternatively that the debt obligations are at least 10,000 euros and are due within a year.

---

[54]   Law No. 3/2012.
[55]   Insolvency Act 1986, s. 267(4) (October 2015). The threshold was previously £750.
[56]   Insolvency Act (Official Gazette RS No. 126-6413/2007), art. 14(3).

Others, in addition or instead, use a debt to income ratio, again such as Slovenia (the ZFPPIPP requires payment default of one or more obligations in total exceeding three times salary and other income received over two months maximum); as does Romania (presumption of inability to pay debt based on a threshold of debt equivalent to a basic minimum income). Income and/or debt to income ratio are also relevant in other ways. Denmark uses a debt/income ratio, not in relation to the definition of insolvency as such, but in deciding whether a debtor may access the debt settlement procedure. In this case, household income and household expenses (which includes responsibilities for dependants) are included. Household expenses are also taken into account in calculating net income in Cyprus, where again, whilst not a strict debt to income ratio assessment, the debtor applies for discharge on the basis that income is below 200 euros per month, and there is inability to meet debts. Hungary's new provisions in the Debt Consolidation Act 2015 provide that the precondition for initiating the procedure is on the basis of a debt to income ratio. Otherwise, whilst inevitably some idea of income not meeting debt is inferred, countries have a more general illiquidity test which is often a permanent inability to pay debts, whether expressed as a minimum period (e.g., at least 12 months from the application or filing of proceedings in Cyprus and Romania), or more generally.

There is, however, also a certain commonality in approach. Whilst not always directly addressed by the returned data, it is clear that definitions are applicable to an individual, rather than a household, although in assessing the ability to pay debts, household expenses and costs of caring responsibilities may be taken into account. Whilst some countries allow debtors to apply jointly, for example, if married or part of the same household, the assessment is still at an individual level (although in Hungary co-debtors' indebtedness can be brought within the assessment). For example, in Finland, spouses, co-debtors and guarantors can apply for joint debt settlement; in Latvia, a debtor can apply jointly with a spouse or other relation; and in Poland, spouses with joint debt can apply to have separate proceedings joined together.

It should be noted at this stage that only Bulgaria, Croatia and Malta do not recognize consumer over-indebtedness in that they have no bankruptcy or debt settlement procedures that cater for consumers. Whilst Malta provides for a specific bankruptcy regime for sole traders, in Bulgaria and Croatia, individuals will only be subject to the general insolvency proceedings as entrepreneurs. In Hungary and Romania, new laws recognizing consumer over-indebtedness have been passed in 2015, although those in Romania only came into force in December 2015, and in Croatia draft laws are being discussed.

In the comparator countries of Norway and the United States, there is no standard legal definition as such, so reflecting the majority position across the EU. In terms of conditions for access to procedures, the comparator jurisdiction of Norway provides both an illiquidity test (debt to income ratio) and insufficiency test (a debt to assets ratio) for bankruptcy, whereas for debt settlement procedures an objective illiquidity test is used (permanently unable to fulfil obligations), together with further subjective elements. In the United States, in contrast, there is no pre-insolvency condition (although there are other eligibility criteria), but the procedures are usually accessed by those who are unable to pay their debts.

Table 8.1 provides a précis of how Member States and the comparator countries approach the definition of consumer over-indebtedness.

8.2.2   Treatment of Over-indebted Individuals and Procedures Available

When a consumer becomes over-indebted there may be a number of procedural options, such as bankruptcy, debt settlement procedures, or informal arrangements. Table 8A.1 (in the appendix to this chapter) provides a basic list of these procedures. The approach to consumers as a 'special case' is mixed across the Member States. For example, the Czech Republic simply applies the insolvency regime that is applicable to all persons, whatever their status; the situation in Germany is similar where only the procedural requirements differ. The remainder also allow consumers access to the general insolvency procedures, but may also provide special regimes.

In Austria, as well as access to debt settlement procedures under the general provisions, natural persons may obtain discharge from the court without creditor approval: in addition consumers' petitions are only handled by district courts rather than higher courts, and the appointment of an IP is not mandatory. In Belgium, it seems that within the general regime, consumers enjoy specific treatment in terms of debt settlement procedures, but are unable to access bankruptcy. In Estonia, Finland, the Netherlands and Sweden, bankruptcy conducted through the court is applicable, but there are special debt settlement procedures for natural persons. The remaining Member States, apart from Bulgaria, Croatia and Malta, also have particular regimes for consumers. This may be as consumers per se, or in the wider context of natural persons, as for example in Ireland, Slovakia and the United Kingdom.

The special procedures in some Member States are not based in bankruptcy but in debt settlement procedures (Belgium, Cyprus, Greece and Luxembourg). Other Member States offer both bankruptcy and debt settlement procedures (e.g. France, Ireland, Latvia, Portugal and the United

Table 8.1 Definition of consumer over-indebtedness

Country	Consumer over-indebtedness definition
Austria	Only test: consumer insolvency–illiquidity as for other debtors
Belgium	No standard definition
	Only test based in procedure access criteria
Bulgaria	Consumer over-indebtedness not recognized
Croatia	No regulation on consumer bankruptcy
Cyprus	No standard definition
	Only test based in procedure access criteria
Czech Republic	No standard definition
	Only test based in procedure access criteria
Denmark	No standard definition
	Only test based in procedure access criteria
Estonia	No standard definition
	Only test based in procedure access criteria
Finland	No standard definition
	Only test based in procedure access criteria
France	*Surendettement*: clear inability to meet non-professional debts in good faith
	Rétablissement personnel (personal rescue): insolvency, i.e. no real possibility of being able to pay debts
Germany	No standard definition
	Only test based in procedure access criteria
Greece	No standard definition
	Only test based in procedure access criteria
Hungary	No standard definition
	Only test based in procedure access criteria
Ireland	No standard definition
	Only test based in procedure access criteria
Italy	Statutory definition: either persistent imbalance between obligations and assets that can be converted to cash, when this imbalance can produce difficulty in meeting debts; or permanent inability to meet debts regularly
Latvia	No standard definition
	Only test based in procedure access criteria
Lithuania	No standard definition
	Only test based in procedure access criteria
Luxembourg	Law of 8 January 2013, article 2, definition of consumer over-indebtedness: manifest inability of debtor to meet the entirety of non-professional debts due or to become due and/or personal guarantees made for debts of sole trader

Table 8.1   (continued)

Country	Consumer over-indebtedness definition
Malta	No definition of consumer over-indebtedness
	No consumer proceedings per se
Netherlands	No standard definition
	Only test based in procedure access criteria
Poland	No standard definition
	Only test based in procedure access criteria
Portugal	No standard definition
	Only test based in procedure access criteria
Romania	No standard definition
	Only test based in procedure access criteria
Slovakia	No standard definition
	Only test based in procedure access criteria, same as for entrepreneurs
Slovenia	Consumer insolvency definition in ZFPPIPP: (i) payment default on one or more obligations which in total exceeds three times salary and other income; (ii) if unemployed, in payment default for at least 1,000 euros
Spain	General insolvency definition: debtor cannot pay debts on regular basis as they mature or expects will not be able to
Sweden	No standard definition
	Only test based in procedure access criteria
United Kingdom	No standard definition
	Only test based in procedure access criteria
United States	No standard definition
Norway	No standard definition
	Only test based in procedure access criteria

Kingdom) or bankruptcy only (Lithuania, Slovenia). The data suggest that these procedures are predominantly court based, although there is provision for out of court mediation, or attempts at out of court settlement in a few Member States before court processes can begin (Estonia, Finland, Germany, Greece, Hungary, Luxembourg and the Netherlands, for more information see below). The justifications for this extra-judicial approach are based in cost and time efficiency.[57] In Sweden for example, the entire process for debtors is handled by the Enforcement Agency, the goal being

---

[57]   Out of court procedures were seen by the INSOL Report on Consumer Debt in 2001 as an efficient and cost saving initiative: J. Kilborn, *Expert Recommendations and the Evolution of European Best Practices for the Treatment*

increased efficiency.[58] Other Member States offer an administrative procedure rather than court proceedings, where the overall debt is below a certain amount, such as in Spain, the United Kingdom and Ireland.

An initial assessment suggests, therefore, that whilst there is divergence in approach, most Member States provide some form of relief from debt for individuals, and that the payment plan is in significant use as a tool.[59] This may even be a 'zero' payment plan such as in Greece, where a debtor has no repayment capacity (e.g. because of unemployment) but is subjected to a structured waiting period before discharge during which he/she is subject to various duties, for example, reporting to the IP.

Nevertheless, the availability of a procedure of itself does not necessarily indicate an effective mechanism for supporting over-indebted consumers and providing opportunities for a fresh start. Both bankruptcy and debt settlement procedures present advantages and disadvantages: bankruptcy may provide a clean slate but still attracts stigma; debt settlement procedures will involve a payment plan, which whilst in theory providing breathing space for a debtor, is still premised on monthly meeting of obligations, potentially stifling initiative.

Aside from this, no procedure is effective unless a debtor is aware of its availability and understands its terms.[60] Whilst bankruptcy may be a concept generally understood by consumers at a basic level, procedures require clear signposting, particularly where there may be a number of options open to the consumer. This is particularly so in relation to out of court procedures, where third parties, such as for-profit debt management or debt advice entities, may act for debtors as IPs, but at high cost.[61] For example, in the United Kingdom, Scotland and Ireland, the various

---

of Over-indebtedness 1984–2010, Law of Business and Finance Series (Deventer, Kluwer, 2011), p. 17.

[58]   *Ibid.* 26.

[59]   Although payment plans are not necessarily seen as efficient: INSOL International, *Consumer Debt Report* (2001); U. Reifner, J. Kiesilainen, N. Huls and H. Springeneer, *Consumer Overindebtedness and Consumer Law in the European Union*, Report for DG Health and Consumer Protection (iff, 2003); Kilborn, *Expert Recommendations* (n. 57 above) 32.

[60]   This may be a particular problem for vulnerable consumers: World Bank, Insolvency and Creditor/Debtor Regimes Task Force, Working Group on the Treatment of the Insolvency of Natural Persons, *Treatment of the Insolvency of Natural Persons* (2013), para. 202 ('World Bank Personal Insolvency Report').

[61]   In the United Kingdom, there is concern about the activities of debt management companies, who may exploit more vulnerable debtors and/or provide poor advice. These are now regulated and supervised by the financial services regulator (the Financial Conduct Authority).

procedures open to a debtor are clearly signposted on government and charity websites. In Sweden, the Swedish Enforcement Agency and in France, the Commission de Surendettement's websites contain information on how to access relief from debt.

Access to procedures may also be complicated in terms of the criteria applied, and may differ depending on whether bankruptcy, a debt settlement procedure or informal arrangement is in question. Again, this is dealt with in more detail below. Where a debtor can petition, Member States may provide relatively open access.[62] However, the basis upon which this is measured differs, with anything from the simple measure adopted in the United Kingdom of an inability to pay debts, to more detailed debt to income ratio assessments, for example in Slovenia and Denmark. Other Member States have more far-reaching restrictions, including a 'good faith' requirement attached to access to procedures, such as in Cyprus.

There is a balance to be struck here. If procedures are too easy to access then issues of moral hazard may arise, with debtors taking on excessive debt in the knowledge that discharge will be gained at a later stage.[63] On the other hand, there is a need to support the 'honest' debtor. The World Bank Personal Insolvency Report refers to open access procedures supporting the 'honest but unfortunate' debtor, who may otherwise 'hesitate' to access the system.[64] Legal conditions, such as minimum debt levels, or less measurable restrictions such as a 'permanent' inability to pay debt (e.g., as required in Greece) may therefore hinder the honest debtor in obtaining discharge. Whilst it is important to prevent dishonest use and abuse of discharge procedures, care must be taken to strike the right balance. The approach of Member States who provide simple eligibility tests to access legal procedures, but restrict the availability of discharge, on the basis of merit, is to be preferred.

8.2.3 Dishonest Debtors

As with second chance for entrepreneurs, the idea behind a 'fresh start' is to aid those who may suffer detriment through no fault of their own, beyond normal circumstances. As was demonstrated in relation to entrepreneurs, most regimes differentiate in some way between unfortunate debtors, and

---

[62] The World Bank Personal Insolvency Report (n. 60 above) explains this as the ability to access a procedure that results eventually in discharge of debts by simply meeting a test, e.g., the inability to pay debts, without further conditions (para. 189).

[63] *Ibid.* para. 193.

[64] *Ibid.* para. 189.

BOX 8.3   CASE HR 10 JANUARY 2003 NJ 2003/195

The debtor lost trade as a result of a criminal conviction. The court held that this was relevant as to the good faith of the debtor, even though the criminal conduct in question was not related to financial activities. The Dutch Supreme Court confirmed that all relevant circumstances should be taken into account when judging whether a debtor is in good faith and entitled to access the debt settlement procedure.

---

those who are dishonest. A similar approach is demonstrated in relation to consumer over-indebtedness. Whilst there is clearly a distinction between debtors who are fraudulent as opposed to debtors who act in a reckless manner, an element of culpability (i.e. intention), for example in relation to knowingly disadvantaging creditors in some way, or taking on debt with no intention of paying and with a view to being discharged, seems to be required in most jurisdictions to exclude access to over-indebtedness procedures. In only a few countries is something less enough to deprive the debtor of the relevant procedure.

In Chapter 7, it was noted that many countries require the good faith of the debtor if discharge is to be allowed. It should be noted here that the absence of good faith has been widely interpreted by some reporters to include incidence of fraud, dishonest behaviour or contravention of disclosure and informational obligations, issues which are relevant in many Member States. There is not a specific test of good or bad faith, but rather a specific list of behaviours that will exclude the debtor from the procedure or discharge. However, it appears that some systems do directly address good faith as a distinct concept, for example, Belgium and France. In the Czech Republic, the debtor's conduct in proceedings is subject to a generally phrased good faith test,[65] but this has been interpreted broadly to include honesty.[66] Cypriot law requires the debtor to be acting in good faith when seeking to rely on the debt settlement procedures although this is not defined; and in the Netherlands good faith is an open norm requiring court judgment (see Box 8.3).

In Greece, Law No. 3869/2010 draws a clear distinction between fraudulent and good faith debtors, and the Netherlands restricts debt settlement in that the debtor must have been acting in good faith in the previous five years. Dishonesty or bad faith attracts serious sanctions and restraints

---

[65]   Insolvency Act, s. 395(1).
[66]   *In Re Petzold*, 29 NSCR 14/2009; *Re Sejckova*, 29 NSCR 71/2013.

in Portugal, and negotiations/conciliation/mediation are not available unless the debtor is in good faith. In the United States, a case under Bankruptcy Code, Chapter 7 or reorganization cases can be dismissed on the ground of the debtor's bad faith, and this is determined by the court. This determination assesses whether the creditors will be deprived of their rights or whether there might be a negative impact on the integrity of the bankruptcy system.

However, where good faith is not directly 'required' in order to access processes or obtain relief from debt, Member States that recognize consumer over-indebtedness require honest, or at the least non-fraudulent, behaviour. Restrictions range from not being able to access processes at all, to curtailing the benefits of procedures. Examples are non-availability of debt settlement procedures in Austria if convicted of fraudulent bankruptcy, with the scope of discharge more limited where discharge is granted without the consent of the creditors and debts arise from crime or tortious acts. In Denmark, the debt settlement procedure is not available if the debtor is found to have acted irresponsibly; and in Estonia, the debt settlement procedure can be refused or cancelled if there is a failure to perform obligations or there is negligence or misconduct in relation to the provision of required information. A similar approach is employed in relation to the availability of discharge where the majority of Member States do not allow discharge that arises from what might be understood more generally as dishonest behaviour (e.g., debts that arise from criminal activity or from intentional torts/wrongdoing).

Overall, there are a range of 'offences' from a failure to comply with obligations, for example in the United Kingdom, Ireland and Slovakia, to withholding or giving false information, which will deprive the debtor of discharge and may result in criminal sanction. In essence, even where there is no specific honesty test, the general requirements of the procedures across the EU aim to prevent dishonest debtors receiving an advantage.

8.2.4   Divergences in Approach

There are similarities in Member States' approach, at a general level, to consumer over-indebtedness, both in terms of eligibility for procedures, the discouragement of dishonest debtors, and a lack of statutory definition of 'over-indebtedness'. Most significantly, in all Member States that have a consumer procedure, definitions of over-indebtedness, such as they are, are clearly embedded in criteria required to enter proceedings and rely on some form of inability to meet debt obligations as the basis of measurement. The differences essentially lie in the parameters of these measurements.

This therefore means that any divergence in approach lies in this initial step. Whilst some Member States use a simple inability to pay debts, which may, or may not, need to be shown to be permanent, others use a debt to income ratio or require a minimum stated amount of debt. Within the debt-income ratio calculation, household expenses may be taken into account – but this is not across the board. To this extent, this may cause some cross-border confusion.

Over-indebtedness is a difficult concept to define. It is therefore not surprising that there is little evidence of a stated legal definition. However, the diverse nature of requirements for accessing procedures may present more of an issue, where a consumer may find he or she is eligible for debt settlement procedures, or bankruptcy in one Member State, and not another. Furthermore, tests of consumer 'insolvency' that rely on minimum levels of debt expressed in a figure, as opposed to a basic calculation, may become out-dated – recent reforms in the United Kingdom suggest this.[67] In this respect, the debt to income ratio may be more appropriate.

In terms of dishonest debtors, divergence here seems to lie in the way in which dishonesty is perceived. This may be regarded as anything from fraudulent behaviour before or during proceedings, to 'negligence' or not complying with all obligations. Some Member States refer to the concept of good faith. However, fluid concepts such as 'negligence', and 'good faith' may have different interpretations, and again may lead to uncertainty. Negligence may, for instance, be equated with irresponsible or reckless rather than careless behaviour (the systems tend to refer to 'gross' negligence, but not in every case), and good faith may stretch from not acting with intention to avoid meeting obligations, to being something measured by a court in the particular circumstances of the case.

8.3 INSOLVENCY PRACTITIONERS FOR CONSUMERS

8.3.1 General Remarks

A wide variety of specific terms are used in the EU to describe insolvency practitioners who are involved in consumer bankruptcy and consumer debt settlement procedures, for example, 'family property supervisor',

---

[67] Level of debt required for creditor's petition increased from £750 to £5,000, and maximum level of debt allowed for a DRO raised from £15,000 to £20,000 in October 2015.

'personal insolvency practitioner' and 'debt administrator'. In this Report, the term 'insolvency practitioner' (IP) is defined broadly to encompass those who fulfil various functions in the different bankruptcy and debt settlement procedures. The definition does not encompass those who merely provide debt advice or counselling to the consumer.

IPs involved in bankruptcies and debt settlement procedures relating to consumers carry out many similar tasks in the different Member States. The tasks, and their objectives, are on occasion similar to those that pertain to IPs in proceedings relating to companies and entrepreneurs. However, their role in relation to debt settlement procedures is often functionally dissimilar to any proceedings that apply to entrepreneurs or companies and therefore the value of comparisons in relation to appointment, remuneration, qualifications and disciplinary measures is questionable.

From the debtor's perspective, the significant divergence between Member States in relation to debt settlement procedures lies in the extent to which the IP has a function in providing some level of assistance in dealing with the procedure and drawing up payment plans which are likely to result in discharge. The fact that the IPs are assisting consumers (or assisting a court to assist a consumer), and in many cases consumers who are impoverished or unskilled with few resources of any kind, results, on occasion, in a different emphasis in the law defining the role and function of the IP and the circumstances of employment of the IP compared with the role in relation to companies. For instance, it is more common to see the IP being a public employee. For low income/low assets cases, the involvement of an IP who is trained in matters relating to accountancy and business recovery is unlikely in practice to be useful or economical. This is recognized in some countries, and for some procedures, by different categories of IPs and/or by different levels of remuneration. In some countries, a new category of regulated IP has been created specifically to deal with consumer bankruptcy and consumer debt settlement procedures with the aims of fostering relevant expertise and reducing costs.

In some Member States, the role of the IP is more obviously focused on assisting the consumer and his or her family and dependants in recovering from severe over-indebtedness and securing a settled and sustainable quality of life. In other Member States, the role of the IP is very much concerned with liquidating assets for the benefit of creditors. In debt settlement procedures, the IP often plays a critical role in liaising with creditors in relation to debt composition proposals, preparing documents for court approval, and in adjusting debt composition proposals which initially fail to satisfy creditors or the court or which require adjustment due to a change in personal circumstances. In some countries, the IP's involvement with the consumer is lengthy because it endures for the life of the payment plan, which may be up to seven years. In Member States where no IP assistance is available to the consumer in debt settlement procedures, this will reduce the availability of the procedure, given that some consumers will lack the skills necessary to draw up the appropriate proposals and documentation. This may well be the case in Germany where, despite recent reform, the new consumer debt settlement procedure appears complicated and bureaucratic. The process provides for very little real assistance to the consumer debtor in terms of preparation for the court hearings.

In some Member States, the IP has a role in ensuring or encouraging the diligence, honesty and scrupulousness of the consumer, both at the initial stage of request for the bankruptcy or debt settlement procedure to be commenced and/or during the life of the debt settlement procedure, when the consumer may be under a continuing obligation to seek or maintain employment or to pass on inherited property to creditors. It is common for consumers taking part in debt settlement procedures to be under obligations to reveal any new assets or fresh source of income; to issue accurate statements of liabilities; not to create incapacity to service debt, and so on. In practice, it will be the IP, if there is one, who has the knowledge and opportunity to police these constraints. Naturally, the ability of the IP to fulfil this role in practice will depend on the resources available to him or her. There appears to have been no or little research on whether this type of obligation is useful on any measure or economically productive in terms of enhancing recovery to creditors or acts as a deterrent of some nature to consumers becoming over-indebted. The potential length of IP involvement and its potentially personally intrusive nature is in contrast to the position of IPs in corporate procedures.

8.3.2 Rules on Qualification, Regulation, Disciplinary Actions, Selection and Conflicts of Interest

In most countries, the general scheme of rules and regulations applying to IPs relating to consumers are largely the same as they are for corporate insolvency proceedings. This similarity applies for Austria (except for garnishee), Cyprus, the Czech Republic, Finland, Germany, Greece, Italy, Lithuania, Luxembourg, the Netherlands (with some exception), Norway (with some exception), Poland, Portugal, Slovakia, Slovenia, Spain (with some exception), Sweden (with some exception), United Kingdom (with some exception) and United States. This is particularly likely to be the case with bankruptcy rather than debt settlement procedures. There is no indication that the law or procedure for selecting or regulating IPs acting in debt settlement procedures for consumers or bankruptcy for consumers are generally presenting difficulty or controversy, either for debtors or creditors. Whilst the procedures for qualification and selection differ between Member States, this is viewed as appropriate given the difference in relevant law and procedure and the differing social and historic positions.

8.3.3   Special Role in Relation to Debt Settlement Procedures

In some countries, there is a special category of IP reserved for debt settlement procedures for consumers or informal arrangements for consumers. This category includes accredited institutions which comply with certain specific resource obligations. For example, in relation to Belgium, the debt administrator must be able to call upon the services of a specially trained or experienced social worker or lawyer. Further examples are Spain, where the out of court adjustment process involves the appointment of an accredited mediator who conducts negotiations with creditors; and the Netherlands, where the administrator in debt adjustment proceedings may be an individual accredited through the Legal Aid Board but need not be a lawyer.

These accreditation methods reflect the position that the drawing up and negotiation of a debt settlement procedure or informal arrangement with a variety of creditors may require patience, tact and diligence and need not always demand high levels of legal knowledge. In some cases, the personal circumstances of the debtor and family may make the task very time-consuming. Some Member States clearly acknowledge that few debtors are capable of carrying out such negotiations effectively without some assistance. The decision on how to fund such assistance, and whether to provide it, differs between Member States. A decision on whether to provide such assistance cannot be divorced from the issue of how to fund it.

In contrast in Germany, no assistance is provided for consumers seeking a debt settlement procedure. The special procedure for consumers, the plan for the settlement of debts, necessitates the preparation by the consumer debtor of extensive documentation, including proposals for a payment plan, asset valuation, lists of creditors, a debt discharge application, and confirmation that an informal arrangement has been attempted and failed. Although some standard forms are provided, they are extremely lengthy. The consumer debtor must also open conventional insolvency proceedings. No assistance is available from the state. Although the court may appoint an IP, this individual is not involved in helping to prepare the documentation or assisting the consumer debtor in any other manner with the process.

Table 8.2 identifies those countries in which the appointment of an

Table 8.2   Appointment of an insolvency practitioner*

Country	Bankruptcy	Debt settlement procedure
Austria	✗	✗
Belgium	N/A	✓
Bulgaria	N/A	N/A
Croatia	N/A	N/A
Cyprus	✓	✓
Czech Republic	✓	✓
Denmark	✓	✓
Estonia	✓	✗
Finland	✓	✗
		(but debt advice available as public service)
France	✓	✓
Germany	✓	✗
Greece	✓	✗
Hungary	✓	✓
Ireland	✓	✓
Italy	✓	✓
Latvia	✓	✓
Lithuania	✓	✓
Luxembourg	N/A	✓
Malta	N/A	N/A
Netherlands	✓	✓
Norway	✓	✓
		(enforcement officer)
Poland	✓	✓
Portugal	✓	✗
Romania	✓	✓
Slovakia	✓	✓
Slovenia	✓	N/A
Spain	✓	✓
		(mediator or notary in out of court process)
Sweden	✓	✓
		(KFM for debt relief mechanism)
United Kingdom	✓	✓
United States	✓	✓

Note: * Countries in which the appointment of an IP of some type is usual in bankruptcy and in debt settlement procedures applying to consumers. In some countries, only one procedure is available and this procedure satisfies some aspects of the definition of bankruptcy and some aspects of the definition of debt settlement procedure. Note that, as defined, bankruptcy entails liquidation of the debtor's assets whereas debt settlement procedure may not.

IP is compulsory in debt settlement procedures and in bankruptcy, both relating to consumers.

8.3.4 Public Body as Insolvency Practitioner

On occasion, the role of IP is fulfilled by a public body. In the case of the draft Croatian proposal (the Draft Consumer Bankruptcy Act), the Financial Agency of the Ministry of Justice has a role in assisting the consumer to prepare for a debt settlement procedure and informal arrangement. The office of the Financial Agency provides a venue for creditors' meetings. The establishment and maintenance of such an agency has resource and cost implications, and in some countries there appears to be little collective or institutional knowledge of insolvency and debt settlement issues and therefore the establishment of such an organization may represent a significant challenge.

In France, the IP role is fulfilled by a public body, the Commission de surendettement (CDS) for all cases except those that involve the liquidation of immovable assets. A key role here for the CDS is to draft the payment plan and send it to creditors, or to submit it to the court with proposals, for instance, to reduce interest rates, impose a moratorium, discharge certain debts, and so on. The CDS also sets the minimum level of income which is appropriate for the debtor having regard to family circumstances. This is a particularly sensitive task. In Hungary, the family property supervisors are government employees and are remunerated as such. They are employed, controlled and regulated by the Hungarian Family Bankruptcy Service in accordance with various provisions set out in statute. Provisions in the Act prevent persons who are connected with the debtor or any creditor being appointed in any particular case. A key role of the family property supervisors is to check that the debtor has the right to bring proceedings and to verify the accuracy of the information provided by the debtor.

In some Member States, debt settlement procedures exist in which it is not usual to appoint an IP (or where the IP provides little real assistance to the consumer) but where substantial assistance is in fact provided to the consumer debtor by state funded debt advice services or by legal aid. This is the case in Portugal (the Consumer Protection Association or DECO), and in Finland (pursuant to the Act on Financial and Debt Counselling 713/2000). In Italy, neither the IP in the Procedure di composizione della crisi da sovraindebitamento (accordo o piano) nor the IP in the Liquidazione dei beni appears to provide real assistance to the consumer debtor, but legal aid is available to consumers with an income of less than 11,369.24 euros, and so, in practice, assistance will be available to low income consumers in relation to these procedures. In the United Kingdom, legal aid is not available but there have been initiatives to extend the range and quality of debt advice services available to consumers through the authorization of debt management companies and debt advice services.

8.3.5   Insolvency Practitioner as Court Assistant

In some instances, an IP role is provided by a court assistant. For example, in Denmark, the court in the debt settlement procedure may appoint an assistant if it sees fit. Here, the court assistant may be an attorney, but need not be. No particular qualification is required. If he or she is an attorney he or she will be subject to the rules of that profession. The role in this case is more limited in that the assistant cannot manage the creditor meetings but provides information and practical assistance to the debtor. The court appoints the assistant and sets the fee based on a specific recommendation. In a similar vein, in Estonian debt settlement procedures, the court may appoint an advisor, who need not be a member of a regulated profession but who is suitably qualified and experienced. The role of the advisor is to impartially inform the court and creditors of the debtor's position and the possibilities of overcoming it and to assist the debtor in drawing up the payment plan. The debtor must pay the fee of the advisor and the level of the advisor's fees is set by regulation.

Table 8.3 provides a functional comparison of IPs' roles in consumer debt settlement procedures between the Member States and the two comparator countries.

8.3.6   Separate Classes of Insolvency Practitioner for Consumers

In some countries, there are two separate classes of IP, for example a general licence is given to those IPs who may be appointed in all cases, including consumer cases, and a special licence applies to IPs able to act in large, complex corporate cases. For instance, this applies in the Czech Republic. In the Republic of Ireland, there is a new separate class of personal insolvency practitioner and a new debt settlement procedure in which the consumer must gain advice and support from someone acting as such.[68] New legislation in the United Kingdom, which came into force on 1 October 2015, provides for the establishment of a separate authorization for IPs who are authorized to act only in cases of personal insolvency. The justifications for these new classes of IP appear to be a need for a greater

---

[68]   See Part 5 of the Personal Insolvency Act 2012.

Table 8.3   Role of insolvency practitioner in debt settlement procedures for consumers

Country	Significant role in assisting the consumer debtor to prepare suitable payment plan	Significant role in assisting the court in assessing suitability of payment plan
Austria	✗	✗
Belgium	✓	✗
Bulgaria	✗	✗
Croatia	✗	✗
Cyprus	✓	✗
Czech Republic	✗ (but amendments proposed which would increase IP's obligations)	✗
Denmark	✗	✓
Estonia	✓	✓
Finland	✓	✓
France	✓	✗
Germany	✗	✗
Greece	✓ (range of professional bodies)	✗
Hungary	✓ (family property supervisor)	✓ (family bankruptcy service)
Ireland	✓ (personal IP)	✗
Italy	✗	✗
Latvia	✓	✗
Lithuania	✓	✓
Luxembourg	✓ (Mediation Commission plus assistance under Law of 8 January 2013, art. 12)	✗
Malta	✗	✗
Netherlands	✓ (administrator)	✓ (supervisory judge)
Norway	✓ (enforcement officer)	✗
Poland	✗	✗
Portugal	✓ (pre-insolvency administrator or DECO)	✗
Romania	✓ (administrator and Insolvency Commission)	✗

Table 8.3 (continued)

Country	Significant role in assisting the consumer debtor to prepare suitable payment plan	Significant role in assisting the court in assessing suitability of payment plan
Slovakia	✗	✗
Slovenia	✗	✗
Spain	✓ (negotiator/mediator)	✗
Sweden	✓ (KFM)	✗
United Kingdom	✓ (debt management organization, nominee)	✗
United States	✓ (standing trustee in Chapter 13)	✗

number of IPs, more specialist expertise, and lower IP fee levels, driven by a more open and competitive marketplace for these consumer IP services.

8.3.7 Fees

Many countries make distinctions between the level of fees that may be charged by IPs in individual cases and those that may be charged in business insolvencies. For example, in the Czech Republic, the IP fee in debt settlement procedures over five years is a fixed amount per month, whereas in bankruptcy, the fee is based on a decreasing sliding scale depending on the level of recovery for all creditors but subject to a fixed floor. In Poland, the fees of the IP are related to the national average monthly salary in the enterprise sector, which is set by reference to a specific Polish index.

The level of IP fees, how they are borne (by the debtor or by the public purse) and whether there must be evidence in advance that the assets are sufficient to bear the fees, are all difficult and controversial issues. This is particularly so in 'no income/no assets' cases where the small size of the debtor's assets bears no relationship at all to the distress and difficulty encountered by over-burdened debtors and their families. The law in many countries struggles to find a solution in these cases. In Sweden, it is a public body, the Swedish Enforcement Agency, that effectively acts as IP. In Romania, the fees are borne by the state and then recovered from the assets of the debtor, and additionally there are no court fees for the petition. In Portugal, the court fees are covered by legal aid.

In the United Kingdom, efforts have been made to make debt settlement procedures more accessible to a larger number of consumers by enabling profit-making companies, as well as charities, to be intermediaries in applications to the Official Receiver for Debt Relief Orders and to assist debtors in other debt settlement procedures. This has led to concerns over conflicts of interest, particularly in relation to consumers being sold unsuitable financial products where the debt management organization has earned a fee or commission from the sale of a financial product such as insurance, a savings plan or a loan. It is hoped that better regulation, which is of course resource dependent, will mitigate this problem.

8.3.8   Comparator Countries

In the comparator country of Norway, in bankruptcy, the court appoints a debt settlement committee to supervise proceedings, which is usually composed of lawyers. In the debt settlement procedure, a public employee takes control of the process and may appoint an assistant who satisfies qualification thresholds and is usually an accountant or a lawyer.

In the comparator country of the United States, in Chapter 7 of the Bankruptcy Code (essentially the bankruptcy procedure), the insolvency practitioner (the trustee), is selected, appointed and remunerated in exactly the same manner as for companies. For Chapter 13 (the debt settlement procedure), each federal district has a list of individuals from which the IP (the Chapter 13 trustee) is selected. In proceedings concerning consumers, the trustees are federal employees and receive a salary from the federal government and in addition are entitled to receive a fixed percentage of all realizations.

8.3.9   Debt Advice

The availability of free advice to consumers on debt and money and the availability of legal aid will, in practice, tend to assist consumers in accessing bankruptcy and debt settlement procedures. Any advice that is provided should be impartial and disinterested and the means of achieving this are varied (e.g. state funding, advice provided by the charitable sector, discretionary regulation). Many other factors are also relevant, including cultural attitudes to debt and to legal processes, literacy, education and geography. Divergences in these issues between Member States will affect the utility of any relevant law on discharge. The existence of impartial debt advice and the provision of legal aid, and relevant measures of equal access to justice for consumers, across the Member States, could usefully be the subject of additional legal and sociological research and falls outside the ambit of this work.

8.3.10 Conclusions on Divergence

The different law and procedure on the appointment, qualification, remuneration and control of IPs in relation to consumer bankruptcy and debt settlement procedures is linked to the different political, social and economic conditions in each Member State and in different assessments of what lies in the public interest. It is evident that skilled and impartial assistance provided to a consumer debtor, by or through an IP of some type, to effect a debt settlement procedure or bankruptcy, is more likely to result in some recovery for creditors and some discharge for the consumer compared to the use of no legal procedure at all and is therefore to be encouraged. Although useful statistics are unavailable, a comparison amongst the Member States and the comparator countries indicates that in Member States where no IP of any type is involved in debt settlement procedures, the debtor is less likely to make use of the procedure or to do so quickly and effectively. Although the alternative of bankruptcy is available in most Member States, and usually requires a lower level of preparation by the consumer debtor, the stigma and compulsory asset liquidation connected with bankruptcy may deter the consumer debtor from using bankruptcy.

Best practice in facilitating a fresh start for over-indebted consumers therefore lies in ensuring that an appropriately qualified and experienced IP of some nature is always involved in applications for debt settlement procedures so as to ensure a swift and appropriate process. The IP may be a public body, or a private individual, a company or a charity accredited in some appropriate manner, a court official or court assistant. Regulation should ensure that the opportunity to exploit conflicts of interest by the IP are controlled. Regulation should ensure that the level of fee charged by the IP, where it must be borne by the consumer debtor, is controlled in some manner so that it does not present a practical barrier to fresh start for consumers. No meaningful comparison is possible in relation to arrangements for remunerating IPs given the differing economic, social and legal conditions present in each Member State and given their widely different roles.

The data suggests there is no indication that the divergent law and procedure in Member States relating to the appointment, qualification, remuneration and control of IPs is having a significant impact on cross-border trade in goods or services or capital or is affecting free movement of persons. The different functions, however, of IPs may create divergence

---

BOX 8.4   CASE STUDY FROM UNITED KINGDOM ON CONFLICT OF INTEREST BY INSOLVENCY PRACTITIONER

A customer approached a debt management organization for help with their over indebtedness of £27,000. The firm assisted them in drawing up a debt management plan but also sold them a fee-charging bank account costing £14.50 per month. This reduced the amount of disposable income the customer had available to pay towards the settlement of their debts each month and therefore extended the life of the debt management plan from 37 years to 47 years. This was not explained to the customer by the debt management organization.[a]

Note: [a] See Financial Conduct Authority, *Quality of Debt Management Advice*, TR15/8 (June 2015), p.30.

---

in access to bankruptcy and debt settlement procedures for consumer debtors in different Member States (see Box 8.4).

Table 8.3 compares, at a very general level, the function of IPs across countries in terms of whether they provide assistance to the consumer debtor to prepare, negotiate and submit a payment plan, and whether they provide assistance to the court either procedurally or by assessing the suitability of any payment plan.[69]

8.4   PROCEDURAL ASPECTS

As was referred to in Chapter 7, the World Bank Personal Insolvency Report, in its discussion of insolvency of natural persons, highlights the distinction between economic concerns of a business insolvency, and the humanitarian concerns of a natural person.[70] This is particularly the case in relation to consumer insolvency, where vulnerability becomes a visible issue, and where the financial difficulty does not emanate from entrepreneurial risk, but from personal circumstances. Yet, as the World Bank Personal Insolvency Report points out, in some respects the rationale

---

[69]   Note that in some countries it is difficult to distinguish between the functions of an IP and the functions of a state funded or supported debt advice service. In these jurisdictions some practical level of advice is available to the debtor but the advisor's role is only partly focused on the legal or administrative process which facilitates discharge and therefore it is difficult to clearly characterize them as IPs as they do not supervise the administration of the debtor's affairs.

[70]   World Bank Personal Insolvency Report (n. 60 above) para. 50.

of insolvency regimes is equally pertinent to all debtors, whether business or consumer.[71] This is reflected in the Recommendation's reference to the fact that some of its principles may also be relevant to consumer 'bankruptcy'.[72] Coherence in initiatives is encouraged[73] and one task of the study is to identify where disparities may lie.

As was originally noted in the report published by London Economics in 2012,[74] it is clear that a number of Member States have introduced, or are introducing in the near future, new measures to assist consumer debtors. Brief details of reform indicated in national reporters' returned data are shown in Table 8.4, together with details from the comparator country of the United States, where recent reform has taken place.

The developments outlined in Table 8.4 seem to show a clear move towards increased discharge for consumer debtors, and providing for debt settlement procedures as a means of rehabilitating the debtor and prompting a fresh start. Even amongst those countries where, procedurally, consumer over-indebtedness is not recognized, both Bulgaria and Croatia have seen pressures for reform to improve the position of the over-indebted consumer. Those countries are introducing completely new frameworks to embrace relief from debt through debt settlement procedures. Reforms of the more established regimes seek to widen access to procedures outside bankruptcy (e.g., in the United Kingdom). This underlines the importance of ensuring such mechanisms are effective to achieve discharge. The EU Member States have come a long way since 2001, when only ten Member States had procedures available for consumers.[75] Table 8.5 shows a broad overview in relation to reforms since 2001, and when countries have introduced new measures or amended their systems/laws in response to consumer over-indebtedness.

The only Member States that have no consumer over-indebtedness

---

[71]   *Ibid.* para. 45.
[72]   Commission Recommendation 2014/135/EU, issued on 12 March 2014, para. 15.
[73]   *Ibid.* paras 10 and 11.
[74]   At that time Austria, Germany, Ireland, Italy, Poland and Slovakia; London Economics, *Study on Means to Protect Consumers* (n. 49 above), Executive Summary, p. ix.
[75]   Noted by the Council in Council Resolution of 26 November 2001 on consumer credit and indebtedness, 2001/C364/01; see also S. Viimsalu, 'The Over-Indebtedness Regulatory System in the Light of the Changing Economic Landscape' (2010) 17 *Juridica International* 218; Viavoice, *Introductory Report* (n. 30 above) 4, 7.

Table 8.4   Recent reforms

Country	Consumer	Entrepreneur	All natural persons
Bulgaria			Draft Bill introduced in 2015 for protection of over-indebted individuals. Not clear if will be accepted by Parliament and Government has suggested will draft new version.
Croatia			Draft Consumer Bankruptcy Act 2015, covers both consumers and entrepreneurs (in relation to smaller size business).
Cyprus			Law on Insolvency of Natural Persons for the Development and Implementation of Personal Repayment and Discharge Plans) 2015, aimed at allowing over-indebted consumers and entrepreneurs a second chance whilst maintaining balance for creditors.
Czech Republic		From January 2014, proceedings on discharge of debts available to consumers, also made available to entrepreneurs (sole traders) if creditor agrees, or debtor has already gone through liquidation or the debt is secured.	

Denmark	New rules on restructuring (primarily apply to entrepreneurs) introduced in 2010, replacing rules on suspension of payments. New rules focus on business rather than the debtor with more influence for creditors.	
Estonia		Debt Restructuring and Debt Protection Act 2010 (in force from April 2011), aims to avoid natural persons with solvency problems having to enter bankruptcy proceedings.
Finland	Act on the Adjustment of Debts of a Private Individual 1993, revised several times. Most recent changes relate to fresh start for diligent/honest entrepreneurs, securing over-indebted individuals housing, and encouraging individuals to seek income whilst on a payment schedule.	

Table 8.4 (continued)

Country	Consumer	Entrepreneur	All natural persons
France	New Law in 2014 which will come into force 2016, reducing the length of the payment plan to seven years (from eight).		
Germany	2013 reform of insolvency law in relation to consumers.		
Greece	Special regime created for consumer natural persons in 2010, Law No. 3869/2010; unlike Insolvency Code, aim is to afford consumer a second chance.		
Hungary	Act on the Debt Consolidation of Natural Persons, June 2015, in force from September 2015, primarily aims to solve problems of mortgage backed loans; preconditions based in mortgage or leasing contract encumbering property used by debtor for habitation with out of court debt consolidation procedure then court led procedure if appropriate.		

| Ireland | Personal Insolvency Act 2012, introduced the Debt Relief Notice, Debt Settlement Arrangement and Personal Insolvency Arrangement. The Bankruptcy (Amendment) Act 2015 reduces discharge to one year and income payment orders to three years, unless there is non-co-operation or concealment of assets by debtor. It also allows the bankrupt person's legal interest in his or her home to re-vest in him three years after the date of bankruptcy, if the Official Assignee has neither sold it, nor applied to court for an order permitting sale of the house, before that date. | |
| Italy | New procedure introduced in Law No. 3/2012 but further radical amendment by Decree Laws 179/2012 and 221/2012. Introduces possibility of only partial payment of secured claims; reduces creditor voting majority; allows for special over-indebtedness procedure for consumer without need for creditor approval; in the Liquidazione dei beni procedure, offers honest/diligent debtor chance of discharge at end of liquidation proceedings. | Reforms include separation of entrepreneur from consumer. |

Table 8.4 (continued)

Country	Consumer	Entrepreneur	All natural persons
Latvia	Over-indebtedness procedure introduced in 2008. Several changes have been adopted. Further reform resisted since then, over concerns for position of creditors and debtors.		
Lithuania	Law on Bankruptcy of Natural Persons 2012, in force 2013. May be further initiatives re shortening of time period for implementing payment plan to three years and debtor to retain home if mortgaged.		
Luxembourg	Law of 8 January 2013 on over-indebtedness, modified several aspects, introduced liquidation phase and discharge of debts, thereby giving some extra protection to debtors.		
Netherlands	Debt Management (Natural Persons) Act 1998 (debt adjustment proceedings) updated in 2008.		

Poland	Revised insolvency proceedings in 2014. Previously insolvency only available if debtor as consumer was in difficulty as a result of exceptional circumstances outside their control.	Restructuring Law amending arts 369 and 370 of the Insolvency Law to reflect EC Recommendation Section IV; allows payment plan and discharge within three years.	Insolvency Act (enacted in 2004) includes a chapter with specific provisions to deal with the insolvency of natural persons. It provides for the discharge of all natural persons.
Portugal	Insolvency Act 2004 provides for possibility of a payment plan for natural persons who are not entrepreneurs or, at least, are not large-scale entrepreneurs, and for a special (procedural) regime for the insolvency of both spouses.		
Romania	New Law, came into force in December 2015. Collective procedures: administrative procedure based on payment plan. Judicial winding up.		
Slovenia	2015 Act on the Conditions for the Implementation of Debt Relief; creditors can write off certain debts without tax effects, and will allow extra consumer to access relief from debt.		

Table 8.4 (continued)

Country	Consumer	Entrepreneur	All natural persons
Spain	Law No. 1/2013, including measures to protect mortgagors, debt restructuring and social housing; amended in 2015 to allow coverage of more problematic cases.	Insolvency law amended in 2013 to allow entrepreneurs access to procedures.	
Sweden		Proposal for amendment to Debt Relief Act 2006 to allow fresh start for entrepreneurs, aims to be in force 2016.	
United Kingdom			The minimum debt threshold for a creditor's petition for a debtor's bankruptcy rose from £750 to £5,000 in October 2015. The maximum debt level at which people can apply for a debt relief order also rose from £15,000 to £20,000.
United States			Last major reforms in 2005, aim to channel debtors away from Chapter 7 into Chapter 13.

Table 8.5 *Chronology of reforms*

Year	Planned or suggested reform not yet adopted	Adopted reforms not yet in force	Reform to existing law (date of adoption)*	No legislation
2002			United Kingdom	Malta
2003			France	
			Estonia	
2004			Portugal	
			Slovakia	
2006			Czech Republic	
			Sweden	
2007			Latvia	
			Slovenia	
2009			Poland	
2010			Austria	
			Denmark	
			France	
			Estonia	
			Greece	
			Latvia	
2011			Slovakia	
			Sweden	
2012			Ireland	
			Italy	
			Lithuania	
			Portugal	
2013			France	
			Germany	
			Greece	
			Luxembourg	
2014			France	
			Poland	
2015	Bulgaria		Cyprus	
	Croatia		Finland	
	Lithuania		Hungary	
			Ireland	
			Romania	
			Slovenia	
			Spain	
			United Kingdom	

Note: * Not all reforms were/are effective immediately.

procedures are Bulgaria, Croatia and Malta.[76] In these countries, the creditors rely on the general civil law relating to debt collection proceedings and enforcement processes.

8.4.1 Scope of Procedures (Including No Income, No Assets) and Their Prerequisites

The general availability of consumer over-indebtedness procedures tends to be in terms of debtor 'persona', whether for the consumer only or to the wider category of natural persons. In terms of actual procedure, there is naturally some difference in approach, yet there are also recurring issues.

8.4.1.1 Scope
As has already been touched upon above, the available range of options open to debtors varies between Member States. Individuals, as debtors, may have access to bankruptcy, either under the general regime, or via a specific framework. In addition they may have access to debt settlement procedures or informal arrangements. Access may also depend on whether they are entrepreneurs or consumers.

The only Member States that do not have bankruptcy accessible to consumers at all are Belgium, Bulgaria, Croatia, France, Greece, Hungary, Latvia, Lithuania, Luxembourg, Malta, Poland, Romania and Slovakia. However, all but Bulgaria, Croatia and Malta either do have a debt settlement procedure for consumers that is akin to bankruptcy (includes the possibility of liquidation), or as in the case of Greece, provide a debt settlement procedure via some form of judicial settlement of debts. Romania's impending reform will allow a consumer to access new bankruptcy proceedings for natural persons. Hungary's new law provides for a debt settlement procedure but there is no avenue for consumer bankruptcy.

However, in terms of insolvency procedures more generally, an initial conclusion that can be made here is that any differentiation of treatment tends to lie in the dividing line between legal and non-legal entity, rather than the type of debt (personal versus business), although there are examples of where business debts owed by an individual restrict the procedures available, e.g. in France and Italy). So, in some Member States whilst consumers may have the bankruptcy option available, this is within the general

---

[76] Whilst a draft Bill has been proposed in Bulgaria, this has not yet been accepted, although the government has indicated it is looking at legislating in this area.

insolvency regime available to all debtors, regardless of their legal status. Such countries are Denmark, Estonia, the Netherlands, Slovakia and Sweden. Alternatively, within the general regime there may be specific procedures for natural persons which will therefore apply to consumers: the United Kingdom and Ireland are examples of this. The position is the same in the comparator countries: in the United States, in theory any debtor can file under, Chapter 7 bankruptcy or the debt settlement procedure under Chapter 11, but Chapter 13 is for natural persons only; and in Norway, any debtor can file for bankruptcy or debt settlement, but there are also specific rules in place for the debt settlement of individuals.

Most Member States have some form of debt settlement procedure, and/or other alternatives, which range from informal arrangements to more structured administrative procedures, and accessibility is based on numerous criteria or prerequisites.

8.4.1.2 Prerequisites/criteria

Criteria for entering any procedure is based, essentially, on the inability to pay debts. Some Member States' conditions put a figure on this (in some cases as one of a number of prerequisites), requiring a minimum level of debt, and this may vary between procedures or depend on who petitions. For example in Cyprus, for bankruptcy to be initiated, the debtor must owe at least 15,000 euros in unsecured debt, in Ireland one of the debt settlement procedures (debt settlement arrangement) requires levels of indebtedness above 20,000 euros. In Latvia, the debt settlement procedure only applies where total debt obligations exceed 5,000 euros, or 10,000 euros if the debtor will be unable to meet all debt obligations that take effect within the following year; and in the United Kingdom, in bankruptcy the debtor must owe £5,000 or more (in England) or £3,000 or more (in Scotland) if the creditor petitions. If the debtor petitions in Scotland, he or she must owe at least £1,500; in England, there is no minimum, although the debtor will need to convince the court there is the requisite inability to meet obligations. In Lithuania, the approach is slightly different, where the minimum is based in a calculation of 25 minimum monthly salaries.

Some Member States also employ a maximum level of debt, for example, in the Republic of Ireland, where a maximum of 3 million euros of debt is allowed for access to the personal insolvency arrangement. In Spain, the out of court procedure has a maximum debt level of 5 million euros. Maximum level of debts and assets are also relevant in relation to the extent to which Cyprus' debt settlement procedure (non-consensual personal repayment plan) is available, where total value of debts must not exceed 350,000 euros and total value of remaining assets (excluding the home) must not exceed 250,000 euros.

However, there seems to be little in the way of specific provision for consumers with no or a low level of income and assets. The exceptions are the Republic of Ireland and the United Kingdom (plus Romania when the new provisions come into force), where the respective debt relief notice and debt relief order (DRO) or (County Court) Administration Order in England are only available to those who have less than a stated amount of debt, assets and income.[77] This is not to say that such debtors are not more broadly catered for elsewhere across the EU. In some respects, protection for consumers with lower levels of income and assets are reflected in other rules within procedures, whether bankruptcy or debt settlement procedures. For example in Greece, debtors with insufficient incomes and little or no property may obtain relief from the majority of debt without entering a payment plan; and Poland has similar provision where debtors with no income or assets, and therefore no means of meeting a repayment schedule, may still obtain discharge. Finally, in relation to low levels of debt, as opposed to income, only the Czech Republic appears to have a relevant mechanism, which allows the court to set monthly repayments in such a case.

In terms of the comparator countries, whilst Norway has no specific provision for low income, low asset debtors, in the United States, debtors whose monthly income is at or below a certain threshold (median family income for a household of their size in the relevant state) are *prima facie* eligible for Chapter 7 bankruptcy. This procedure is not available for debtors who have sufficient capacity to repay at least some proportion of their debt.

8.4.1.3 Voluntary versus compulsory procedures: who can petition

There seems to be a delineation between voluntary procedures and compulsory procedures, primarily based on whether the creditor can initiate a procedure. Debtors in most Member States have the option to petition for their own bankruptcy or debt settlement procedure and compulsory subjection to procedures tends only to occur where the creditor is entitled to petition. An exception to this is Slovenia, where a debtor is 'obliged' to file for bankruptcy once they have reached the insolvency threshold of payment default on one or more obligations which in total exceed three times salary and other income, or if unemployed, in payment default for at least 1,000 euros. It is notable that debt settlement procedures can usually

---

[77] Ireland: debts of 20,000 euros or less, net income of 60 euros per month or less and assets of 400 euros or less. United Kingdom: £15,000 of debts or less, £59 of net income per month or less, £300 or less of assets. The (County Court) Administration Order (England) is only available where outstanding debt is less than £5,000.

Table 8.6   Who may petition

	AT	BE	BG*	CY	CZ	DE	DK	EE	IE	EL	FI	ES	FR	HR*	HU
Bankruptcy				×			×	×	×						
Debt settlement	×	o		o	o	×	o	o	o	o	o	~	o		o
Out of court /administrative procedure				o						o			o		+

	IT	LT	LU	LV	MT*	NL	PL	PT	RO	SE	SK	SI	UK	US	NO
Bankruptcy	o					×	×	×	×	×		×	×	×	×
Debt settlement	o	o	o	o		o	o	o	o		×			×	o
Out of court /administrative procedure							o			o			o		

Notes:
× = Both creditor and debtor can initiate proceedings
o = Debtor only can initiate proceedings
+ = Joint application
~ = Administrator initiates proceedings
* = No provision

only be initiated by the debtors. Table 8.6 illustrates who may apply for which procedure.

Some Member States require a previous out of court settlement of some kind to have been attempted first. In Finland, before debt settlement procedures can be opened, the debtor must have attempted a negotiated settlement with the creditors, if appropriate. In Germany, the debtor must be able to show there has been an unsuccessful attempt to settle the claims out of court; and in Greece, in order to access the judicial settlement element to the debt settlement procedure, the debtor may first seek an out of court settlement with creditors, either informally or through mediation. Hungary's new law requires an out of court debt consolidation procedure first, before court proceedings; and Luxembourg's Law of 8 January 2013 has a mediation phase as its first stage of the debt settlement procedure. In the Netherlands, debt settlement can only be requested if an out of court composition is offered but no agreement has been reached; and in Spain, the obligation to have reached or attempted an out of court settlement features in the majority of options.

Indeed, a number of Member States provide for out of court procedures, or informal arrangements such as mediation, whether or not a prerequisite. Such approaches would seem to encourage solutions that sit outside the court's purview, or restricting court involvement to an appeal or 'rubber stamping' role, something observed in the London Economics Study in 2012[78] and seen in relation to the option of 'administrative procedures' across a number of Member States. As has already been observed, this may be seen as both cost and time efficient. This does not mean, however, that out of court/administrative procedures will necessarily be free for the debtor (see below).

8.4.2 Role of the Court, Administrative Bodies and Creditors

8.4.2.1 Role of the court and other bodies

Limits on court-based activity are not only reflected in the encouragement of out of court procedures. Avenues for the debtor that do not entail bankruptcy are often overseen by administrative bodies such as an IP, with the court having a relatively limited role, often simply being involved in approval of payment plans already agreed between the relevant parties.[79] Examples are Cyprus, where the court's only role is to sanction the payment plan and the IP's decisions; and in France, the Commission de surendettement opens and controls the consumer over-indebtedness procedure (procedure de surendettement), with the court supporting the process through imposing specific measures recommended by the Commission, or hearing appeals against Commission decisions. In Ireland, the debt relief notice is applied for through an intermediary and issued by the Insolvency Service, while the debt settlement arrangement and personal insolvency arrangement proceed through an IP, with approval by the court.

Portugal's special revitalization procedure does not directly involve the court, but is run by an IP with the court only being involved in the application for the opening of proceedings and then in the later stage in terms of confirming the restructuring plan. In the United Kingdom, an English IVA is run by a nominee, with the court's role being primarily in terms of being able to revoke or suspend a creditor's approval in certain circumstances and to receive notice once the IVA is complete (unless the debtor applies for an interim order, in which case the court's role is greater,

---

[78] London Economics, *Study on Means to Protect Consumers* (n. 49 above) Executive Summary, p. x.
[79] An observation also made in *ibid*.

in that it considers the application and then decides whether or not an order should be given). With regard to the English DRO of the Official Receiver's actions, if the creditor applies for such. In Scotland, in relation to the Protected Trust Deed, which is similar to the English IVA, the court's role is primarily as an avenue of appeal, in certain circumstances, against decision made either by the trustee, creditors or the accountant in bankruptcy.[80]

Sweden's procedures are again notable in this regard in that, outside bankruptcy, the debt settlement procedures are almost entirely run by the Enforcement Agency, the KFM, which draws up the proposal for creditor approval, and decides whether to grant relief (even if there is creditor dissent). The court is only involved if there is an appeal against a decision by the KFM. In contrast, the role of the court is much more prevalent in relation to consumer bankruptcy procedures, and this may be because in a number of Member States, individual bankruptcy procedure seems to broadly follow the pattern of corporate /business insolvency.

8.4.2.2 Role of creditors

The creditors' role in consumer over-indebtedness procedures, and their involvement, is dictated by the procedure concerned. Whilst in the majority of cases a creditor may bring a bankruptcy petition and has voting rights if its claim is registered, creditors' influence is much more limited in relation to other procedures where a payment plan is involved. Payment plans may be part of an out of court arrangement, where the creditors and debtor come to an agreement on the schedule of payments, or may be part of in court debt settlement procedures, where the plan is imposed by the court. Of course, in any mediation or out of court settlement, creditor involvement is essential, but in relation to debt settlement procedures, creditors have less or no influence on the schedule that is applied by the court. An example is the Danish debt settlement procedure (debt rescheduling), where creditors have no input, or the Italian Procedure di composizione della crisis da sovraindebitamento del consumatore (Piano) where the proposal is confirmed by the court without need for creditor approval. In other countries, creditors may be given the chance to comment or vote on a payment plan, but dissenting creditors may have the plan imposed upon them, for example, if a majority of the creditors are in favour of the proposal. The creditors' rights are protected, however, to

---

[80] The Accountant in Bankruptcy is the Scottish Government Agency responsible for overseeing the trust deed process and approving its protected status.

the extent they may have a right of appeal, and generally this seems to be the case across the various procedures.

It also seems that in bankruptcy, or where assets are liquidated, the ranking of creditors may reflect the ranking within business/corporate insolvency, particularly in relation to secured creditors. These creditors, in a number of Member States, stand apart from other creditors in that the realization of the security is treated separately: funds from the sale of the secured asset are used to satisfy the secured debt before any other debt. There are exceptions; in Belgium, secured creditors are treated the same as other creditors in the collective debt settlement (debt settlement procedure for consumers only); and in Ireland, secured debts can be restructured within the personal insolvency arrangement (debt settlement procedure for natural persons).

Of interest here is the new reform in Hungary, based in mortgage debt.[81] The new Debt Consolidation Act is aimed at solving the problems of mortgage backed loans for the acquisition of a home and the procedures are therefore designed for the situation where the debtor is party to a mortgage or leasing contract secured on the home. The mortgagee acts as the main creditor and, whilst it is for the debtor to initiate proceedings, the mortgagee has control of the required out of court procedure, where agreement on a payment plan must be attempted. A court based debt consolidation is only resorted to where such agreement cannot be reached between creditor and debtor.

Similarly, in Portugal, the regulatory framework provides a more targeted approach to particular types of debt, beyond simple preference in favour of secured obligations, as is the case in most countries. Here, there is an extraordinary regime for debtors (a negotiation procedure) where the debt in issue is a housing loan, and the debtor is in a 'very difficult economic situation'. This interestingly is not just in relation to secured creditors, however. There are also two specific procedures where bank debt is at stake. These are the action plan for the prevention of risk of default and out of court debt restructuring procedures, both being based in an agreed plan to restructure the debt, the former being a preventative mechanism, and the latter to allow some form of repayment within the debtor's means.

---

[81]   Prompted by the global financial crisis in 2008, which led to the national currency being devalued. This left a large number of Hungarian citizens unable to pay monthly instalments, as these were calculated on the exchange rate applicable when the instalment was due.

8.4.3 Practicalities: Average Length of Proceedings, Publicity and Costs

8.4.3.1 Length of proceedings

Many reporters have confirmed that there are no official statistics that confirm the average length of procedures. Here is meant, not the average length of a payment plan, but how long the overall process takes, whether bankruptcy or debt settlement. Evidence from reporters suggests that the length of proceedings varies, dictated partly in terms of the legal requirements in this regard and the practicalities of court procedure. For example, in Denmark, where statistics were available from the Danish Court Administration, it was estimated that the average processing time for the debt settlement procedure in 2014 was 5.3 months, but a restructuring procedure was up to 11 months, with an average processing time for bankruptcy being 15 months, and the complete proceeding lasting up to two years. This accords with Germany where, although there are no statistics as such, procedures are estimated normally to be six months and two years. For other countries, the overall length of proceedings, where for example a payment plan may be involved, can be much longer. A couple of reporters also mention that court delays can also lengthen the process.

8.4.3.2 Publicity

All Member States, with the exception of Belgium and Italy, publish details of the various procedures in some form. The divergence in approach lies in whether bankruptcy only is advertised, who the information is available to, and for how long. Nevertheless, the majority of countries have some time limit, for example in Cyprus, where information on the bankruptcy remains on the debt discharge register for a year after the order is made; or the Czech Republic, where the entire insolvency file in debt settlement procedures is available online for the duration of the case and five years after closure. In contrast in the United Kingdom, bankruptcies, IVAs and debt relief orders (debt settlement procedures) are removed three months after discharge or the end of the payment plan. A further contrast can be made between countries such as Slovakia and Slovenia, where there is no time limit on how long information may be available, although this is a minority approach. The policy behind this appears to broadly lie in the tensions between protecting the interests of current and future creditors, and those of the debtor. This is both in terms of fresh start and confidentiality. However, this does not mean to say that information may not still be available via other avenues, for example, credit score mechanisms.

In the comparator countries, publicity of procedures is also required. In Norway, debt settlement procedures (apart from voluntary proceedings under the Bankruptcy Act) are registered and announced in the *Official Gazette*. In the United States, there is no formal process for publicizing bankruptcy, however, there is wide public access to court proceedings. This is only curtailed in very limited circumstances (protection of trade secrets and confidentiality) or where there is a risk to the debtor's person or identity. This also reflects the position in Norway, where a court may decide an announcement of debt settlement procedure should not be allowed if it would cause damage to the debtor.

8.4.3.3   Costs

Cost of proceedings can inevitably be a barrier to debtors accessing procedures and can affect efficiency. The data suggests a number of Member States require the debtor to pay something, with only Greece and Slovenia exonerating the debtor from any charges; and in Sweden, where there is no charge for debt settlement or the service of counsellors in relation to debt relief. However, there may be support available for the debtor; for example, in some Member States where the debtor is liable, there is the opportunity for state help through legal aid or other means. Alternatively, costs may be met elsewhere for some procedures, as for example in France, where fees are only due from the debtor if a liquidator is appointed under the rétablissement personnel avec liquidation, but, if the debtor has no means of paying this, public funds are used to pay the liquidator's fees.

There are a variety of methods of calculating fees, from a set court fee for presenting a petition or applying for a procedure, to administration costs calculated on the basis of the value of the estate. The 'set' costs differ widely across Member States, with set fees ranging from 10 euros (debt settlement and bankruptcy initiated by debtor in Estonia) to 1,800–2000 euros in Germany.

In the comparator country of Norway, there is no set administrative fee for debt settlement procedures and in bankruptcy the court approves the fee of the insolvency administrator and fees of other advisors are settled by agreement. In the United States, court fees for Chapter 7 proceedings are US$335, and US$310 for Chapter 13. There is also the availability of fee waiver (Chapter 7 only).

8.4.3.4   Advantages and disadvantages of various procedures

Bankruptcy may provide a clean slate but still attracts stigma and will mean the liquidation of all assets and potentially the loss of the family home. It is arguable this is inappropriate where there is no value in the estate from which creditors can be paid. Debt settlement procedures will involve a payment plan, which whilst in theory provides breathing space for a debtor, involves monthly financial obligations, potentially stifling initiative and trapping the debtor in a low standard of living. However, it could be argued that these debt settlement procedures are more adaptable to the debtor's individual situation and are therefore to be preferred over bankruptcy, provided the length of the payment plan is not too great.

Beyond this, the following initial comments can be made:

- Debt settlement procedures allow a range of options that may not necessitate the liquidation of assets; the most flexible procedures are best in terms of allowing adaptability to the individual debtor.
- Informal arrangements may be preferable in terms of reduced cost and time (court delays can lengthen the process).
- Out of court procedures may have the same advantages and be less daunting for the debtor.
- It is more appropriate to treat all natural persons under the same legal regime to allow for consumers that may have some entrepreneurial debt and who may have used private income and assets to support the failing business.
- Criteria for debtor initiation of legal procedures should be simple and not too restrictive.
- There should be some control on the costs and fees that fall on the consumer debtor.
- All procedures should result in discharge.

However, it is important to consider the role and position of the creditor to ensure a balance is maintained. Whilst debt settlement procedures as opposed to bankruptcy may be a better option for consumers, it is important to ensure that creditors have a place in proceedings, particularly where it is only debtors that may bring an application. The extent of creditor involvement may be best placed in terms of appealing against a proposal rather than allowing creditors control over the proposal itself (as, e.g., in Italy), as this provides the debtor or the administrator with the flexibility to frame something suitable for the individual debtor. By the same token, it may be appropriate to impose an arrangement on creditors where the debtor has very little income.

The difficulty with the informal arrangement is that there may be no effective mechanism to protect creditors against default. In the same way, debtors may find creditors do not adhere to the agreement.

8.4.4 Conclusions on Divergence

Outside the general categories of bankruptcy and debt settlement procedures, inevitably there will be divergence in the mechanics and detail of proceedings available to debtors.[82] The rate of development of Member States' consumer insolvency systems has differed across the EU, and as legislation adapts or innovates, this will lead to variation. For example, an attempt at an out of court settlement or mediation may be required before the procedure can be accessed. However, the benefit of this may be dubious, being, rather, a prolongation of the debtor's problems and an unhelpful delay. Such divergence, however, is unlikely to cause a major cross-border issue.

Prerequisites/criteria also vary, and this has been discussed above. However, the greatest divergence appears to be in terms of time-line and cost, particularly the latter where extremes are demonstrated, from nothing at all to the hefty costs of the German system. A preliminary analysis suggests that it is these two aspects of procedures that may have more of a cross-border impact. This is likely only to be the case if the difference is so great that a consumer is prepared to move countries to access the procedure, presuming of course that he/she is aware of another country's beneficial process. The other element of cost is, of course, its impact on access to relief. If costs of a procedure, whether bankruptcy or debt settlement, are prohibitive, this can effectively exclude a debtor, for whom the procedure is most appropriate. This is something that has been highlighted, for example in the United Kingdom, in relation to the deposit and other fees payable in order to access bankruptcy.[83] Best practice would be for such debtors either to have recourse to other options, or be ensured of assistance/discount, as appropriate.

8.5   GUARANTORS

Several issues relating to insolvency law and procedure arise in relation to guarantors, sureties and co-debtors of consumer debt. In this section, the term 'debtor' will refer to the consumer who has incurred the debt to the supplier of goods or services. The term 'guarantor' will refer to the

---

[82]   Observable even within the United Kingdom, where there are some differences between England and Wales, Scotland and Northern Ireland.

[83]   Christians Against Poverty, *Too Poor to Go Bankrupt: A Report on CAP's Insolvency Demographic and the Problems Posed by the Current Debt Relief Order (DRO) Eligibility Criteria* (2014), available at https://capuk.org/fileserver/downloads/policy_and_government/too_poor_to_go_bankrupt_report.pdf; see also www.mirror.co.uk/money/personal-finance/goverment-to-review-bankruptcy-fees-89698. The issue of fees was connected to the drive for reform to allow greater access to alternatives to bankruptcy, i.e. the DRO.

entity which has guaranteed this debt in some manner (whether or not the creditor is obliged as a matter of law to call upon the debtor first before calling upon the guarantor to meet that obligation; and whether or not the liability of the guarantor is affected by any compromise, dispute or alteration in relation to the debt owed by the debtor).

8.5.1 Undue Influence and Guarantee Set Aside

In relation to consumer debt, the providers of guarantees (and the co-debtors if there are any) may well be relatives or spouses or cohabitees of the consumer. The guarantor may or may not have shared in the benefits that flowed from the assets, goods or services acquired by the consumer from the various creditors. Relations between the consumer and the guarantor may have been such that the guarantor had little real choice over whether to grant the guarantee and may have been coerced, explicitly or implicitly, into granting the support. This issue is particularly sensitive from a public policy perspective when a guarantee is secured on the family home.

8.5.2 Recourse of Guarantor to Consumer

The law in most countries permits any guarantor who has paid a creditor under the terms of the contract of guarantee to have recourse to the consumer for the sums paid out under the guarantee (and possibly costs incurred). This claim is normally subject to the conventional limitation periods that apply in that country. The issue that therefore arises is that the guarantor may seek recourse from the consumer after the conclusion of, or outside the terms of, any insolvency proceedings that apply to the consumer, thus escaping any procedure which discharges the consumer's debt. If legal advice and assistance is not available, the consumer may not be aware of the right of recourse against him/her and may not therefore voluntarily bring that liability into the bankruptcy or debt settlement procedure. Some countries have law that permits a guarantor to escape liability under the contract of guarantee on the grounds of duress or undue influence but this will only come into play, in many countries, if the guarantor makes an application to the court to have the guarantee set aside.

8.5.3 Consequent Insolvency of Guarantor

Where claims under the guarantee push the guarantor into insolvency, it may be appropriate to link the bankruptcy or debt settlement procedure of the guarantor with the bankruptcy or debt settlement proceedings

---

BOX 8.5   AUSTRIAN APPROACH TO FAMILY MEMBER AS GUARANTOR

In Austria, the Consumer Protection Act permits guarantees given by family members to be quashed by the court in certain circumstances (e.g. the guarantor's assumption of liability was inappropriate in the light of his or her income or the guarantor gained no personal benefit from the obligation). However, the issue is not considered *ex officio* in the course of bankruptcy and any discharge gained by the consumer following bankruptcy does not affect guarantees given by family members. Therefore the bankruptcy and discharge of a consumer may well be closely followed by the bankruptcy of his or her spouse because the creditor will enforce the guarantee against the spouse which will push him or her into bankruptcy.

---

applying to the consumer, so that discharge or compromise is provided to both parties on the same terms and taking account of the assets available to both guarantor and consumer and the income needs of all relevant parties. This may be appropriate for spouses or other parties who share a household. If the law does not allow the procedures to be dealt with together, the scope for unfairness to one or other party is enlarged since the court, or other authority, may take account of different evidence or give different weight to relevant issues. This may result in different decisions over discharge or compromise. In addition, two separate sets of proceedings, examining common issues, is inefficient. Where consumer and guarantor are in the same family, with common dependants, the differing outcomes of two sets of proceedings may cause unforeseen hardship, as well as stress, to dependants (see Box 8.5).

8.5.4   Current Insolvency Law and Procedure Relating to Guarantees

8.5.4.1   Family guarantors
In most of the countries examined, there is no special law or procedure that applies to guarantees, which relate to insolvent or over-indebted consumers. The general law on the enforceability of the guarantee applies so that the creditor can enforce the liability against the guarantor, whether or not they are a family member. This is the case in Austria, Belgium, Bulgaria, Croatia, Denmark, Estonia, Germany, Greece, Hungary, Ireland, Italy, Latvia (but different law applies to a different category of guarantor: sureties), Lithuania, the Netherlands, Poland, Portugal, Romania, Slovakia, Slovenia, Spain, Sweden, the United Kingdom and the United States. The only proviso to this is that in some of these countries, for example

the United Kingdom, Austria, Belgium and the United States, there is scope for the guarantor to escape liability on the grounds of undue influence or duress or, in the case of Belgium, where there was no benefit to the guarantor or where there was a discrepancy between the level of the debt and the level of the debtor's income. However, this issue will usually not be considered *ex officio* (as a matter of convention and procedure by the insolvency court or relevant administrator of its own initiative). Therefore, an application to a court by the guarantor is necessary. Any procedure which rests on the guarantor making an application to court (or to an administrator) is unlikely to be as effective in providing appropriate relief to family guarantors.

It seems likely that Council Directive 93/13 of 5 April 1993 on unfair terms in consumer contracts applies to contracts of guarantee. This would ensure that the contract could be reviewed by a court, upon application, in order to determine whether it is unfair having regard to the guarantor's weak bargaining power and level of knowledge of the real commercial position relating to the terms of the deal between the consumer and the creditor. However, despite the large number of recent European cases relating to financial consumer contracts, this point has not arisen to date and so the law is unsettled. In particular, it is uncertain whether a guarantor would be held to be a consumer within the meaning of the Directive given the absence of a good or service being provided to him or her by the creditor, although this point would turn on the facts in any particular case.[84]

8.5.4.2   Right of recourse to consumer

Some countries deny a guarantor recourse to the insolvent consumer. The guarantor is simply liable under the guarantee to the creditor and if he or she cannot pay, he or she may be pushed into insolvency him/herself as a consequence. The countries in which this applies are the Czech Republic (where recourse proceedings are automatically prevented against a consumer in debt discharge proceedings); the Netherlands (if payments to other unsecured creditors will be reduced as a consequence);

---

[84]   See, e.g., C-537/13 *Siba* relating to asymmetry of information between the consumer and the supplier in a financial transaction, and C-26/13 *Kasler* v. *OTP Jelzalogbank Zrt* relating to foreign currency mortgage loans, both of which construe the law so as to give the consumer a right of review in relation to the detrimental term or circumstance in the financial services contract. See the various discussions on unconscionability in M. Kenny, J. Devenney and L. Fox Mahoney (eds), *Unconscionability in European Private Financial Transactions: Protecting the Vulnerable* (Cambridge, Cambridge University Press, 2010).

Poland (recourse prevented); Spain (where there is no recourse if there has been a grant of discharge to the consumer in relation to that debt); and Sweden (where the recourse is reduced in proportion to any debt discharge granted).

8.5.4.3 Special law relating to enforceability of guarantees of obligations under consumer financial contracts

Some countries appear to wish to deter the use of guarantees by creditors and so have provisions that render enforcement of guarantee obligations difficult in some circumstances. Latvia has specific law preventing unfair contract terms in contracts of surety given by consumers. Cyprus bars enforcement claims against a guarantor after two years. Belgian law provides that any guarantee may be annulled if there is a discrepancy between the amounts borrowed and the debtor's means or if the guarantee provided no benefit to the guarantor.

8.5.4.4 Procedures which allow, encourage or compel guarantor/co-debtor obligations to be dealt with in the bankruptcy or debt settlement procedure relating to the consumer

A few countries specifically provide law and procedural rules relating to the guarantors' liability and for the guarantors' claims for recourse against the consumer and/or for the position in relation to co-debtors. This may be motivated by the public interest being served by quickly settling ownership and occupation rights to residential family property. This appears to be the case in France, where the Commission de surendettement is obliged to make enquiries of the consumer debtor about guarantees and then to notify the guarantors of the bankruptcy or debt settlement procedure which has been commenced. In Hungary, any guarantors or co-debtors may join in the bankruptcy and, to that extent, his or her assets will be liquidated to meet claims. If they do not join the process and they pay out under the guarantee or joint liability, they may enforce a full right of recourse against the consumer debtor after the closure of the debt consolidation process, unless their claim is by that time barred by the limitation period. Time does not continue to run during the bankruptcy. Co-debtors (such as spouses jointly liable under mortgage debt) are contacted by the Family Bankruptcy Service, and encouraged to participate in the bankruptcy, so that the family's position in relation to the debt (usually in respect of the family home) can be resolved. In Finland, co-debtors may file a joint petition for a debt settlement procedure in respect of joint secured or joint ordinary debts. Provision is also made for consumer debtors and guarantors to file joint applications for debt settlement procedures and in that event a payment plan will be settled applying to the guarantor's liability as well as the consumer debtor's liability. Specific provisions are set out in the Act on the Adjustment of the Debts of a Private Individual.

The comparator country Norway has specific legislation covering the enforceability of guarantees in favour of financial institutions. These impose on the institution good faith obligations to provide information to the guarantor at the time of grant (including advice on whether the guarantee is appropriate) and during the life of the guarantee. In addition, the guarantee is unenforceable if the institution has withheld significant information from the guarantor or otherwise misled him/her. In the United States, guarantee liabilities are treated in the same way as other debts. Liability may be avoided due to duress, undue influence or the failure to comply with an applicable Statute of Frauds.

8.5.5 Conclusions on Divergence

The law differs between Member States in the extent to which the obligations under guarantees and the obligations of co-debtors are dealt with in relation to consumers that are subject to bankruptcy and debt settlement procedures. The position is summarized in Table 8.7. There are very few countries in which these liabilities are dealt with *ex officio* in the course of the relevant insolvency proceedings. Any provisions which oblige or allow, as a matter of course, the consideration of the liabilities of co-debtors and guarantors will inevitably widen the scope and therefore the expense of proceedings. Many consumers do not have the resources to pay the costs and fees of the relevant insolvency proceedings and therefore there are public interest considerations in relation to widening the remit of bankruptcy and debt settlement procedures.

The law differs between Member States in relation to the availability of remedies, under the general law and not connected to insolvency proceedings, to co-debtors and guarantors of consumer debt which has been adjusted or discharged. In addition, the conditions of access to such proceedings between Member States differ widely (e.g. in relation to the availability of legal aid and advice for consumers). This is due to the very different private law history, legal institutions and legal culture between the Member States.

From the data received, there appears to be little or no evidence that divergent law and procedure relating to guarantees is affecting the free movement of consumers or the free movement of capital or financial services between Member States.

It may be the case that financial institutions are less willing to provide consumer credit in Member States where recourse against co-debtors and guarantors is prevented as a matter of law, but again the data gathered

Table 8.7 *Law in relation to co-debts and guarantor liability in the context of the bankruptcy or entry into debt settlement procedure by a consumer*

Country	Special rules for guarantee liability
Austria	Discharge leaves guarantors unaffected, but special provisions to absolve family guarantors on the grounds of undue influence. Independent of insolvency proceedings.
Belgium	Guarantee may be annulled or discharged if discrepancy between debt and debtor's income and assets or if guarantee did not benefit guarantor.
Bulgaria	None
Croatia	None
Cyprus	Two-year limit on enforcement proceedings against a guarantor.
Czech Republic	Debtor not liable to guarantor in recourse proceedings.
Denmark	None
Estonia	None
Finland	Guarantor may petition for payment plan on guarantee liability.
France	Guarantors may make submissions to the CDS in respect of their guarantee obligations. Discharge may be granted to insolvent guarantor.
Germany	None
Greece	None
Hungary	Guarantors and other obligors (security holders) may join in debt consolidation process. Otherwise right of recourse remains after closure of debt consolidation process.
Ireland	None
Italy	None
Latvia	Law prohibits unfair contractual terms in sureties given by consumers. Independent of insolvency proceedings.
Lithuania	None
Luxembourg	Professional creditor may not enforce personal security (*'cautionnement'*) against guarantor or co-debtor if it was manifestly disproportionate in light of certain parameters.
Malta	None
Netherlands	Rights of creditors against co-debtors and sureties not affected by proceedings. In relation to recourse claims (by co-debtor who has paid out under surety/guarantee), admittance restricted.
Norway	Obligations of good faith apply between creditor and guarantor which compel the creditor to provide the guarantor with information about the loan and other relevant circumstances. The financial institution is obliged to inform the guarantor if the borrower is unsuited to the loan agreement. Obligation on

Table 8.7   (continued)

Country	Special rules for guarantee liability
	financial institution to advise a consumer against providing guarantees if he /she is unfit in the light of his/her financial position. Obligation to inform guarantor if there is change in borrower's financial circumstances, e.g. reduction in liquidity. Length of liability under guarantee given by consumer limited to five years (secured) or ten years (unsecured). Guarantee void if financial institution misled consumer or withheld important information.
Poland	Rights of recourse by guarantor/surety/co-debtor extinguished against a creditor, subject to debt discharge/repayment schedule. Insolvent co-debtor/surety/guarantor must file for insolvency proceedings in his/her own right.
Portugal	None
Romania	Debtor's relief from debt under insolvency proceedings does not benefit co-debtor or guarantors and no stay on enforcement proceedings against them. Full right of recourse to co-debtor/guarantor.
Slovakia	None
Slovenia	None
Spain	Guarantors and co-debtors have no right of subrogation against the consumer where there has been a grant of discharge.
Sweden	If the consumer has obtained relief, the guarantor's recourse claim against the consumer is reduced proportionately.
United Kingdom	None
United States	None. Guarantee liable to be set aside for duress, undue influence, non-compliance with a relevant Statute of Frauds.

here suggest little evidence that this is the case. Any law reform that inhibited the rights of creditors under contracts relating to the provision of consumer finance would need to be justified by reference to very good evidence on distortion of access to consumer finance between Member States and by reference to opinions on the desirability of increasing access to consumer finance.

Best practice jurisdictions: those jurisdictions, such as the Czech Republic, Poland and the Netherlands, that limit the recourse of the guarantor or co-debtor to a consumer debtor who is, or has been, subject to bankruptcy or a debt settlement procedure provide the consumer debtor with a better opportunity for an effective discharge and fresh start. However, the restriction of recourse in this manner may, of course, have the effect of pushing the guarantor or co-debtor towards consumer over-indebtedness.

8.6 LEGAL AND PRACTICAL CONSEQUENCES OF OVER-INDEBTEDNESS PROCEDURES

The consequences of over-indebtedness itself are well documented and have been referred to earlier in the Report. Health issues, social exclusion and lack of economic contribution to the community are all likely consequences of consumer over-indebtedness. The balance between ensuring creditors' interests are protected and allowing productivity, re-admission into the community and fresh start is a fine one. Beyond the obvious various benefits of consumer over-indebtedness procedures, such as stay of enforcement processes and debt discharge, there are a number of less positive legal consequences which follow from bankruptcy and debt settlement procedures. Other practical consequences often result from the proceedings.

The majority of Member States provide for certain obligations or restrictions on a consumer following an over-indebtedness procedure. Primarily, but not exclusively, the consequences with the biggest impact, at least in the short term, seem to emanate from bankruptcy. The only Member States that have no legal consequences at all are Lithuania, Germany and Slovakia, although Austria and the Czech Republic report that restrictions are limited following bankruptcy. In Austria, many of the original restrictions have been lifted, in the last two decades, and for instance, a debtor is now only prohibited from carrying on a business or trade if the bankruptcy proceedings could not be opened due to lack of means. However, a bankrupt is not able to practise as a lawyer or notary. A very similar approach is adopted in the Czech Republic.

Restrictions following bankruptcy are observable across the countries that are members of the EU. Obligations and rules that directly relate to the procedural aspects are mostly connected to issues of control: the consumer debtor loses control of the estate, cannot enter transactions relating to the estate (or only with the consent of the IP), and there may be prohibitions on accessing new credit (e.g., in the United Kingdom, a bankrupt cannot borrow more than £500 unless he/she informs the lender of the bankruptcy; in Ireland, 650 euros). These restrictions are also evident in Estonia, Hungary, Latvia and Slovenia. Non-compliance with an obligation in the bankruptcy may even result in arrest and imprisonment (e.g., in Estonia and the United Kingdom). The other restriction that features heavily relates to the ability of the bankrupt to hold certain offices, whether as a director of a company or public office, or practise certain professions (e.g., as a lawyer). Cyprus, Denmark, Estonia, Ireland, Italy, Latvia and the United Kingdom all have these restrictions.

In relation to debt settlement procedures, the legal consequences for the consumer debtor are more mixed. For example, in Belgium, the debt settlement procedure also requires the administrator to take control of the debtor's estate, and the debtor is no longer able to administer his or her own income, although allowance is made in terms of the debtor having enough money to live. In Finland, the legal consequences of the debt settlement procedure are an obligation to provide information and make notifications. Ireland's restrictions on access to credit apply to all procedures and the debt relief notice imposes a requirement for the debtor to notify change in circumstance (if an improvement, to allow the Insolvency Service to pay creditors more). In Italy, restrictions may be imposed (primarily in relation to obtaining or using further credit) during the Accordo procedure, by agreement. In Romania, a debtor under the debt settlement procedure will not be able to obtain new credit unless there is a serious emergency in relation to his or her personal situation or that of the family. In the United Kingdom, the IVA and DRO also puts the debtor under a number of restrictions, including obtaining new credit, and imposes an obligation to disclose any change in circumstances which may swell the debtor's income/estate allowing creditors to be paid more.

For the Member States where regimes are new, or there have been recent reforms, the practical consequences of over-indebtedness procedures are still difficult to gauge at this stage (Lithuania, Hungary, Ireland, Italy, Luxembourg, Romania). One notable approach is that of Poland, where restrictions beyond the 'economy' of a bankruptcy can also be seen in the impact on marriage, in that all assets of a new spouse subject to the 'marital community property regime' would become part of the bankruptcy estate. This, potentially, may dissuade individuals from getting married. Otherwise, one practical consequence of procedures to be noted here is in relation to the debt settlement procedure. Whilst this tool is often used as a means to avoid bankruptcy, it may bring its own detriment. Where a payment plan within the debt settlement procedure may continue for a number of years, a consumer debtor may find he or she is unable to improve his or her financial circumstances, particularly where income may be barely enough to cover the monthly payments imposed.

However, the issue that has perhaps the greatest practical impact is publicity. All Member States (bar Austria, Belgium and Lithuania) provide that notice of bankruptcy must be entered into some form of Official Register, and some Member States also impose publicity obligations in relation to debt settlement procedures (see above). Apart from the personal stigma that may still arise from this, the most negative impact of a publicity requirement may be long-term exclusion from meaningful or affordable credit. This is observed by a number of reporters, although there is little evidence to confirm this conclusion. There is in most Member States a time limit, in that, for example, the debtor's details can be removed after a stated period of time.

In addition, the recast Insolvency Regulation[85] obliges Member States to publish relevant information in relation to insolvency proceedings listed in Annex A[86] on a publicly accessible electronic register from 26 June 2018, although there are certain exceptions in relation to consumers (as opposed to entrepreneurs).[87] The register will be accessible to individuals, including banks and creditors, in other Member States from 26 June 2019. There is considerable scope for distorting effects if some Member States include details of all insolvency procedures affecting individuals (including those that do not entail asset liquidation) whilst others restrict entries to the most formal procedures (such as bankruptcy). Regulations which oblige all Member States to remove information from the register within a specific timeframe would assist debtors in making a fresh start and discourage distorting effects between Member States.

The negative effects of publicity may, however, be felt for some time after proceedings have ended, in that private databases such as credit reference agencies may keep the data beyond time periods relevant to official registers. In the United Kingdom, there are several private credit scoring agencies and they are very widely consulted by prospective landlords, employers and creditors. The credit score produced by these agencies for a debtor subject to any procedure, whether bankruptcy, IVA, DRO or Administration Order, will be affected for at least six years. This can have a chilling impact on fresh start. In relation to bankruptcy, creditors will

---

[85]   Regulation on Insolvency Proceedings 2015/848 ('recast Insolvency Regulation').

[86]   Member States decide which proceedings are listed.

[87]   Recast Insolvency Regulation, art. 24(4): Member States are not obliged to include in the insolvency registers the mandatory information laid down in art. 24 or to make such information publicly available provided that 'known foreign creditors are informed of the court before which and, where applicable, the time limit within which a challenge of the decision opening insolvency proceedings is to be lodged': art 24(2)(j).

sometimes ask whether a debtor has been bankrupt in the last ten years. In Austria, details of bankruptcy may be available for up to seven years. France is notable here, in that whilst registration of debtors is required, and may last for eight years (or seven years under a personal rescue procedure) banks are legally prohibited from terminating credit support during procedures, unless the debtor has behaved badly.

It is not just access to credit, however, that can be affected by a bad credit score. Other aspects of the consumer debtor's life are detrimentally affected. Access to housing, including social housing, insurance, buying goods on credit or even mobile phones may, in effect, be restricted, and in certain cases, some types of bank accounts may not be accessible. Procedures that take control of assets and income normally allow a debtor a basic income for living. However, it is often the case that a bankrupt debtor will not be able to keep a family home beyond a temporary period. Other avenues for housing must therefore be protected. These are all issues that lead to social and financial exclusion, and their impact should not be underestimated.

In the United States, there are few direct legal consequences, and there is no formal denial of further credit, whilst in Norway, a bankrupt may be unable to obtain a licence to practise professions, such as the law and accountancy, and may be subject to director's disqualification (detailed in Chapter 1) and arrest if there is a chance he/she may abscond, or obligations are not complied with. In terms of publicity, there are safeguards in place, which are designed to mitigate the impact of publicity, where the interests of the debtor are likely to be severely harmed. However, in reality it is likely such safeguards are infrequently invoked.

8.6.1 Conclusions on Divergence

Legal obligations to publicize the names of consumers subject to bankruptcy and debt settlement procedures on Official Registers and to make those registers publicly accessible are clearly designed to protect the interests of creditors and prospective creditors. There may be distorting effects on the opportunity for fresh start for consumers if the legal obligations relate to different types of insolvency proceeding in different Member States and if there are different time periods beyond which the names of consumers must be removed. For instance, if one Member State compels removal of a name from the register after only one year, consumers in that Member State will have a greater opportunity for fresh start than consumers in a Member State where the law compels removal of a name from the register after eight years.

8.7 DEBT DISCHARGE

8.7.1 Introduction

Discharge from debt is the key desired outcome for any individual debtor entering insolvency proceedings. The legal environment for debt discharge for individuals in the EU is very diverse and reflects to a degree the political and social attitudes towards the incurrence of debt by an individual (and the effect on his or her family and dependants), and the ethical approach of each society towards debt and personal responsibility for it. In recent years, most countries have seen a sharp rise in the availability of personal credit and a rise in personal over-indebtedness. In some countries, this has driven legal change to deal with attendant social problems, and in others, legal change is being considered at present. In some Member States, legal change has been driven by a sudden increase in a particular type of credit such as mortgage finance, for instance in Hungary, or credit cards in the case of Croatia, and in increases in rates of default in respect of mortgage debt, personal loans and credit card debt for example in Hungary, Croatia[88] and Portugal.

Many newer debt settlement procedures oblige the preparation of payment plans which may endure for many years in theory. Many debtors find it difficult to draw up reasonable and appropriate payment plans which are likely to be acceptable to creditors and/or the court (if necessary). Appropriate and realistic needs assessments are a crucial part of these.[89] The resources needed to undertake good needs assessments (taking into account dependants' needs and unusual or infrequent expenditure) and to draw up sustainable and realistic payment plans is considerable. Few Member States provide the necessary resource free of charge. Methodically sound research is needed on whether obliging consumer debtors to earn debt discharge by adhering to payment plans in debt settlement procedures over a period of time is genuinely in the public interest on any measure. It may be that such plans do in fact increase the amounts paid to creditors (even taking costs into account), or assist debtors in acquiring good spending habits, or are beneficial due to some other factors. On the other hand,

---

[88] Financial Agency of the Ministry of Finance of Croatia reported 322,498 insolvent consumers in Croatia on 31 December 2014 out of a total population of approximately 4.2 million. See Croatian national report.

[89] E.g., there is a lack of free and impartial debt advice to consumers in the United Kingdom, despite very high levels of personal indebtedness. See Step Change Debt Charity, *An Action Plan on Problem Debt* (2015), and recent work by the Financial Conduct Authority in relation to debt management services.

they may merely satisfy punitive and retributive norms which rest on the assumption that over-indebtedness is immoral and great effort should be made by the consumer debtor and family to repay what has been borrowed. A family unit is very different from an economically productive business entity and the social and economic objectives to be furthered in consumer insolvency proceedings, and the balance to be struck between competing objectives, are likely to differ in each country. These differing norms are reflected, to some extent, in the different law applying to discharge of consumer debt between Member States.

8.7.2 Debt Discharge Periods

The simplest cases are countries where legal proceedings are instituted (or terminated) and discharge, in respect of all admissible debts, follows on automatically at a specific date in the future, that is there is no requirement for a further application to the court. In these most simple cases the procedure is usually the terminal procedure of bankruptcy, involving liquidation of all the debtors' assets, rather than any payment plan over a number of years. The countries offering this type of simple discharge include the United Kingdom and Ireland (one year discharge period)[90] and the comparator jurisdiction of the United States (Bankruptcy Code, Chapter 7: 60 days after the date set for the initial creditors' meeting). These proceedings have the advantage of relative simplicity and speed for the debtor and family. Whether the adverse consequences of becoming bankrupt (as opposed to entering into one of the debt settlement procedures) will outweigh the advantage of simplicity and speed will differ in each jurisdiction and will depend on economic and social conditions in that jurisdiction (e.g. ease of access to housing, whether loss of employment will follow automatically from bankruptcy, and the social stigma attached to bankruptcy), as well as the formal legal consequences of appearing on a register of bankrupt individuals (such as losing the opportunity to borrow or being prevented from holding office as a director or in some cases public office).

It should also be noted that discharge may be challenged and therefore to that extent is not guaranteed. For example, in the Republic of Ireland, if the court accepts the valid objection to discharge, the period during which the debtor is not discharged can be extended by up to eight years.[91]

---

[90]   In Ireland, this has been reduced from three years to one year by the Bankruptcy (Amendment) Act 2015.

[91]   The Bankruptcy (Amendment) Act 2015 extends this to 15 years if the debtor's non-co-operation is serious enough.

In many countries, there is no access to discharge for consumers other than through a debt settlement procedure involving a payment plan, coupled with some type of oversight over economic activity and circumstances (e.g., an obligation to reveal inheritances, an obligation to seek work, not to dissipate assets, etc.). In the majority of cases these payment plans are agreed between debtors and creditors or between debtor and an IP or a court. In these cases, repayment periods are set at anything between ten years (the maximum that applies in Finland); eight years in France (over-indebtedness procedure); seven years in Austria (in the Zahlungsplan) and Hungary (in specific circumstances); five years in Belgium, Cyprus (personal repayment plan), the Czech Republic and Denmark; and three years in Latvia. The precise calculation of timeframes differs, as do the consequences of the debtor failing to adhere to the terms of the payment plan (which must become more likely as the length of the payment plan increases given the greater chance of changed circumstances). Changed circumstances will result in the revival of negotiations and discussions and further court applications. In many instances, for example in Italy and Poland, the court has the difficult job of determining how much income the debtor and family should be allowed for basic needs over this (often long) period and this discretion is often unfettered, which leaves the debtor and family in a vulnerable position.

In some countries, discharge is not available at all to consumers. This applies to Malta, Bulgaria and Croatia, although in Bulgaria and Croatia draft legislation is under discussion.

Some countries require the debtor to make special application to the court or administrative authority for discharge once the primary liquidation or insolvency proceedings have been instigated or reached a certain stage. This occurs in Spain where an additional court application for discharge is required. Even if granted, the discharge may be annulled on the application of a creditor in the five-year period following discharge. Alternatively, more flexible systems such as in Ireland allow application to the court within stated time periods, on the basis that certain requirements, relating to full or partial payment of creditors, are met.

8.7.3   Debt Discharge Dependent on Payment Plan or Asset Liquidation

In all countries where discharge is possible it is dependent either on liquidation of the debtor's assets or on compliance with a payment plan as part of a debt settlement procedure. In many countries, procedures entail an initial attempt to agree a composition with creditors (usually with the possibility of agreeing to liquidate some assets in order to obtain creditor approval) followed by an application to the court if consent from creditors cannot be obtained.

8.7.4 Assets Excluded from Liquidation

In most Member States, personal and household effects needed by the debtor and family are excluded from liquidation, as are goods, including a vehicle in some cases, that are necessary to pursue employment. These aspects are generally uncontroversial.

The position in relation to the home, whether subject to mortgage debt or not, is inevitably linked to the law on security and property rights in each Member State. Rates of home ownership vary within the EU and the availability of suitable alternative rented accommodation will also be very different.[92] The social impact of large numbers of homeless debtors is obvious and will have become more so in some countries since 2008. In Finland, the family home will not be sold, regardless of whether it is subject to security, if a reasonable alternative residence is not available or if selling it would provide insignificant additional funds for ordinary debtors. In Greece, the court may exclude the house from being liquidated if its value is below a certain threshold, with instalment payments being set by the court instead.[93] In Hungary, if the debtor and co-debtors express a wish to retain a property as a main residence on more favourable credit terms, this will be taken into account by the court (although how this will work in practice is not yet apparent as the Debt Consolidation of Natural Persons Act 2015 only came into force on 1 September 2015).

In Latvia, the home will not be liquidated for the benefit of all creditors if the debtor comes to a separate arrangement with the mortgagor.[94] In the United Kingdom, in bankruptcy proceedings, there is some protection against surrender of particular types of residential tenancy.[95] In addition, where a trustee in bankruptcy is seeking an order for possession of a family home, an application must be made to the bankruptcy court. The bankruptcy court is compelled to take into account the needs of the

---

[92] For statistics on home ownerships in the EU see EUROSTAT, *Population by Tenure Status* (2013) which showed home ownership to be highest in Romania, Croatia, Hungary and Slovakia and lowest in Germany, Austria, Denmark and France.

[93] Law No. 3869/2010.

[94] Although in Latvia there is a proviso that the other creditors may not be adversely affected by the arrangement, which seems very difficult to put into effect in practice.

[95] Insolvency Act 1986, s. 335A.

BOX 8.6   *FOYLE* V. *TURNER* [2007] BPIR 43 (UNITED KINGDOM)

F and W were declared bankrupt in 1991. F and W continued to live in the family home. The trustee in bankruptcy was unsuccessful in selling the home, which was of very low value. The bankruptcy was discharged in 1994 but the Official Receiver continued as trustee of the estate. In 2004, the value of the house had risen and the Official Receiver obtained an order from the court permitting him to sell the property. F appealed against the order for sale but the appeal was dismissed. The court held that, despite the delay, the interests of the creditors had not been out-weighed by exceptional circumstances and it was just and reasonable to make an order for sale.

---

spouse and children, as well as the interests of the creditors, in considering whether to grant the possession order. After a period of one year from the date of the first vesting of assets in the trustee in bankruptcy, the court will assume, unless the circumstances are exceptional, that the interests of the creditors outweigh those of the family members (see Box 8.6). In Ireland, recent legal change provides that the home will be re-vested in the discharged bankrupt three years after the bankruptcy adjudication if the Official Assignee has not sold it.[96]

In contrast, in Poland the debtor must give up his or her home together with all other assets. However, unlike the entrepreneur for whom there is no special provision, proceeds from the sale of the home are separated and put into a fund for the use of the accommodation needs of the debtor, which is equivalent to the average rent in the area for residential property for a term of one to two years. The aim here is to provide some protection against homelessness for the debtor and family.

In the United States, a homeowner may opt, in Chapter 7 bankruptcy, to affirm the mortgage contract under section 524(c) of the Bankruptcy Code, in which case the mortgage contract and its terms will be renegoti-ated under court scrutiny so that the debtor remains in possession of the house. The right of the secured creditor remains in place but the terms of the loan agreement as to interest (and repayment of accrued interest) are likely to be more favourable in the future for the debtor and family under the renegotiated contract. In Norway, under procedures under the Debt Settlement Act the debtor is permitted to keep his or her house provided its value does not exceed what is reasonable given the size of the debtor's household. However, the rights of secured creditors to enforce their

---

[96]   Bankruptcy (Amendment) Act 2015, s. 10(b), (c).

security are unaffected so in practice this only assists debtors who own their own home and have not granted a mortgage or other charge over it.

The other socially significant asset is the pension fund. It may be the case that in the majority of Member States, pensions are provided by the state or by employers under arrangements where no rights to a pension vest until retirement age is reached. In these arrangements the law is unlikely to regard the fund (if any is identifiable) as a liquidated asset which is available to creditors. In some Member States, such as the United Kingdom, recent changes in pensions law have given individuals more flexible rights over individual pension funds, such as the right to take benefits in a variety of forms and at earlier ages and in stages. This means that the fund is more obviously under the debtor's control at an earlier age (or could be so if he/she elects), and so may in law fall into the debtor's estate for the benefit of creditors. The law is currently uncertain and is the subject of appeal.[97]

In the United States, where there is a longer history of individual pension funds being treated as personal assets rather than as a collective entitlement that fall in at a specific age, there is a specific disregard of US$1,245,475. This permits the individual debtor to retain his or her retirement fund, up to this limit. This retirement fund may then be used by him or her at retirement to purchase an annuity or other financial products to generate an income in retirement. The trustee will have no rights over this fund or the income generated from it.

Pension funds and residential property are assets where there is a great capacity for significant distortion if Member States have differing approaches on the balance to be struck between debtor and creditor and between individual and collective property rights. Distinctions could have a severe impact on free movement of people, services and capital. More comparative detailed legal and socio-economic research is needed in both areas for the benefit of debtors, creditors and those providing advice and to ensure that any law reform reflects real social and economic conditions.

8.7.5 Exclusion of Discharge

The ideal position for an over-indebted individual is for an insolvency procedure to relieve them of all debts, however incurred, for which they

---

[97] The High Court in *Horton* v. *Henry* [2015] 1 WLR 2488, in December 2014, held that the trustee in bankruptcy could not obtain an income payments order in respect of a pension income which had not actually fallen into payment. This contravened the earlier decision of *Raithatha* v. *Williamson* [2012] 1 WLR 3559. The decision of the High Court in *Horton* v. *Henry* has been appealed to the Court of Appeal.

are personally liable. If some debts are excluded (e.g., those that relate to liability for a negligent act), the debtor and his/her family will not obtain a fresh start and will continue to be burdened by debts which have collectively pushed him or her into insolvency. It is notable that the list of debts which are not discharged in an insolvency procedure appears to be increasing in many countries, for instance in the United Kingdom. The prospect here is that the stigma and legal and factual restrictions attached to bankruptcy or a debt settlement procedure are present but the procedure itself does not in fact provide the conditions for a genuine fresh start. Statistics on successive insolvency procedures (where the same debtor or family enters into successive different or similar insolvency procedures over a number of years) are not available for any jurisdiction. Careful research is needed to reveal whether the non-discharge of debts in bankruptcy and debt settlement procedures is tending to push debtors into repeated over-indebtedness proceedings because they continue to be burdened by these obligations and this burden is in fact precluding fresh start for debtors and their families.

In many countries, debts relating to maintenance liabilities for children and other dependants are excluded from discharge. This is the case in all the countries reviewed except for Cyprus, the Czech Republic, Greece, the Netherlands (for debt adjustment) and Slovakia.

In most countries, fines, compensation orders and penalties relating to criminal behaviour are not discharged and/or cannot be included in any scheme of arrangement, as for example in Greece. This is presumably because the fine or penalty has been imposed in the place of some other criminal sanction such as imprisonment or community service. It would be unacceptable as a matter of public policy on criminal justice were this penalty to be dispensed with in the course of insolvency proceedings and may in fact distort sentencing if this were not the case. The position in relation to damages for personal injury or death consequent on negligence and for administrative fines and penalties and for tax debts is far more diverse between Member States, and the norms behind the individual approaches are not apparent. In some countries in which access to tertiary education is encouraged by the provision of student loans from the state (or with state support), student loans will not be discharged. This is the case in the United Kingdom and the Netherlands.

In the United States, there are 21 categories of non-dischargeable debt. These include tax debts; domestic support obligations; consumer debts aggregating more than US$650 for luxury goods and services incurred on or within 90 days before bankruptcy; cash advances aggregating more than US$925 that are extensions to consumer credit granted on or within 70 days prior to bankruptcy; debts arising from wilful or malicious damage to person or property; certain fines, penalties and forfeitures payable to government; and student loans, except where undue hardship would be imposed on the debtor and his/her dependants. In Norway, only maintenance and tax obligations are excluded from discharge. Secured debt is also not discharged to the extent that it is covered by the value of the secured asset (so the creditor enforces the security to recover the sums due).

8.7.6 Discharge Automatic

The ideal position from the debtor's viewpoint is that discharge occurs automatically upon the expiry of a particular time without the need for a court application or administrative procedure. This produces certainty for debtors and for creditors and reduces costs associated with administrative procedures and court applications. If the discharge is recorded in a public register this produces certainty for all. Discharge occurs in this way in Austria, Belgium, Denmark (in respect of debt rescheduling), Finland, France, Ireland, Slovenia, Sweden and the United Kingdom. One point should be made here, however: even discharge does not necessarily mean the debtor is completely free. For example, in the United Kingdom it is possible for the court to require the debtor to make payments from income or assets for a period of up to five years after the discharge. This period is three years in Ireland.[98]

In the comparator country of Norway, discharge is automatic (no further procedure or application required). In the same way in the United States, in Bankruptcy Code, Chapter 7 (the liquidation procedure), discharge is automatic in the absence of any objection. In Chapter 13 proceedings (payment plan), discharge is granted by the court upon receipt of a certificate from the debtor and trustee that all payments under the plan have been made. Under both procedures, discharge is conditional upon the debtor having attended a course in personal financial management.

8.7.7 Conclusions on Divergence

From the debtor's perspective, clear advantage lies in obtaining discharge, without further application to the court, after the expiry of a specific, short, period from a clearly identifiable point in time. The UK bankruptcy procedure, where discharge is obtained after one year, can be viewed

---

[98] The Irish Bankruptcy (Amendment) Act 2015 has reduced this to three years from five, unless the debtor has failed to co-operate or hidden assets.

as providing best practice here. However, this may be unacceptable to countries in which the overriding cultural and normative context in which the law operates is one of retribution. From a creditor's perspective, there are some indications that few creditors actively participate in legal processes which allow them to vote on payment plans. This may indicate that creditors regard participation in such processes as lacking in value from a cost/benefit perspective and in fact expect little or no recovery. Debt may well be written off by creditors once legal proceedings are initiated. This is an issue of behavioural finance which should be addressed in carefully designed research that identifies creditor behaviour and its impact on credit markets. If creditors do not in fact expect repayment once proceedings have commenced, little purpose is served by lengthy and burdensome processes that are designed to achieve it.

The helpful effect of discharge in assisting fresh start will be severely affected if more debts are excluded from discharge as a matter of law in each Member State. Best practice lies in keeping this category of non-dischargeable debts to a minimum. However, this is a difficult issue as distorting effects could follow if, for example, maintenance debts and student loans are routinely included in discharge. This may well encourage large numbers of people to enter bankruptcy or debt settlement procedures and shift the burden of providing these benefits onto the state. The following categories of debt are commonly excluded from discharge and consideration could be given to encouraging the adoption of common practice in all Member States: maintenance and child support; criminal penalties and criminal compensation orders; student loans; secured debt. The following types of debt are treated more variably between Member States: awards of damages in civil proceedings; debts relating to tax; civil fines and penalties due to the state.

There is some indication that the different conditions for debt discharge between Member States have a very small distorting effect in encouraging over indebted consumers to move to a Member State in which discharge is easier or quicker to obtain (see further Box 8.7). Greater correlation of conditions for obtaining discharge through bankruptcy and debt settlement procedures would reduce or eliminate this effect.

The position on debt discharge is summarized in Table 8.8.

8.8   BALANCE BETWEEN COMPETING OBJECTIVES

Until relatively recently, legal procedures relating to consumer bankruptcy and consumer over-indebtedness did not attract such sustained political and legal attention as company insolvency in the EU. This may

---

BOX 8.7   INCIDENCE OF BANKRUPTCY TOURISM

The likelihood of bankruptcy tourism, particularly in relation to German and Irish debtors travelling to the United Kingdom to take advantage of its short discharge period of one year in bankruptcy, has attracted comment but there is little evidence that it is common. Informal statistics maintained by the UK Insolvency Service in 2012 show that only 217 debtors appeared to have moved their centre of main interest (COMI) to the United Kingdom in order to open bankruptcy proceedings in England and Wales. Of these, 134 emanated from Germany, 35 from Ireland and 48 from other countries. The law restricting the availability of proceedings to those debtors who have established a permanent COMI in the United Kingdom which is ascertainable by third parties is settled and appears to work effectively.[a]

Note: [a] Informal statistics reported in J. Niemi, 'A Minimum Standard for Debt Discharge in Europe?' (2013) 26(102) *Insolvency Intelligence* 7. For relevant UK case law applying centre of main interest test to cases of bankruptcy see, e.g., *Sparkasse Bremen AG v. Armutcu* [2012] EWHC 4026 (Ch); *Irish Bank Resolution Corp. Ltd v. Quinn* [2012] NI Ch. 1; and *Official Receiver v. Mittelfellner* [2009] BPIR 1075.

---

be because corporate insolvency regimes are more obviously linked with economic regeneration and with the legal environment for the provision of credit to companies by banks and other large professional lenders. Banks will not lend to companies unless they are confident of their standing in any insolvency and this requires a legal framework. Larger levels of professional involvement with corporate insolvency are present because funds are available to professionals to undertake the insolvency and restructuring work entailed with companies. High levels of professional engagement ensure that the law is kept under review and is subject to change and adaptation to suit economic conditions. On the other hand, individual over-indebtedness provides comparatively little remunerated work for professionals but represents a burdensome social problem to the individual countries.

Personal lending has historically been supported by charges, pledges and liens over movable and immovable property and it therefore may have been less necessary to develop any additional legal framework. Debts have been settled by the enforcement of security. Some countries had no history of the provision of goods and services on credit to individuals, other than by family members, until very recently (e.g. Bulgaria and Croatia) and so there has been no need to develop effective over-indebtedness legal procedures. Sharp rises in the availability of credit and the fall in asset prices in 2007/08 has changed this landscape. The attendant social problems have necessitated discussion, although not always legal change given the conflicting normative framework. The continuing provision of personal

Table 8.8 Summary of debt discharge

Country	Debt discharge timeframe	Debt discharge dependent on asset liquidation or repayment plan	Assets excluded from liquidation for discharge	Debts excluded from discharge	Discharge automatic (no further application or procedure)	Special rules to assist fresh start
Austria	(1) Zahlungsplan (most common for consumers): <7 years from acceptance of plan by creditors (2) Sanierungsplan (rare): <2 years from acceptance of plan (3) Garnishee (income assigned to trustee): <7 years from opening but can be up to 10 years	(1) Assets sold on opening of initial court procedure (2) Not sold but requires majority creditor approval of restructuring plan which indicates 20% creditor repayment in 2 years (3) Proceedings will only be opened if debtor has no assets	Personal clothing and furniture	Generally only debts that were not revealed in bankruptcy due to fault of debtor; but in garnishee, claims arising from criminal or tortious acts and maintenance claims may be excluded from discharge	Zahlungsplan: if plan adhered to Sanierungsplan: if plan adhered to Garnishee: made by court on filing of report by trustee Automatic if 10% debt discharge; otherwise requires application by debtor	There is an official insolvency database and information is removed from this one year from end of payment plan or garnishee period
Belgium	Five years from establishment of settlement plan (by creditors or if necessary by the court)	Asset liquidation normally part of plan if discharge is included and not merely delay in repayment. Voluntary	Household goods necessary for humane existence excluded	Maintenance to children and former spouse; debts linked to crimes for personal injury	On completion of settlement plan	

liquidation of some assets may assist viable settlement plan

Bulgaria	None	None	None	None	None	None
Croatia	Nothing at present, draft in discussion					
Cyprus	PRP: <60 months debt discharge mechanism: immediate but stringent conditions Discharge order after bankruptcy: court considers official receiver's report	PRP: dependent on successful fulfilment DDM: no but stringent minimum asset and income conditions Discharge after bankruptcy order: <3 years after bankruptcy order	Tools and equipment for business or trade <6,000 euros Vehicle <3,000 euros if necessary for daily activities Necessary household appliances for debtor and family members	Secured debts; credit cards and bank overdrafts and 10% of secured loans	Court application needed except for PRP	Applications can be made to official receiver to publish notice of discharge
Czech Republic	In the debt discharge route, the legislative limit is 5 years; the court sets the payment plan (evidence that usual period is much lower, 17 months). Tight timeframe for creditors filing claims (30 days). Alternative route is liquidation	In either route (liquidation or debt discharge) discharge conditional on repayment of 30% debts other than in exceptional circumstances upon order of the court	Debtor's personal effects	Criminal penalties for intentional crimes; civil damages if consequent on intentional behaviour	Subject to an order of the insolvency court; debtor must apply for this Opportunity for creditors to object and for debtor to apply early if circumstances exceptional	No, following debt discharge, file available on register for 5 years

Table 8.8 (continued)

Country	Debt discharge timeframe	Debt discharge dependent on asset liquidation or repayment plan	Assets excluded from liquidation for discharge	Debts excluded from discharge	Discharge automatic (no further application or procedure)	Special rules to assist fresh start
Denmark	Debt rescheduling: 5 years and commences month after debt rescheduling order made (unless court fixes later date). Debt reduced to amount actually repayable (relates to debt incurred prior to decision of court to reschedule)	Debt rescheduling: creditors paid out of income over life of payment plan. Rescheduling may be delayed by court until assets realized or costs reduced (e.g. house move). Debtor released from debts by court order	Assets necessary to maintain modest home and lifestyle for debtor and family are protected (other than real estate)	Debt rescheduling: secured by charge to extent of charge	Debt rescheduling: court order is definitive	No
Estonia	Debt restructuring: no specific time limits Bankruptcy: 1–8.5 years given that bankruptcy is followed by a special discharge procedure	Debts are discharged according to the repayment plan Bankruptcy: debts remaining after the bankruptcy proceedings are subject to a special discharge procedure	No	Debt restructuring: maintenance support claims and claims for compensation for damage caused by wilful act cannot be discharged,	No, court application needed	No

Finland	Ordinarily 3 years but if debtor released from obligations it is 5 years; may be over 5 years if debtor remains in own home; must not exceed 10 years	In debt adjustment, assets will be liquidated if necessary other than essentials; owner occupied house will not be sold if reasonable alternative not available or proportion of debts repaid will not be significantly increased	Owner occupied home (unless debt can't be paid over 10 years), furniture, personal effects of debtor and family, working implements	although payment terms can be extended Maintenance debt Secured debt not affected unless secured assets are liquidated	Operates automatically at end of payment plan but 2-year window in which creditor can apply to court if financial circumstances have improved	Entry in Legal Register Centre's register of debt adjustment is removed when payment schedule completed
France	Over-indebtedness procedure: discharge on completion (limit of 8 years and 7 years from 2016) of plan Personal rescue procedures (with or without liquidation): court settles discharge; may be immediate	Over-indebtedness procedures: discharge upon completion of plan; plan may require sale of assets by debtor Personal rescue: discharge occurs when procedure is closed	Personal rescue procedure with liquidation: debtor keeps assets essential for livelihood and assets without economic value	Maintenance; criminal damages; criminal penalties; secured debts on movable assets; debts paid by guarantor; debts incurred after commencement	Yes	No

Table 8.8 (continued)

Country	Debt discharge timeframe	Debt discharge dependent on asset liquidation or repayment plan	Assets excluded from liquidation for discharge	Debts excluded from discharge	Discharge automatic (no further application or procedure)	Special rules to assist fresh start
Germany	Six years from opening of insolvency proceedings provided attachable part of salary has been assigned to trustee. Reduced to 3 years if debtor has paid 35% of debts plus costs	Dependent on asset liquidation	Some assets excluded and non-attachable part of income	Liabilities resulting from intentional torts; maintenance obligations; tax obligations where criminal court has sanctioned for non-payment; debtor's fines; liabilities from interest free loans provided to pay costs of proceedings	Requires court decision	No
Greece	Where court orders a repayment plan it may also at the same hearing discharge debts. Discharge remains effective so long as payment plan complied with	Court may make discharge dependent on payment plan and asset liquidation. If assets available, liquidation order likely	Debtor may request court to exclude main residence provided it does not exceed certain value and income/ assets of debtor fall below thresholds	Civil law penalties and fines; tax and revenue debts owed to public sector, local government, national insurance	Yes, no further court application required	Court register is cleared of information, 12 months after application approved. Debtor's debt record is

Hungary	5 years plus an additional 2 years in special circumstances if minimum statutory repayment sums have been received; creditors who have not registered claims will be effectively time-barred from enforcement	For both out of court and in court procedures, a payment plan is normal and asset liquidation possible; debts may be compromised; a consensus is reached. In the court led process, the consolidation process is subject to creditor voting	Court may order repayment of up to 80% of value of house to creditors. Assets and income will be excluded: decree awaited. Debtor's preference as to main residence taken into account	Maintenance if set by court and up to a limit; damages; housing expenses linked to housing co-operatives and condominiums up to a limit; real property insurance; taxes	No, but family property supervisor organizes court hearing	removed from state's Teiresias archives after 3 years. Family property supervisor reports procedure completion to government agencies, including new Central Credit Reporting Agency and to Family Bankruptcy Service
Ireland	Debt relief notice : 3 years (but earlier if half is settled) Debt settlement	Debt relief notice: all listed debts discharged, certificate issued	DRN: vehicle of <Euro 2,000. DSA and PIA: principal private	Maintenance under court orders, court fines for criminal	No. Court application necessary. Register present	Removal from relevant registers. Assistance

Table 8.8 (continued)

Country	Debt discharge timeframe	Debt discharge dependent on asset liquidation or repayment plan	Assets excluded from liquidation for discharge	Debts excluded from discharge	Discharge automatic (no further application or procedure)	Special rules to assist fresh start
Ireland	arrangement (unsecured debts only): 5 year repayment period (extendable to 6 years), discharged on completion Personal Insolvency Arrangement (secured and unsecured): Unsecured discharged over <6 years (extendable to 7 years). Secured can be restructured Bankruptcy: reduced to 1 year	Debt settlement arrangement: listed debts settled on completion of plan. Register of Debt Settlement Arrangements (kept by ISI) records discharge Personal IA: listed debts settled on completion but secured debts subject to claw back if provided for in plan for up to 20 years. Register of Debt Settlement	residence and assets used for business or employment including potentially a vehicle Bankruptcy: home now reverts to bankrupt (subject to any mortgage) after 3 years unless sold by Official Assignee in bankruptcy before that date	offences, personal injury / death damages obligations, liabilities relating to fraudulent loans. Require consent of creditor: Tax, local government charges, health charges, service charges relating to residences, rates, and household charges		of Personal Insolvency Practitioners. Increased support and advice to consumers through the Money Advice Budgeting Service

410

Italy	by Bankruptcy Amendment Act 2015 For liquidation: 4 years minimum from filing of application subject to conditions For debt settlement procedure: no debt discharge but new obligations to repay adjusted debts arise through payment plan; no time limit on payment plan	Arrangements records discharge Bankruptcy: normal duration of payment plan now 3 years Debt discharge dependent on court application at close of liquidation process; dependent on asset liquidation and payment plan; subject to stringent conditions	Assets required by debtor and family	Maintenance debts; tortious damages; criminal and administrative sanctions not limited to expired debts; and tax debts in certain circumstances	No	No
Latvia	Up to 3.5 years from the application to commence over-indebtedness procedure. First liquidation of assets occurs (within 6 months), then the discharge plan is settled. Timeframe	Dependent on both: liquidation of assets followed by payment plan if necessary	Property essential for gaining income; if residence subject to mortgage, house is excluded if debtor comes to separate arrangement with mortgagor provided other creditors not compromised	All debts included in payment plan, including those incurred during procedure; administrator prepares list of debts	Not automatic; court takes decision at hearing	No, information kept on public register for 10 years. Individual credit institutions may keep for longer

Table 8.8 (continued)

Country	Debt discharge timeframe	Debt discharge dependent on asset liquidation or repayment plan	Assets excluded from liquidation for discharge	Debts excluded from discharge	Discharge automatic (no further application or procedure)	Special rules to assist fresh start
	depends on estimate of percentage of remaining debts that can be settled in specific period; maximum period: 3 years					
Lithuania	5 years from commencement of payment plan	Payment plan approved by creditors or court; may include asset liquidation	Assets necessary for business or employment can be preserved and must be specified in payment plan; plan must state income needed each month for debtor and family to satisfy needs	Damages for death/personal injury; child maintenance; fines for criminal acts or administrative offences	Depends on bankruptcy administrator issuing a certificate of completion in relation to payment plan and this being confirmed by the court	None

Luxembourg	Judge may order immediate remission of some debts in the rétablissement judiciaire (phase 2); otherwise, maximum length of payment plan is 7 years. Complete discharge of all debts only possible in third phase: judicial restructuring	Repayment plan approved by creditors or by the court; may include asset liquidation. Complete discharge only possible in third phase, judicial restructuring, which is reserved for situations where debtor is completely compromised; all assets will be liquidated in this phase and all debts discharged (unless insufficient funds to pay costs)	Movable assets necessary for life or professional activity	Debts settled by guarantor or co-debtor; maintenance obligations; damages/ compensation owed to victims of intentional violence	Automatic upon decision of judge at the end of third phase (if entered into) or in accordance with decision of judge in second phase	Removal of entry in register occurs 7 years after the decision of the judge to end the proceedings
Malta	No provisions for consumers					
Netherlands	Bankruptcy: no discharge for unfulfilled debts which are enforceable after close of proceedings; discharge may only result from a composition	Bankruptcy: no discharge Composition: discharge dependent on terms of the composition with creditors approved by court Debt adjustment: asset liquidation occurs	Debt adjustment: assets that the debtor acquires and it is agreed he/she may keep: reasonable household effects; amounts needed for daily living	Debt adjustment: secured creditors may exercise rights; student loans excluded; amounts due consequent on commission of criminal offence (fines,	No automatic discharge: requires court approval (at termination of debt adjustment proceedings)	The state provides a register of credit-worthiness for individuals; creditors obliged to notify successful

Table 8.8 (continued)

Country	Debt discharge timeframe	Debt discharge dependent on asset liquidation or repayment plan	Assets excluded from liquidation for discharge	Debts excluded from discharge	Discharge automatic (no further application or procedure)	Special rules to assist fresh start
	approved by creditors and court proceedings: discharge may occur at termination which will in general be within maximum 3 years from the opening of the proceedings	prior to termination (including assets acquired during debt adjustment period); discharge flows from termination		compensation, payments to victims); loans secured by mortgage on residential property		completion of debt adjustment proceedings; duration of registration is 5 years
Norway	Debt settlement proceedings under Bankruptcy Act (voluntary or compulsory): in accordance with composition agreed; no time limit or guidelines Debt settlement proceedings under	Debt settlement under Bankruptcy Act (compulsory) may involve partial debt reduction, delay in payment, a liquidation with or without debt reduction. If voluntary, other terms may be agreed	All processes: clothes and personal effects; equipment needed for a profession or education	Maintenance and tax obligations incurred after proceedings opened (for Debt Settlement Act only for individuals); fines and orders relating to criminal offences;	Debt settlement proceedings: generally debt is discharged by court hearing and no need for new court application once payment plan complete;	Duration of 'payment remarks' is 4 years; duration of registration of bankruptcy is 5 years

	Debt Settlement Act only for individuals: 5 years or a longer period up to 10 years if the court so orders Bankruptcy: consumer normally remains liable for debts not settled by dividend payments	Debt settlement under Debt Settlement Act (only for individuals): liquidation of assets compulsory and debt settlement may be partial or total Bankruptcy: all assets liquidated	secured debt excluded insofar as security covers indebtedness; but under Debt Settlement Act, debtor may keep house provided value is reasonable given position of debtor and family		discharge revoked if plan not complied with by debtor Bankruptcy: debt not normally discharged but a compulsory composition may be sought	Duration of 'payment remarks' is 4 years; duration of registration of bankruptcy is 5 years
Poland	Up to 36 months which is the maximum initial period of a payment plan; debtor can apply to court to extend by further 18 months. No payment plan if debtor manifestly unable to perform	Generally dependent on due performance of payment plan which follows from asset liquidation. Exceptions to payment plan on humanitarian grounds and then debt discharge immediate. Debtor obliged to behave in honest /diligent manner during repayment period	No assets excluded (residence not excluded); amount awarded out of proceeds to pay rent in similar location for 12/24 months	Maintenance; pension benefits connected with liabilities for illness, incapacity, injury or death; fines and restitution orders connected with criminal conviction; damages linked to criminal conviction; claims concealed by debtor with intent	Requires court order in order to verify performance and honesty/ diligence; court arranges (not responsibility of debtor)	Entry in register of insolvent debtors is deleted upon final court decision to discharge; no action by debtor required

Table 8.8 (continued)

Country	Debt discharge timeframe	Debt discharge dependent on asset liquidation or repayment plan	Assets excluded from liquidation for discharge	Debts excluded from discharge	Discharge automatic (no further application or procedure)	Special rules to assist fresh start
Portugal	5 years from the termination of the insolvency proceedings if court so orders	Dependent on liquidation of assets and then passing income to fiduciary who discharges debts of the estate	Exempt property: no value assets plus those essential for pursuing professional activity; court assesses income that may be retained during insolvency and discharge period	Maintenance; damages for intentional wrongdoing; fines and penalties resulting from crimes/ administrative offences; tax; no exception for residence; secured debt not dealt with differently	Dependent on very early request to court for discharge; then dependent on discharge period being granted (and not revoked). Subject to discharge order by court at end of discharge period provided conditions complied with	None, removal from register occurs at termination of proceedings

Romania	Compliance with payment plan/ simplified insolvency: after 60 days of closure debtor may request discharge of the court; closure will follow 5 or 6 years of payment plan. Discharge may be immediate on decision of court Winding up judicial procedure: 1 year if paid 50% debts; 3 years if 40% of debts; 5 years if less than 40% of debts	Repayment plan: 5–6 year payment plan Simplified procedure (no assets/low income): 3 years Winding up: assets liquidated	Non-traceable assets and income; personal and household goods; religious artefacts; a vehicle subject to maximum value; articles assisting debtor in performance of work (including animals, seeds, etc.)	Maintenance obligations (subject to threshold linked to median salaries); criminal and administrative liabilities; no effect on collateral so mortgagor may sell home	Requires court application and involvement of Insolvency Commission; ensures compliance with payment plan or payment of minimum level of claims	When discharge decision published in Bulletin for Insolvency Proceedings, all limitations of rights are removed and the decision is communicated to all relevant institutions
Slovakia	3 years from court hearing	All property must be liquidated; dependent on honest intent of debtor and related to efforts to secure employment/ income. Few guidelines but normally dependent on payment plan	List related to household and employment needs	No debts are automatically excluded from discharge	No, debtor must make specific court application for discharge and make efforts to repay creditors for 3-year period	No

Table 8.8 (continued)

Country	Debt discharge timeframe	Debt discharge dependent on asset liquidation or repayment plan	Assets excluded from liquidation for discharge	Debts excluded from discharge	Discharge automatic (no further application or procedure)	Special rules to assist fresh start
Slovenia	Bankruptcy: court sets probation period of 2–5 years from lodging of request for debt discharge by debtor Settlement for entrepreneurs: depends on terms of compromise and work out agreed with creditors	Bankruptcy: no clear guidelines for judges who set length of discharge period; linked to age, family status, health, other personal matters, cause of insolvency	Personal and household necessaries; live-stock, farm machinery, seeds; assets necessary for work/employment; some cash; medals/ military honours; objects needed by disabled persons; some income/cash payments are ignored such as humanitarian aid; payments to foster parents; assets received from the state for under employment policies	Discharge affects all subordinated debts even when claims not lodged; following priority claims not discharged: wages for 3 months prior to bankruptcy; compensation for work related accidents; compensation for termination of employment; salaries to employees whose employment terminated due to bankruptcy; taxes and duties; also maintenance; damages for personal injury/death	No separate application necessary; court *ex officio* issues resolution on debt discharge upon expiry of probation period	Information remains on public register even after debt discharge is recorded; no grounds apparent for removing entries from register

| Spain | Application for discharge follows termination of insolvency proceeding which will involve liquidation of assets (if any). Only natural persons can apply for it and it is granted provided that the debtor had attempted to reach an out of court restructuring plan and pays all claims against the estate, the privileged claims, and, if he/she had not attempted to reach an out of court plan, at least 25% of the ordinary claims | In some cases, dependent on 5-year repayment plan for privileged claims and others such as tax, social security, maintenance claims | There are only rules that prevent seizure of income that fall within monetary limits relating to minimum wage | Maintenance obligations; public law and privileged claims (which must be paid in the 5-year repayment plan phase); secured debts are not included in the discharge; no bar to enforcing security | Court application required and can be challenged by creditor in following 5-year period on grounds of debtor behaviour, improvement in income/ assets, existence of hidden assets. Once 5-year period over, another court application is required to confirm discharge | Final discharge must be published in Public Insolvency Register |

Table 8.8 (continued)

Country	Debt discharge timeframe	Debt discharge dependent on asset liquidation or repayment plan	Assets excluded from liquidation for discharge	Debts excluded from discharge	Discharge automatic (no further application or procedure)	Special rules to assist fresh start
Sweden	Bankruptcy: no discharge Debt settlement for natural persons: 5-year relief plan for debts included in plan; may be extended to 7 years	Bankruptcy: asset liquidation Debt settlement: repayment plan	The home is not excluded; Swedish Enforcement Authority (KFM) decides which assets to sell	Maintenance obligations; debts for which creditor has pledge, lien or other preferential right; claims that have not yet been quantified can be declared not subject to process (e.g. student loans, damages claims)	Automatic upon decision of KFM but is subject to revocation and review, e.g. on application of creditor or the debtor; period may be extended to 7 years	Register amended after proceedings completed, including repayment plan
United Kingdom	Bankruptcy: 1 year IVA: in accordance with composition DRO: normally one year from date of order County Court administration order: debts scheduled to order discharged in accordance with order of the court	Bankruptcy: discharge automatic, will follow asset liquidation IVA: as agreed and may include repayments and discharge County Court administration order: repayment plan is normal; asset	Bankruptcy: tools; books; vehicles and other items of equipment if necessary for employment, business or vocation; clothing, bedding, household effects for debtor and family; property held on trust;	Criminal fines; obligations to pay maintenance or child support; confiscation orders made in connection with crime; liability to repay loans from social fund; liabilities for fraud/breach of	Bankruptcy: no order required All other procedures: operates automatically and no court order or other procedure is necessary	None

	Debt management plan: in accordance with plan	liquidation very rare Debt Management Plan: repayment plan is usually involved but liquidation is not	certain categories of protected and residential tenancy; pension funds: uncertain at present in law Other procedures: not relevant as no asset liquidation	trust; damages for personal injury; student loans discharge has no effect on the ability of the secured creditor to enforce security against residential or other property		Extent of assets excluded from liquidation assists fresh start
United States	Chapter 7: 60 days after date set for initial creditors' meeting unless objection or petition to dismiss Chapter 13: 3 or 5 years from order of the court confirming the plan	Chapter 7: requirement to surrender assets but discharge is not conditional on asset sale Chapter 13: discharge dependent on fulfilment of plan obligations	Chapter 7: State law governs exemptions (some States exempt residential property, States set differing levels of wage exemption); federal exemptions (which debtors can choose to be bound by in place of State law in this regard unless their State has opted out) specify exempt values for residential property and a motor vehicle; household effects up to a limit; unmatured life insurance contracts; damages payments; retirement funds up to US$1.2 million	Secured creditors can still enforce rights *in rem* but debtors have option to redeem or surrender or enter into reaffirmation; long list of debts excluded from discharge	Chapter 7: automatic in absence of objection Chapter 13: court grants discharge on certification of completion of plan	

credit must be balanced against personal responsibility for debts incurred, the need to encourage return to economic activity and some protection for family and social life. Many countries have struggled to find, or articulate a discussion on, the right balance to be struck.

Many national reporters have expressed the view that discharge periods, coupled with obligations to make repayments, are too long and should be shortened. This applies to Austria; Germany (despite recent reform); France (where the comment is that debtors often find it difficult to draft payment plans and adhere to them); Latvia; Lithuania; Portugal; and to Spain, where the five-year surveillance period is burdensome. There appears to be little evidence on whether payment plans merely serve an educative, retributive and symbolic function and are not in fact economically effective in terms of repaying debt.

The Danish report comments that of 5,974 relevant cases in 2014, only 2,014 were accepted for debt rescheduling and this indicates that the procedure is not providing adequate assistance to the relevant population. Recent reforms in Finland have been motivated by a desire to assist individuals to continue to live in the family home. Reforms are being discussed in Lithuania relating to the debtor's housing needs.

In Luxembourg, resort to formal over-indebtedness procedures is very low and this is noteworthy and interesting. Only 25 new over-indebtedness cases were examined by the competent court in the last year. No explanation for this low incidence is suggested. In Slovakia, the incidence of personal insolvency is still very low.

Many countries have very recently reformed their over-indebtedness and personal insolvency law and some national reporters in these countries express the view that it is too early to assess the effectiveness of the new regime as there is insufficient evidence on which to base conclusions. There simply has not been a sufficient number of cases to gain an impression of the impact of the reform. This applies, for example, to Italy, Hungary, Poland, Romania and Estonia, and in Cyprus, where very recent reforms were prompted by the serious national over-indebtedness that came to the fore in 2012 and where a package of reforms, including insolvency law reform, was agreed between the European Commission, the IMF and the government of Cyprus.

In many Member States, there appear not to be active charities, consumer groups and lobbyists who keep legal change and its social impact under review. This is in contrast to the United Kingdom, where organizations such as Step Change Debt Charity, the Consumer Association and the Citizens Advice Bureau are well organized (if under-resourced) and provide valuable, informed discussion. Latvia also has interested civil organizations that lobby in relation to personal insolvency law reform.

The Association of Commercial Banks of Latvia and the association representing over-indebted consumers (Latvijas Kreditnemeju Apvieniba) have both been very active in discussing legislative change. In Malta, the consumer interest group Caritas Malta has campaigned for new over-indebtedness law but change is still awaited. The Romanian banking industry has lobbied hard against new law. The Swedish banking industry has also lobbied very effectively against legal change. There is an indication that in Portugal, law reform to assist consumers (the Portuguese Consumer Code) has been prevented by effective bank lobbying. There is little current evidence of other groups that lobby for change and carry out research in this area. More research is needed on the existence of appropriate civil society organizations, representing consumers or those seeking debt relief advice, who are well informed of the conditions actually pertaining to consumers.

In some jurisdictions, personal insolvency law and procedures are not dealing well with the over-indebtedness of spouses because the procedures and law treats each spouse as an individual and there is little law, guidance or procedure on how to deal with pooled assets, responsibilities and income (the family home, the maintenance of children and dependants, income from various sources). This is the case in Poland and in the Czech Republic, where very recent law reform has attempted to solve the problem but where the national reporter comments that comparative investigation, in other EU countries, would be very helpful.

A concern in the Czech Republic and in the United Kingdom is that debt advice providers in the private sector are over-charging unsophisticated debtors for debt advice services and providing poor quality advice. In the United Kingdom, there is evidence that some debt management companies persuade the debtor to purchase poor quality financial products which are unsuitable to that particular debtor at that time. Choice in debt management and debt advice has been increased but quality has not necessarily been improved and this has often worked against the debtor's interest. Regulation is discretionary and resource intensive and will never be entirely effective in controlling poor advice to vulnerable individuals.

Poor advice is more likely when the legal regime is complex and where there are many different choices and procedures available to debtors and where repeated filings, discussions and applications are needed. In addition, lengthy and complex regimes are likely to be more resource intensive from the Member State's perspective. The German reporter comments that the German procedure is still too complex and bureaucratic. In Slovenia, recent changes have been aimed at procedural simplification and exoneration from court fees. The French report comments that frequent legal change in France has made the law more unstable and difficult for consumers to understand and gain advice on. The relevant law was reformed in 1989, 2003, 2010, 2013 and 2014. It compares unfavourably with some simpler regimes applying to commercial liquidation procedures and law available in Alsace and Moselle. No good comparison is available between consumers who simply renegotiate indebtedness outside legal procedures and those that engage with the legal framework to provide relief. However, the reporter opines that the opportunity for the Commission de surendettment or judge to reduce interest rates on loans has acted as an incentive for banks to be careful in credit decisions. In Hungary, the very recent new procedure is not available to consumers with debts below a minimum threshold due to the costs entailed in the procedures (which are financed by the state). The motivating force in Hungary has been the need to deal with housing loans and the new procedures do not deal adequately with motor vehicle and finance lease debtors and this is viewed as regrettable. In Ireland, the new procedure is compelling debtors to engage with bank creditors (in relation to secured housing debt) before they can achieve discharge and this is delaying their ability to achieve a fresh start. However, as with Greece, the imperative here is to protect the economic interests of struggling banks as well as the interests of consumers.

In Greece, the opinion expressed is that recent reforms went too far in protecting debtors, particularly in respect of preventing recovery by banks against the residential property of debtors by enforcing security. This limitation is perceived as having affected the solvency of Greek banks adversely and it is to be noted that very recent reforms to Greek insolvency law are designed with an aim of improving the availability and efficiency of the relevant procedures to Greek companies.[99] The Netherlands appears to be a country where the general consensus is that the new law, as amended in 2008, is working well. This is the conclusion of the Association for Debt Counselling and Social Banking in a report of 24 April 2014.

---

[99]   Law No. 4336/2015.

8.9 REMAINING ASPECTS OF OVER-INDEBTEDNESS: INTERNAL MARKET, COLLECTION OF DEBT AND REMAINING MATTERS

8.9.1 General Aspects and the Internal Market

Consumer over-indebtedness can have an impact on consumer welfare (health and financial/social exclusion) and productivity in the wider community. It has numerous causes but can be exacerbated by high interest rates, and unfair lending practices. The Civic Consulting Report identified five 'key messages and lessons for policymakers'. These are that consumer over-indebtedness as a concept is complex, and arises from a number and combination of factors; there is a need for further data; there is a benefit to be derived from prevention, attention to, and resolution of consumer over-indebtedness: these all have importance as an aim of policy development; there is a need for 'a multi-dimensional and integrated government policy response'.[100]

The question posed in this study, however, is the extent to which consumer over-indebtedness legal procedures themselves impact on the above issues and on movement between Member States. Where reporters have provided an opinion, views have been mixed in terms of the extent of impact and success of their country's procedure. As discussed above, certainly for Member States where reforms have been recent, for example Hungary, it is too early to properly assess these questions. Doubts have already been raised, for example, in Romania as to the efficiency of reforms. Criticisms have been levelled at the lack of clarity in the new law and the length of the procedure.

However, there seems general consensus that consumer over-indebtedness procedures are likely to lead to more careful lending (assessment of credit-worthiness) and potentially a restriction on access to credit. It should, however, be borne in mind that other factors besides insolvency regimes may impinge on credit availability.

There are arguments that divergence of approach to personal insolvency may result in hindrance to free movement and relocation of citizens within the EU.[101] For example, discharge may be allowed in some Member States

---

[100] Civic Consulting, *The Over-Indebtedness of European Households* (n. 2 above) ch. 9.

[101] Niemi, 'Consumer Insolvency in the European Legal Context' (n. 37 above) 443, 456.

but not others; the residence requirement may effectively exclude EU citizens from other Member States' procedures; and inconsistency in the recognition of payment plans from other Member States may be indirectly discriminatory.[102] On the other hand, favourable insolvency and consumer over-indebtedness regimes may encourage consumers to move to such countries. Evidence of this lies in the experience of England and Wales, where the bankruptcy system is a particular choice of Irish and German nationals.[103]

However, it is interesting to note at this stage of the analysis that insolvency 'tourism' was reported as isolated, with cases referred to in Slovakia, Hungary, Italy, the United Kingdom, Ireland[104] and Germany. These are not viewed as representing a general trend.

Again, in relation to fiscal matters, opinion is divided. Whilst there are some concerns raised that easy access to procedures may have a negative impact on fiscal discipline, other views suggest that effective insolvency procedures should have the imposition of fiscal discipline as part of their rationale. It is interesting to note here that the cost of procedures may have an impact on the country's economy. For example, it has been suggested privately that the new Romanian law, where administrators' fees are covered by the state, could have an impact of as much as 217 million euros in five years, calculated on the basis that there may be up to 800,000 insolvencies over that period.[105]

In other countries, wide use of insolvency procedures is also in evidence. Available statistics show that in 2014, over 116,000 individual petitions for debt settlement were filed in Finland; in Denmark there were 5,974 debt rescheduling applications (although not all were accepted); and in Greece, since the reform in 2010, it is estimated that 200,000 applications

---

[102] *Ibid.* 453.

[103] See, e.g., *Official Receiver* v. *Eichler* [2007] BPIR 1636; *Official Receiver* v. *Mitterfellner* [2009] BPIR 1075, discussed in A. Walters and A. Smith, '"Bankruptcy Tourism" Under the EC Regulation on Insolvency Proceedings: A View from England and Wales' (2010) 19(3) *International Insolvency Review* 181. Reasons for this are the automatic discharge provisions, the straightforward process and eligibility criteria (pp. 191–3).

[104] Although this has been stated as a reason for the new amendments being brought forward by the Bankruptcy (Amendment) Act 2015, see www.irishtimes.com/business/personal-finance/new-bankruptcy-law-single-most-positive-thing-for-debtors-1.2449328.

[105] A. Stanescu (World Bank consultant), 'Romania's Personal Insolvency Law Not Precise Enough', *Romania Insider*, 22 September 2015, available at http://globalinsolvency.com/headlines/world-bank-consultant-romania-s-personal-insolvency-law-not.

for some sort of compromise have been lodged with the court. In Slovenia, it is estimated that approximately 5 per cent of the population will meet the conditions required for relief from debt. In the United Kingdom, recent statistics show that in the second quarter of 2015, there were a total of 18,866 individual insolvencies in England and Wales; 1,606 individual insolvencies in Scotland; and 696 individual insolvencies in Northern Ireland.[106] In the United States, for the period ending 30 June 2015, 551,808 Chapter 7 applications and 301,802 Chapter 13 applications were made.[107]

8.9.2 Collection of Debt

The majority of Member States have some form of protection in place in relation to action for the collection of debt. Some of these protections are based in suspension of enforcement actions, and indeed this tool is evident across the EU. In Austria, during bankruptcy, all enforcement of debt is stayed; in Belgium, there is a bar against collection of debt in collective debt settlement procedures; and in Cyprus, a debtor can apply for a temporary protection order to suspend repayment, enforcement proceedings or a sale of the family home.

Denmark's system provides that once the debt settlement procedure starts, no execution or attachment is allowed or possession of debtor's mortgaged property, and within restructuring, there are restrictions on being able to seek satisfaction for debts. Estonia has a similar approach, where during the debt settlement procedure there may be a prohibition of creditors from exercising rights (although the court may allow some actions). In Germany, individual enforcement is banned during insolvency proceedings and during and after the discharge period. The same picture is seen across the EU, with Latvia, Luxembourg, Portugal, Romania (when the law comes into force), Slovakia and the United Kingdom all having similar stays, where creditors who have been part of the procedure, whether bankruptcy or otherwise, are prevented from enforcing certain debts. One further particular protection, referred to above, is prevention of eviction from the family home. This (albeit as a temporary measure) features in many Member States such as the United Kingdom, Ireland, Latvia, Luxembourg, the Netherlands, Poland, Portugal and Spain, and

---

[106] Although this shows a downwards trend: Insolvency Service, *Insolvency Statistics* (April–June 2015), available at www.gov.uk/government/uploads/system/uploads/attachment_data/file/448858/Q2_2015_statistics_release_-_web.pdf.

[107] See www.uscourts.gov/statistics/table/f-2/bankruptcy-filings/2015/06/30.

reflects a policy that recognizes the potential vulnerability of the debtor and the debtor's family.

There is little data on the control of actual debt collection procedures, but it is reported that Greece, Sweden and the United Kingdom all regulate the providers of debt collection services and relevant agencies to ensure fair procedures and control possible abuses. This is also the case in the United States.

8.9.3   Additional Comments

In order to measure the impact of consumer over-indebtedness legal procedures, it is important, as a starting point, to understand what they are trying to achieve. As has been outlined earlier in the Report, consumer over-indebtedness, however it is defined as a concept, is rooted in financial difficulty. The question as to how this detriment, particularly for consumers, can be prevented, or its impact reduced, is complex and is informing reform across the EU. For example, in the United Kingdom, in the years leading up to the 2006 reforms of the Consumer Credit Act 2006, the UK government set up a Task Force to look into the reasons for and consequences of consumer over-indebtedness, this being seen as one of the 'main drivers' behind the consultation on legislative amendment.[108] More recently, reforms have taken place in other EU Member States with the aim of addressing this issue.

Consumer over-indebtedness procedures have a number of objectives:

- reduction of the risk of financial and social exclusion;
- relief from unmanageable debt;
- rehabilitation of the debtor;[109]
- fresh start and returning the debtor to productivity.

All of these objectives are geared towards the benefit of the debtor, although the creditor also benefits from a controlled access to debtor funds and potentially a more efficient recovery of at least some debt.[110] It is arguable that creditors are more likely to be concerned about consistent application of discharge provisions rather than the fact its availability may be automatic without need for further application or procedure.

---

[108]   DTI, *Tackling Loan Sharks* (n. 26 above) para. 1.2.

[109]   E.g., seen as an objective of the UK Insolvency Service: J. Tribe, 'The *Kekhman* Quintessence: What is English Personal Insolvency Law For?' (2015) 3 *Nottingham Insolvency and Business Law e-journal* 18.

[110]   World Bank Personal Insolvency Report (n. 60 above) para. 1.8.

Certainty of discharge periods allows the creditor to assess exposure and act accordingly.[111] There are, however, potential negative consequences of such procedures, for example, the risk of reduced access to credit where creditors see a greater risk in not being able to recover their debts. Credit availability, however, may be affected by other factors, for example, the regulation of the credit provision itself.

A good example of this might be the 'payday lending' market in the United Kingdom. This type of credit consists of high cost short-term loans, more often than not offered over the Internet, and has attracted intense criticism in relation to cost, sales practices and lack of proper affordability checks for customers. As a result, the UK Financial Conduct Authority has introduced new rules, restricting charges, the ability to 'roll over' loans[112] and how payments are collected. It has been this regulation of the lender that has, in effect, reduced the access to this type of credit,[113] rather than bankruptcy and debt settlement procedures.

The general opinion from the reporters, where expressed, is that making more legal procedures available to more over-indebted consumers and traders has not so far acted so as to impede the supply of personal credit to the marketplace. However, there is a lack of methodologically sound research which investigates the link between recent law reforms in this area and the behaviour and responses of entities that supply credit and goods on credit.

There are other potential negative aspects to these procedures outlined by the World Bank Personal Insolvency Report such as moral hazard, debtor fraud and stigma.[114] However, it is clear from the Member States' procedures, both in bankruptcy and debt settlement, that debtor fraud is dealt with robustly, with many procedures being unavailable should this occur. Indeed, this is the approach not only in relation to fraudulent behaviour but also dishonesty and/or negligent disregard of obligations.

The question of stigma is more difficult. Whilst the drive behind consumer over-indebtedness procedures is to provide the debtor with a fresh start, publicity can not only provide a disincentive, but can delay some of the real benefits of accessing the procedure. Nevertheless, publicity

---

[111] Tribe, 'The *Kekhman* Quintessence' (n. 109 above) 344.

[112] Where a borrower is offered further finance to pay off outstanding debt as well as a further sum. This contributes to spiralling debt.

[113] The FCA estimated that the price cap on payday lending would reduce the number of borrowers who would still have access to this type of credit by 11 per cent: FCA Consultation Paper, *Proposals for a Price Cap on High Cost Short Term Credit*, CP14/10 (July 2014).

[114] World Bank Personal Insolvency Report (n. 60 above) part 1.9.

requirements can bring benefits. Publicizing debtor's bankruptcy and/ or other debt settlement procedures provides a protection for future creditors and can potentially increase creditor confidence in lending to individuals. It can also assist creditors in a better assessment of a debtor's credit-worthiness, and therefore can help prevent the debtor from falling back into debt. This demonstrates, as with all aspects of consumer over-indebtedness procedures, that the balance between creditor and debtor interests is a fine one.

APPENDIX: DATA TABLE

Table 8A.1 List of procedures

Country	List of procedures for consumers only	List of procedures for entrepreneurs	Consumers and entrepreneurs
Austria			Bankruptcy Debt settlement proceedures: restructuring plan if debtor's assets not to be sold (minimum quotas); if assets sold debtor can submit payment plan Rejection of payment plan: garnishee proceedings instead
Belgium	Debt settlement procedure: collective debt proceedings	Bankruptcy Judicial re-organization	
Bulgaria	No proceedings	Bankruptcy but no discharge	
Croatia	No proceedings	Bankruptcy Restructuring plan	
Cyprus		Debt settlement procedure: Co-ordinated Repayment Plan	Bankruptcy Debt settlement procedures: personal repayment plan; debt discharge mechanism
Czech Republic			Bankruptcy ('liquidation route') Debt settlement procedure ('instalment route')
Denmark		Debt restructuring	Bankruptcy Debt settlement procedure
Estonia			Bankruptcy Debt settlement procedures

431

Table 8A.1 (continued)

Country	List of procedures for consumers only	List of procedures for entrepreneurs	Consumers and entrepreneurs
Finland		Bankruptcy	Debt settlement procedure: adjustment of debt under Act on the Adjustment of the Debts of a Private Individual
France	Debt settlement procedures: Procedure de surendettement; Rétablissement personnel sans liquidation; Rétablissement avec liquidation (bankruptcy)	Bankruptcy	
Germany	Special rules for consumers are mandatory in terms of procedure		Debt settlement procedure: plan for settlement of debts as part of insolvency proceedings
Greece			Two-stage debt settlement procedure: out of court mediation; if unsuccessful, judicial settlement
Hungary			Debt settlement procedures: out of court debt consolidation procedure; court led procedure
Ireland			Bankruptcy Debt settlement procedures: debt relief notice; personal insolvency arrangement
Italy	Procedure di composizione della crisi da sovraindebitamneto del consumatore (Piano)		Liquidazione del beni Procedure di composizione della crisi da sovraindebitamento del consumatore (Accordo)

Country			
Latvia	Debt settlement procedure	Must file for insolvency proceedings of legal persons first; once removed from the Commercial Register can then access debt settlement procedure for natural persons (consumers)	
Lithuania			
Luxembourg	Debt settlement procedure in 3 stages: mediation; judicial settlement; judicial restructuring	Bankruptcy	Debt settlement procedure
Malta	No proceedings		
Netherlands		Bankruptcy proceedings Suspension of payments	Bankruptcy Debt settlement procedure
Poland	Debt settlement procedure: liquidation and repayment plan Action plan for prevention of risk of default Out of court bank debt restructuring	Bankruptcy under Insolvency Law, arts 369–370	
Portugal			Debt settlement procedures: liquidation and payment plan; special revitalization proceedings; payment plan Simplified bankruptcy procedure
Romania	Debt settlement procedures: repayment plan, simplified insolvency procedure Bankruptcy		
Slovakia			
Slovenia		Bankruptcy of independent entrepreneurs and professionals; simplified compulsory settlement of independent entrepreneurs	Debt settlement procedure Bankruptcy (natural persons)

Table 8A.1 (continued)

Country	List of procedures for consumers only	List of procedures for entrepreneurs	Consumers and entrepreneurs
Spain			Bankruptcy Debt settlement procedure: out of court repayment or restructuring plan if under 5 million euros Fast-track procedure
Sweden		Business reorganization	Bankruptcy Debt settlement procedures: debt relief for natural persons (payment plan)
United Kingdom			Bankruptcy Debt settlement procedures: IVA; DRO; (County Court) Administration Order; debt management plan; court enforcement procedures
United States			Bankruptcy under Chapter 7 Debt settlement procedures under Chapter 13 and Chapter 11
Norway			Bankruptcy proceedings under Bankruptcy Act Debt settlement proceedings under Bankruptcy Act Debt settlement proceedings under Debt Settlement Act for individuals

Appendix 1: First questionnaire

European Commission, Directorate-General Justice

Study on a new approach to business failure and insolvency. Comparative legal analysis of Member States' relevant provisions and practices

JUST/2014/JCOO/PR/CIVI/0075

First Questionnaire for National Reporters, April 2015

This questionnaire relates to the law relating to companies and other legal entities commonly used by Entrepreneurs in your jurisdiction to carry out businesses for the purpose of making profit. If necessary and appropriate, each question should be answered in relation to each type of director/ Entrepreneur and each type of legal entity. The numbering used in this questionnaire must be adopted in your report as it is necessary for the Team to be able to compare the situation in each Member State.

1. Directors' liability and disqualifications
a. What are the duties of directors at the following times:
    (i)   before insolvency (such as duties to ensure the existence of plans for preventative actions to avoid insolvency and identifying possible insolvency problems);
    (ii)   nearing insolvency (such as decisions on taking preventative actions);
    (iii)   insolvency without the commencement of any formal insolvency procedure; and
    (iv)   after an insolvency procedure is commenced?
    Is there any shift in duties at these points in time compared with when companies are clearly solvent? Does the type of insolvency procedure opened have an impact on the potential liability of directors?

b. What are the possible sanctions against directors for non-compliance with insolvency related duties? For example in relation to transactions carried out and decisions made in the period immediately prior to insolvency or when insolvent? Provide recent significant examples of sanctions imposed in your Member State. Is enforcement action frequently taken during insolvency proceedings against directors for breach of insolvency related duties? Provide a description of the body that undertakes enforcement activity and some statistical evidence of the activity undertaken by it in the last 2 years. Do shareholders of the company have a role in initiating enforcement?

c. What are the obstacles to such enforcement by any party (such as lack of incentive for liquidators, legal costs, lack of standing for shareholders, difficulty in obtaining evidence, etc.)?

d. What law determines the directors' liability for insolvency related duties in your Member State? Does the law in your Member State draw a clear distinction between insolvency law and company law duties? Is tortious liability also engaged for breach of insolvency-related duties?

e. Has the absence of uniform rules at EU level for directors' liability created any practical problems? Please provide examples of cases where companies or their directors have chosen to initiate insolvency related proceedings in one EU Member State rather than another because of differences in law. Please provide examples where compliance has been difficult due to divergent rules on director liability between Member States?

f. Are directors of insolvent companies removed, and if so under what circumstances (for example, always in case of insolvency, in case they are found unfit to perform their duties)? Provide recent examples.

g. Are directors of insolvent companies prevented from participating in business activity in the future in any circumstances (for example, by disqualification)? Do disqualifications operate by virtue of a legal provision or by virtue of a judicial or administrative decision? What are the possible grounds for director disqualification that relate in any way to insolvency? For how long do disqualifications orders typically last in the case of insolvency-related disqualification? Provide recent examples.

h. What are the national rules on jurisdiction for issuing a removal or disqualification order against directors (for example, is it restricted to companies that have their registered office in that Member State or have their central administration or principal place of activities in that Member State or where there are other connecting factors?)

i. How is the information on director disqualifications dealt with in the

Member State (e.g. is it made public or not, in a register or otherwise, for how long is the information kept on the register)?

j. Is there a reliable procedure for ensuring that directors that have been disqualified are not appointed as directors either for a new or existing company? Does this procedure deal with foreign disqualification orders effectively? Is there any procedure for checking whether foreign or home disqualification orders have been applied for?

k. Has the absence of European rules ensuring the transparency of disqualification orders amongst Member States and recognition of disqualification orders made in other Member States created problems in practice?

2. Insolvency Practitioners (administrators, liquidators, supervisors, mediators, etc.)

a. To what extent does the legal system rely on qualified Insolvency Practitioners and to what extent does it rely on specialist courts for ensuring the optimal functioning of the insolvency system? If there are no specialist insolvency courts or Insolvency Practitioners, what legal or administrative mechanisms encourage fairness, efficiency, business rescue and public and creditor protection?

b. What law, if any, governs the qualification (including training), status and powers of Insolvency Practitioners? Are Insolvency Practitioners part of a regulated profession?

c. What are the rules, which govern disciplinary action against Insolvency Practitioners? For example, rules on fines, loss of status as an Insolvency Practitioner, warnings for poor conduct? Are these disciplinary actions public or private? Who may commence such disciplinary proceedings?

d. What are the professional rules and/or law on liability insurance for Insolvency Practitioners? For example, is it compulsory in any type of insolvency or other proceedings commenced, and are there minimum limits on the extent of insurance cover?

e. How are Insolvency Practitioners chosen and appointed in a given case? By creditors, the court? To what extent and under what conditions can Insolvency Practitioners from another Member State be appointed?

f. What is the law that governs conflicts-of-interests which Insolvency Practitioners might experience? How is compliance with these rules ensured and by which body? Has there been any recent controversy or difficulty in relation to conflicts of interest of Insolvency Practitioners? If so, has the situation been satisfactorily resolved?

g. What are the rules on the remuneration of Insolvency Practitioners?

On what basis are Insolvency Practitioners remunerated (time involved, percentage based on property sold, etc.)? Has there been any recent prominent line of discussion that has suggested that Insolvency Practitioners are paid too much or too little or inappropriately in some other manner, and whether this relates to payment before, during or after appointment. Provide supporting information.

3. Ranking of claims and order of priorities
a. What are the rules on ranking of claims/order of priority and what are the rationales or the policy considerations behind those rules? Are financial claims (from banks or other entities that provided the business with capital) and commercial claims (from trade creditors, landlords, suppliers of good and services, for instance) treated differently?
b. How are claims from employees treated? (for example, for salary, holiday pay, pension contributions, etc.). If there is no preference for employees' claims, is there any other legal or social mechanism which protects employees against financial loss in the event of their employer's insolvency? Are self-employed agents treated any differently from other trade creditors?
c. How are claims for tax and claims for social security contributions treated? If there is any priority granted to such claims, what are the policy reasons that have been given for this?
d. How are shareholders' claims treated in formal insolvency proceedings? How are shareholders treated in preventative procedures (that is, procedures designed to prevent the onset of formal insolvency proceedings)?
e. Is there a super-priority rule for new financing which is provided when the company is in an insolvency procedure or in a preventive procedure or is close to either? What priority is given in these circumstances? Is this generally considered to work well so as to foster corporate rescue? Have any particular difficulties been identified with the super-priority provisions? Provide recent examples which are illustrative of typical difficulties and advantages of these provisions.

4. Avoidance and adjustment actions
a. What types of transaction, that occurred prior to insolvency or prior to and during preventive proceedings, can be impugned, adjusted, set aside or challenged in law? What are the conditions under which a transaction by the company in the period prior to the inception of insolvency proceeding can be avoided, impugned, set aside or challenged? What type of sanctions are provided for and what is their effect (e.g. automatic or non-automatic nullity, etc.)?

b. Is there a presumption that certain transactions, which took place in a 'suspect' period before the opening of insolvency or preventative proceedings, should be set aside? If so, what is the length of the suspect period? To what type of transaction does the presumption apply? What effect does the presumption have?

c. Is there a specific time period (or several time periods depending on the situation) within which a transaction can be challenged? If so, how long is it and what is the point (filing or opening of insolvency proceedings or the existence of other criteria) at which the time limit starts to run? Give one or more illustrations of how this works in practice.

d. Can new financing given in the context of a restructuring plan be challenged under the rules on avoidance if insolvency proceedings are subsequently opened? What are the criteria for a successful challenge? If the court has discretion to avoid new financing contracts, what guidelines are there on how the discretion will be exercised?

e. Has the divergence of the rules on avoidance/adjustment actions within the EU created problems in practice? Identify these problems and whether they are or will be entirely addressed by the provisions in the Insolvency Regulation (recast).

5. <u>Procedural issues relating to formal insolvency proceedings</u>

a. Opening of insolvency proceedings

(i) Is there an insolvency/illiquidity test which triggers certain obligations for the debtor company/directors (such as to file for insolvency)? How is the insolvency and/or illiquidity test defined?

(ii) Is there an obligation on the debtor company/directors to open insolvency proceedings (whether in court or out of court) and what is the time limit for doing so? What are the circumstances that require the debtor company/directors to open proceedings?

b. Involvement of creditors

(i) Can creditors initiate insolvency proceedings against the debtor and if so, under what conditions? What are these proceedings?

(ii) How are creditors informed of the opening of insolvency proceedings?

(iii) What are the time limits on creditors filing claims in insolvency proceedings?

(iv) Does the law provide for the establishment of creditors' committees? What are the laws on their establishment, composition, powers and working methods?

(v) Does the law provide for different classes of creditors, in the sense that different classes have different powers in relation to the progress of the insolvency (for example, power to vote on proposals, power to replace the Insolvency Practitioner, etc.)?

(vi) What are the voting rules in relation to creditors' committees and creditors' meetings which wield power in relation to the course of the insolvency procedure?

c. Liquidation of the Insolvent Estate

(i) Is the sale of the business as a going concern promoted in your jurisdiction? What law and other measures further this purpose? Are there so-called 'pre-pack sales' in your Member State? Please describe the main features of such procedures.

(ii) Where the outcome of proceedings is the piecemeal sale of the insolvent estate, what rules apply to such sale (e.g. rules on public auctions, valuations)?

(iii) Are there any measures to speed up the sale of assets (such as low value assets) or to dispense with the need to sell all assets, e.g. those of low value and/or low quality?

(iv) Has there been any recent controversy on the liquidation of insolvent estates in general? For example, informed comment suggesting that the process works poorly or to the unfair disadvantage of one party or another.

d. Special arrangements facilitating insolvency proceedings for SMEs

(i) Are there any special fast or low cost insolvency procedures which apply only to small companies or new ventures or any other subcategory of business?

(ii) Are there any standard forms or templates which relate to any step of these procedures (e.g. filing for opening of procedure, filing of claims, a restructuring plan)?

(iii) In your opinion are these procedures or procedural elements useful and effective for encouraging the quick rescue of small businesses?

e. Costs of formal insolvency proceedings

(i) What are the costs of formal insolvency proceedings (for example, court fees, other administrative fees)? How are the professional fees of the Insolvency Practitioner (or other supervisor or mediator) calculated? How are these fees and costs borne?

(ii) What are the rules on legal costs incurred by Insolvency Practitioners in the course of the proceedings? For example, for legal advice provided on his or her duties or liabilities or in relation to transactions carried out during the insolvency proceedings such as sales of the business or assets?

(iii) What methods are there to ensure that professional fees are not disproportionately high? Are these methods effective? Please provide an illustration and examples.

6. Progress on the Implementation of Commission Recommendation of 12 March 2014 on a new approach to business failure and insolvency

The Commission adopted on 12 March 2014 a Recommendation on a new approach to business failure and insolvency addressed to the Member States concerning the national rules on insolvency. The Recommendation proposed that each Member State should ensure that a framework is in place by 14 March 2015 (a) to enable efficient restructuring of viable enterprises in financial difficulty, and (b) to give honest Entrepreneurs a second chance to run a successful business.

The Member States are invited to implement the Recommendation by 14 March 2015.

The following questions are designed to enable the Commission to assess which Member States have either adopted the recommendations; are proposing to do so; or finally, need take no action because their law already reflects the desired position.

a. Preventive Restructuring Framework

Do debtors now have access to a preventive restructuring framework which complies with that described in Section III of the Recommendation in particular in that:

(i)   It allows the debtor to restructure its debts before it is insolvent and with the aim of avoiding insolvency.

(ii)   It allows the debtor to remain in control of its business.

(iii)   It permits a temporary stay of enforcement actions.

(iv)   It provides for a restructuring plan to bind dissenting creditors if it is approved by a court.

(v)   It permits new financing, sales of certain assets and debt equity swaps to be included in restructuring plans and ensures that they are not declared void, voidable or unenforceable.

(vi)   Courts can confirm restructuring plans quickly and by written procedure.

(vii)   If debtors do not currently have such access, is new law proposed which effects these changes? What is the expected timescale for enacting this law? Are any parts of the proposed new law controversial?

Please list each procedure if there is more than one and explain the conditions of access to each such procedure.

b. Second Chance for Entrepreneurs (natural persons only)

(i)   Is the law now such that Entrepreneurs may be fully discharged of their debts within 3 years in the manner set out in Section IV of the Recommendation?

(ii) Are there more stringent provisions in national law which fulfil one of the aims set out in paragraph 32 of the Recommendation?

(iii) If this is not currently the law, is new law proposed which effects these changes? What is the expected timescale for enacting such law? Are any parts of the proposed new law controversial?

c. National statistics

Are any reliable national statistics available on the number of insolvency procedures opened, the length of the procedures and the outcome of the procedures opened? Please refer to both preventive restructuring and formal insolvency procedures.

d. Obstacles to the EU internal market

Please identify one (or more) relevant insolvency law or rule or practice in your Member State which, in your opinion, has the greatest potential to hinder or discourage the proper functioning of the EU internal market (for example, the free flow of capital across borders, cross-border trade and investment).

e. Other important matters that might be addressed

Are there any other issues relating to insolvency or preventive proceedings which, in your opinion, are important and relevant to the proper functioning of the EU internal market? These may be issues that are relevant to directors, investors, creditors, debtors, employees, agency workers, Consumers, shareholders, the courts or the EU economy as a whole. Please explain the issue fully.

Appendix 2: Second questionnaire

European Commission, Directorate-General Justice

UNIVERSITY OF LEEDS

Study on a new approach to business failure and insolvency.
Comparative legal analysis of Member States' relevant provisions and
practices

JUST/2014/JCOO/PR/CIVI/0075

Questionnaire for National Reporters: Task 2, June 2015

This questionnaire relates to the law on Consumer over-indebtedness
and Consumer bankruptcy in your jurisdiction. The numbering used in
this questionnaire must be adopted in your report as it is necessary for
the Team to be able to compare the situation in each Member State.
Guidelines to reporters are at the end of the questionnaire.

1. Consumer over-indebtedness – general aspects
a.   Is there a standard definition of Consumer over-indebtedness in your
     jurisdiction? If there is, what is it? Is it applicable to a household or to
     an individual? Does it make use of debt to income ratios or other tests
     of illiquidity? Does it depend on subjective and objective assessments
     of outgoings or of Consumer/household need or living costs? Does it
     differ if there are children or other dependants in the household?
b.   Please explain how Consumer or household over-indebtedness is
     treated in your jurisdiction. For example, does it fall under a general
     insolvency regime, or are there special procedures for over-indebted
     individuals or households that apply generally or to limited categories
     of individuals or in certain limited circumstances.
c.   Where special procedures exist for over-indebted individuals or house-
     holds, do the same rules apply to Entrepreneurs (i.e. natural persons

incurring debt while pursuing a business, trade, profession, craft, etc.) or do different rules apply? Does it make any difference whether the business, trade, profession or craft is carried out with others in a partnership or in some other business vehicle that has separate legal personality rather than as a sole trader?

d. List all the procedures and specify whether these are out of court, administrative or court procedures, or some combination of these. Specify if these procedures are compulsory. Is there a series of procedures that may be gone through in a specified sequence (for example, an obligation to go through mediation before court proceedings are commenced)?

e. Are dishonest/bad faith/fraudulent debtors treated distinctly in these procedures, and if so how? What is the legal test for the dishonest/bad faith/fraudulent conduct in national law and what is the procedure for applying this test. Is the test generally considered to be good, reliable and relatively easy to apply? Please supply illustrations and examples.

f. Describe how natural persons are treated in cases where they have both personal debts and debts that relate to a business, trade, profession or craft carried on alone or together with others. Provide one or more illustrations of how this works in practice.

2. Insolvency Practitioners (administrators, liquidators, supervisors, etc.)

a. Where the procedures necessitate the appointment of an Insolvency Practitioner, are the rules applying to these practitioners different from those that apply to corporate insolvency which are described in the answers to questionnaire 1? If they are different, describe them in detail by reference to the questions asked under question 2 in questionnaire 1.

3. Procedural aspects: to be described for each of the procedures listed in answer to question 1.d.

a. What is the scope of each procedure in terms of the court's (or other administrator's) power to bring persons within the jurisdiction of the procedure? To whom can it apply and in what circumstances?

b. What are the conditions for accessing these procedures and in what timeframe do they operate?

c. What role does the court or other administrative body play?

d. Are particular procedures applied to specific categories of Consumer such as no-income, no-asset Consumers or Consumers who have a low level of debt? Please describe these specific procedures.

e.   What is the involvement of creditors, including the possibility of creditors filing for the procedure, their role in the drawing up of repayment plans (whether or not these plans include debt relief), the voting majorities when plans are adopted by creditors and the rights of dissenting creditors?

f.   What are the rules on ranking of claims/order of priorities in Consumer over-indebtedness procedures? How are secured creditors treated compared to unsecured creditors?

g.   What is the average length of the procedure? When is the procedure considered to have ended? In your opinion is the procedure unnecessarily long and is this due to asymmetry of information between over-indebted Consumers and well informed creditors? Provide information on the source of your statistics on the average length of the procedure.

h.   Publicity of procedures: is information about the over-indebtedness procedures made public? If so, where, to whom, under what conditions and for how long? What are the policy considerations behind such publicity?

i.   What are the costs of over-indebtedness procedures in terms of court or administrative fees? Are there special arrangements for Consumers who cannot afford to pay the costs of procedures?

4.   Guarantors

a.   What are the special rules, if any, applicable to guarantees for a Consumer's or an Entrepreneur's debt? Do these special rules only apply to a guarantee given by an individual?

5.   Consequences of over-indebtedness procedures

a.   What are the legal consequences for a debtor of an over-indebtedness procedure? For example, exclusion from obtaining credit, exclusion from a profession or public position, prevention from opening a bank account or using payment systems, the inclusion in a debtor's database. For how long do these restrictions last? Do these restrictions also apply to any different Entrepreneur procedure?

b.   What are the additional practical consequences for a debtor of an over-indebtedness procedure? For example, difficulty in obtaining housing, reduced employment prospects. What evidence is there for these practical consequences and their severity? Do these restrictions also apply to any different Entrepreneur procedure? Will any debt discharge process have an impact on these practical consequences?

6. Discharge of debt

a. What debt discharge provisions apply under the procedures mentioned in question 1.d and under what conditions and timeframe? Please specify the start point(s) of the discharge period(s) or the method of calculation of discharge periods.

b. Is debt discharge dependent on the liquidation of the debtor's assets, the fulfilment of repayment plan or a combination of the two?

c. Is the debtor entitled to keep any assets out of a liquidation process and does this have an impact on the discharge?

d. Are any debts excluded from the discharge (for example, debts relating to maintenance obligations or tax obligations)? How is secured debt dealt with under the discharge regime?

e. Does discharge operate automatically (e.g. at the time of concluding a liquidation of assets procedure) or is a new court application necessary (e.g. after a repayment plan had been completed)? If an additional application is required, does it add unnecessary difficulties for debtors in your opinion or does it fulfil a necessary function?

f. Are there other consequences linked with the debt discharge aimed at giving Consumers a fresh start (e.g. removing information from certain registers)?

7. Overall assessment of balance between competing objectives

Please provide an overall assessment of how your jurisdiction is reconciling the need to allow over-indebted Consumers a fresh start with the traditional objective of insolvency law of maximising the return to creditors. Please also identify recent (in the last five years) trends in national reforms regarding the treatment of over-indebted Consumers including trends reflected in reforms which are currently under discussion or being implemented into national law. Where reform initiatives failed, please explain what they consisted of and for what reasons they were unsuccessful. Are there any particularly powerful interest groups or lobbying groups which in your opinion have affected the direction of law reform?

8. Internal market dimension

In your opinion, what impact do over-indebtedness procedures, and in particular the discharge regime, have on: the reduction of non-performing loans; fiscal discipline; Consumer spending/purchasing power; evolution of interest rates and lending practices; the welfare of Consumers; productivity in terms of more Consumers having a fresh start and returning to the active economy; decision of Consumers to move to another Member State; any other aspect not mentioned already? Please justify your answer.

9. <u>Other aspects</u>
a. Please explain whether the collection of debt in relation to an over-indebted household is regulated and how it is regulated. For example, there may be a bar on the eviction of vulnerable people in the household or a provision requiring all individual enforcement actions to be suspended during the procedure.
b. Please explain what other aspects of law and regulation relating to the over-indebtedness of Consumers may have, in your view, an impact on the internal market and/or Consumer welfare and which have not been touched upon in the questions above.

Glossary

'absolute priority' rule: This is a principle requiring that creditors and other claimants against the debtor's estate should be paid in the same order under a restructuring plan as they would be paid in a liquidation of the debtor's business.

actio pauliana: An avoidance action derived from Roman law which provides for the avoidance of transfers of property that are made to defeat or delay the claims of creditors or to put the property beyond the reach of creditors.

avoidance rules: Those rules included in legislation that enable certain kinds of pre-insolvency transactions to be challenged, and if the action is successful, the transactions are usually set aside.

balance sheet insolvency: The value of the liabilities of a company or a person exceed the value of their assets.

bankruptcy: A legal process in which the debtors' assets are liquidated and the proceeds of sale are distributed to creditors. The debtor's debts, unless specifically exempted by law, are discharged unconditionally. The process can be commenced by the debtor. A moratorium on enforcement processes occurs.

bankruptcy trustee: A person who in a US bankruptcy context takes control of the debtor's affairs.

carve-out: A proportion of recoveries under a security interest set aside for the benefit of parties other than the secured creditor.

cash flow insolvency: A company or a person is unable to pay their debts as they fall due.

centre of main interests (COMI): The place where main insolvency proceedings commenced under the European Regulation on Insolvency Proceedings must be opened.

connected person: A person or a company that is connected to the insolvent, usually through association or blood.

consumer: Natural person who is not an entrepreneur.

consumer over-indebtedness: Generic term for being unable, or having difficulty in meeting, payment obligations, whether temporarily or permanently.

debt advice: Advice provided to a debtor for the purpose of facilitating debt discharge.

debt relief: Procedures outside bankruptcy or debt settlement procedures, including an informal arrangement, which provide for agreed debt repayments which may or may not result in discharge. Such procedures can be voluntary and/or administrative.

debt settlement organizer: An individual who acts in a debt settlement procedure to organize the collection of periodic repayments, asset liquidation (if any) and debt discharge (if any).

debt settlement procedure: A legal process in which the debtor makes periodic debt repayments to a court or administrator in order to discharge one or more debts. The debtor's assets may be liquidated in the legal process and outstanding debts may be reduced. Debt discharge will depend on the debtor's actions over a period of time, to an extent. A moratorium on enforcement processes occurs in respect of the debts that are subject to the procedure.

Delaware: A small US State on the Eastern seaboard. It is regarded as the foremost US jurisdiction as far as corporate law is concerned and the place where more than 50 per cent of US listed companies are registered.

discharge: Permanent release from an obligation. This may be straight discharge (unconditional freedom from debt) or conditional discharge (dependent upon some payment of debt).

disqualification: A process that leads to a director being unable to act as a director and, in some jurisdictions, act in other capacities.

dissenting creditors: Creditors who object to the terms of a restructuring plan.

enforcement process: A procedure under the control of a court for collecting debt in respect of which there has been a court order, which may include seizing assets.

entrepreneur: An individual, with unlimited liability, carrying out a trade, profession, craft or business as a natural person.

equitable subordination: A principle whereby a shareholder loan may be deemed to constitute a disguised capital contribution and is therefore subordinated to ordinary unsecured claims on this basis.

European Regulation on Insolvency Proceedings: It came into force on 31 May 2002 and it seeks to foster co-operation between countries in the EU as far as insolvency proceedings are concerned. The Regulation has been 'recast' and the recast version will come into force generally from 26 June 2017.

examiner: A person who in a US bankruptcy context carries out the investigations that have been entrusted to it by the Bankruptcy Court.

going-concern value: The value of the debtor's business if it is kept alive rather than liquidated.

harmonization: Rules on a particular issue are the same across the EU and compliance is required save where safeguard measures are needed.

household: A group of related individuals living under one roof.

illiquid: A company or a person is unable to pay their debts as they fall due.

impaired claims or interests: In the US bankruptcy context, refers to a situation where there is an alteration in the rights that the holder of a claim or interest would enjoy outside bankruptcy.

informal arrangement: Any contractual settlement of debts which is agreed without any involvement of a court.

insolvency practitioner (IP): Any person or body whose function it is to represent the collective interest of creditors and to administer or liquidate the assets of which the debtor has been divested or to supervise the administration of the debtor's affairs.

lex concursus: The law of the place where insolvency proceedings have been opened.

lex situs: The law of the place where property is located.

liquidation: A process where the assets of an insolvent company are sold and after the paying of expenses the balance is paid out to creditors according to the provisions of the appropriate statute or other legal provision.

liquidation or 'best interests' test: This is a test which requires that creditors should receive at least as much under a restructuring plan as they would receive in a liquidation of the business.

'loan-to-own' strategy: This describes a situation where a lender advances money to a business with a view ultimately to acquiring an ownership stake in that business.

mediator: A person who assists the debtor and creditors in negotiations on a restructuring plan.

moratorium: A legal bar on creditors commencing or continuing legal action to recover debt.

new finance: Finance that is provided to a person or company in financial distress or even when insolvent.

no creditors worse off: This refers to a situation where creditors would receive at least as much under a restructuring plan as they would do in a liquidation of the business.

non-adjusting creditors: Creditors who are unable to adjust the explicit or implicit lending terms to take into account the fact that the borrower has granted security.

opening of insolvency proceedings: The point when insolvency proceedings are first commenced.

out-of-the-money creditors and shareholders: Parties who on a restructuring of a debtor's business would not receive any payment or other consideration if the normal scheme of liquidation priorities were applied.

over-indebtedness: A company or a person's assets do not cover their liabilities.

pari passu principle: This involves the payment of creditors in a collective insolvency on an equal and rateable basis.

payment plan: Schedule of payments over a specified time period agreed between the debtor and creditor or imposed by the court.

pre-insolvency transaction: A transaction entered into by a company before it has become subject to some form of formal insolvency proceedings.

pre-pack: An agreement for the sale of all or part of the debtor's business or assets which is entered into before the commencement of formal insolvency proceedings.

priority (preferential) creditors: Creditors who by virtue of insolvency laws and regulations are given priority over some or all other creditors in the event of the debtor entering insolvency proceedings.

second chance: The opportunity to start again in terms of entrepreneurial activity.

security interests: Rights over property to ensure the payment of money or the performance of some other obligation.

supervisor: A person who oversees the activities of the debtor and takes the necessary measures to safeguard the legitimate interests of creditors and other interested parties.

suspect period: A period before a company or person enters formal insolvency proceedings during which transactions may be avoided.

tortious liability: Liability because of the commission of a civil wrong.

transaction defrauding creditors: Any transaction that was entered into by a debtor who subsequently becomes subject to formal insolvency proceedings and there was some intention to put creditors at a detriment as a result of the transaction. This derives from the *actio pauliana*.

trustee in bankruptcy: An individual who acts in a bankruptcy to liquidate assets and distribute proceeds of sale to creditors.

Bibliography

Akerlof, G., 'The Market for "Lemons": Qualitative Uncertainty and the Market Mechanism' (1970) 84 *Quarterly Journal of Economics* 488

Armour, J., 'Should We Redistribute in Insolvency?' in J. Getzler and J. Payne (eds), *Company Charges: Spectrum and Beyond* (Oxford, Oxford University Press, 2006)

Armour, J., 'The Law and Economics Debate about Secured Lending: Lessons for European Lawmaking?' (2008) 5 *European Company and Financial Law Review* 3

Ayotte, K., 'Bankruptcy and Entrepreneurship: The Value of a Fresh Start' (2007) 23 *Journal of Law, Economics and Organisation* 161

Ayotte, K. and D. Skeel, 'Bankruptcy or Bailouts' (2010) 35 *Journal of Corporate Law* 469

Baird, D., 'Bankruptcy's Uncontested Axioms' (1998) 108 *Yale Law Journal* 573

Baird, D. and T. Jackson, 'Corporate Reorganizations and the Treatment of Diverse Ownership Interests: A Comment on Adequate Protection of Secured Creditors in Bankruptcy' (1984) 51 *University of Chicago Law Review* 97

Bebchuk, L. and J. Fried, 'The Uneasy Case for the Priority of Secured Claims in Bankruptcy' (1996) 105 *Yale Law Journal* 857

Bebchuk, L. and J. Fried, 'The Uneasy Case for the Priority of Secured Claims in Bankruptcy: Further Thoughts and a Reply to Critics' (1997) 82 *Cornell Law Review* 1279

Blum, B.A., 'The Goals and Process of Reorganizing Small Business in Bankruptcy' (2000) 4 *Journal of Small and Emerging Business Law* 181

Bridge, C., 'Insolvency Office Holders: A New Study by the EBRD Provides Insight into Creditors' Rights in Insolvency' (2014) *Law in Transition* 2

Brouwer, M., 'Reorganization in US and European Bankruptcy Law' (2006) 22 *European Journal of Law and Economics* 5

Brown, S., 'Using the Law as a Usury Law: Definitions of Usury and Recent Developments in the Regulation of Unfair Charges in Consumer Credit Transactions' (2011) 1 *Journal of Business Law* 91

Carballo Piñeiro, L., 'Towards the Reform of the European Insolvency

Regulation: Codification Rather than Modification' (2014) 2 *Nederland Internationaal Privaatrecht* 207

Carruthers, B. and T. Halliday, *Rescuing Business: The Making of Corporate Bankruptcy Law in England and the United States* (Oxford, Clarendon Press, 1998)

Clifford Chance, *European Insolvency Procedures* (London, Clifford Chance LLP, 2012)

Dahiya, S., K. John, M. Puri and G. Ramirez, 'Debtor-in-Possession Financing and Bankruptcy Resolution: Empirical Evidence' (2003) 69 *Journal of Financial Economics* 259

Davydenko, S. and J. Franks, 'Do Bankruptcy Codes Matter? A Study of Defaults in France, Germany and the UK' (2008) 63 *Journal of Finance* 565

De Weijs, R.J., *Harmonisation of European Insolvency Law and the Need to Tackle Two Common Problems: Common Pool and Anticommons* (19 October 2011), available at http://ssrn.com/abstract=1950100

De Weijs, R.J., 'Towards an Objective European Rule on Transaction Avoidance in Insolvencies' (2011) 20 *International Insolvency Review* 219

Eidenmuller, H., 'A New Framework for Business Restructuring in Europe: The EU Commission's Proposals for a Reform of the European Insolvency Regulation and Beyond' (2013) 20 *Maastricht Journal* 133

Eidenmuller, H. and K. Van Zweiten, *Restructuring the European Business Enterprise: The EU Commission Recommendation on a New Approach to Business Failure and Insolvency*, European Corporate Governance Institute (ECGI) Law Working Paper No. 301/2015, Oxford Legal Studies Research Paper No. 52/2015

Eisenberg, T. and L.M. LoPucki, 'Shopping for Judges: An Empirical Analysis of Venue Choice in Large Chapter 11 Reorganizations' (1999) 84 *Cornell Law Review* 967

Faber, D., N. Vermunt, J. Kilborn and K. van der Linde, *Treatment of Contracts in Insolvency* (Oxford, Oxford University Press, 2013)

Finch, V., 'Security, Insolvency and Risk: Who Pays the Price?' (1999) 62 *Modern Law Review* 633

Finch, V., 'Pre-packaged Administrations: Bargains in the Shadow of Insolvency or Shadowy Bargains?' (2006) *Journal of Business Law* 568

Franken, S., 'Three Principles of Transnational Corporate Bankruptcy Law: A Review' (2005) 11 *European Law Journal* 232

Gallagher, A. and A. Rousseau, 'French Insolvency Proceedings: La Revolution a Commence' (2014) *American Bankruptcy Institute Journal* 20

Garrido, J.M., 'No Two Snowflakes are the Same: The Distributional Question in International Bankruptcies' (2011) 46 *Texas International Law Journal* 459

Gerner-Beuerle, C., P. Paech and E. Schuster, *Study on Directors' Duties and Liability* (London, LSE, prepared for the EC, April 2013), available at http://daccess-dds-ny.un.org/doc/UNDOC/LTD/V13/807/89/PDF/V1380789.pdf?OpenElement

Hahn, D., 'Concentrated Ownership and Control of Corporate Reorganizations' (2004) 4 *Journal of Corporate Law Studies* 117

Haines, J.B. and P.J. Hendel, 'No Easy Answers: Small Business Bankruptcies after BAPCPA' (2005) 47 *Boston College Law Review* 71

Harris, S.L. and C.W. Mooney, 'Measuring the Social Costs and Benefits and Identifying the Victims of Subordinating Security Interests in Bankruptcy' (1997) 82 *Cornell Law Review* 1349

Hart, O. and J. Moore, 'Default and Renegotiation: A Dynamic Model of Debt' (1998) 113 *Quarterly Journal of Economics* 1

Jackson, T. and D. Skeel, 'Bankruptcy and Economic Recovery' in M.N. Baily, R.J. Herring and Y. Seki (eds), *Financial Restructuring to Sustain Recovery* (Washington, DC, Brookings Institution Press, 2013)

Keay, A., 'In Pursuit of the Rationale Behind the Avoidance of Pre-Liquidation Transactions' (1996) 18 *Sydney Law Review* 56

Keay, A., 'Preferences in Liquidation Law: A Time for a Change' (1998) 2 *Company Financial and Insolvency Law Review* 198

Keay, A., 'The Recovery of Voidable Preferences: Aspects of Restoration' (2000) *Company Financial and Insolvency Law Review* 1

Keay, A., 'Balancing Interests in Bankruptcy Law' (2001) 30 *Common Law World Review* 206

Keay, A., *Company Directors' Responsibilities to Creditors* (Abingdon, Routledge, 2007)

Keay, A., 'The Prescribed Part: Sharing Around the Company's Funds' (2011) 24 *Insolvency Intelligence* 81

Keay, A., *McPherson's Law of Company Liquidation* (3rd edn, London, Sweet and Maxwell, 2013)

Keay, A., 'Directors' Duties and Creditors' Interests' (2014) 130 *Law Quarterly Review* 443

Keay, A., 'The Public Enforcement of Directors' Duties: A Normative Inquiry' (2014) 43 *Common Law World Review* 89

Keay, A., 'Wrongful Trading: Problems and Proposals' (2014) 65 *Northern Ireland Legal Quarterly* 63

Keay, A., 'The Shifting of Directors' Duties in the Vicinity of Insolvency' (2015) 24 *International Insolvency Review* 140

Keay, A., 'Security Rights, the European Insolvency Regulation and Concerns about the Non-application of Avoidance Rules' (2016) 41 *European Law Review* 72

Keay, A. and P. Walton, 'The Preferential Debts Regime in Liquidation

Law: In the Public Interest?' (1999) *Company, Financial and Insolvency Law Review* 84

Kempson, E., *Over-indebtedness in Britain, A Report to the Department of Trade and Industry* (Personal Finance Research Centre, 2002)

Kenny, M., J. Devenney and L. Fox Mahoney (eds), *Unconscionability in European Private Financial Transactions Protecting the Vulnerable* (Cambridge, Cambridge University Press, 2010)

Kilborn, J., 'La Responsibilisation de l'economie: What the United States Can Learn from the New French Law on Over-indebtedness' (2005) *Michigan Journal of International Law* 619

Kilborn, J., *Expert Recommendations and the Evolution of European Best Practices for the Treatment of Over-indebtedness 1984–2010*, Law of Business and Finance Series (Deventer, Kluwer, 2011)

Kilborn, J., 'Reform, Counter Reform and Transatlantic Rapprochement in the Law of Personal Bankruptcy' (2015) 3(12) *Nottingham Insolvency and Business Law e-journal* 235

Kolmann, S., 'Thoughts on the Governing Insolvency Law', paper presented at the Conference on the Future of the European Insolvency Regulation, Amsterdam, 28 April 2011, available at http://www.eir-reform.eu

La Porta, R., F. Lopez de Silanes and A. Shleifer, 'The Economic Consequences of Legal Origins' (2008) 46 *Journal of Economic Literature* 285

La Porta, R., F. Lopez de Silanes, A. Shleifer and R. Vishny, 'Legal Determinants of External Finance' (1997) 52 *Journal of Finance* 1131

La Porta, R., F. Lopez de Silanes, A. Shleifer and R. Vishny, 'Law and Finance' (1998) 106 *Journal of Political Economy* 113

Lawless, R.M., 'Small Business and the 2005 Bankruptcy Law: Should Mom and Apple Pie Be Worried?' (2007) 31 *Southern Illinois University Law Journal* 585

Lawless, R.M., A.K. Littwin, K.M. Porter, J.A.E. Pottow, D.K. Thorne and E. Warren, 'Did Bankruptcy Reform Fail? An Empirical Study of Consumer Debtors' (2008) 82 *American Bankruptcy Law Journal* 349

Levitin, A.J., 'Bankrupt Politics and the Politics of Bankruptcy' (2012) 97 *Cornell Law Review* 1399

LoPucki, L.M., *Courting Failure: How Competition for Big Cases is Corrupting the Bankruptcy Courts* (Ann Arbor, MI, University of Michigan Press, 2005)

LoPucki, L.M. and J.W. Doherty, 'Bankruptcy Survival' (2015) 62 *University of California Law Review* 970

LoPucki, L.M. and S. Kalin, 'The Failure of Public Company Bankruptcies in Delaware and New York: Empirical Evidence of a "Race to the Bottom"' (2001) 54 *Vanderbilt Law Review* 231

Madaus, S., 'The EU Recommendation on Business Rescue: Only Another Statement or a Cause for Legislative Action Across Europe?' (2014) *Insolvency Intelligence* 81

Markell, B., 'Clueless on Classification: Toward Removing Artificial Limits on Chapter 11 Claim Classification' (1994) 11 *Bankruptcy Developments Journal* 1

McAlinden, S. and D. Menk, *The Effect on the U.S. Economy of the Successful Restructuring of General Motors* (2013), available at www.cargroup.org/assets/files/the_effect_final.pdf

McCoid, J., 'Bankruptcy Preferences and Efficiency: An Expression of Doubt' (1981) 67 *Virginia Law Review* 249

McCormack, G., 'Super-priority New Financing and Corporate Rescue' (2007) *Journal of Business Law* 701

McCormack, G., 'Rescuing Small Businesses: Designing an "Efficient" Legal Regime' (2009) *Journal of Business Law* 299

McCormack, G., *Secured Credit and the Harmonisation of Law* (Cheltenham and Northampton, MA, Edward Elgar Publishing, 2011)

McCormack, G., 'Universalism in Insolvency Proceedings and the Common Law' (2012) 32 *Oxford Journal of Legal Studies* 325

McCormack, G., 'Conflicts, Avoidance and International Insolvency 20 Years On: A Triple Cocktail' (2013) *Journal of Business Law* 141

McCormack, G., 'World Bank Doing Business Project: Should Insolvency Lawyers Take It Seriously' (2015) *Insolvency Intelligence* 119

Michaels, R., 'Comparative Law by Numbers? Legal Origins Thesis, Doing Business Reports and the Silence of Traditional Comparative Law' (2009) 57 *American Journal of Comparative Law* 765

Miller, H., 'Chapter 11 Reorganization Cases and the Delaware Myth' (2002) 55 *Vanderbilt Law Review* 1987

Milman, D., *Personal Insolvency, Personal Insolvency Law, Regulation and Policy* (Abingdon, Routledge, 2005)

Milman, D., *The Governance of Distressed Firms* (Cheltenham and Northampton, MA, Edward Elgar Publishing, 2013)

Milman, D. and R. Parry, 'Challenging transactional integrity on insolvency: an evaluation of the new law' (1997) 48 *Northern Ireland Legal Quarterly* 24

Mindel, D. and S. Harris, *The Pursuit of Harmony Can Easily Lead to Discord: Why Local Insolvency Laws are Best Developed Locally* (Ernst and Young, April 2015)

Mucciarelli, F., 'Not Just Efficiency: Insolvency Law in the EU and Its Political Dimension' (2013) 14 *European Business Organization Law Review* 175

Niemi, J., 'Personal Insolvency' in G. Howells, I. Ramsay and

T. Wilhelmsson, with David Kraft (eds), *Handbook of Research on International Consumer Law* (Cheltenham and Northampton, MA, Edward Elgar Publishing, 2010)

Niemi, J., 'Consumer Insolvency in the European Legal Context' (2012) 35 *Journal of Consumer Policy* 443

O'Dea, G., J. Long and A. Smyth, *Schemes of Arrangement: Law and Practice* (Oxford, Oxford University Press, 2012)

Omar, P., 'Insolvency, Security Interests and Creditor Protection' in I. Davies (ed.), *Security Interests in Mobile Equipment* (Aldershot, Ashgate, 2002)

Paterson, S., 'Bargaining in Financial Restructuring: Market Norms, Legal Rights and Regulatory Standards' (2014) 14 *Journal of Corporate Law Studies* 333

Paterson, S., *Rethinking the Role of the Law of Corporate Distress in the Twenty-First Century*, Law Society and Economy Working Paper Series WPS 27-2014 (December 2014)

Payne, J., *Schemes of Arrangement: Theory, Structure and Operation* (Cambridge, Cambridge University Press, 2014)

Peng, M.W., Y. Yamakawa and S.-H. Lee, 'Bankruptcy Laws and Entrepreneur-Friendliness' (2010) 34 *Entrepreneuership Theory and Practice* 517

Pfeiffer, P., 'Article 13 EIR: Avoidance, Avoidability and Voidness' in *External Evaluations of Regulation No. 1346/2000/EC on Insolvency Proceedings*, JUST/2011/JVC/PR/0049/A4

Pochet, C., 'Institutional Complementarities Within Corporate Governance Systems: A Comparative Study of Bankruptcy Rules' (2002) 6 *Journal of Management and Governance* 343

Ramsay, I., 'Regulation of Consumer Credit' in G. Howells, I. Ramsay and T. Wilhelmsson, with David Kraft (eds), *Handbook of Research on International Consumer Law* (Cheltenham and Northampton, MA, Edward Elgar Publishing, 2010)

Rasmussen, R. and R. Thomas, 'Timing Matters: Promoting Forum-shopping by Insolvent Corporations' (2000) 94 *Northwestern University Law Review* 1357

Reifner, U., J. Kiesilainen, N. Huls and H. Springeneer, *Consumer Over-indebtedness and Consumer Law in the European Union*, Report for DG Health and Consumer Protection (iff 2003)

Reifner, U., J. Niemi-Kiesilainen, N. Huls and H. Springeneer, *Over-indebtedness in European Consumer Law Principles from 15 European States* (Books on Demand GmbH, 2010)

Rhee, D.J., 'The Principle of Effective Protection: Reaching Those Parts Other [Principles] Cannot Reach?', paper presented at BEG/ALBA

Conference, Athens, 29–30 May 2011, available at www.adminlaw.org. uk/docs/sc%2012%20Deok%20Joo%20Rhee.pdf

Ringe, G., 'Capital Markets Union for Europe: A Commitment to the Single Market of 28' (2015) 9 *Law and Financial Markets Review* 5

Rodano, G., N. Serrano-Velarde and E. Tarantino, *Bankruptcy Law and Bank Financing* (2014), available at www.igier.unibocconi.it/files/547. pdf

Roe, M. and F. Tung, 'Breaking Bankruptcy Priority: How Rent-Seeking Upends the Creditors' Bargain' (2013) 99 *Virginia Law Review* 1235

Sarfaty, G., 'Why Culture Matters in International Institutions: The Marginality of Human Rights at the World Bank' (2009) 103 *American Journal of International Law* 647

Skeel, D., 'What's So Bad about Delaware?' (2001) 54 *Vanderbilt Law Review* 309

Sobol, R., *Bending the Law: The Story of the Dalkon Shield Bankruptcy* (Chicago, IL, University of Chicago Press, 1991)

Sorensen, K., 'Disqualifying Directors in the EU' in H.S. Birkmose, M. Neville and K.E. Sørensen (eds), *Boards of Directors in European Companies: Reshaping and Harmonising Their Organisation and Duties* (London, Wolters Kluwer, 2013)

Stiglitz, J. and A. Weiss, 'Credit Rationing in Markets with Imperfect Information' (1981) 71 *American Economic Review* 393

Tabb, C.J., 'Bankruptcy After the Fall: US Law under s 256' (2006) 43 *Canadian Business Law Journal* 28

Tabb, C.J. and C. Jordan, 'The Death of Consumer Bankruptcy in the US?' (2001) 18 *Bankruptcy Developments Journal* 1

Tilley, A., 'European Restructuring: Clarifying Trans-Atlantic Misconceptions' (2005) *Journal of Private Equity* 99

Triantis, G., 'A Theory of the Regulation of Debtor-in-Possession Financing' (1993) 46 *Vanderbilt Law Review* 901

Tribe, J., 'The *Kekhman* Quintessence: What is English Personal Insolvency Law For?' (2015) 3 *Nottingham Insolvency and Business Law e-journal* 18

Trumbull, G., *Consumer Lending in France and America: Credit and Welfare* (Cambridge, Cambridge University Press, 2014)

Vallender, H., H. Allemand, S. Baister, P. Kuglarz, H. Mathijsen, B. O'Neill, E. Collins and S. Potamitis, 'A Minimum Standard for Debt Discharge in Europe?' (2013) *Insolvency Intelligence* 7

Van Zwieten, K., *Restructuring Law: Recommendations from the European Commission* (2015), available at www.ebrd.com/downloads/research/ law/lit114e.pdf

Vermeille, S., *The Legal System and the Development of Alternative Methods of Financing to Bank Credit; Or How French Law has Failed to*

Adapt to the Evolution of the Economy and Finance (2012), available at http://papers.ssrn.com/sol3/papers.cfm?abstract_id=2090036

Viimsalu, S., 'The Over-indebtedness Regulatory System in the Light of the Changing Economic Landscape' (2010) 17 *Juridica International* 217

Vriesendorp, R. and F. van Koppen, 'Transactional Avoidance in the Netherlands' (2000) 9 *International Insolvency Review* 47

Walters, A. and A. Smith, '"Bankruptcy Tourism" Under the EC Regulation on Insolvency Proceedings: A View from England and Wales' (2010) 19 *International Insolvency Review* 181

Walton, P., 'Pre-Packaged Administrations: Trick or Treat' (2006) *Insolvency Intelligence* 113

Ward, T.M. and J.A. Shulman, 'In Defence of the Bankruptcy Code's Radical Integration of the Preference Rules Affecting Commercial Financing' (1983) 61 *Washington University Law Quarterly* 1

Warren, E., 'Bankruptcy Policymaking in an Imperfect World' (1993) 92 *Michigan Law Review* 336

Warren, E., 'Making Policy with Imperfect Information: The Article 9 Full Priority Debates' (1997) 82 *Cornell Law Review* 1373

Warren, E. and J.L. Westbrook, 'Financial Characteristics of Businesses in Bankruptcy' (1999) 73 *American Bankruptcy Law Journal* 499

Warren, E. and J.L. Westbrook, 'The Success of Chapter 11: A Challenge to the Critics' (2009) 107 *Michigan Law Review* 603

Warren, E., T.A. Sullivan and J. Lawrence Westbrook, *The Fragile Middle Class American in Debt* (New Haven, CT, Yale University, 2000)

Wehinger, G., 'SMEs and the Credit Crunch: Current Financing Difficulties, Policy Measures and a Review of Literature' (2013) *OECD Journal, Financial Market Trends* 2

Wessels, B., 'Harmonization of Insolvency Law in Europe' (2011) 8 *European Company Law* 27

Wessels, B., 'Themes of the Future: Rescue Businesses and Cross-Border Cooperation' (2014) *Insolvency Intelligence* 4

Westbrook, J., 'Two Thoughts About Insider Preferences' (1991) 76 *Minnesota Law Review* 73

White, M.J., *Bankruptcy Reform and Credit Cards*, NBER Working Paper No. 13265 (July 2007)

Williams, R., 'What Can We Expect to Gain from Reforming the Insolvent Trading Remedy?' (2015) 78 *Modern Law Review* 55

Wilson, T., 'The Responsible Lending Response' in T. Wilson (ed.), *International Responses to Issues of Credit and Over-indebtedness in the Wake of Crisis* (Farnham, Ashgate, 2013)

Zywicki, T., 'Is Forum-Shopping Corrupting America's Bankruptcy Courts?' (2006) 94 *Georgetown Law Journal* 1141

Index